FORGING THE GOLDEN URN

Studies of the Weatherhead East Asian Institute, Columbia University

STUDIES OF THE WEATHERHEAD EAST ASIAN INSTITUTE,
COLUMBIA UNIVERSITY

The Studies of the Weatherhead East Asian Institute of Columbia University
were inaugurated in 1962 to bring to a wider public the results of significant new
research on modern and contemporary East Asia.

Forging the Golden Urn

THE QING EMPIRE AND THE POLITICS OF REINCARNATION IN TIBET

Max Oidtmann

Columbia University Press
New York

Columbia University Press wishes to express its appreciation for assistance given by the Wm. Theodore de Bary Fund in the publication of this book.

Columbia University Press
Publishers Since 1893
New York   Chichester, West Sussex
cup.columbia.edu

Cataloging-in-Publication Data available from the Library of Congress
ISBN 978-0-231-18406-9 (cloth)
ISBN 978-0-231-54530-3 (electronic)

Cover design: Guerrilla Design
Cover image: Finding of a Dalai Lama, 19th Century. Album leaf; ink, color and gold on paper; painting proper: 33.9 x 28.8 cm (13 3/8 x 11 5/16 in.) Harvard Art Museums/Arthur M. Sackler Museum, Bequest of the Hofer Collection of the Arts of Asia, 1985.863,6. Photo: Imaging Department © President and Fellows of Harvard College

In all their settlements, the abilities of the people are sure to be varied as a result of differences in heaven and earth, heat and humidity,
and the breadth of valleys and streams. The people born in them have
different temperaments: firm or yielding, frivolous or stern, unhur-
ried or punctual. Their tools are differently made, their clothing varied yet suitable. Their teachings were reformed without changing
their customs; and the governmental arrangements were rectified, but
without affecting their suitability.

THE BOOK OF RITES, "ROYAL REGULATIONS," XXXV

The conformity of hearts and of sentiments is always preferable to a
uniformity of customs.

NICOLAS DE CORBERON, PRESIDENT OF THE CONSEIL

SOUVERAIN D'ALSACE, 1719

There are those who find a way to be free,
yet some constantly suffer under the rule of others.
Oh, how the just is outweighed by the unjust,
and the sentient beings of this land can find no peace!

Keep [one's people] from mixing with one another,
and they will not bring injury upon each other.
Nurturing each separately without altering their traditions,
that is the way for ruling the sentient beings.

JU MIPHAM NAMGYEL GYATSO, 1895

Contents

Contents

Preface and Acknowledgments

This book started with two small copybooks originally produced in the office of the Qing imperial residents (the *ambans*) who were stationed in Lhasa between 1875 and 1900. Now part of the collection of the Harvard-Yenching Library, these two artifacts offer a rare view of the business the officials conducted in Tibet in the name of the dynasty. The copybooks do not contain a complete record—far from it—and much of the information is bureaucratic boilerplate. But for me they did contain two surprises. The first was that they were written in Manchu. Although Manchu was the official language of the Qing state, I had been under the impression that its day-to-day use, even in official contexts, had largely ceased by the late nineteenth century as a result of the acculturation of the Manchus to the culture and language of China. Yet here it was, still in use among officials stationed in Lhasa. The second remarkable thing was that despite the formulaic quality of the reports, they hinted at a lively and sustained interaction between Qing colonial officials and indigenous elites—primarily hierarchs of the Geluk church and local Tibetan aristocrats. Moreover, they documented multiple occasions when Qing officials had used the Golden Urn lottery to identify the rebirths of prominent reincarnate lamas. Here again, I had been under the impression that the Golden Urn, which had originated with the Qing state and not indigenous Tibetan traditions, had been employed in Tibet only in the face of

[ix]

considerable protest and only in the event of a search for rebirths of the Dalai Lama or Panchen Lama.

In the West, standard histories of Tibet present Qing rule in the nineteenth century as anemic and distant—more concerned with the appearance of control than its exercise. To some degree this kind of narrative has been dictated by the desire of many Tibetologists to downplay "Chinese" influence in Tibet or Tibetan regions prior to the Communist "liberation" of Tibet in 1951. And indeed, there are good reasons to be skeptical of claims of either Chinese or Manchu influence in Tibet during the late Qing. There were rarely more than a couple thousand Qing civil and military personnel in Tibet at any given time during that period. Qing officials may very well have papered over their limited authority with fictitious accounts of actions taken. The use of the Golden Urn would seemingly have been no exception, and reports of it may be fabrications. But these two copybooks suggested otherwise. At the very least, they indicated that there was a wider world of Manchu-language materials from Tibet that had yet to be investigated and compared to Tibetan-language sources.

Subsequent research using archives from the Qing imperial government in Beijing, imperial outposts on the Sino-Tibetan frontier, Geluk monasteries, and the Ganden Podrang government of the Dalai Lamas has turned up an unexpectedly complex record of interactions between Qing authorities and Tibetan Buddhist subjects. Moreover, as I juxtaposed government reports in Manchu with the Tibetan-language chronicles of monastic authorities, it sometimes became possible to discern whispered secrets that would have otherwise been inaudible. These "codes" were the shared possession of the Qing elite and facilitated the production of a set of uniquely Qing instutions and rituals such as the Golden Urn.

This book argues that Qing officials did have an impact on Tibetan society, and that it was in the interest of many Tibetan elites to see to it that they did. Conversely, many thousands of Tibetans, primarily Buddhist monks, traveled into China during the Qing and had their own impact on the culture and politics of Chinese society. It was in the interest of many Chinese, Manchus, and Mongols to see to it that these monks were as influential as possible. A full account of the interactions and exchanges that were fostered (or imposed) in the context of Qing colonialism is beyond the scope of this book. It is my intent here to offer a limited account of this encounter by focusing on the history of one key ritual that could both bind and divide Qing elites: the Golden Urn. Where did the idea come from? How did contemporaneous Tibetans and Qing officials think it worked? Why was it used or rejected?

My attempt to answer these questions has incurred many debts. The research could not have begun without the support of Mark C. Elliott, in whose seminar on Manchu-language materials I first encountered the Manchu-language copybooks from Lhasa. Special gratitude is due to those colleagues who took up the daunting task of reading the book manuscript (or portions of it) and offered critical advice on how to improve it: Pär Cassell, Devin Fitzgerald, Edward Kolla, Anatol Lieven, James Reardon-Anderson, Peter Schwieger, Michael Szonyi, Gray Tuttle, Benno Weiner, Leonard van der Kuijp, Karine Walther, and the anonymous reviewers at Columbia University Press. The book would never have been completed without Brenton Sullivan's advice on database organization and his careful editing of the manuscript at numerous stages. Dorjé Nyingcha and Tsering Tashi helped correct my translations of Tibetan sources. The revision process also benefited enormously from the feedback I received after presenting my research at the Oxford University China Centre in March 2017. Thanks to Matthew Erie and Henrietta Harrison for organizing this seminar. Others who gave generously to this project through friendship, expertise, and conversation include: Abdullah Al-Arian, Sonia Alonso Saenz de Oger, Christopher Atwood, Robbie Barnett, Jim Bonk, Wesley Chaney, Chen Qingying, Pamela Crossley, Devon Dear, Josh Freeman, Ying Hu, Jia Jianfei, Macabe Kelliher, Loretta Kim, Benjamin Levey, James Millward, Matthew Mosca, Fernanda Pine, Eric Schluessel, Per Sørensen, Hannah Theaker, Liu Wenpeng, Ulan (Wu Lan), Stacey Van Vleet, Yang Hongwei, Yumkyab, and Laurence Zhang. Carole Sargent at the Georgetown Office of Scholarly Publications, Susan Bohandy, and Leslie Kriesel at Columbia University Press all played critical roles in navigating this book through the editing process and into publication. The mistakes that remain are entirely my own.

Financial support for research and writing has come from several sources: the Harvard University Asia Center and Fairbank Center for Chinese Studies provided funds for several summers of research and language study; a Fulbright–Hays Doctoral Dissertation Fellowship facilitated two years of uninterrupted fieldwork in China; and Faculty Research Grants sponsored by Georgetown University and the Qatar Foundation financed further research as well as editing and indexing. Further thanks are due to the Harvard University Art Museums, the Rubin Museum of Art, and Lark

Mason Associates for sharing art images. Law Alsobrook designed the accompanying map and reformatted images for publication.

The greatest debt lies with my family: Jenny, Henry, and Helen, who are always ready for adventure; my parents, Linda and Ernst; my sister, Margaret; and my in-laws, Erik and Diana, all of whom have sacrificed much worry and heartache because my work has often separated us. This book is dedicated to my beloved wife, Jenny.

A Note on the Archives

The Qing state's successful consolidation of power over first China and then the Outer Regions (Mongolia, Kökenuur, Xinjiang, and Tibet) relied not only on astute messaging but also on the management of information. The careful curation of official correspondence and the sequestration of internal deliberations in *dangse* (archives) by early Manchu rulers was a stark contrast to the situation in the preceding Ming state, where the debates of the Chongzhen court (1627–1644) leaked out into society and government officials absconded with official materials, often publishing them in polemical broadsides aimed at opposing factions.[1] Beatrice Bartlett, Philip Kuhn, Mark Elliott, and several other scholars have pointed to the creation of a secret extrabureaucratic communications network to manage the empire. The Palace Memorial System and ad-hoc Inner Court advisory bodies such as the "Office for Handling Military Exigencies" (aka the Grand Council) were among the key tools that allowed the Yongzheng and Qianlong emperors to discipline the bureaucracy and direct the empire's resources to the realization of imperial objectives such as the conquest of the Junghar state in the 1750s and the defeat of the Gurkhas in 1792.[2]

In Tibet, colonial rule rested on the supervision of communications between Geluk authorities in Lhasa and lay and monastic elites elsewhere in Inner Asia. The seizure of the indigenous postal system in 1751 and the attempt to channel the external communications of the Ganden Podrang government and other local administrators through the office of the *ambans* from the 1790s on were manifestations of the Qing rulers' concern with information. In practice, the Qing never completely monopolized the flow of information in Inner Asia, and certainly not within the Geluk school itself. Yet they did create a remarkably efficient system of imperial communications: in 1793, news about the Golden Urn, dispatched at the most urgent pace of 600 Chinese *li* (approx. 160 km) per day, could arrive in Beijing in 30 days or less.[3]

Since the mid-1990s, the People's Republic of China has similarly prioritized the management of historical data from Qing-era Tibet. This book, much like other recent attempts to reconstruct Tibetan history, has been fundamentally shaped by the evolving policies of party-supervised archivists at the First Historical Archive (FHA), the primary depository of Qing-period documents, located within the Forbidden City, and other scholarly institutions charged with promoting the official narrative of Chinese history such as the China Tibetology Research Center and the Qing History Project run by the Institute for Qing History at Renmin University. For instance, in the early 2000s, the FHA and the Qing History Project simultaneously began initiatives to digitize the archives of the Qing court. No longer able to examine original documents in their original context—packed into bundles organized by date and, occasionally, topic, by Qing-era secretaries and clerks—researchers are limited to "key word" searches guided by the parameters set by archival authorities. Since 2009, "provisional" restriction of all memorials categorized as "ethnic" (Ch. *minzu lei* 民族類) has meant that vast quantities of materials from the Qing's Outer Regions are now inaccessible, essentially placing the history of Mongolia, Tibet, and Turkestan off limits. A search for the memorials of Qing officers stationed in frontier regions, for instance, will return reams of reports on grain prices and the weather, but little else.

For most scholars, both inside and outside of China, the work-around has been the compendiums of historical documents published by the FHA and other government agencies such as those mentioned above. A second approach, adopted by far fewer scholars, has been to turn to the Manchu-language materials and especially the copies of the Manchu-language Palace Memorials made by the clerks who staffed the Grand Council. This archive can still be consulted using old-fashioned microfilm rolls and through the digitized version, which came online (within the FHA only) in 2013. Since Manchu-language materials are by definition "ethnic," the FHA has found it unseemly to sequester an entire class of materials, especially since these materials, amounting to between 1,600,000 and 3,000,000 items, represent perhaps 20 percent of their entire holdings.[4] Yet even here, the digitization has had consequences, most importantly severing the original reports from the many attachments—maps, confessions, supplementary letters in indigenous languages such as Tibetan or Mongol, and top-secret addenda—that originally accompanied them. Several of the documents essential to the argument of this book, for instance, were attachments and therefore are now much more difficult, if not impossible, to locate in the new digital database.[5]

This state of affairs leads to two observations. The first is that to their credit, the archivist-officials of the PRC have been remarkably even-handed in their application of the rules: Chinese and foreign scholars face the same restrictions. However, circumscribing research on the Qing borderlands or "ethnic" issues to the minority of students willing to learn Manchu has served to discourage the study of the non-Han parts of what has become China and parochialized the concerns of Chinese historians—much the same way that the use of Manchu by the Qing elite and censorship by the Qing state during the seventeenth and eighteenth centuries severed Chinese elites—the Han literati—from investigation of the empire's new territories in Inner Asia.[6]

Second, the story told here has inevitably been sculpted by the mechanics of the modern archives and the policies of PRC archivist-officials and—at least in the first two acts—is strongly oriented around the views expressed in Manchu and Chinese by the Qing's ruling elite. Luckily, much like the records of other imperial enterprises, these documents are sufficiently replete with contradictions, ambiguities, and anxiety about the underlying realities of their own normative claims that they can still serve to undermine reductive proclamations of imperial sovereignty and superiority made by representatives of the Qing and the People's Republic. Future scholars will inevitably offer alternative and conflicting interpretations of this period, on the basis of their own individual fortunes in the archives.

Note on Transliteration and Nomenclature

The Qing-period encounter between Tibetans and agents of the Qing government unfolded in a variety of languages and dialects. For the purposes of this study, materials in three languages have been consulted: Manchu (Ma.), Tibetan (Tib.), and Chinese (Ch.).

Chinese words and names are transcribed in Pinyin. Manchu words and names are transcribed according to the conventions of Jerry Norman's *Comprehensive Manchu–English Dictionary* (2013). Where only the Chinese version of a Manchu name is known, a hyphen separates syllables of the Pinyin romanization. Tibetan words and names are transcribed in the main body of the book according to the conventions of the Tibetan and Himalayan Library Simplified Phonetic Transcription of Standard Tibetan established by David Germano and Nicholas Tournadre (2003). Wylie equivalents are available in the list of orthographic equivalents and in the notes. Mongol names and terms are transcribed according to the form given in Christopher Atwood's *Encyclopedia of Mongolia and the Mongol Empire* (2004). Generally, I refer to individuals according to the English transcription of their name from their native language. Thus, the name of the chief representative of the Qing court in Lhasa from 1792 to 1795, Heliyen, is written according to the transcription of his Manchu name and not his Chinese name (He-lin 和琳).

The Tibetan term *trülku* (Tib. *sprul sku*, Ma. *hūbilgan*, Mo. *khubilgan*, Ch. *hu-bi-le-han* 呼畢勒罕), literally "emanation body," is used throughout to refer to reincarnate lamas. Terms or titles that appear frequently in multiple languages have been rendered according to the standard Manchu-language transcription. Thus, the Mongol-language title for reincarnate lamas, *khutugtu* (meaning "holy" or "blessed one") is consistently rendered *kūtuktu* following the standard Manchu transcription. Similarly, the Mongol-language title *nomunkhan* is written using a slightly modified Manchu transcription: *nomunhan* (Ma. *nomun han*). Tibetans often referred to *kūtuktu* and *trülku* in general as *rinpoché* ("precious one"). In general, I use the title *kūtuktu* to refer to those *trülku* who had received that title from Qing rulers. In translating Tibetan sources, however, I preserve the source's choice of appellation, usually either *kūtuktu* or *rinpoché*. I also retain the more familiar English "Pandita" for the Sanskrit title *Paṇḍita* (Mongol *bandida*, Ma. *bandida*, Tib. *mkhas pa*), meaning "scholar" or "master of the five sciences." While these decisions have resulted in some perhaps ungainly combinations of Tibetan and Manchu (for example, the Demo *kūtuktu* or Erdeni Pandita *kūtuktu*), it is hoped that the improved clarity and consistency enhances the reading experience.

Abbreviations

BLRYP = Chap spel tshe brtan phun tshogs, *Bod gyi lo rgyus rags rim g.yu yi phreng ba*

BMNT = Brag dgon pa dkon mchog bstan pa rab rgyas, *Yongs rdzogs bstan pa'i mnga' bdag rje btsun bla ma rdo rje 'chang 'kon mchog rgyal mtshan dpal bzang po'o zhal snga nas kyi rnam par thar 'dod 'jug ngogs* [Life of Belmang Könchok Gyeltsen]

DLNT08 = De mo 08 ngag dbang thub bstan 'jigs med rgya mtsho, *'Jam dpal rgya mtsho'i rnam thar* [Life of the Eighth Dalai Lama, Jampel Gyatso]

JQ = *Jiaqing reign* 嘉慶朝, 1796–1820

JYZP02 = Gung thang bstan pa'i sgron me, *Kun mkhyen 'jam dbyangs bzhad pa sku 'phreng gynis pa rje 'jigs med dbang po'i rnam thar* [Life of the Second Jamyang Zhepa]

JYZP03 = Mkhan po ngag dbang thub bstan rgya mtsho, *Kun mkhyen 'jam dbyangs bzed pa sku 'phreng gsum pa'i rnam thar* [Life of the Third Jamyang Zhepa]

MSCB = Brag dgon pa dkon mchog bstan pa rab rgyas, *Mdo smad chos 'byung* [Oceanic book]

MWLF = *Manwen lufu zouzhe, Junjichu*, First Historical Archives (Beijing). Unless otherwise indicated, citations are of microfilm slide numbers.

MWJXD = *Qianlong chao manwen jixindang*

QL = *Qianlong reign* 乾隆朝, 1736–1795

QSL = *Qing shi lu* [Qing veritable records], Zhonghua shuju ed., 1985

YHGSL = Zhongguo diyi lishi dang'an guan, ed., *Qingdai Yonghegong shiliao*

YYZDZZ = Zhongguo Zangxue yanjiu zhongxin et al., eds., *Yuan yilai Xizang difang yu zhongyang zhengfu guangxi dang'an shiliao huibian*

FORGING THE GOLDEN URN

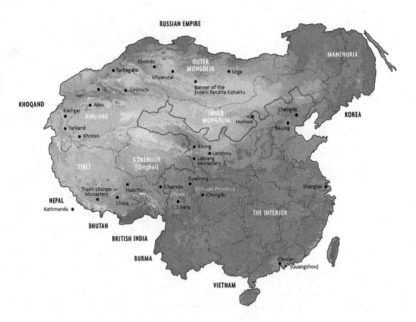

The Qing Empire circa 1820

Introduction

The Great Qing State and the
Entanglements of Reincarnation

In the predawn hours of November 29, 1995, a delegation of officials from the highest echelons of the People's Republic of China secretly assembled in the inner sanctuary of the Jokhang Temple in Lhasa to oversee the identification of the reincarnation of the Tenth Panchen Lama (1938–1989). To ensure that the Communist Party retained possession of the personage of the next Panchen Lama and to exclude the Fourteenth Dalai Lama (1935–) and his government-in-exile from exercising any role in the identification process, the government had resurrected a ritual that had not been employed in Tibet since 1908—the Golden Urn lottery. According to one witness, the temple grounds had been emptied of their customary caretakers and guards had been posted to keep out the usual morning pilgrims.[1] Despite careful preparations, the government was still clearly nervous about its ability to manage the ritual and control the results.

The tightly choreographed ceremony unfolded as follows. The names of three government-approved children were affixed to ivory lots, wrapped in cloth, and placed in the urn. Then, as the dignitaries looked on, Bumi Rinpoché, the government-approved head of the Geluk school of Tibetan Buddhism, prostrated before the statue of Śākyamuni Buddha, turned to the table holding the urn, and quickly drew a lot from within. The monk then passed the lot to Luo Gan, the Secretary-General of the State Council of the People's Republic of China, who had flown in from Beijing just hours before. As the senior representative of China's executive government, he had the duty to unwrap the lot and inspect the name. Having certified the result, he then handed the lot to Gyeltsen Norbu, the governor of the Tibetan Autonomous Region, to read aloud.

With this ceremony, the PRC recast the Golden Urn lottery as both symbol and proof of Tibet's indivisibility from China. At the same time, the central government also committed itself to a long-term effort to persuade both domestic and foreign audiences that the procedure was legitimate and the children selected in the lottery were genuine rebirths of prominent lamas. The policy of using the Golden Urn to identify reincarnated lamas of the Geluk church had commenced well before 1908: it was first introduced in 1792, after Tibet had been incorporated into the Qing empire (1644–1911). With this long history in mind, contemporary advocates for the procedure in the PRC have framed it in ways that have re-created the atmosphere of the late eighteenth and nineteenth centuries. For example, a large-scale mural depicting the 1995 ceremony normalizes the supremacy of officials from Beijing over those in Lhasa by deploying the same visual motifs that one sees in the imperial portraits produced in the Qing palace workshops. Luo Gan, disproportionately sized, tight-lipped, and armored with a rigid black suit, looms solemnly over the lesser figures of local Tibetan cadres and Buddhist monks. The premise behind both this painting and the formal promulgation in 2007 of the Golden Urn as a national law by the State Bureau of Religious Affairs was that the use of the ritual during the Qing period was sufficient justification for the People's Republic to reimpose it in the twenty-first century. According to this logic, diligent attempts to re-create the original ritual using the genuine artifact (rescued from the warehouses of the Museum of the Tibetan Autonomous Region) should persuade the public that it can be once more a legitimate tool for identifying true reincarnations, most importantly the future Fifteenth Dalai Lama.

The Communist Party's rediscovery of the Golden Urn has necessitated the production of a substantial and still-expanding body of historical studies of reincarnation in Tibetan Buddhism, documentary collections, and museum exhibitions in Beijing, Lhasa, and other major cities.[2] The scale of this carefully orchestrated endeavor reflects the difficulty of erasing the irony of an avowedly socialist and atheist state's attempt to resurrect the

Detail of A-Zha 阿扎, Han Shuli 韓書力, and Yu Xiaodong 于小冬, "Jinping cheqian 金瓶掣簽" (The Golden Urn Lottery)

"feudal" institutions and "superstitious" customs of the imperial past among its ethnic minorities.[3] Yet, despite their industriousness, state-sponsored scholars and government cadres have made little effort to understand the origins of the ritual in the 1790s or do much more than chart its use over the course of the nineteenth century.

Outside of China, researchers have vociferously disputed the idea that the Golden Urn was ever a widely used or legitimate procedure, arguing that from the outset it faced stiff opposition from Tibetan Buddhist communities.[4] Moreover, these scholars tend to portray the nineteenth century as a period of declining Qing influence in Tibet—a characterization with which even some PRC scholars concur.[5] In his 1973 study of the Tibetan government, Luciano Petech characterized the nineteenth century as a period of "stagnation, with little apparent change" during which both local Tibetans and Qing agents slumbered in a "somnolent peace."[6] In this vein, scholars have dismissed reports about the Golden Urn from Qing officials stationed in Lhasa as the artifice of an increasingly shambolic empire. Confident that this "foreign" imposition was ignored from the moment of its invention, non-PRC historians have felt little need for a history of the ritual's origins.

The project of this book is to return to the original polyglot conversations of the Qing era and test these long-standing assumptions. The modern-day stage managers of the PRC have skillfully restored the sets and props of the Qing empire, but have written a new script for their actors. Anachronistic and foreign ideas have been imposed on both officials of the late-eighteenth-century Qing state and its Tibetan Buddhist subjects. What were the original pressures that forged the urn and shaped its use as an instrument of imperial rule?

Using the Manchu-language correspondence of the empire's colonial officials as well as the Tibetan-language chronicles of the Tibetan Buddhist monastics they encountered, this book traces the trajectory of the Golden Urn from the Qing capital to Lhasa and then on into the home communities of reincarnate lamas in Tibet and Mongolia from 1792 through the early 1800s. As the urn passed from hand to hand, secret memorandum to public edict, Manchu to Chinese to Tibetan, and from factory to temple, it underwent several profound transformations and took on a range of diverse and sometimes contradictory meanings. Viewed from one perspective, a lottery for allocating jobs in the mundane world of the Chinese bureaucracy became for a time a legitimate Tibetan divination ritual and an integral part of the recognition process for numerous prominent lamas over the nineteenth century. Viewed from another perspective, a device that had originated in a Ming-era (1368–1644) anticorruption campaign had been repurposed as an instrument for asserting Qing imperial sovereignty over both church and state in Tibet and Mongolia.

The multiple transformations of the Golden Urn reveal how people in the "Great Qing State" (Ma. *Daicing gurun*, Ch. Da Qing Guo 大清國) navigated two interrelated tensions particular to all colonial orders. The first arose between the impulse on the part of an imperial power and its agents to reform, assimilate, or otherwise "civilize" the colonial subject and the desire to keep them separate, distinct, distant, and traditional. The second was the frictions that arose from indigenous interests in preserving political and cultural autonomy and the desire to use the instruments of the empire for personal and institutional aggrandizement. In this case, I am referring to the desire of the Geluk hierarchs to both deepen and broaden the reach of their political and religious administrative system. The Golden Urn originated in the desire of the Qing emperor to assert his control over the Tibetan arts of divination and prognostication. But it succeeded ultimately for very different reasons. Tibetan and Mongol elites, both lay and monastic, saw within the new ritual the possibility of further expanding and consolidating their own authority. As a result, between 1792 and 1911 approximately eighty reincarnations in Tibet and Mongolia were identified using the Golden Urn ritual, and few Tibetan elites overtly contested the legitimacy of the "Great Empire of China" (Tib. *gyayül gyelkhap chenpo*) during this period.[7] Understanding the history of the Golden Urn, therefore, should shed some light on why Qing rule over its sprawling Eurasian possessions was remarkably durable.

The Imperial Gift

Our story begins north of the Great Wall at the mountain palace of the Qing emperors in Chengde, where only the invigorating rumble of distant thunder and the sweat-stained liveries of messengers from the capital might spark thoughts of the sweltering plains to the south. It was here in August 1792 that the Qianlong emperor (r. 1735–1796, lived 1711–1799) and his councilors made a surprising—and to many contemporaries, perplexing—equivalence between two very dissimilar parts of their great empire. Faced with what appeared to be an epidemic of corruption among the hierarchs of the Geluk school of Tibetan Buddhism—monks and aristocrats in Tibet and Mongolia were suspected of colluding to identify their kinsmen as reincarnate lamas—the emperor turned to the Chinese bureaucratic tradition for a solution. His novel idea was that a lottery for allocating official posts across the provincial administration of China proper could be repurposed as a ritual for identifying "true and authentic" reincarnations of the Geluk lamas of Inner Asia.[8]

The appointment lottery had its roots in the preceeding dynasty, the Great Ming. Since 1594 the Board of Civil Appointments in Beijing had from time to time allocated vacant magistracies in the provinces by drawing lots. The locations of various posts would be written on wooden strips and placed in a tall, cylindrical vase. Having shuffled the lots, officials from the Board of Civil Appointments then placed the vase on a high ceremonial table. Expectant officials were invited in turn to kneel before the table, reach up, and draw out a lot. The idea, of course, was that unable to see the lot and read the destination, neither the candidates nor the bureaucrats of the board would have the opportunity to prearrange the appointments and thus profit from the process. The impetus for the invention of the "appointment lottery" in the late Ming had been the increasingly widespread view among the official class that landing a plum post had little to do with merit but everything to do with who one knew and how much one could afford to pay. The corruption of the appointment process was understood by all as a potentially fatal blow to the efficacy and legitimacy of the Ming bureaucracy—an institution already riven by factional politics.[9]

It should come as no surprise that in such a climate, a lottery for allocating official posts was instantly controversial. Ming bureaucrats argued over the degree to which it posed an obstacle to appointing officials to posts that matched their abilities. Would the state suffer if inexperienced men were dispatched to challenging and strategic offices? Was it a waste if talented candidates were deployed to provincial backwaters? There was also suspicion that this device too could be manipulated. These fears persisted among officials who entered the bureaucracy of the Ming's successor, the Qing dynasty (1644–1911). In his memoirs, Gabriel de Magalhães, a Portuguese Jesuit who had been stationed in Beijing, recalled that in 1669 a certain mandarin had caused an uproar when, having drawn the name of a forlorn outpost in the distant southwest corner of the empire, he lost all composure and, while violently belaboring the presiding official with his fists, demanded to know what had become of the "City of great Trade" [*sic*] and the bribe he had paid to procure it.[10]

Despite such scandals, by the early eighteenth century debate subsided and the use of the appointment lottery had not only become routine and unremarkable but also been adopted by other ministries such as the Board of War.[11] Thus, during the summer of 1792, the Qing ruler fixed his mind on the idea that the apparent corruption of the process of identifying reincarnations among Tibetan Buddhists could be analogized to the venality of Ming officialdom, and it was therefore entirely appropriate to export the lottery to Tibet. On August 18, the emperor instructed eunuchs in the imperial workshops to produce five ivory lots and a gold-plated copper vase cast in the shape of a traditional Tibetan-style urn, referred to in Chinese as a "benba" pot after the Tibetan term *bumba*.[12] Over the next two months, the emperor repeatedly intruded into the manufacture of the urn, ordering the replacement of lotus-petal decorations with Chinese-style auspicious clouds, arranging the inscription of the Kalachakra mantra on four sides, and finally, personally selecting the precious stones and corals for the lid.[13] Just days before the completed "Golden Urn" (Ma. *aisin bumba*, Tib. *ser bum*) emerged from the factory, the emperor began issuing instructions about how it was to be used. To the Mongol aristocracy he wrote: "After one of your long-cherished [reincarnations] passes away, with regard to their rebirth, consult the prophecies of the four oracles of Tibet. Once they have identified several [candidates], write their names and dates of birth on lots and place them in the Golden Urn. The Dalai Lama and Panchen Lama, along with our ministers resident in Tibet will then make a selection. That will be the reincarnation."[14]

In his later reminiscences, the Qianlong emperor found little to trouble him about appropriating a technology from the Chinese administrative tradition and imposing it on Tibetan Buddhists in Tibet, Mongolia, and other parts of the Qing empire in Eurasia. Nor did he shy away from the controversies that had dogged the administrative lottery during the Ming. Lest there be any confusion about the origin of the idea, the emperor took advantage of the publication of his *Collection of Poetry and Prose on the Ten Complete Victories* in 1794 to explain his train of thought:

[The Golden Urn lottery] is similar to the manner in which lots are drawn in the boards of Civil Appointments and War. When established during the Ming there were those who mocked [the procedure], calling the Board of Civil Appointments the "Board of Lots." [. . .] However, if this matter had been entrusted to the ministers of those two boards, fair and honest ministers would have been unable to avoid pleasing some and offending others; self-interested ministers would ultimately have handed out posts according to what they took in! There was no alternative but to institute [the lottery] to eliminate these maladies. My decree that the lamas must also draw lots is truly a replication of this.[15]

But were things really so simple? Could a Ming anticorruption measure be successfully exported to Lhasa? Camouflaged as a Tibetan ritual object, would the Golden Urn find acceptance among Tibetan Buddhists? The Qianlong emperor believed that he had struck the correct balance between imposing the laws of the Qing state and protecting indigenous traditions. Citing from the *Book of Rites*, the classical Chinese guide to ritual and governance, he wrote:

Although I supported the teachings of the Yellow Hats [i.e., the Geluk church], I have done so according to a passage that appears in the *Royal Regulations*: one should improve their teachings, not replace their teachings. One should improve their laws, not replace their traditions.[16]

This statement appeared in the emperor's first public justification of the new law, the *Discourse on Lamas*. Translated from Chinese into Manchu, Mongol, and Tibetan, this proclamation was ultimately inscribed on a massive stone pillar that stood at the heart of the Yonghegong Tibetan Buddhist monastery complex in Beijing—metaphorically anchoring the Geluk church to the Qing ship of state. Although a Tibetan reader would have understood that "Yellow Hat" (Tib. *zha ser*) referred to the distinctive, mustard-colored hats of the Geluk monks, the *Discourse*'s Confucian allusions would have been perplexing at best. Moreover, they would have found it difficult to ignore the emperor's implicit attack on the authenticity of many leading reincarnate lamas. Indeed, proclamations such as this tell us very little about how lay and monastic communities in Tibet and Mongolia, as well as members of the Qing court and its colonial officers, comprehended the procedure. How ultimately would Qing subjects navigate the contradictions inherent in the emperor's dictat? Could the state and its agents "improve" Tibetan Buddhism without imposing an alien culture or antagonizing its adherents? Could the Qing state govern Tibet without transforming it?

These questions matter because the smooth succession of religious and political authority from one reincarnation to the next was of enormous consequence for the daily lives of tens of thousands of Qing subjects. The reincarnate lamas of the Geluk church were also rulers, jurists, landowners, and even occasionally merchants and bankers in addition to being spiritual authorities. For this reason I find it useful to think of the Geluk not simply as a school of religious teachings or a monastic order, but rather as a "church" that paralleled the roles and reach of the Catholic establishment in early modern Europe.[17] The most prominent Geluk hierarchs—the Dalai and Panchen lamas—were major statesmen. In 1792 the Eighth Dalai Lama (1758–1810) ostensibly governed Tibet from his headquarters in the Potala Palace in Lhasa. For most of his life a series of regents had overseen day-to-day administration, but these regents were themselves for the most part also reincarnate lamas. The Panchen Lamas in west-central Tibet (the province of Tsang) and the Jebtsundamba Lamas of Outer Mongolia were also temporal rulers, although on a somewhat smaller scale. The emperor's new ritual might guarantee smoother transitions from generation to generation, but it also threatened to upend what in some cases were centuries of local traditions for identifying rebirths. And the question of whether it could successfully "improve their laws, not replace their traditions" only grew in importance as the Qianlong emperor quickly doubled down on the Golden Urn: shortly after the first urn was sent to Tibet, a second urn was commissioned with the intention that it be used at Yonghegong in Beijing to identify rebirths of lamas from Inner and Outer Mongolia.

The Emperor's Wager

What was at stake when the Qianlong emperor made the decision to forge the urn? Even for contemporaneous observers, the new policy seemed unrelated to the exigencies of recent crises, most importantly the wars with the Gurkhas of Nepal. In 1791, the Gurkhas had launched a large-scale invasion of Tibet from Nepal. The Gurkhas had attacked Tibet once before in 1788, but according to the Qing court's understanding of things, the invasion had been easily blunted by a determined show of strength by Qing military forces. This time, however, the Gurkha army had marched nearly unopposed across several hundred miles of Tibet; occupied its second largest city, Shigatze; sacked the seat of the Panchen Lamas, Trashi Lhünpo monastery; and thrown the Tibetan government and its Qing advisors into turmoil. To add insult to injury, the Gurkhas carted off the immense treasure of Trashi Lhünpo, a great portion of which had recently been personally donated by the Qianlong emperor. Upon receipt of this news, Bajung, the emperor's chief advisor on Tibetan issues, who had only recently returned from Tibet, committed suicide. It was subsequently learned that instead of vigorously beating back the Gurkhas' first invasion, the emperor's officers in Tibet had stood idly by while the Tibetan government bought off the invaders with cash payments. The honor of the Great Qing State lay in fragments amid the rubble of Trashi Lhünpo.

But the Gurkhas had grossly miscalculated on this second foray into Tibet. By the early spring of 1792, Qing military forces from around the empire had converged on Lhasa. Led by Fuk'anggan, an experienced field commander and Manchu confidant of the emperor, a mixed army of twelve thousand Tibetan and Qing soldiers recaptured the border town of Kyirong in June and then proceeded to mount a well-organized counterattack on the Gurkhas. By the end of September, the Qing military together with its Tibetan allies had occupied much of central Nepal and extracted a humiliating surrender from the Gurkha commander, Bahadur Shah.[18]

Well before the conclusion of the military campaign, the emperor, his advisors in Beijing, and his agents in Tibet had begun discussing possible measures to reform the administration of Tibet and prevent further invasions from across the Himalayan frontier. From the perspective of the court's resident officials in Tibet, the difficulties of the region had seemed primarily military and administrative in nature. As early as 1789, Bajung, together with Ohūi, the commander of the Qing military forces stationed in neighboring Sichuan Province, had submitted to the emperor a series of proposals to strengthen the Tibetan military and enhance Qing supervision of the Tibetan government. These ideas would ultimately form the basis of a sweeping set of twenty-nine reforms to the administration of Tibetan government adopted by the Qing court in 1793. Yet to what was evidently the great perplexity of many civil and military officials, in the spring and summer of 1792 the emperor and his inner circle of advisors at court directed their attention first to the matter of reincarnation and the perceived corruption of the Geluk hierarchs. The emperor disseminated the first explanations of the Golden Urn procedure to officials in Mongolia and Tibet in October 1792. The first reincarnations were identified using the new measure in March 1793. It was not until the following month that Fuk'anggan presented a finalized list of twenty-nine reforms to the Dalai Lama. Heading this list was the new statute introducing the Golden Urn. The fact that the Qing government directed its ire at the Geluk monks and lamas seemed strange, especially because many of these same men had earned the public praise of the emperor for their assistance to Qing military forces as they launched the counterattack. Moreover, among the emperor's closest confidants were voices that dismissed the Golden Urn as an unnecessary and dangerous wager of imperial prestige.[19]

Why, then, take this risk, especially when the empire's military victory had already resolved the border conflicts with Nepal and provided the political capital to reform other aspects of local administration in Tibet? For the edification of the imperial bureaucracy, the emperor had prepared the aforementioned *Discourse on Lamas*. Here, he cast aspersions on the authenticity of a number of contemporaneous reincarnations and even on the underlying principle itself. The Buddha, he acidly observed, had not been reborn. It was entirely appropriate, therefore, for the emperor to take charge of this matter and, by extension, place the Geluk monks more generally under the jurisdiction of the emperor's laws. Turning to history, Qianlong argued that the Mongol rulers of the Yuan dynasty (1271–1368) had made the critical mistake of allowing "lamas" to act above the "royal law." His readers would have understood the implied relationship between this mistake and the fleeting and turbulent nature of Mongol rule. The importance of the lamas demanded that the Qing ruler act to shore up the Geluk church. This oft-quoted and much reproduced edict did not explain, however, why the emperor was so concerned about the perceived corruption within the Geluk church and the faith of its adherents.

Looking back at the major events of his reign, the Qianlong emperor should have had little to fear from the Geluk. Hierarchs of this school of Tibetan Buddhism had proven themselves allies of the emperor in some of the key moments of his reign. In the successive wars to pacify the Tibetan-speaking people of Gyelrong, for instance (also known as the Jinchuan campaigns of 1747–49 and 1771–76), the Geluk had mobilized logistical support for the Qing military, propagandized on behalf of the Qing cause, and even brought their spiritual weaponry to bear on the enemy.[20] Another test had presented itself in the late 1750s when, with few exceptions, the most prominent lamas had backed the Qing in a much more complex and dangerous war: that with the empire's most obstinate foreign enemy, the Junghar Khanate—a foe of the Qing with whom the Geluk had at many times in the past been on friendly terms. Even the Seventh Dalai Lama (1708–1757), who along with prominent family members had been suspected of Junghar sympathies, was by the end of his life a trusted proxy for the Qing state and largely left to his own devices. From the death of the Seventh Dalai Lama right down to the early 1790s, the Qianlong emperor had had enough confidence in the successive regents to grant them considerable leeway in managing the affairs of Tibet.

Yet despite this seemingly harmonious relationship, the Qianlong emperor could not but have been aware of the fact that the Geluk church remained the largest organization in the empire not directly supervised by the imperial bureaucracy or otherwise centered on the Qing court. The Geluk church's political control of central Tibet[21] and near monopoly of the religious life of Inner Asia predated the Qing conquest of China, and its institutional history stretched yet further into the past. The government of the Eighth Dalai Lama, known as the "Ganden Podrang," could trace its roots to an eponymously named palace that had come into the possession of the lineage of the Dalai Lamas in the early 1500s. In 1792, the Geluk core curriculum and educational system, ritual apparatus, communications systems, procedures for evaluation and promotion of monks and other personnel, military forces, and the bulk of its financing still existed largely outside the purview of the Qing government. By contrast, although the rural Chinese gentry of the Qing "interior domains"—the former Ming territories—greatly outnumbered the Geluk monks, their education, social status, and advancement into the profitable world of the bureaucracy were carefully regulated by the civil service exams.[22] The monks of the various Daoist and Buddhist temples and monasteries of the Qing interior similarly outnumbered those of Inner Asia, but none belonged to an order that could match the geographic scope, curricular or ritual uniformity, and centralization of the Geluk. Nor did their monastic endowments result in the kinds of administrative responsibilities that the Geluk hierarchs shouldered. With the exception of imperially sponsored temples in Beijing and a handful of other religious sites scattered across the Qing interior, Buddhist and Daoist establishments remained largely local affairs, funded and staffed by neighboring communities. Moreover, since the early eighteenth century,

Qing administrative codes had banned the construction of new Buddhist and Daoist temples and severely proscribed the number and public activities of the Chinese clergy.[23] These ambitious measures of social control—although never fully realized—had as yet no parallel in Mongolia or Tibet.

During the second half of the eighteenth century, in the midst of the self-proclaimed "Prosperous Age," the Qing government could bestow titles on prominent lamas, regulate to some degree their peregrinations between Tibet and Mongolia, sponsor their sojourning in Beijing and at other religious sites within the empire, review appointments within the bureaucracy of the Ganden Podrang, underwrite major works of Buddhist scholarship, or patronize aspects of ritual life by constructing monasteries and hosting ritual services. Yet although these levers were influential, few Qing rulers—and certainly not the Qianlong emperor and his councilors—had deluded themselves into believing that they fully controlled the Geluk machine. Since the late 1720s, Qing rulers had installed imperial residents (the *ambans*) in Lhasa to keep an eye on things. On three occasions (1720, 1727, 1751), these rulers had dispatched large-scale military expeditions to Tibet. In the aftermath of the campaigns Qing agents had insisted on certain changes to the basic structure of the Ganden Podrang administration in Lhasa. However, these measures quite intentionally had little impact on either the internal administration of the Geluk church or local governance outside of Lhasa. Even among the Mongols, the group with which the Qing state had perhaps the longest administrative experience and among whom it had established a wide network of allied indigenous nobility, there were countervailing and troubling trends. A growing portion of military-aged men lived in monasteries that were directly and indirectly linked to Lhasa and other centers of Geluk authority through patterns of pilgrimage, shared texts, ritual practices, and higher education either at the great monastic universities in Lhasa and Amdo (the northeastern Tibetan plateau region including Qinghai and the highland regions of Gansu Province) or by teachers dispatched by those institutions.[24]

On the eve of the Gurkha invasion, from the point of view of the Qianlong emperor and those Qing officials with experience in Inner Asia, the Geluk lamas were a mashup of somewhat contradictory characters: lieges of the Manchu ruler, erudite but preachy schoolmasters, conjurers of uncertain ability or possibly shamans, and at best, bodhisattvas possessed of a genius that tied them to the eternal truths of Buddhism. The Geluk church was the loyal, if occasionally roguish friend of the imperial house, obliged as a guest to observe its etiquette and shibboleths. But it was not its hand-maiden (or "bondservant," if our metaphor is to remain within a Manchu paradigm).

Yet to conclude here that the Qing emperor's greatest fear was an insur-rection built around the Geluk's administrative capacity and funded with the social capital that came from being the chief purveyor of spiritual sal-vation across Inner Asia would be a serious misreading of the historical record. During the last decades of his reign, the Qianlong emperor only rarely expressed concern about the loyalty of the Geluk, either in public or in private among his senior advisors. Indeed, such a fear would have been far-fetched in the post-Junghar era. After the conquest of the Junghar khan-ate in 1757, there no longer appeared to be any dangerous foreign state that might seek to turn the Geluk against the Qing. Moreover, during the 1790s the Geluk church had not as yet been weaponized as an instrument of Tibetan nationalism. The Geluk counted among its monks and adher-ents not just Tibetans but also people from across Eurasia and the Qing empire. The establishment of the Ganden Podrang government in Lhasa during the mid 1600s had relied heavily on the military and financial support of the Mongols, for example. The archival holdings of the Potala Palace reveal that during the Qing period, much of the business of the Geluk church was conducted in the Mongol language. The idea that the Geluk church would be the vehicle for the realization of a Tibetan ethno-state would have been difficult for either the Qianlong emperor or Tibetan elites to imagine.

Instead, what appears to have kept him up at night—or perhaps more accurately, got him up in the pre-dawn hours to compose missives to his staff in sharp red ink—was the belief that the dynasty's lack of oversight of the Geluk might lead to a schism within the church. If the venality of high-ranking prelates or doubts about the authenticity of the Geluk's reincar-nated lamas were to lead to a breach, the overall stability of the empire would be at risk. The Geluk juggernaut was a reliable foundation for Qing rule, provided that its claims to virtue and orthodoxy remained unques-tioned, or alternatively, that any doubters remained quarantined within the geographically and politically marginalized (for the time being) alternate schools of Tibetan Buddhism.

"An Avignon Dalai Lama." "A schism within the Geluk church." While these analogies to European history would have been meaningless to the Qianlong emperor and his advisors, not to mention Geluk monks, they did not need to leaf far through their own histories for a refresher on doctrinal strife. The Geluk had originally referred to themselves as the "Gendenpa," meaning the "virtuous ones."[25] Their order had coalesced in the late 1400s as a righteous insurgency against what they perceived as the poor scholarship and lax discipline of the then dominant schools of Tibetan Buddhism. The result was a dramatic revival of piety and mass monasticism, but also considerable violence culminating in a civil war that tore apart the fabric of Tibet in the late 1500s and early 1600s. In the early 1700s, two competing Dalai Lamas had provided justification for a series of external military adventures in Tibet led in turns by the Qing state and the Junghar Khanate. It was therefore the hidden fault lines of the Geluk church, not its apparent strength—the divisiveness to which all teachings ultimately seemed prone, not the superficial unity of the "Yellow Teachings"—that I believe drove the elderly Qianlong emperor and his officials into a possible collision course with the Geluk in 1792. Church and state were neither separate nor equal, the emperor argued in the *Discourse on Lamas*, and by using the Golden Urn he hoped to take unequivocal control over both.

The Orthodoxies of Nationalist History

Much as in the Qing period, the Geluk church remained at the turn of the twenty-first century arguably the largest—in terms of both geographical scope and informal membership—extrabureaucratic, nongovernmental organization in the PRC (although during the Qing the idea of a NGO would have made little sense). This is despite the fact that the Maoist revolution of the 1950s through 1960s caused the death of many monks and permanently stripped the Geluk church of most of its assets, administrative responsibilities, and legal privileges. However, the fears that prompted the PRC to revive the Golden Urn in the 1990s and have subsequently animated the scholarship of Chinese Tibetologists are entirely different from those of the 1790s. A brief comparison helps explain why the scholar-cadres of the latter state have been so reluctant to investigate the origins of the Golden Urn ritual or the controversies surrounding its use.

Unlike Qianlong and his ministers in the late 1790s, for whom the preservation of orthodoxy in its various forms presented the greatest challenge, scholars in the PRC must manage the conflicting claims of Tibetan and Chinese nationalisms. From the perspective of the contemporary

Chinese state, the Geluk church is an obstacle to the assimilation of the Tibetans, a bridgehead for Tibetan nationalism, and the potential foundation of an independent Tibetan state. Aspirations to independent Tibetan statehood clash with the official position of the PRC since the 1990s that China has, "since ancient times," been a "unified, multiethnic nation-state." As a result, PRC historians are forced to reconcile the history of Qing empire building and its attendant violence and tensions with the demands of contemporary Chinese nationalism—in other words, to present the Qing as just one incarnation of "China." Contemporary China's Tibetologists therefore, have construed the invention of the Golden Urn in 1792 as the inevitable culmination of "China's" efforts to "perfect" (Ch. *wanshan* 完善) Tibet's indigenous government system and "realize" (Ch. *shixian* 實現) its sovereignty in the region.[26]

In the teleological world of contemporary PRC historical scholarship, the fifty-six ethnic groups that comprise the modern Chinese nation have been delimited with precision, yet the apparently inescapable historical process by which these groups melded into the singular "Chinese people" (Ch. *Zhonghua minzu* 中華民族) is measured in reference points that become increasingly wooly the further one gets into the past.[27] To investigate the origins of the urn or the debates that attended its creation and implementation, among either Qing officials or Tibetan elites, is to insinuate that the urn might not have been forged and that an alternate set of relations between the metropole and the periphery could have emerged and, in fact, might still emerge. Tracing the origins of the lottery to the mundane arena of late Ming bureaucrats would be an unsettling reminder of the alienness of the imperial bestowal and desacralize the Qing monarch's inspiration. As an icon of the fusion of Tibetans into the Chinese nation, the Golden Urn is a gift that cannot be returned.[28] Thus for PRC historians, the goal since 1995 has been to prove its existence, not probe its origins.

For the Qianlong emperor, though, as well as for most of his descendants until the late nineteenth century, the idea that the Han, the Manchus, and even possibly the Tibetans constituted a single Chinese "nationality," "race," or "ethnicity"—all possible translations of the Chinese word *minzu*—did not exist. The term *minzu* itself did not enter the Chinese vocabulary until the late 1890s, and the emperor would have strongly disagreed with the notion that the Manchus and other non-Han people of the empire were assimilating into an undifferentiated "Chinese" whole.[29] The Qing empire organized its populations into several administrative categories: the Manchus, Mongols, *Hanjun* ("Chinese martial") and other "bannerpeople," the core of the conquest elite; the Mongols of the "outer regions" of the empire; Muslims; Tibetans; and the Han "commoners," i.e., the predominantly Chinese subjects of the former Ming state. In the paternalistic language of Confucianism, Qing rulers could speak of these groups as belonging to a "single family," but not as a single "people," "nation," or "race." Moreover, when the court considered these groups, it rarely thought about them as internally undifferentiated "interest groups" or "constituencies."[30] On the contrary, Qing rulers addressed themselves primarily to indigenous elites with whom they shared personalistic bonds and a common imperial enterprise.

Ironically, many contemporary observers outside of China who have been critical of the modern revival of the Golden Urn have shared a key assumption with Chinese Tibetologists: the existence of a coherent Tibetan *minzu* or ethnicity in the eighteenth century. However, in contrast to mainland PRC scholars, those outside believe the purported existence of this emergent Tibetan nation entailed irreconcilable differences and tensions between Tibetans and the Manchus or Tibet and "China." According to this logic, Tibetans axiomatically rejected the Golden Urn as a foreign interference in Tibetan Buddhism.[31] An early articulation of this argument can be found in the influential diaries of Sarat Chandra Das, the British agent who traveled extensively in central Tibet between 1879 and 1881 and, in the interest of legitimating British objectives north of the Himalayas, was predisposed to find the Qing representatives and their regulations widely reviled and ineffective.[32] The most influential modern commentator on the urn, however, was Tsepon W. D. Shakabpa (1907–1989), who mustered a variety of nineteenth-century Tibetan sources to argue that the Qing authorities were little more than "political observers" and that the Tibetan people vigorously resisted their interference in the process of identifying lamas.[33]

Shakabpa's perspective cannot be easily dismissed. However, Tibetan-language sources do not uniformly reject Qing involvement—several contradictory statements can be found within even a single source—nor can one find within these sources a notion of the Tibetan people or Tibet that readily matches the ideals of either twentieth-century Tibetan nationalists or PRC historians working within the *Zhonghua minzu* paradigm. This is not to deny that influential ideas about Tibet as a geopolitical place or the "people of Tibet" (Tib. *Bod gyi mi*) can be found in pre–twentieth-century

Tibetan sources. It is rather to point out that these ideas were varied and inconsistent (and remain so down to the present) and that we need to be more attentive to how they interacted with other notions of political legitimacy, geography, and group identity that circulated across the Qing empire.[34]

Another reason for the widespread lack of attention to the origins and life of the Golden Urn is that historians both within and outside of China have largely ignored the Manchu sources on the subject. Contemporary PRC Tibetologists are awash in the modern rhetoric of nation-building and in the ruling language of the PRC, Chinese, rather than the legitimating ideologies of the empire and the languages of the empire's colonial elites. Prior accounts of the Golden Urn, therefore, have almost entirely relied on on the Chinese language and especially a handful of prominent (and literally monumental) public edicts such as the *Discourse on Lamas*.[35] The *Discourse* was not, however, the emperor's definitive statement on Tibetan Buddhism and the rationale for the new procedure for identifying reborn lamas. An articulation of a particular message at a particular point in time, it carefully hid the traces of debate and doubts about the Golden Urn procedure and provided neither the last word on how the Golden Urn was to be used nor any indication of the additional measures the dynasty would ultimately resort to in order to implement the new policy.

Even the Qianlong emperor himself obliquely signaled that Chinese-language sources told only one version of the story: the non-Chinese versions of the *Discourse*—the Tibetan, Manchu, and Mongol versions—stated that it had been composed for the benefit of "some Chinese, who said that I placed excessive importance on the teachings of the Gelukpa."[36] In other words, the *Discourse* was a response to those Chinese officials who criticized the expenditure of the dynasty's resources on Tibetan Buddhism and might have reasonably wondered who served whom in the exchange. The Tibetan translation of the *Discourse* never circulated within central Tibet and thus provides few clues about how Tibetans might have learned about the urn. It would take nearly a year from the time that Qianlong ordered the forging of the urn for a formal proclamation of the new ritual to be translated into Tibetan and promulgated across Tibet.[37]

If we take Qianlong's hint, then we must search for the rationale for the urn among the non-Chinese language records of the officers and agencies that dealt with Inner Asia. The task of managing Tibetan Buddhists fell not to the civil officials of the capital bureaucracy—the Six Boards and affiliated agencies that handled the affairs of the eighteen provinces of China proper—but to monks resident at Yonghegong and other imperially sponsored monasteries in and around Beijing, and, above all, the Manchu and Mongol military officers who staffed the Court of Colonial Affairs or "Court for Governing the Outer Domains" (Ma. *tulergi golo be dasara jurgan*; also known in English-language studies as the "Court for Managing the Frontiers," "Bureau of Colonial Dependencies," or "Lifan yuan 理藩院" from the Chinese name for the institution). These officers served the empire at garrisons scattered across the steppes, deserts, and mountains of Inner Asia.[38] Their work was conducted in the Manchu, Mongol, Tibetan, and Turkic languages, in addition to Chinese.

The Qianlong emperor preferred to deal with his Inner Asian subjects not from within the palaces of the Forbidden City, but while in residence at his summer retreat at Chengde. There, removed from the scrutiny of Beijing's bureaucracy, the emperor played host to monks and aristocrats from Mongolia and Tibet and in June 1792, first floated the idea of confirming the identity of reincarnations through a lottery. The early discussions of the urn, therefore, commenced not in Chinese but in Manchu—the official language of the Qing state and its conquest elite. Even after the urn had been dispatched to Tibet and the Qianlong emperor had passed away, when Qing officials dealt with the business of reincarnation they did so primarily in Manchu. This practice continued well into the first decade of the twentieth century.

Three Acts and Three Themes

My account unfolds in three acts. Act 1 begins with the aftermath of the second Gurkha invasion of Tibet (1791) and explores the deliberative process that lay behind the invention of the Golden Urn over the spring, summer, and fall of 1792. During this period, the Qing ruler became convinced that the problems of Tibetan governance could only be solved if the imperial center took a more direct role in Tibetan administration, and that such a role could only be sustained if it possessed a monopoly over the arts of divination and prognostication. In the winter of 1792, the urn was escorted to Lhasa and a second urn was installed at the Yonghegong monastery in Beijing. However, to the emperor's dismay, his officials soon reported that the Tibetans and Mongols not only did not share his sense of crisis but also had continued to seek rebirths of prominent lamas according to existing traditions. In response, the emperor ordered his officials to promote the use of the urn and discredit the oracles of central Tibet and other indigenous divination practices. Act 2 reconstructs the evolution of this campaign into a full-scale assault on the credibility of the Dalai Lama, show trials of the oracles in Lhasa, and a propaganda effort that stretched from Beijing to Tibet and Mongolia.

Act 3 arrives at the scene of our story's denouement: Labrang Trashi Khyil, a massive monastic university at the crossroads of China, Tibet, and Mongolia. In February 1797, the monastery leadership's desire to locate the third-generation rebirth of their founding lama, the Jamyang Zhepa *kūtuktu*, independently according to their own procedures collided with the emperor's new law. Upon receipt of the request to exempt the Jamyang Zhepa from the Golden Urn lottery—and despite having formally abdicated to his son a year earlier—the "retired emperor" swung back into action. Emperor Qianlong ordered a covert operation to ensure that the Golden Urn was used and that the leading candidate, the child favored within the domains of the Jamyang Zhepa, would not be selected. Told from the perspective of secret Manchu-language dispatches and Tibetan-language chronicles, this final act reveals the previously unseen manipulations of Qing officers stationed in Lhasa, the codes by which Qing elites—both Manchu and Tibetan—communicated, and the essential role of influential lamas allied to the Qing court. Ultimately it was Tibetan elites themselves who found a home for the urn within indigenous traditions of divination and erased from the historical record doubts about its use.

In presenting this story, I am concerned throughout with three interrelated and recurring themes: sovereignty, faith, and law. This book will not tell you when Tibet became part of China. Instead, it asks how Qing officials, emperors, and Tibetan Buddhists wrote about the thing we now refer to as "sovereignty." The fact that the Qing government and its elites functioned in a polyglot environment with multiple traditions of political thought resulted in diverse and sometimes incommensurate understandings of how different parts of the empire related to each other politically. Moreover, much like Tsarist authorities in the Caucasus or agents of the British East India Company before the 1770s, Qing officials and locals alike had trouble identifying or agreeing upon when, where, and how imperial rule had been established. Acts 1 and 2 trace the emergence of a distinctive imperial view of sovereignty that argued that the emperor's authority in Tibet hinged on the domination of shamans, oracles, and the technologies of divination more generally. This new sovereign claim meant that the Qing state would henceforth attempt to do much more than patronize the Geluk.

Previous scholarship on the Qing's Eurasian empire has observed that much of the dynasty's legitimacy seemed to derive from its broad support for Tibetan Buddhism and its skill at presenting Qing rulers not simply as patrons but even as bodhisattvas.[39] But the Qing state did not simply speak in a Buddhist idiom in order to gain the trust and loyalty of its Tibetan and Mongol subjects. It actively sought to remold its subjects' faith. The campaign to promote the use of the Golden Urn entailed an overt effort to build belief in the new Qing ritual and shatter trust in indigenous traditions of divination. In this respect, Qing colonialism bore many similarities to the governing practices of its southern neighbor, British India, and other contemporaneous imperial enterprises. Much as the British set about codifying "authentic" Islam and Hinduism in South Asia, the Qianlong emperor and his successors, together with their agents, set about reifying and protecting "orthodox" Buddhism as well as "shamanism."[40] As with the concept of sovereignty, understandings of "faith" and theories of how belief works were situated in specific historical encounters and cultural traditions. The imposition of the urn and the resulting conflicts provide an opportunity to observe how Tibetan elites and Qing officials thought about the nature of faith.

Our discussion of faith raises several additional questions. First, how did elite Tibetans view their Qing patrons? As Johan Elverskog has pointed out in his study of Qing-period Inner Mongolia, we should not assume that patronage of the Geluk teachings automatically translated into legitimacy for those rulers who entered into preceptor-donor relations with Geluk lamas or otherwise patronized the church.[41] Moreover, previous studies of Qing patronage of Tibetan Buddhism have failed to disentangle the actions and ideals of the dynasty's colonial officer corps, mostly drawn from the ranks of the capital's garrison of Manchu and Mongol bannermen, from the actions, ideals, and representations of the emperor. Did the faith and religious practices of these intermediaries matter to Geluk hierarchs? And what did the Qing's colonial officers think about Tibetan Buddhism? These issues come to a head in acts 2 and 3, where I examine discussions among both Tibetans and Qing authorities about what was the most effective method for identifying authentic and credible reincarnations: the Golden Urn or the prophecies of the oracles.

The Golden Urn was not simply a new procedure for identifying reborn lamas, it was also a regulation—a law, with several attendant subclauses, adjusted over time and tailored to particular reincarnate lineages. In imposing this law, official documents spoke of not only restoring faith but also a sense of fairness to the phenomenon of confirming reincarnations. In this respect, the introduction of the Golden Urn was one aspect of a broader campaign to legitimize Qing rule through promises of a cleaner legal order—a strategy the Qing shared with neighboring empires, but one that has been largely overlooked in scholarship of Qing-period Tibet.[42] Moreover, from an official perspective, the extension of law was a key mark of expanded imperial sovereignty. By this measure, Tibet had not truly "entered the map" (Ch. *ru bantu* 入版圖) until it had been sewn into the legal fabric of the empire.

Early Qing Views of Tibet

Just who were these incarnate lamas, and what had their relationship to the Qing state been like before the Qianlong emperor exported the Golden Urn to Tibet? Two essential observations must be made as we begin addressing these questions. The first is that from the perspective of Qing rulers and their field officers, Tibet and Tibetan Buddhism were always a secondary and subsidiary concern to their overwhelming priority, the security of their state vis-à-vis the Mongols. Second, Qing rulers understood "Tibet" primarily through categories and interpretations borrowed from the Mongols. Even as late as the 1790s, knowledge of central Tibet within the empire's capital bureaucracy was limited to the handful of Manchu or Mongol bannermen who had served as the emperor's personal emissaries in Lhasa and the small coterie of Tibetan-speaking lamas the emperor housed in Beijing, most of whom hailed from Gansu Province, Qinghai, or the Mongol leagues.[43] The result was that Qing rulers and their advisors understood no existence of "Tibet" distinct from its contemporaneous configuration as a domain of the Geluk church and its "Yellow Doctrines" (Ma. *suwayan šajin*).[44] Imperial advisors were primarily concerned with a church and its precepts, not a nation and its people.

The earliest Manchu-language texts referred to Tibet using terms borrowed directly from the Mongols: usually *Tanggūt* and occasionally *Tubet*. From the 1630s through the early 1700s, these terms indicated not a clearly delimited geographical place, but rather a high culture—a language, script, and body of texts and teachings. Qing sources dating to the 1620s mention a "Tanggūt state" (Ma. *tanggūt gurun*), placing it in a category equivalent to their own state and that of the Ming. In contrast to their portrayal of neighboring states, with which the first Manchu rulers saw themselves as contending for survival, the "Tanggūt state" was qualitatively different. Whereas relations with neighboring powers are a complex dance of marriages, hostages, diplomatic emissaries, petty feuds, and short, sharp wars, Tibetans appear only as the occasional "lama," and their lay governing tradition is invisible—despite the fact that central Tibet was under the dominion of the lay kings of Tsang at the time. According to one entry in the "Old Manchu Archives" from the reign of Hong Taiji, the "Tanggūt state" lay at the extremity of the known world. It was a place to be not conquered but "relied upon."[45] In these documents, the "people of the Tanggut state" (Ma. *tanggūt gurun i niyalma*) were not "Tibetans" in any modern sense—they were not a *volk* or race sharing common descent, but rather people who resided on the Tibetan plateau and were fluent in implicitly Buddhist "Tanggut" culture.[46] Over the eighteenth century, Manchu-language discussions of Tibet absorbed a number of labels that originated in the Chinese language—*wargi dzang* (Western Tsang) or *wei dzang* (Ü-Tsang) from Chinese *Xizang* (西藏) and *Weizang* (衛藏), respectively, to refer to the domain of the Dalai Lamas, and *Fandze* (Ch. *fanzi* 番子 or *xifan* 西番) to refer to the people[47]—but these terms only seem to have added to the ambiguity of just where, what, and who was Tibetan. For instance, during the latter years of the Qianlong reign and into the early nineteenth century, official publications increasingly referred to all Tibetan-speaking peoples as *Fandze*, yet simultaneously distinguished *Fandze* as a class of people residing in the border regions of Sichuan, Gansu, and Qinghai, different from the "Tanggūt people" (Ma. *tanggūt i urse* or *tanggūt irgen*, Ch. *tanggute min* 唐古忒民) who inhabited Lhasa and its environs.[48] On occasion, Qing official sources distinguished "Fan language" from "Tanggūt language," presumably indicating some knowledge of the difference between the languages spoken in Amdo and central Tibet.[49] Secret communications between Qing field officers and the court were even more likely to distinguish Tanggūts from Fandze.[50] Moreover, Qing internal reports were also inclined to see critical differences between "tribal Fandze" (Ma. *aiman i fandze*) who lived a predominantly nomadic lifestyle and other Tanggūts or Fandze who made their livings from trade or agriculture.[51] In the 1720s, the Qing state began delimiting a boundary for the territory administered by the government of the Dalai Lamas. In the aftermath, being Tanggūt or Fandze also implied a particular legal identity: these were people who by definition lived under administrative and legal orders distinct from those of the empire's Chinese interior.[52] Although Qing authors noted that historically the "Tufan" empire had unified much of the Tibetan plateau and seriously threatened both the Tang and the Song states, they did not see contemporary Tanggūt or Fandze as an inherently unified and belligerent people—a view that contrasted quite sharply with assumptions about the Mongols, and the western Mongols or Oirats in particular.[53] In short, from the perspective of Qing imperial sources dating to the late 1700s through early 1800s, while individual Tibetan "tribes," households, or communities might be a nuisance in the borderlands, it was the "Tanggūt sutras" (Ma. *tanggūt nomun*) and "Yellow Doctrines" that required careful management and constant attention at the highest levels of the imperial government.

Qing authorities were most concerned, therefore, with managing relations with the class of incarnate lamas who, as the hierarchs of the various orders and schools of Tibetan Buddhism, were often also administrators of large lay populations or were perceived as exerting enormous influence over the hereditary nobility of Mongolia and Tibet. These incarnate lamas were, as noted above, entitled by the Qing state to the status of *kūtuktu*—itself a term borrowed from Mongol. In both Mongol and Manchu, *kūtuktu*, or "noble one," was a term of veneration for important *hūbilgan*, the Mongol and subsequently Manchu translation of the Tibetan concept of *trülku*.[54]

The *Trülku* Institution in Tibetan History

In its most simple and colloquial sense, a *trülku* was a being capable of directing their own rebirth or incarnation as a result of his (and occasionally her) mastery of the Buddhist teachings. As a result, Tibetans also referred to such people as *yangsi*, "conscious rebirths." More formally, the term *trülku* refers to the "emanation body" of a buddha (*Nirmāṇakāya* in Sanskrit)—the manifestation or emanation of a buddha that is visible in the mundane world and able to bring his compassion to bear on the affairs of ordinary human beings. By the late seventeenth century, Tibetan Buddhists could divide *trülku* into different ranks and types, the most important of which were considered manifestations of powerful bodhisattvas or buddhas. The Dalai Lamas and Jebtsundamba Lamas of Outer Mongolia, for instance, were understood as emanations of the bodhisattvas Avalokiteśvara and Vajrapāṇi, respectively, and the Panchen Lamas were associated with the buddha Amitābha. Since bodhisattvas and buddhas were capable of creating multiple worldly manifestations, it was entirely possible for several *trülku* to claim to be emanations of the same one. Among the lesser ranks of *trülku* were those humans whose mastery of the teachings had given them the ability to take control over transmigration and thus continue to aid their disciples and patrons in future lives. Most *trülku* belonged to this category. However, the boundaries between these two categories of *trülku* were blurred, and disciples of *trülku* from the latter category often identified famous historical figures from classical India or the Tibetan Buddhist tradition as antecedents of their master, thus establishing more ancient and august roots. Moreover, it was also possible for *trülku* to claim to be not only an emanation of a bodhisattva but also the incarnation of a historical person (or persons). Thus, in the late 1600s, the regent Sanggyé Gyatso described the Great Fifth Dalai Lama as the fifty-fourth rebirth of a lineage that had begun with the bodhisattva of compassion, Avalokiteśvara, and then continued through a chain of succession that included a series of ancient Indian princes, Tibetan emperors such as Songtsen Gampo, the seventh-century ruler credited with overseeing the first transmission of Buddhism to Tibet, and many other Buddhist adepts from both India and Tibet.[55]

The first Tibetan Buddhist order to begin systematically identifying their leading monks as *trülku* in a chain of deliberate rebirths (or "rosary of bodies") were the Karma branch of the Kagyü order in the late thirteenth century. Although the Third Karmapa, Rangjung Dorje (1284–1339), the chief hierarch of the Karma Kagyü, is generally understood as being the first to explicitly identify himself and be acknowledged by his disciples as the rebirth of earlier Karmapas, Schwieger cautions that the idea of the Karmapa as a lineage of reincarnations and the use of the term *trülku* were not widely accepted until the life of the Fourth Karmapa (1340–1383).[56] Although it emerged relatively late in Tibetan history, the idea that certain humans might control their rebirth had deep roots in the Mahāyāna theories of the bodhisattva that had emerged in the fourth century CE. For instance, the Buddha Śākyamuni, whom Mahāyāna Buddhists considered a bodhisattva, was credited with the ability to recall and recount previous births.[57] Later, during the era of the second transmission of Buddhism to Tibet, the Indian scholar and refugee Atiśa (982–1054) had argued in his magnum opus *Bodhipathapradīpa* (A Lamp for the Path to Enlightenment) that humans who had mastered the Buddhist teachings could choose their future rebirths.[58] It should come as no surprise, then, that the earliest extant claims of *trülku*hood, which date to the late twelfth century, were made by members of the Kadam, the Tibetan Buddhist order directly inspired by the teachings of Atiśa.[59] The Kadampa were also responsible for popularizing the notion that the bodhisattva of compassion, Avalokiteśvara, was the primary protector of Tibet and that several of the most prominent masters of their order had been reincarnations of this bodhisattva.[60] The politically dominant Sakya school made a claim that their own founding patriarch, Sachen Künga Nyingpo (1092–1158), had also been a reincarnation of Avalokiteśvara.[61]

The popular culture of this period also contained practices that can be considered precursors to the development of the *trülku* institution. Tibetan sources from the twelfth through thirteenth centuries contain numerous accounts of religious adepts who were able to transfer their consciousness to animals or the bodies of other people.[62] Widely shared understandings of death and reincarnation—most importantly the idea that after death one's consciousness still lingered relatively intact for an additional forty-nine days before dissolving into a new life—meant that it should be possible for consciousness to be transferred to another body.[63]

The idea of the *trülku* offered the Karma Kagyü a number of strategic advantages. It enhanced the prestige of their leadership, who were now not simply followers of the Buddha but rather emanations of powerful and transcendental beings—buddhas and bodhisattvas in their own right. It helped keep the order from fracturing—instead of going their separate ways, disciples would stick around to learn from the rebirth. And, perhaps most importantly, it represented a means of reproducing religious and political authority in a manner at least somewhat independent of aristocratic households and lay rulers, whose whims might be fickle and whose fortunes could wax and wane. Prior to the invention of *trülku* lineages, noble households with religious pretensions such as the leaders of the Sakya had frequently attempted to pass down their authority through sons or nephews, with uneven degrees of success. In 1355, therefore, the Karma Kagyü quite consciously established another *trülku* lineage—the Zhamarpa, the first of whom had been a disciple of the Third Karmapa—and over the next two centuries, all the other major orders of Tibetan Buddhism adopted the practice.[64]

The Geluk, the dominant church of Tibetan Buddhism at the time of the founding of the Qing state in the mid 1600s, had been slow to establish its own leadership as *trülku*. Moreover, the monk credited with establishing the doctrines that would ultimately develop into the Geluk order, Tsongkhapa (1357–1419), did not become the progenitor of a new incarnation line. On the contrary, the initial strength of Tsongkhapa's order derived from the institution building that accompanied his scholarly brilliance and personal charisma. In what was conceptualized as a thorough reform of contemporaneous Buddhist culture, the Geluk reasserted the importance of mass monasticism and monastic discipline, constructed monasteries, reformed old ones, and established a unified curriculum, centralized education system, and shared ritual repertoire to maintain the unity of the movement over time and space.[65] Not until the late 1400s did the Geluk began identifying *trülku* lines among the second- and third-generation disciples of Tsongkhapa. Among these were the monks subsequently seen as the starting points for the Dalai Lama and Panchen Lama lineages, as well as several other incarnate lineages that would figure prominently in future relations between the Geluk, the Mongols, and the Qing: the Tatsak, Pakpalha, and Demo *rinpochés* (later honored with the title *kūtuktu* by Qing rulers). By the mid-1500s, the new norm among the Geluk was that *trülku* were the legitimate leaders of the church. Moreover, monks who rose to positions of prominence but lacked *trülku* status were assumed to possess the credentials to direct their rebirth in the future, thus leading to the proliferation of new incarnation lines. For instance, by the seventeenth century, it had become common for monks who held the position of *Ganden Tripa*—abbot of Ganden monastery and administrative head of the Geluk educational system—to be posthumously acclaimed as *trülku*.

Incarnation lineages were not simply a stream of rebirths or re-emanations but also corporate estates (Tib. *labrang*) passed from generation to generation. In the case of the leading *trülku* hierarchs, these estates consisted of accumulated personal effects—books, clothes, paintings, ritual objects, et cetera, along with often substantial real estate—monastic residences and in some cases entire monasteries, farms, pastures, and other revenue-generating properties that had been donated by patrons and disciples in order to sustain religious endeavors. Since these estates could be geographically dispersed and were often inhabited by substantial lay populations, even entire farming villages or herding communities, *trülku* generally retained "treasurers" (Tib. *chakdzö*), "stewards" or "overseers" (Tib. *nyerpa*), and other permanent staff to help manage their affairs and keep track of the diverse obligations of their lay and monastic subjects.

Labrang staff were generally drawn from among the clergy and shouldered substantial responsibilities, especially during the *trülku's* minority. The task of searching for and authenticating rebirths of the deceased also fell to these men. The fact that even among the Geluk there was neither a standardized procedure for identifying candidates nor a centralized authority for verifying *trülku* meant that the job was fraught with difficulties. If the searchers were lucky, an aged or dying *trülku* would have provided a testament indicating the location and situation of his future rebirth. Without such clues or in the event of a sudden or untimely death (not uncommon when epidemic diseases and smallpox in particular took a ferocious toll on Mongol and Tibetan children), searchers might begin by scouring the last acts or utterances of the deceased lama, or even examining the deportment of the corpse, for hidden signs. Other typical aspects of a search might include examining auspicious weather events, unusual natural phenomena, or even the dreams of women who had recently given birth, and consultation with other *trülku* or influential lamas—especially those who had had relations with the deceased or had been involved in previous searches. At various stages the searchers might also seek the advice of oracles, either locally or at important religious centers such as Lhasa. Oracles, or more accurately, the human spirit mediums (Tib. *kutenpa*, Ch. *gu'erdanba* 古爾丹巴) who possessed the ability to serve as the voice of gods, deities, and other supernatural beings, offered unique insights into processes of transmigration that might be otherwise invisible to humans. Moreover, laypeople, monks, *trülku*, and oracles could employ a wide range of divination technologies to gauge the progress of the search and the veracity of the candidates.

Searchers furthermore had to contend with the fact that there were also a variety of ways of transmigrating. A rebirth or re-emanation could emerge simultaneously in multiple children or even before a *trülku* had passed away. It was also conceivable that the physical process of "rebirth" itself could be avoided. Such was the case with the prominent Third Tongkhor Lama, Gyelwa Gyatso (1588–1639), who, "having no need to take existence in the womb, instead, upon encountering the body of a nineteen-year-old partially Chinese boy that was being carried to the charnel ground near the Sug river, like a bird in flight passed instantly [to the boy's body], which suddenly exclaimed, 'I'm the Tongkhor!' Both [the boy] and the corpse of the [lama] were taken to Tongkhor monastery."[66] The chronicler Drakgönpa Könchok Tenpa Rapgyé then added that en route to the monastery, the monks encountered another influential local *trülku* who upon testing the boy, immediately ordained him and gave him a new name, then received teachings from the incarnation. A later account added that remarkably, the boy, who had previously received no instruction in Tibetan, not only could suddenly read and write in the language but also thoroughly understood the texts.[67] According to both observers, this sort of "transfer of consciousness" (Tib. *drong juk*) was highly unusual. But even a cursory perusal of Tibetan texts, especially of *namtar*, the ubiquitous biographies of *trülku* and other Buddhist saints, reveals that every search unfolded in its own idiosyncratic way, shaped primarily by the precedents set by previous reincarnations in the lineage and the sentiments and concerns of the *trülku's* monastic community and lay subjects or patrons.[68]

It should come as no surprise, therefore, that these searches could be highly contentious. Whereas reincarnation initially appeared as an elegant solution to the problems posed by prior methods of reproducing religious and political authority, in practice it quickly engendered its own unique dilemmas. In the case of the Fourth Tongkhor Lama, the young, formerly "Chinese" man's mastery of Tibetan-language texts evidently laid to rest most concerns about the veracity of his claim to the Tongkhor's estate. No less an authority than the Great Fifth Dalai Lama himself testified to the lama's authenticity.[69] Yet a hundred years later, in the 1750s, two different toddlers were identified as candidates to be the sixth incarnation of the Tongkhor Lama, and the lineage split permanently into two separate streams, one in Amdo and one in Kham. For the Tongkhor lamas, the split proved largely amicable, but in many other communities—as will be discussed in act 3—conflicts among candidates and their supporters could turn violent. Moreover, the extended regencies required to raise a child to adulthood and the substantial economic and political resources available to those who controlled the *trülku's* estate provided ample incentives and opportunities for internal strife and destabilizing interventions from outside.

The Geluk Church and the Qing State

In the winter of 1652–53, the Shunzhi emperor (1638–1661) hosted the Fifth Dalai Lama, Ngawang Lozang Gyatso (1617–1682), in Beijing for the first of what would be only two face-to-face encounters between Dalai Lamas and Qing rulers during the course of the empire's history. Much was at stake in this meeting, especially for the young emperor. Having declared an end to the regency just a year earlier, Shunzhi was only fourteen years old. Surrounded by the battle-hardened uncles and other relatives who had overseen the initial conquest of the Ming state in 1644 after almost thirty years of warfare, the emperor was only barely in control of the throne, presiding tenuously over a bureaucracy riven by questions of how power would be shared between the conquest elite and the Han literati. Beyond the walls of the capital, the "great enterprise" of subjugating China had only just commenced. In the provinces, much authority had been delegated to former Ming military commanders of questionable loyalty, and in the far south and on the island of Taiwan, members of the Ming royal family still lurked, rallying widespread anti-Qing sentiments.[70] Moreover, from the north and west pressed other powerful rulers, most importantly the khans of the Khalkha and Oirat Mongols, who might reasonably be expected to worry the Qing's Inner Asian borders or even follow the Manchus into China, if the new Qing empire displayed signs of weakness. Cognizant of the Dalai Lama and the Geluk church's intimate alliances with the Mongol rulers, the Shunzhi emperor directed enormous material and human resources to the visit, despite the criticism of several prominent Han advisors in the court.[71]

Although it can be reasonably asserted that the Fifth Dalai Lama had less riding on the meeting, coming as he was at the entreaty of the Qing emperor and representing a incarnate lineage and a religious order with an institutional history stretching back to the early 1400s, his government in Lhasa was more fragile and novel that it first appears, having been established just two years before the Qing invaded China. By the early 1600s, the Gelukpa had grown into perhaps the largest among the competing traditions of Tibetan Buddhism, yet they held no monopoly over the religious landscape or the political and economic resources of lay rulers and nobles.[72]

During the Fifth Dalai Lama's youth, a century of sporadic violence between the leading families of the provinces of Ü and Tsang for the control of central Tibet boiled into full-scale civil war.[73] This conflict took on sectarian hues from an early stage. The leading families of Tsang, first the Ringpungpa and subsequently the household of Karma Püntsok Namgyel (1587–1620/21), the first Tsang "king," had long supported the Karma Kagyü, as well as several other groups, while the families of Ü—and especially those of its chief city, Lhasa—had channeled their sympathies toward the Geluk. In the year following the birth of the Fifth Dalai Lama, the Tsang king's military forces finally prevailed over those of Ü. Karma Püntsok Namgyel and his successor, Karma Tenkyong (1606–1642), proscribed the Geluk teachings and attempted to prevent the search and recognition of the Fifth Dalai Lama. Even after the Tsang king reluctantly sanctioned the identification of the incarnation in 1621, the boy's survival remained no sure thing—a fact that could never have been far from the child's mind, since his own father had perished at the hands of the first Tsang king shortly after his conquest of Ü in 1618.[74]

The historical sources for this period are highly partisan, but it is clear the ongoing violence in Tibet was never purely sectarian, secular, regional, or even ethnic, and all combatants quickly attempted to enlist outside powers despite the well-recognized dangers such a strategy might pose. Since the mid 1500s, both the Karma Kagyü and the Gelukpa had sought patronage among the Mongols, especially with the Tümed and their ruler Altan Khan (1507–1582), who had risen to preeminence among the eastern Mongols. An accord between Altan Khan and the Third Dalai Lama, Sönam Gyatso (1543–1588), sealed with an exchange of titles (including, famously, "Dalai Lama") at a meeting near Kökenuur Lake in 1578, proved particularly beneficial for the Geluk: missionaries and Geluk monasteries began to proliferate in the Kökenuur region and elsewhere within the domains of the Tümed and their allies; wealth, pilgrims, and, in several instances, Tümed cavalry flowed back toward central Tibet and the main Geluk monasteries in Lhasa. The identification of a great grand-nephew[75] of Altan Khan as the Fourth Dalai Lama, Yönten Gyatso (1589–1616), would have further solidified this alliance, had the fortunes of the Tümed not declined precipitously shortly thereafter when they were defeated by another eastern Mongol ruler, Ligdan Khan of the Chahar Mongols. The Tsang king, Karma Tenkyong, took advantage of this turn of events to solidify his newly established kingdom and, starting in the early 1620s, forged alliances first with Ligdan Khan and subsequently his successor, Choktu Taiji, a ruler from the northern Khalkha Mongols. The hegemonies of both Choktu Taiji and the Tsang king, however, were to prove short lived.

In 1637 Güüshi Khan, at the head of an alliance of Oirat tribes from western Mongolia, attacked the rich pastureland of Kökenuur and killed Choktu Taiji. Although the Geluk had only been active among the Oirat confederation since 1615, the ruling families of the Khoshud and Junghar tribes had become staunch supporters. During a pilgrimage to Lhasa following his military victory, Güüshi met repeatedly with the now twenty-year-old Fifth Dalai Lama, ultimately taking the monk as his chief preceptor and dedicating himself to the protection and advancement of the Geluk tradition. After protracted campaigning in Amdo and Kham, the khan—now the "King of the Dharma who upholds the Teachings"—delivered on his promise and invaded Tibet in 1642. Together with local Geluk Tibetan allies, the Oirat military forces brought the Tibetan civil wars to a close, executed the king of Tsang, and, to the best of their abilities, either dismantled institutions of the Karma Kagyü or forcibly converted their followers. In a striking demonstration of his faith, in 1642 Güüshi Khan directly granted the "Thirteen Myriarchies"—a metaphor for the Tibetan provinces of Ü and Tsang, along with some neighboring areas of Ngari (western Tibet) and Kham (eastern Tibet), to the estate of the Dalai Lama. The Dalai Lama and his contemporaries perceived Güüshi's gift as having transformed central Tibet into the personal fief of the Dalai Lama and the administrative center of his estate—the Ganden Podrang manor at Drepung monastery—into the *de jure* central government of Tibet.[76]

Having themselves barely survived the contest for the rulership of Tibet, the Fifth Dalai Lama and his advisors were not complacent about the future of their newfound authority. Recent history had demonstrated the utility, for instance, of Mongol allies, but also their unreliability. With this in mind, the Fifth Dalai Lama, citing the prophecies of the oracles of Lhasa, repeatedly warned Güüshi Khan and his descendants, the Khoshud nobility of Kökenuur, that any lapse in their dedication to the Geluk would result in the collapse of their principalities.[77] However, in addition to threatening the Mongols with divine retribution, the Dalai Lama personally oversaw an elaborate effort to popularize his rule through art, architecture, and literature. At the core of this project was the still radical idea that the Dalai Lama was an incarnation of both Avalokiteśvara and the ancient Tibetan emperor Songtsen Gampo and thus the sole legitimate ruler and protector of Tibet. This message was conveyed on a monumental scale by the construction of a new seat for the Ganden Podrang government in Lhasa on the ruins of the hilltop palace-fort of the ancient Tibetan emperors. The designation of this spectacular fortress as the Potala—a reference to the abode of Avalokiteśvara—was a transparent declaration of imperial ambitions in both the mundane and spiritual realms. This endeavor to scale up "bodhisattvacratic governance," to use David Seyfort Ruegg's terminology, from a model for estate management to the administration of Tibet in its entirety was unprecedented in Tibetan history.[78]

The joint Oirat–Geluk conquest of Tibet had required substantial long-term planning and discipline, as well as coordination across the lonely and harsh topography of Inner Asia. Above all, however, it was built upon a shared vocabulary—a unifying ideological program of legitimacy and justice. The key building block of this program was the idea that human activity must be guided by two distinct "traditions" or "laws" (Tib. *luk nyi* and *trim nyi*, respectively), usually articulated in Tibetan texts of the sixteenth through nineteenth centuries as the "Dharma" (Tib. *chö*) and "statecraft" (Tib. *si*), in this order.[79] Not without justification, scholars of Tibetan history have referred to the two traditions through the shorthand of "religion" and "politics." To the degree that the contemporary Western concept of "politics" refers to the sometimes morally problematic arts of dividing, regulating, punishing, and otherwise exercising dominion over other human beings, it is a reasonable match for the usage of *si* by Geluk authors. In contrast to the post-Enlightenment Western concept of "religion," however, *chö* is not a separate and parallel set of human-generated beliefs and activities about the divine, but rather the underlying and all-encompassing principles of the cosmos as revealed in the teachings of Śākyamuni, the historical Buddha. Unlike the inferior and superficial laws that attempt to guide and restrain human behavior, the Dharma constitutes a path toward action that is truly impartial, moral, and with enduring consequences. The Geluk argument was that for the "royal" or "kingly" laws (Tib. *gyeltrim*) to be genuinely august, a would-be Caesar needed to ground their decisions in the laws of the Dharma (Tib. *chötrim*).

The Geluk justified this principle on both their understanding of Buddhism and their views of key historical precedents, most importantly the achievements of the "Buddhist Kings" of the ancient Tibetan empire and, more recently, the relationship between Pakpa Lama (1235–1280) of the

Sakya church and Qubilai Khan (1215–1294), the founder of the Yuan state. The Geluk construed the Qubilai–Pakpa relationship as the archetypical instantiation of the *chöyön* bond: a concordat between a preceptor or officiant (Tib. *chöné mchod gnas*) from the monastic community and a lay "donor" (Tib. *yöndak*) or "benefactor" (Tib. *jindak*). According to the Gelukpa, sealing such a bond assumed the willingness of the lay ruler to submit (or "convert") to the tutelage of the lama-preceptor and support the general "salvation project" of the Geluk.[80] From the perspective of the Great Fifth Dalai Lama, the relationship also entailed no submission of the monk to the political diktats of the lay ruler/donor. On the contrary, it ideally guaranteed the security of the monk's own temporal administration. This was, of course the Great Fifth's view of his own relationship with Güüshi Khan and his descendants, as well as his predecessor the Third Dalai Lama's relationship with Altan Khan.

Archival materials from the Yuan period suggest that the Pakpa Lama and other leaders of the Sakya church were the political vassals of Qubilai and obeyed the khan's edicts or otherwise cited his authority when issuing commands. However, Geluk hierarchs such as the Great Fifth and his companions asserted that the *chöyön* relation in no way compromised their claims to kingship. This shift reflected the fact that over the fifteenth through sixteenth centuries, reincarnate lamas had, through the acquisition of ever larger *labrang*, emerged as rulers in their own right.[81] This was especially true in the region around Kökenuur Lake (Amdo or Domé in Tibetan sources). At the same time as the Fifth Dalai Lama was establishing his regime in Lhasa, Geluk lamas in Amdo began to identify themselves as "princes" among the Mongol aristocracy and governed substantial polities.[82] Thus Tibetan authors began to characterize such lama-lords as representing the "syzygy of Dharma and statecraft" (Tib. *chö-si zungdrel*).[83] The Great Fifth seems to have been particularly concerned with clarifying the nature of his relations with lay rulers. With regard to Güüshi Khan, the Dalai Lama went as far as to assert that even the preceptor–donor framework did not pertain to him. Instead, he argued that Güüshi had bound himself to Sönam Rapten (1595–1658), the former treasurer of the Dalai Lama's *labrang* and the chief administrator (Tib. *depa*) of the Ganden Podrang government.[84] When recollecting his journey to Beijing to meet the new Qing ruler, he wrote that when he arrived at the Qing frontier, the emperor's kinsmen showed him such deference that, "It was a sign that I was the legal and unparalleled king of Tibet."[85]

At this point, a question could be reasonably raised about what exactly a monarch stood to gain from committing to such an alliance. In the case of the Shunzhi emperor, it is clear that at least some of his contemporaries—primarily Han court officials—viewed the Dalai Lama's visit as a dangerous affront to the majesty of the emperor. As I hinted above, the answer probably lies in the obstacles the emperor had encountered to the secure exercise of his supposedly autocratic power. Engagement with the Geluk church brought with it a number of benefits. First, as Samuel Grupper has argued, in addition to any personal satisfaction that might derive from having placed one's spiritual well-being in the hands of an acclaimed *trülku*, the Dalai Lama offered the young Manchu ruler the opportunity to "re-sacralize" his rule.[86] Beginning with Altan Khan, the Gelukpa had identified their royal patrons as Cakravartin kings or Dharma kings.[87] Recognition as a Cakravartin placed Shunzhi in a lineage that included the near-mythic Indian ruler Aśoka as well as Chinggis and Qubilai khans. Such associations might legitimize his rule, but also provided justification for further expansion—the Cakravartin was, by definition, a world conqueror. Moreover, several of these rulers also became themselves re-envisioned as emanations of bodhisattvas.[88]

The relationship had other practical benefits. The commitment to Buddhist governance and the advancement of the Geluk teachings had the potential to serve as a unifying project, binding diverse populations with a common purpose and solidifying the foundations of the state. Similarly, beyond Qing borders, the pursuit of Buddhist governance could either cement alliances with neighboring powers or head off competitors who might also seek recognition as as Cakravartins. That fact that a powerful being—the worldly emanation of the Bodhisattva Avalokiteśvara (i.e., the Dalai Lama)—and potentially thousands of other monks would be dedicating their prayers and other spiritual resources to the preservation of the state was also important. As we will see in the discussion that follows, Qing rulers through Qianlong took this function very seriously. And finally, it should not be forgotten that such practices were not entirely "foreign"—the Ming state had also cultivated the support of powerful Tibetan lamas such as the Karmapa lamas and Tsongkhapa, and even as early as the Tang, Chinese emperors had sought recognition as Cakravartins from domestic Buddhist authorities.[89] Thus Shunzhi adopted the language of Buddhist governance and committed himself to *chöyön* relations with the Geluk hierarchs.

Although Shunzhi was the first Manchu ruler to bind himself to the Geluk, his efforts built on patterns set by his father, Hong Taiji (r. 1626–1643) and grandfather, Nurhaci (r. 1616–1626). The dynastic founder Nurhaci had been the first to engage the services of a "Tanggūt" lama—a monk from the Sakya school to whom he granted the title "Dharma master" of his newly established "Latter Jin" state. Hong Taiji deepened the relationship with the Sakya. In the aftermath of military victory over the last Chinggisid ruler in eastern Mongolia, Hong Taiji constructed a temple in his new capital of Mukden to honor the Sakya protector deity Mahākāla, imitating Qubilai Khan's patronage of the Sakya and proclaiming his domain the legitimate successor to the Yuan. It was in this temple that many of the ceremonies honoring the founding of the new "Qing" (Ma. Daicing) state and the consolidation of his Jurchen subjects as the renamed "Manchu" people were undertaken in 1636. Although the Dalai Lama declined several invitations from Hong Taiji to visit Mukden, he did deliver a valuable gift: formal recognition of the Manchu monarch as an emanation of the bodhisattva Manjuśrī, an identification that was extended to subsequent Qing rulers.[90]

But did the early Qing emperors understand the *chöyön* relationship in the same way that the Geluk hierarchs did? Were they truly prepared to subordinate their political agenda to the religious goals of the Geluk church, or at least recognize the parity of the emperor and his preceptor in their respective spheres? Ishihama argues that Hong Taiji took his obligations to Buddhism seriously, quoting several letters exchanged among the Qing ruler, the Dalai Lama, Güüshi Khan, and other Mongol nobles in which the flourishing of the Geluk teachings is portrayed as an essential precondition for the success of the state.[91] Yet even in these letters, the authors have subtly reversed the underlying language: where Tibetan-language texts speak of "Dharma and statecraft," the Manchu and Mongol texts discuss "statecraft and the Dharma," explicitly placing the lay ruler and patron above the church.[92] Despite sharing a vocabulary of Buddhist governance and rhetoric about the purported "parity" of temporal statecraft and spiritual mentoring, both Tibetan and Manchu sources always saw an implicit hierarchy. In contrast to much prior scholarship, Schwieger observes that even the Great Fifth Dalai Lama may have felt that subsequent to his exchange of titles and seals with Shunzhi his temporal authority derived from the Qing emperor. Although during the lifetime of the Fifth Dalai Lama neither the Shunzhi nor the Kangxi emperor ever directly interfered with the administration of the Ganden Podrang, the Fifth Dalai Lama often invoked the Qing emperor's authority in his commands to subordinates.[93] Until further research is conducted in the archives of the early Qing state, it is difficult to write with authority on the underlying motivations of Qing rulers and their advisors in pursuing the *chöyön* bond.[94]

Colonial Tibet

Between Shunzhi's nervous rendezvous with the Fifth Dalai Lama and the beginning of our story in 1792, nearly one hundred and forty years had passed and much had transpired between the Qing court, the Geluk church, and the Ganden Podrang government in Lhasa. In 1696, in the aftermath of the Junghar khan Galdan's failed attack on the Qing, the Kangxi emperor (r. 1662–1721) learned from captured Junghar soldiers that the Fifth Dalai Lama had been deceased for fourteen years. On the pretext that the Dalai Lama was on a particularly rigorous meditative retreat, the regent, Sanggyé Gyatso, had continued to rule in his name and also identified and raised in secret his purported rebirth, the Sixth Dalai Lama, Tsangyang Gyatso (1683–1706). The revelations not only severely damaged relations between the Ganden Podrang and Kangxi, who had been relying on the Dalai Lama to broker the long-simmering tensions among the Junghars, the Khalkha Mongols, and the Qing state, but also plunged Tibet into two decades of political upheaval. The Sixth Dalai Lama did Sanggyé Gyatso few favors. He refused to take the vows of ordination in 1702 and stated quite explicitly that he did not believe himself to be the incarnation of the Great Fifth.[95] Within three years, the regent was dead—assassinated by Lhazang Khan, a descendent of Güüshi Khan who appeared interested in taking his role as "king" in Lhasa more seriously. Shortly thereafter the young Sixth Dalai Lama lost his life in mysterious circumstances while being escorted to Qing territory. Lhazang Khan, who had been behind Tsangyang Gyatso's extradition to Beijing, then presented an alternate Sixth Dalai Lama to the public.[96]

In the years that followed, the debate that swirled around the identification of the Sixth or Seventh Dalai Lama (depending on one's perspective) resulted in successive invasions of Tibet. The Junghars made it to Lhasa first in 1717 and, having killed Lhazang Khan, established their own military government in collaboration with much of the Geluk establishment.

The Qing launched their own campaigns to dislodge the Junghars in 1718 and again in 1719–1720. The second attempt succeeded, largely because the harshness of Junghar rule had turned many residents of central Tibet against them, but also because Qing military forces subsequently escorted to Lhasa a youth who had been widely acclaimed as the legitimate Seventh Dalai Lama, Kelzang Gyatso (1708–1757).[97] Having planted a new Dalai Lama in the Potala Palace, Kangxi was insistent that neither the Dalai Lama nor the descendants of Güüshi Khan exercise further political authority in Tibet. A council of aristocratic ministers replaced the Dalai Lama and his regent at the pinnacle of temporal governance, and Lhazang Khan's would-be successor, Lubsang-Danzin, was returned to his base in Kökenuur with none of the honors he had expected.[98]

Despite major defeats in 1696 and 1720, the resilient Junghar khanate continued to pose a strategic threat to the security of the Qing state—a concern that bore directly on relations with the Geluk church and the Ganden Podrang. Although Kangxi's son and grandson, the Yongzheng and Qianlong emperors respectively, proved willing to sanction a variety of political arrangements in Lhasa, they also demonstrated that they would not tolerate even a hint of support for the Junghars or overt hostility to the Qing. When strife within the council of ministers devolved into outright civil war in Tibet in 1727, the Yongzheng emperor dispatched a Qing expeditionary force to support the faction of minister Polhané, who had persuaded the court that he best represented their interests. Thus, until his death in 1747, both Yongzheng and Qianlong were content to leave the day-to-day administration of Tibet to Polhané, eventually conferring the title of "king" on him in 1740. The Seventh Dalai Lama, having been associated with the anti-Polhané faction, was exiled to Kham. Although Yongzheng permitted him to return to the Potala in 1735, he remained formally excluded from exercising the political prerogatives of the Fifth and Sixth Dalai Lamas.[99]

Similar to events in 1727, the attempt by Polhané's son Gyurmé Namgyel to realign the Tibetan government with the Junghars in 1750 was met with prompt action: Qing agents in Lhasa assassinated the king and yet another military expedition marched on Lhasa. In the aftermath of this crisis, the Qing court chose to recognize efforts undertaken by the Seventh Dalai Lama to prevent Gyurmé Namgyel's revolt and calm the situation before Qing troops arrived. The Dalai Lama was once again given a political mandate—Luciano Petech argues that the Qing court and its agents saw this as a restoration of the authority that former Dalai Lamas had enjoyed—but this time would govern with the assistance of a council of ministers (the *kashag*).[100] After his death in 1757, the Qing court allowed the return of a regent, although with considerably circumscribed powers in comparison to those of the seventeenth-century regents of the Great Fifth. This revived version of the Ganden Podrang government consisted of the Dalai Lama, regents drawn from a select number of Geluk *kūtuktu* (who had usually been screened personally by the Qing emperor after a period of residency in Beijing), four councilors or *kalön* sitting atop a small Lhasa-based bureaucracy, and a field administration of Lhasa-appointed district officers. It took shape through intensive discussion between Tibetan lay and monastic elites, Qing field officials, and the court in Beijing over the 1750s and remained the basic government structure until the 1950s.[101]

Qing rulers adopted stronger measures, however, to diminish the influence of the Ganden Podrang government in the borderlands between China and Tibet and limit possibilities for independent communication with the Junghar Khanate and Mongolia more generally. In this respect, it was the Great Fifth Dalai Lama's old allies, the descendents of Güüshi Khan and the other Kökenuur-based Khoshud nobles, who were required to make the greatest sacrifices. In 1720, Kangxi stripped them of their control over territories in Kham (Eastern Tibet). In 1724, victory in war with the grandson of Güüshi Khan, Lubsang-Danzin, provided the Yongzheng emperor and his generals with the opportunity to permanently dismantle what remained of the Khoshud khanate in Kökenuur. Following a policy of "planting the banner and delimiting the land" (Ch. *Chaqi dingdi* 插旗定地), the Mongol nobles and their retainers were assigned to fixed territories in the pastures surrounding Kökenuur Lake and, in the place of their own indigenous chief, would henceforth be overseen from the neighboring town of Xining by a plenipotentiary military officer dispatched from Beijing—the Xining or Qinghai *amban*.[102] The main corridor between Tibet and Mongolia had now "entered the map" of the Qing state.[103] Yongzheng furthermore approved the extraction of the Khoshud nobles' non-Mongol, Tibetan-speaking subjects. These communities and territories were placed under the administration of civil officials in the neighboring provinces of Gansu and Sichuan. In 1726, Yongzheng approved the newly delimited borders for the Dalai Lama's government, marking, at least on paper, the end of what had been a contiguous zone of Mongol–Geluk collaboration stretching from the pastures of Kökenuur to the valleys of Kham and across the provinces of central Tibet.[104] The early 1720s thus witnessed the introduction of Qing colonialism throughout the Tibetan plateau.

Why label Qing policies in Tibet colonial? This was not an interpretation that Qing authorities would use themselves, at least not until the turn of the nineteenth century when they began to self-consciously compare their administration of the "outer regions" of the empire to the overseas colonies of the Netherlands, England, and France.[105] Qing-period Tibet was also never a destination for the resettlement of Han commoners from China proper nor the focus of large-scale efforts at economic extraction by either the Qing state or private Chinese businesses. And to speak of "Manchu colonialism" in Tibet would seem at first glance absurd: no Manchu populations ever settled permanently in Tibetan regions and Manchu bannermen were at least nominally restricted by law from any direct engagement in commerce. Yet the sustained and long-term efforts by Qing rulers, the metropolitan bureaucracy, and civil and military field officers, as well as nonofficial people from the Qing interior, to assert and maintain the dominance of the Qing imperial house and, increasingly in the late 1700s, "China" (*Zhongguo* 中國) over the Geluk church and the peoples of the Tibetan plateau merits comparison to the contemporaneous efforts of neighboring regimes such as the British in India and the Romanov dynasty elsewhere in Eurasia.

Placing Qing imperial practices and ideologies within the category of colonialism makes sense given the degree to which studies of European empires in the seventeenth through nineteenth centuries have come to emphasize the processes of cultural creation and social differentation that facilitated the political dominance of the metropole or elite minorities over an indigenous majority.[106] In a recent synthesis of this scholarship, Jürgen Osterhammel asserts that the distinguishing feature of "modern colonialism" was not colonies but rather political domination of the imperial periphery and the degree to which the metropolitan elite claimed their right to rule on the basis of cultural superiority.[107] Only a minority of European colonial endeavors resulted in "successful" economic exploitation or large-scale migration from Europe.[108] As Partha Chatterjee has pointed out in the case of British India, imperial rule rested not only on maintaining the privileged status of the ruling elite but also on reifying local cultures and limiting contact among subordinate peoples.[109] This "politics of difference" is what distinguished empires from the homogenizing principles of the nation-state (in which equal citizenship is prized over the variegated privileges of royal subjects), regardless of whether the empire's possessions sprawled across the seas or neighboring continental interiors. In this book, therefore, "colonialism" refers to the ideas that justified the superiority of the metropole and explained the differences among the empire's subject peoples, as well as to the administrative institutions, laws, and policies that embodied those ideas. Colonialism was usually based on the pretensions of a civilizing project that promised the potential transformation or assimilation of subject peoples to the ways of the ruling elite but in practice served to accentuate perceived differences between rulers and ruled.[110] Colonialism describes imperial governance irrespective of whether its subjects view their submission as legitimate or fair.

In the Qing case, well before the conquest of the Ming state early Qing rulers were deeply conscious of maintaining what they perceived as the distinctive martial and moral qualities of the Manchu banner elite. Having entered China, successive Qing rulers remained highly sensitive to the prospect of acculturation to Chinese ways and, as both Pamela Crossely and Mark Elliott have demonstrated, embarked on diverse initiatives to preserve the élan of the conquest elite. Segregated living arrangements, an edifice of legal distinctions, and repeated efforts to reify difference in historical chronicles, genealogies, and other ritual observations were remarkably successful at preserving a sense of separateness between banner people and Han commoners down to the twentieth century.[111] In this respect, Qing rule over China could be as "colonial" as its governance in the outer regions. From the perspective of the Qianlong emperor, it was nothing less than the unique attributes of the Manchu people—honesty, frugality, and martial valor, among other virtues—that enabled them to revive orthodox Confucian rule within China—a task at which the native Ming dynasty had evidently failed.[112]

Several earlier studies have interpreted the Qing state through the lens of colonialism.[113] Peter Perdue in particular has highlighted four characteristics of the Qing state that resembled other colonial systems: the institution of separate administrative regimes for different colonial regions, the cultivation of indigenous elites to serve in these separate administrations, careful management of immigration from China proper into the colonial territories (although this policy vastly expanded during the late Qing), and finally, extraction of natural resources and other local products, when possible.[114] Laura Hostetler has argued that the Confucian universalism espoused by seventeenth- and eighteenth-century Qing rulers and the imperial bureaucracy was a colonial ideology. The Qing court sponsored the creation of maps, histories, and ethnographic scholarship that served the bureaucracy's need for information about the realm's assorted peoples while simultaneously placing them within a civilizational hierarchy according to their purported assimilation to Confucian norms. These objects impressed upon the viewer the emperor's magnanimity and his right to rule as the epitome of a Confucian sage-king.

For the purposes of this book, the utility of thinking of the Qing as a colonial empire is twofold. First, studies of imperial authority elsewhere suggest that it was, almost as a rule, unevenly exercised. The justifications for imperial rule were similarly articulated and understood with remarkable diversity by both colonial agents and indigenous subjects at different points in time and in different places. Qing colonialism had different ramifications for Amdo and Kham than it did for central Tibet or Ngari in the remote far west. Agents of Qing colonialism could and did draw on more than one epistemology to justify submission to the Qing state. Documents collected for this study record the Qing ruler and his officials idiosyncratically mixing idioms from both Confucian and Buddhist traditions. Moreover, as recent studies of European colonial practices by Lauren Benton, Lisa Ford, and Elizabeth Kolsky have pointed out, initiatives to increase the authority of the imperial government over the frontier territories or otherwise encourage assimilation to the culture of the metropole most often began with settlers and local officials of various sorts or the indigenous elites themselves.[115] This observation leads to the second advantage of embarking on a study of Qing colonialism in Tibet: it draws attention to the contingent encounters between indigenous elites and representatives of the ruler on the edges of the empire. As James Hevia has aptly put it, Qing rule was a "continuing achievement" that hinged on the careful management of relations between indigenous elites and Qing agents (and on a regular basis, the emperor himself) and the subsequent representation of these meetings in official and unofficial documents.[116] Much as the unavoidable incorporation of Han literati into the new Qing administration of the former Ming territories exacerbated anxieties about the assimilation of the Manchus, the inclusion of Inner Asian elites in the Qing's system of frontier governance, even if only indirectly, also raised fears about the dilution of the authority of the Manchu and Mongol bannermen and doubts about just how far they should go to accommodate themselves to the customs and beliefs of local elites such as the prelates of the Geluk church.[117] These tensions only became more acute because in the late 1700s the colonial elite was itself expanding, as Han literati began to write and commentate on the affairs of the outer regions, join the entourages of banner officers, or even in rare cases serve in posts along the western provincial frontiers.

For these reasons, my study has focused on tracking relationships between Tibetan Buddhists and Qing colonial agents. This narrow focus on their specific and repeated encounters reveals the degree to which Qing colonial rule, much like that of other colonial regimes, was far from static or assured. Over the limited period documented in this book, the agendas, goals, and even the vocabularies of these individuals changed dramatically, reshaping the politics of both the metropole and the periphery. And even among Qing officialdom there were diverse and even contradictory notions about the goals and reach of Qing control.

The establishment and maintenance of Qing ascendancy in Tibet was the result of a series of historically contingent personal relationships and alliances, astute information management, episodic military campaigns, occasional institutional tinkering, tactical compromises, and quite a bit of "muddling through" on the part of frontier officials. These officials and their supervisors in the Qing capital premised their right to intervene in Tibet and the affairs of the Geluk church on an enduring sense of cultural and ethnic supremacy. Osterhammel writes that "colonialism is not just any relationship between masters and servants, but one in which an entire society is robbed of its historical line of development, *externally manipulated* and transformed according to the needs and interests of the colonial rulers. . . . Rejecting cultural compromises with the colonized population, the colonizers are convinced of their own superiority and of their ordained mandate to rule."[118] Osterhammel's definition captures the ambitions of many Qing officials in the 1790s and growing numbers of Han literati later in the nineteenth century. However, the Qianlong emperor and his advisors ultimately chose to impose their dominion by working, as they saw it, *within* indigenous cultural paradigms and with indigenous elites. They argued that they had the right to edit and revise religious practices in Tibet because they had developed superior knowledge of Buddhism. Furthermore, evidence from this study suggests that in both central Tibet and Amdo, far from arresting the development of Tibetan society, efforts by Qing colonial authorities to "improve" Tibetan Buddhism and local administration—and maintain the subjugation of Tibetan Buddhists to the Qing ruler—both consolidated and altered salient features of Tibetan society, inevitably introducing certain elements on the basis of their governing experience in China. In the case of the Golden Urn, Qing officials, Geluk prelates, Tibetan and Mongol aristocrats, and a variety of local notables played an integral part in making the new procedure into an old routine and, with differing degrees of intentionality, helped sustain both Qing and Geluk rule. Let us turn now to a quick overview of the chief characters.

Dramatis Personae

The Emperor: For much of the first and second acts, the voice of the Qianlong emperor—or the "Divine Lord Supported by Heaven" (*enduringge ejen abkai wehiyehe*), as he was referred to in Manchu—dominates. In the fall of 1792, Hungli (the emperor's personal name in Manchu) was eighty-one years old and had ruled for fifty-seven years. In 1795 he formally abdicated to his son, Yongyan, who took over as the Jiaqing emperor (r. 1795–1820). However, the elderly emperor was explicit that he had absolutely no intention of handing "state matters" over to his successor and continued to rule until his death in 1799 as the "supreme emperor" (Ch. *taishang huang* 太上皇).[119] This period is of critical importance to the narrative, yet the accumulating years and infirmities—loss of memory and physical decline—raise questions about whether it is really Qianlong's voice that we hear. Such questions are particularly acute for this period because the challenges facing the empire were many and complex and the emperor relied extensively on a single advisor, the chief grand councilor Hešen (和珅 1750–1799). As the head of the empire's highest deliberative body and president of three of the six main government ministries, Hešen not only controlled much of the information that reached the emperor but also drafted many of the imperial instructions: "court letters" (Ch. *tingji* 庭寄) to the Grand Council to be passed on privately to leading officials in the provinces and outer territories and "edicts" (Ch. *shangyu* 上諭) to the general population.

It can be difficult to be certain, therefore, where Hešen ended and Qianlong began. Hešen eventually stood accused of usurping imperial prerogatives and wielding the imperial brush. However, the quantity of Qianlong's "vermillion rescripts"—short, personalized responses written directly on the secret reports sent to the throne by select high-ranking officials in China proper and in the Outer Regions—and other vermillion edits and interlinear comments on the documents concerning the Geluk church and the Golden Urn dating from 1792 through 1797 indicates a relatively high degree of personal attention. Much of the argument in acts 1 and 2 rely on Qianlong's personal comments and edits on documents circulating between him, Hešen, and other confidants in Beijing and Chengde. If imperial rescripts can be used as a measure, direct personal engagement by the emperor seems to have ended in late 1797 as his health failed, and his brush disappears from view. In contrast, with the ascension of the Jiaqing emperor, the affairs of Tibet, Kökenuur, and the Geluk church in general received far less attention and were almost as a rule marked by the emperor with only the most perfunctory "noted."

The Inner Circle: The importance of Tibetan affairs to the Qianlong emperor is best indicated by the degree to which he appears to have delegated these matters to a handful of officers from an inner circle of elite Manchu families with long histories of personal service to the throne. Overall command of the 1792–93 military campaign in Tibet and Nepal and subsequent investigation of the Ganden Podrang government was handed to Fuk'anggan (福康安 1753–1796), the son of Fuheng (福恆 d. 1770), a celebrated military commander and grand councilor of the 1750s–1760s. Fuk'anggan had proven himself by leading the suppression of a major rebellion in Taiwan in 1788.[120] Among the first officials to learn about the emperor's plans for the Golden Urn was Agūi (阿桂 1717–1797), a former grand councilor and stalwart of the Qianlong reign who had also served the ruler in every major military campaign since the 1740s. Hešen, whom we have already met, was perhaps the most notorious official of the Qing period. His reputation for corruption was confirmed after Qianlong's death when it was discovered that he possessed a personal fortune of over four million taels—a sum equivalent to approximately 6 percent of the empire's treasury reserves.[121] His influence on Qing Tibet policy during the last decades of the eighteenth century should also not be underestimated, especially since it was his brother, Heliyen (和琳 1753–1796), who followed Fuk'anggan to Tibet and who, as chief Lhasa *amban* from 1793 to 1795, personally conducted the investigation of Tibetan affairs and the campaign to legitimize the Golden Urn.

The *Ambans*: In the aftermath of brief civil war in central Tibet in 1727, the Yongzheng emperor saw fit to establish a permanent mission in Lhasa for observing Tibetan affairs. Generally led by one or two high-ranking

Hešen
Detail from *Yubi pingding Taiwan ershi gongchen xiangzan*, 1788

plenipotentiary officials "personally dispatched" (Ch. *qinchai* 欽差) by the emperor from among the commanders of the capital's Mongol and Manchu military units, the office of the "*amban* resident in Tibet for handling matters" (Ma. *dzang de tefi baita icihiyara amban*, Ch. 駐藏大臣) acquired a more formal structure in the late 1740s and early 1750s. In 1747, Qianlong instituted the pattern of overlapping three-year appointments of junior and senior *ambans* to ensure that two officials were usually serving contemporaneously.[122] Following the Gyurmé Namgyel affair of 1751, the same imperially sanctioned articles that returned leadership of the Tibetan government to the Seventh Dalai Lama also, in article 2, elevated the authority of the *ambans*. Henceforth, when the Ganden Podrang's council of ministers dealt with "very important tasks," decisions had to be sanctioned with the seals of both the Dalai Lama and *ambans*.[123] Although the *amban* was charged with overseeing the work of the council of ministers, the job was still inherently a military posting. If not already of military rank, *ambans* were almost always simultaneously given military commissions as "commanders" or "vice-commanders" (Ch. *dutong* 都統 or *fu dutong* 副都統, respectively) and were, from 1751, in charge of the Qing military garrison in Lhasa, a force of ostensibly 1,500 soldiers and officers.[124]

However, as several Qing officials noted in the late 1780s and early 1790s, the two *ambans* resident in Lhasa exercised little leverage over the Tibetan administration, a situation they contrasted to the decision-making power of *ambans* stationed in Mongolia, Turkestan, Kökenuur, and the former Junghar pastures. Served by a skeleton crew and with no formal mechanism for inserting themselves into the business of the Ganden Podrang or asserting discretion over its finances, the *ambans* struggled even to stay abreast of current events. According to Agūi, the job was an "empty post."[125] As a result, the *ambans* had difficulty tracking developments both within Tibet and along its frontiers and, blindsided by events such as the first Gurkha invasion in 1788–89, were subsequently blamed by the court for a series of perceived mistakes and blunders by both themselves and the Tibetan government. Qianlong did little to help the situation by sacking and substituting officials with unprecedented speed: between 1786 and 1794, thirteen different men were appointed to serve as junior or senior *ambans*.

Beginning in 1789, a series of officials including Bajung (巴忠 1788–89) and Ohūi (鄂輝 1791–92) began drafting proposals to reform the Ganden Podrang government and hopefully add teeth to the *amban*'s theoretical oversight of the *kalön*.[126] Fuk'anggan, Heliyen, and Cengde (成德 1792–94), built upon these suggestions when they introduced their proposals in 1793. The aforementioned Twenty-Nine Articles attempted to establish mechanisms for ensuring that the *ambans* were truly the political equals of the Dalai Lama. The *ambans* were given the right to dictate decisions to any officials in the Ganden Podrang and further imperial oversight over appointments. Most importantly, these new regulations established the *ambans* as the sole channel for communication between Beijing and the Ganden Podrang government and the Geluk hierarchs in Lhasa, as well as supervision over all external communications with other rulers and states such as the Gurkhas in Nepal. The authority of the *ambans* would—in theory—be secured through their monopoly over information. Shortly thereafter, two new *ambans*, both Mongol bannermen with considerable prior governing experience, Hening (和寧1741–1821, assistant *amban* from 1793–1800) and Sungyun (松筠 1752–1835, senior Lhasa *amban*, 1794–99) were transferred to Lhasa and tasked with the job of transforming these proclamations into some sort of reality.[127]

The Beijingers: In addition to the Manchu and Mongol bannermen resident in the "Tatar City" surrounding the imperial palace, the emperor also turned to Beijing's resident *kūtuktu* and other Geluk monks for advice. The practice of inviting Geluk hierarchs to Beijing for long-term residence had begun during the late Kangxi reign, probably in response to nagging doubts about the Fifth Dalai Lama and his liaisons with the Junghars and anti-Manchu rebels in southwest China. In 1686, for instance, Kangxi began cultivating the Second Changkya *trülku*, Ngawang Lozang Chöden (1642–1712), as his chief Geluk minister, dispatching him first to Tibet and then Inner Mongolia before finally retaining him in Beijing as a semipermanent "state preceptor" in 1706.[128] The need to reassert the dynasty's commitment to Buddhist governance in the aftermath of the annexation of large Tibetan populations in Amdo and Kham in the 1720s, combined with consideration of the weaknesses of the Sixth and Seventh Dalai Lamas, resulted in an expanded effort to attract lamas to Beijing under the Yongzheng and Qianlong emperors. In the 1790s, therefore, archival documents reveal the emperor consulting with several *kūtuktu*, many of whom hailed from the pivotal crossroads region of Amdo. In the late spring of 1792, the three most prominent *kūtuktu* in the Beijing area were the Galdan Siretu *kūtuktu* (Ma. *G'aldan siretu kūtuktu*, 噶勒丹錫呼圖呼圖克圖)[129] and two monks from the Amdo region, the Gomang *kūtuktu* (Ma. *G'umang kūtuktu*, 果蟒呼圖克圖)[130] and the Sixth Tongkhor *kūtuktu* (Ma. *Dungk'or*, 洞科爾呼圖克圖), Jamyang Tendzin Gyatso (1753–1798).[131] Two other "Beijing *kūtuktus*" were also instrumental in smoothing the way for the use of the Golden Urn in the late 1790s and early 1800s, although they were not long-term residents of the capital during this period. These were the Third Tukwan *kūtuktu* (土觀呼圖克圖), Lozang Chokyi Nyima (1707–1802), and the Third Gungtang (貢唐呼圖克圖) *kūtuktu*, Könchok Tenpé Drönmé (1762–1823).

The Ganden Podrang: Formally invested with the seals of his office in 1781, the Eighth Dalai Lama, Jampel Gyatso (1758–1804), could have expected to rule unassisted, in the manner of the Seventh Dalai Lama from 1751 to 1757. In practice, however, because either he did not wish to assert his administrative prerogatives or he was prevented from doing so, the burden of governance was shouldered by a series of regents—a situation that, although not anticipated in the constitutional arrangements of 1751, was probably not disadvantageous to the Qing court. Ngawang Tsultrim (1721–1791), a highly educated monk from Amdo who had personally tutored the Qianlong emperor from 1762 to 1777, took over the position of regent in 1777. Entitled the (Ma.) *erdeni nomunhan* by the emperor and concurrently installed as the Ganden *tripa*, Ngawang Tsultrim governed until he return to Beijing in 1786.

For the next three years, the Eighth Dalai Lama ruled assisted only by the four *kalön*, as outlined in the constitutional arrangements of 1751. In Qing reports the Dalai Lama emerges as an inscrutable character.[132] The focus of near constant suspicion, accused of nepotism toward his relatives, and stained by association with ministers blamed for mishandling relations with Nepal and provoking the first Gurkha invasion in 1788–89, he was also, as we shall see, the recipient of imperial accolades in 1791–92. In 1789 the Qianlong emperor reappointed a regent, this time explicitly ordering the *kalön* to follow the regent's instructions. This move should be read less as proof of the innate governing abilities of the Dalai Lama than as an indication of the degree to which the emperor struggled to trust someone about whom he could only gather partial and indirect knowledge. The new regent, the Eighth Tatsak *kūtuktu*, Lozang Tenpé Gönpo (1760–1810), hailed from a lineage of incarnations that had been closely associated with the Qing court since the Kangxi reign.[133] In the 1750s the Seventh Tatsak *kūtuktu* had served as the abbot of the new imperial monastery at Yonghegong.[134] According to Qianlong's 1786 rankings, the Eighth Tatsak was among the four most important *kūtuktu* resident in Beijing.[135]

In a demonstration of how difficult it was to maintain the confidence of the Qing court, the Eighth Tatsak *kūtuktu* was himself recalled to Beijing in 1790 on the basis of rumors that he had become complicit in the designs of the Dalai Lama and his family. The elderly Ngawang Tsultrim returned to Tibet to take the reins, yet unfortunately passed away within months of his arrival. In the midst of this crisis, suddenly compounded by a second invasion from Nepal, the Tatsak *kūtuktu* was sent back to Lhasa. He was retained as regent until his death in 1810.[136] The Qianlong emperor rewarded the Tatsak *kūtuktu* for his services by endowing and constructing on his behalf a new "Royal Monastery" in Lhasa—Kündeling, which would thereafter be the official residence of future Tatsak incarnations and regents.[137] Also present in Lhasa for many of the key events of this book was the Eighth Demo *kūtuktu* (Ma. *Dimu kūtuktu*, 第穆呼圖克圖), Ngawang Tubten Jikmé Gyatso (1778–1819). Although only fifteen years old in 1793, he had inherited an estate with a tradition of political service—his predecessor, the Seventh Demo *kūtuktu*, had been regent between 1757 and 1777. As tutor to the Ninth Dalai Lama (1806–1815), regent from 1811 to 1819, and, perhaps more importantly, author of the biographies of the Eighth and Ninth Dalai Lamas, he played a crucial role in implementing the Qianlong period reforms and interpreting their legacy.

The Locals: The imperial campaign to stamp out reliance on the oracles and indigenous "shamans" (Ma. *saman*) focused on the four state oracles of central Tibet, the Nechung, Lamo, Gadong, and Samyé oracles. During the era of the Great Fifth, all four were commissioned as fourth-rank officials in the bureaucracy of the Ganden Podrang and frequently consulted on affairs of state.[138] The Qianlong emperor and his agents fixated on the human medium and his assistants at Lamo monastery who channeled the "Dharma protector" (Tib. *chökyong*; Ma. *cuijung*, Ch. *chuizhong* 吹忠/垂仲/吹仲) deity known as Tsangpa or "the Brahmā with the conchshell topknot."[139] Chinese and Manchu documents frequently elide the distinction between the human medium and the protector deity, referring to both generically as the "Lamo Chökyong."[140]

As the Qianlong emperor and his officials attempted to promote the use of the Golden Urn and suppress the oracles, the searches for three different rebirths posed critical tests in three key regions. These were the searches for the Third Erdeni Pandita *kūtuktu* (1793) in Outer Mongolia, the Eighth Pakpalha *kūtuktu* (1796) in Kham, and the Third Jamyang Zhepa *kūtuktu* (1797) in Amdo. As indicated by the shared title of *kūtuktu*, all three lineages received imperial sponsorship. However, unlike the "Beijingers" described above, they rarely resided for long periods of time in either Chengde or Beijing. Their status as *kūtuktu* primarily reflected their importance to the dynasty's system of local administration in Tibet and Mongolia.

The Erdeni Pandita lineage (Ch. *E'erdeni Bandida hutuketu* 額爾德尼班第達呼圖克圖) dated to the seventeenth century. In the 1650s the First Erdeni Pandita, Lozang Tenzin Gyeltsen (1639–1702), a descendant of the Chinggisid ruler Dayan Khan (1464–1517), founded the monastery of Lamiin Gegeenii Khuree in the Khangai Mountains of Mongolia after returning from a period of study in Tibet. During the life of the Second Erdeni Pandita (1703–1788), the *trülku*'s properties coalesced into the second largest ecclesiastic estate among the Khalkha Mongols.[141] If the search for the Third

Erdeni Pandita *kūtuktu* was the court's first chance to promote the Golden Urn among the Khalkha, the death of the Seventh Pakpalha *kūtuktu* (1755–1794) presented a similar opportunity in eastern Tibet. The Eighth Pakpalha was heir to a large estate centered at Jyampaling monastery in the town of Chamdo, where it had grown rich from its strategic location on the main trading route between Tibet and Sichuan. Conceived of as emanations of Avalokiteśvara, the lineage had been influential teachers and the focus of devotion and salvation in Kham since the 1500s.[142]

Although the construction of Labrang Trashi Khyil, the monastic seat of the Jamyang Zhepas, dated only to 1711, by the 1790s it was already a major center of Geluk learning and pilgrimage in Amdo. Under the tenure of the Second Jamyang Zhepa, the monastery had expanded to encompass four different teaching colleges, housing two to three thousand monks depending on year and season.[143] His estate directly administered and taxed six to twenty-four thousand laypeople scattered across neighboring farming and herding communities and was the focus of donations—both regular and irregular—from a much wider network of supporters scattered across Amdo.[144]

Labrang monastery
Rubin Museum of Art, C2012.4.3 (HAR 1097)

In the context of managing these searches, the Qing state was forced to deal with a range of additional local elites: lay notables, headmen, and householders (parents of prospective *trülku*) as well as the *labrang* estate treasurers, stewards, and chamberlains, monastery abbots, and other monks who might be involved in locating the rebirths of their former master. These individuals represented the upper tier of indigenous elites and were therefore the primary target of Qing policies and messaging. In the case of the Erdeni Pandita, the Qing initially dealt with the treasurer of his estate, Nawangdasi (Ch. Nawang zhashi 那旺札什),[145] who had already been investigating the rebirth of his teacher since 1791. In the case of the Pakpalha *kūtuktu*, Qing authorities coordinated the search with the Fourth Zhiwala *kūtuktu*, another lama from the same region. During the search for the Jamyang Zhepa in 1796–97, a much wider range of characters emerge from contemporaneous documents, most importantly the treasurer of the *trülku*'s estate and several other prominent local *trülku*. Among these was a future abbot of Labrang monastery, the Second Belmang Pandita Könchok Gyeltsen (1764–1853), who led the monastery's delegation to Lhasa to observe the Golden Urn ritual.

The Troublemakers: An upstart power in the Himalayan region, the Gurkha king Prithvi Narayan Shah (1723–1775) successfully unified the small states of the Katmandu valley under his control in the 1760s. Under his successor Bahadur Shah, tensions grew between Nepal and Tibet over the value of the coinage used to transact cross-border trade as well as the treatment of merchants. These tensions were exacerbated when a feud among the relatives of the Sixth Panchen Lama (1738–1780) over the wealth of the deceased lama's estate spilled over the border. In 1788, the deceased Panchen Lama's stepbrother, the Tenth Zhamarpa, Chödrup Gyatso (1742–1793), fled to Nepal, bringing with him not only a considerable number of followers but also detailed information about the lay of the land north of the border. The Gurkhas invaded in 1788 and, having dealt several defeats to the Tibetan military, accepted an agreement—the terms of which were kept secret from the Qing court, but were not entirely unknown to the *ambans*—to receive a yearly stipend from the Tibetan government in return for their withdrawal. In 1791, the Ganden Podrang's failure to pay precipitated the abduction of two *kalön* who had been sent to renegotiate the treaty and a large-scale invasion of Tibet by Gurkha military forces. This event, in turn, catalyzed the events of this book.[146]

ACT I

The Royal Regulations

In December of 1794, the Qianlong emperor handed down a striking set of instructions. The emperor's newly appointed chief representative to Tibet, Sungyun, was given strict orders not to prostrate when meeting the Eighth Dalai Lama. Sungyun could not have been unaware of the delicacy of the issue since he had helped manage the embassy of Lord Macartney, the English ambassador whose reluctance to prostrate before the Qing ruler had caused so much trouble in Beijing just a year earlier.[1]

The Qianlong emperor feared that "Sungyun, a man of the Mongol banners who reveres the Yellow Doctrines," might show too much humility in the presence of the Dalai Lama and fail to uphold the precedent set by the previous chief *amban*, Heliyen. Reports of Heliyen's decision not to prostrate when meeting the Dalai Lama in 1792 had been received with approval at the Qing court. The Qianlong emperor provided the following explanation to Sungyun:

Heliyen did not prostrate before the Dalai Lama, yet regardless [those in attendance] were extremely obedient and respectful to him. Although the Tatsak and Demo *kūtuktus* did not kneel before [Heliyen], I have received subsequent memorials reporting that all the others, from the *kūtuktus* to the *kalön*, knelt. Heliyen's behavior is very pleasing. If any *ambans* were to act in such a haughty and arrogant manner in other places, I would probably find it unacceptable. Yet for the past several years the customs of Tibet have been in decline. The only reason things are not completely in tatters is because in reality it is the *ambans* who have been entrusted with containing all the problems [the Tibetans] have encountered. Thus since the *ambans* have rectified matters, authority [*toose*] resides in them. Since they have only just found a basis for managing affairs, it is acceptable that they have not been able to pin [everything] down.[2]

These instructions succinctly encapsulate the dramatic shift in Qing perspectives on the political authority of the Dalai Lama and the administration of the Ganden Podrang government in Lhasa between 1791 and 1794. As he considered the affairs of the proceeding three years, Qianlong clearly felt that they had culminated in the permanent transfer of sovereignty to the dynasty. This and other related documents expressed this political change using the Manchu word *toose*—a term generally translated into English as "power," but which in the hands of the Qianlong emperor and his ministers connoted the authority to make the final decision. However, the establishment of more direct rule and the overt assertion of sovereignty in Tibet in the context of encounters between Tibetans and Qing officials was not inevitable; nor had this policy initially been the goal of Qing officialdom, even in the immediate aftermath of the Gurkhas' attack on Tibet and the collapse of indigenous defensive forces in the winter of 1791–92. On the contrary, the unprecedented articulation of Qing sovereignty in Tibet was intimately linked to the emperor's new interest in controlling the arts of divination. Act 1 traces the rise of the Qing court's concern with Tibetan divination practices—a concern that culminated in the argument that the practical exercise of Qing authority over all matters Tibetan required as a prerequisite a monopoly over the use of divination.

The imposition of Qianlong's designs for the Golden Urn, however, was not unimpeded. From the outset, court confidants such as Agūi and the Galdan Siretu *kūtuktu* expressed concern that the new procedure would either not achieve its desired goals or have to be modified. Most significantly, the emperor's advisors prevented him from proscribing the role of the oracles of central Tibet in the selection process. The Qianlong emperor's most famous statement on Tibetan Buddhism and reincarnation, the *Discourse on Lamas*, issued in mid November 1792, papered over these internal debates. This examination of the deliberations that lay behind the public statements finds that the Qing government's ambitions went much further than simply disciplining the reborn lamas of the Geluk school. Intent at first on establishing control over the arts of divination, Qianlong and his advisors ultimately found themselves arguing for the termination of temporal rule by monastic authorities.

Cooperation: Fuk'anggan and the Eighth Dalai Lama

Prior accounts of Qianlong's reform of the Geluk church and the Ganden Podrang government generally begin with the assumption that imposing a more direct form of imperial control in Tibet was a perennial objective of the Qing court. By Qianlong's own account in the *Discourse on Lamas*, the reforms had been a long time coming: he had merely been waiting for a "fortuitous moment" to implement his "brilliant decisions."[3] The archives, however, tell a different story. In 1789 and 1790, in the aftermath of the first short conflict with Nepal, the court had in fact received two sets of proposals for reforming the Ganden Podrang government from Bajung, a Tibetan-speaking Manchu whom the emperor had personally dispatched from the Court of Colonial Affairs, and Ohūi, the highest-ranking military commander in the southwest. The proposed measures tackled a range of issues such as the military preparedness of Tibetan troops, enhancing the ability of the *ambans* to oversee the work of the *kalön* and approve appointments within the Tibetan bureaucracy, but they were not adopted or implemented. Instead, deliberations focused primarily on the purported corruption of the relatives of the Eighth Dalai Lama and a handful of other Tibetan officials and ultimately resolved that hauling off a couple of the Dalai Lama's cousins to Beijing for punishment and appointing a trusted regent—the Tatsak *kūtuktu*—would be sufficient to rectify matters.[4] Considering this track record of inactivity and neglect of Tibetan affairs, Qianlong's 1793 lecture on acting at a "fortuitous moment" reads more like an attempt to explain why he had not taken action earlier. Moreover, despite expressing considerable distrust of the Eighth Dalai Lama on several different occasions between 1789 and 1790, the emperor does not appear to have entirely given up on him. The replacement of the governing Geluk hierarchs with Qing appointees from the imperial metropole was not on the agenda when Qianlong first learned of the Gurkha invasion of Tsang in late September 1791.

Initially Qianlong and his ministers were impressed by the manner in which the Dalai Lama and the abbots of the major monasteries in Lhasa faced the threat of a Gurkha attack. In truth it was the apparent witlessness of the serving Lhasa *ambans*, Bootai and Yamantai, that most vexed the court. As the Gurkha forces marched across the Tibetan frontier and then sacked Trashi Lhünpo, the *ambans* urged the Dalai Lama to flee with the young Panchen Lama northeast to Amdo. The Dalai Lama resisted this suggestion and after traveling to the Jokhang Temple to perform his own prognostication, announced that the Gurkhas would not make it to Lhasa. His biographer, the Eighth Demo *kūtuktu*, records the Dalai Lama as berating the *ambans* for their lack of resolve.[5] Upon receiving their report that the Dalai Lama had refused to budge from the Potala, Qianlong wrote, "It is fortunate that the Dalai Lama and the abbots are decisive and will tenaciously defend Buddhism. The people will be fortified through their unity and not take to flight at the slightest fright. This bestirs my heart, reward them!"[6] The *ambans*, however, were promptly cashiered.

Inspired by the Dalai Lama's fortitude, representatives of the monastic community of Lhasa proposed opening a second front in the war against the Gurkhas: "If we are unable to destroy those demons of rage [the Gurkhas] who threaten the body of the Glorious Lama [i.e., the Dalai Lama] this will be a major sin against the jewel vehicle of us Buddhists. We lamas by means of a violent device will cut [the Gurkhas] off from the deities who support their domain and visualize their painful death."[7] The deployment of prayer against the Gurkhas quickly received the full support of the Qing court. Qianlong certainly assumed that the Gurkhas would bring to bear whatever magical weaponry they could muster. In this escalating prayer war, a flurry of communications passed between Qianlong, Agūi, Hešen, and the Dalai Lama concerning the sponsorship of major ceremonies in both central Tibet and Beijing in the winter and spring of 1791–92. In a court letter passed to the Dalai Lama via the Grand Councilors Agūi and Hešen, the emperor stressed the important contribution that "earnest and sincere recitation of sutras" could have on the progress of the war. He already credited the work of the monks of Ü with "pinning down the squirming Gurkha bandits" when the latter's campaign failed to reach Lhasa.[8] He was particularly concerned about the abilities of the renegade Zhamarpa Lama, who was living under the protection of the Gurkhas. He warned the Dalai Lama: "As for the Zhamarpa, he is an evil lama of the Red Hats, a deceitful person who is an expert at wielding harmful magic. At this time it cannot be predicted what sorts of futile magic there will be, so [you] must be ready to intercept and repel."[9]

When Fuk'anggan and the vanguard of the Qing expeditionary force arrived in Lhasa on February 14, 1792 (QL 57/01/22), Fuk'anggan and Qianlong were as yet undecided about what comportment would be appropriate when meeting the Dalai Lama. In the previous decades it had been customary for the Qing officials to prostrate before the Dalai Lama, especially on the occasion of their first audience upon arriving in Lhasa to take up the post of *amban*.[10] Although it is unlikely that the officials had been performing the *ketou* (磕頭), the elaborate routine of bowing and "head-knockings" undertaken at formal audiences with the emperor, the language used in Fuk'anggan and the emperor's discussion of this issue made no semantic distinction between the two—it was all "prostration" (Ma. *heng-kilembi*, Ch. *zhanli* 瞻禮, or *xingli* 行禮). And regardless of how it was conducted, they agreed that prostration conveyed a political message and needed to be carefully considered. However, in contrast to his instructions to Sungyun two years later, the emperor allowed Fuk'anggan to use his own discretion:

> Since you have the rank of general and are traveling to Tibet to settle affairs, when you first meet in order to convey my instructions, it is naturally not necessary to prostrate [Ch. *xingli*] before him. Yet the Tibetans [Ch. Fan] of Tibet take etiquette seriously; therefore it is not inadvisable to show a bit of respect. You should deliberate on this matter and by your comportment make the right impression and preserve their system.[11]

It is clear from these instructions that privately Qianlong believed that Fuk'anggan as both general and representative of the imperial personage outranked the Dalai Lama, but they do not imply that at this time the emperor or his courtiers envisioned the transfer of authority from the Dalai Lama to court-appointed officials in the way that they would one year later. And even if Qianlong did believe that the *toose* of Tibetan officials had shifted, then he certainly felt it was not yet the time to force the issue.

Both Fuk'anggan and the Demo *kūtuktu*, who witnessed this event and authored the biography of the Eighth Dalai Lama, write that upon arriving for the audience the general had prepared to prostrate. However, according to the Demo *kūtuktu*, the Dalai Lama prevented Fuk'anggan from performing the act out of respect for the "customs of the interior" and the general's status as the "fruit of the vision" of "the emperor who is truly

Fuk'anggan
Detail from *Yubi pingding Taiwan ershi gongchen xiangzan*, 1788

Manjusri, the father of all Buddhas."[12] Fuk'anggan's report agrees at least partly here with that of the Demo *kūtuktu*. The general wrote that the Dalai Lama stated, "A monk like myself will not accept being prostrated to by an unusually important official such as yourself."[13] Yet the Dalai Lama's deference to Fuk'anggan was finely calibrated. According to the Demo *kūtuktu*, the Dalai Lama and the general exchanged ceremonial scarves "as equals," after which the visitor was ushered to a seat positioned slightly lower than those of the Dalai and Panchen lamas.[14] The general simply notes that this seat was "exceedingly proper."[15]

Although it is not recorded in the Tibetan-language account, Fuk'anggan reported that before taking his seat he delivered orally an edict from the emperor. According to this summary, the edict reassured the Dalai Lama that the purpose of the military expedition was to protect the Geluk church.

The statement furthermore reiterated the emperor's praise for the Dalai Lama's fortitude in the face of the Gurkha assault and criticism of the *ambans*. Yet it was not all compliments: Fuk'anggan concluded by relaying the emperor's judgment that because "those people in Tibet who govern affairs are unable to think long term and only concern themselves with the short term" and the "Tibetan troops are much too cowardly," in the future, "after the bandits have been pacified and eliminated, with regard to the matter of reconstruction, it will be necessary to design and establish new laws to ensure that the border is tranquil and there are no further disasters."[16] Since the Demo *kūtuktu* did not include this remark in his summary of the event, it is difficult to know if it was actually communicated. However, from Fuk'anggan's subsequent reports, this was primarily directed against the lay representatives of the Ganden Podrang administration. Fuk'anggan implied that it would be the responsibility of the Dalai Lama and Panchen Lama to promulgate and enforce the future laws.

In a separate memorial filed on the same day as the audience, Fuk'anggan drew on information supplied by the Dalai Lama to offer his own explanation for the Gurkha invasion. He blamed the conflict first of all on the Gurkhas, who had taken advantage of weak Tibetan defenses to attempt to resolve a dispute over exchange rates with force. The general apportioned blame to the *kalöns* and chief *amban* Bajung as well, singling them out for spinelessness and for signing a separate and secret treaty with the Gurkhas that they clearly had no intention of following through on. Yet in Fuk'anggan's analysis the Dalai Lama emerged unscathed, a testament, perhaps, to the impression that the lama and his attendants had skillfully made on the general prior to and during his audience. Where the Dalai Lama and his advisors, especially the former regent, Ngawang Tsültrim (the First Tsemonling *kūtuktu*, 1721–1791), were resolute, uncompromising, and willing to prosecute hostilities to their conclusion, Tibet's secular ruling elites were "cowardly and unable to think long term about the implications of their decisions." He characterized the Dalai Lama as an effective administrator and commended his skill at organizing supplies for the military force. Fuk'anggan also offered that he found the ten-year-old Panchen Lama so attractive and charming that it was hard to believe he was not really a reincarnation. Therefore Fuk'anggan suggested that the centerpiece of any reform effort must be to establish supervision over the council of ministers (the Kashag).[17]

From the tone of these reports, it appears that the court was preparing a rationale for reform, but not a sweeping transfer of political authority. The emperor's own message, for instance, was itself vague: both the *ambans* and the chief ministers (*kalöns*) of the Tibetan government had been the target of the emperor's withering criticism, not the Dalai Lama. If anything, Fuk'anggan's comments suggest an interest in enhancing the authority of the Dalai Lama at the expense of other indigenous elites. Moreover, consideration of concrete measures to improve the governance of Tibet was, according to Fuk'anggan, "not an urgent matter at present."[18] His request to postpone further discussion of reforms was a sign that at the very least he had not yet fixed ideas of what a post–Gurkha war Tibetan government would look like.

Sources of Doubt Before 1792

The initial impetus for the urn ritual came not from a desire to assume the political authority of Tibetan Buddhist monks (this would come later and only in fits and starts) but from profound feelings of insecurity fed by the unpredictable nature of reincarnation and the seemingly capricious and unconstrained behavior of the oracles, the handful of individuals whose skills at spirit possession and divination frequently provided the final word on the identification of reincarnated lamas and even Tibetan government policy more generally. The idea for the urn arose first among Qianlong and his inner circle of advisors. This group included Hešen and his brother Heliyen; the old stalwart of the Qianlong reign, Agūi; and other trusted and influential lamas who resided in Beijing. When examining the origins of the Gurkha war they determined that the root cause was a scramble for wealth on the part of a corrupt group of interrelated nobles and reincarnated lamas. If these lamas were fraudulent, then the oracles who had identified them were clearly charlatans as well. Moreover, the court blamed defeatist divinations for the quick collapse of defenses around Trashi Lhünpo monastery. They worried that a political order that hinged on faith in reincarnation was fragile if the process of identification was not reliable. If the subject populations of the various monastic domains of Inner Asia started to doubt the legitimacy of their lama-lords, or, even worse, if conflict broke out between different parties supporting different candidates, there might be grievous strategic consequences for the dynasty. The

Gurkha war was thus understood first as a domestic crisis and only secondarily as a foreign crisis. The latter followed naturally, but it is highly indicative that the Qing reform efforts began by tackling what they perceived to be the core problem—restoring faith in the authenticity of reincarnation. Only months later did the court begin pulling together a program for the reform of the Tibetan administration. As Fuk'anggan had pointed out, the superficial squabbles over trade and coinage were to be handled later. Understanding the motives of the Gurkhas and punishing their transgressions were secondary to dealing with the seeming moral collapse of the Tibetan ecclesiastic elite.

Doubts about the ability of disciples of powerful Buddhist adepts to accurately locate their rebirths were as old as the institution of the *trülku*. No less an authority than the Great Fifth Dalai Lama gave voice to these misgivings. He began his delightfully irreverent autobiography with the observation that he had taken the throne of his predecessor, "like a donkey clothed in a leopard's skin." Such humility was *de rigueur* in the autobiographical writing of *trülku*—it was unbecoming for a lama to boast (this was the job of his biographers). But the Great Fifth's criticisms of *trülku* were particularly cutting:

> Here in Tibet, which is unlike India, there are two kinds of lamas, one hereditary and the other reincarnate. The first are learned in the two traditions, like a son capable of continuing his father's heritage. There is no interruption and his followers can have peace of mind. The second one is the reverse; he is afraid that he may not receive gifts from the people, both the living and the dead, like the *manipa* who collects alms with his box of sacred objects. His followers worry that they may not find the reincarnate after the lama's death. They go forth and precipitously recognize boys put forward by pretentious parents. People get carried away, like the rabbit in the story startled by the *chal* noise; they see things as if they were snakes that are in fact ropes. These lamas are really foxes disguising themselves as lions.[19]

If this was not enough, the Fifth Dalai Lama claimed to have no recollection of his previous lives and suggested that his own identification in 1621 was a somewhat arbitrary affair. Such doubts may have contributed to his extensive efforts at self-deification: the construction of palaces, historical narratives, and art that associated him with the Bodhisattva

Avalokiteśvara and previous Tibetan rulers and Buddhist masters. Even among these projects, however, there were ideas that might cause problems for future Dalai Lamas. In the mid-seventeenth century, for instance, the Fifth Dalai Lama began to advance the notion that there would be only seven Dalai Lamas. In making this claim, the Great Fifth was borrowing a popular prophecy from the Kadam school of Tibetan Buddhism that had predicted the arrival of Seven Buddhas who would promote the teachings and protect the world.[20] After the death of the Fifth Dalai Lama, the regent, Sanggyé Gyatso, further promulgated this idea, even including it in a letter to the Qing court that attempted to justify his own rule in Tibet.[21]

Members of the Qing court shared the doubts of Tibetan elites. The *Discourse on Lamas*, for instance, echoed a sarcastic comment in the Fifth Dalai Lama's autobiography that called into question the notion of conscious rebirth by noting that, "there is neither *trülku* of the Buddha nor of Tsongkhapa."[22] Yet it is clear that Qianlong personally believed that there were real *trülku*. His close advisor and "state preceptor" (Tib. *gur gyi loppön*, Ch. *guoshi* 國師), Changkya *kūtuktu* Rolpé Dorjé, was the most famous example.[23] As the case of the Zhamarpa lama demonstrates, Qianlong still feared the powers of even those lamas upon whom he publicly cast aspersions.[24] Thus the important matter is not faith in reincarnation per se but the credibility of the recognition process. And there is good evidence that this issue had been a concern of the emperor for several decades.

The best-known precedent for an intervention into the recognition process was the 1758 decree that forbade the followers of the Jebtsundamba *kūtuktu* from searching for his reincarnation among the aristocracy of Mongolia. Qianlong alluded to this precedent when he described in *Discourse on Lamas* the prediction of the Tüsiyetü Khan that his wife's unborn child would be the next Jebtsundamba and subsequent embarrassment when the child turned out to be a daughter. Peter Perdue has argued that the 1758 prohibition and the subsequent Golden Urn lottery were both motivated by the strategic desire to head off the possibility that a powerful incarnation would emerge within the household of a great Mongol lord, thus creating a potent challenge to the hegemony of the Qing emperors in Inner Asia.[25] This interpretation makes good sense because the 1758 edict followed closely on the suppression of the Chinggünjab rebellion of 1756–57. During this incident, a disaffected Khalkha prince, Chinggünjab, had attempted to gain the support of the Jebtsundamba for his armed resistance to Qing military levies. In 1792, Qianlong and his ministers may have continued to worry about the convergence of military and religious authority among indigenous elites, but this line of reasoning does not appear in the records of their deliberations.

According to the Tukwan *kūtuktu*'s 1798 biography of Changkya Rolpé Dorjé, during the early 1760s, the search for the reincarnation of the Seventh Dalai Lama may also have briefly raised alarms within the Qing court. Qianlong dispatched Rolpé Dorjé to Tibet to coordinate the search with the Sixth Panchen Lama. However, although the candidate selected by these two eminences was duly recognized by the emperor and enthroned in 1762, Tukwan wrote that supporters of an alternate candidate continued to protest. Fortunately, the Changkya *kūtuktu* was able to soothe local feelings and prevent the extradition of the troublemakers to Beijing for punishment.[26] There is no mention in either Qing or Tibetan sources about whether the discord that emerged during this search stemmed from the Great Fifth Dalai Lama's prediction that there would be only seven Dalai Lamas. Although this notion appears to have been buried by the late eighteenth century, it is hard to imagine that there were not still some well-read Geluk elite who nursed their suspicions in private. The challenge of persuasively identifying a future Ninth or Tenth Dalai Lama could not, therefore, be underestimated.

A court letter from Qianlong concerning the reincarnation of the Changkya *kūtuktu* in 1786 is perhaps an early articulation of the concerns that would become prominent in 1792. In the aftermath of Changkya Rolpé Dorjé's death in 1785, the bereaved emperor took great interest in the process of locating the *kūtuktu*'s rebirth. Rolpé Dorjé had left instructions that his rebirth would occur in a place known as "Ralo" under the jurisdiction of the Xining *amban*. Thus Qianlong instructed Bufu, the Xining *amban*, to coordinate with the Chuzang *kūtuktu* (Changkya Rolpé Dorjé's younger brother) in the search. Qianlong warned the *amban* to beware of corruption: "When the rebirth emerges, it cannot be foreseen whether there will be petty quarrels over which person it is. At the time when the *kūtuktu*'s disciple (Ma.) Gelek Namk'a returns to the pastures, it is unacceptable for him, having accepted any goods, to come to an identification of the reincarnation according to his own feelings."[27] This represents the articulation of two concerns that would become more prominent over the next couple of years: first, the emperor worried about the potential for local conflicts over different candidates. Second, he feared that those charged with assisting in the search could be corrupted by the potential for personal gain. A year and a half later, Qianlong ordered that the name of the candidate located by Chuzang *kūtuktu* be sent to Tibet for confirmation by the Lamo Chökyong oracle.[28] In May 1788, Qianlong received word that the oracle had sanctioned the child in question.[29]

Overall, although the archival record demonstrates that the Qing court kept close track of searches for important rebirths, there is no evidence from before 1792 that suggests a desire for a major intervention into the process or acute suspicions of the oracles or other divination arts of central Tibet. In fact, the evidence suggests that on the contrary, the Qianlong emperor had considerable respect not only for the oracles of central Tibet in general, but specifically for the oracle of Lamo monastery. The registers of the imperial workshops note that in 1781 the emperor had received a Tibetan-style *tangka* painting depicting the Lamo protector deity as a gift from an emissary of the Drungba *kūtuktu* (of Trashi Lhünpo monastery). Moreover, the third Changkya *kūtuktu* had relayed gifts to the emperor directly from the Lamo oracle and, as recently as 1792, the Grand Council had bestowed gifts in return.[30]

The Sack of Trashi Lhünpo and the "Concocted Prophecy"

The collapse of the defenses at Trashi Lhünpo monastery in Tsang and the subsequent plundering of the monastery not only provided the Qing dynasty with *casus belli* for launching an expeditionary force against Nepal but also resulted in a key imperial pronouncement on divination and the position of lamas under Qing law that would shape the thinking behind the emperor's *Discourse on Lamas*. The court's search for culpability in the immediate aftermath of the debacle at Trashi Lhünpo resulted in the execution of an unlikely figure: a senior monk *jedrung lama* Lozang Tenpé (Ch. Luobuzang danba 羅布藏丹巴)[31]—one of only nine monks who remained behind in the monastery to attempt to defend it from the Gurkhas.

The fall of Trashi Lhünpo was a major embarrassment for the court. Just two days before the Gurkhas captured the monastery, the chief *amban*, Bootai (Ch. Bao-tai 保泰), who had arrived to escort the young Panchen Lama back to Lhas,a filed a firsthand report from the front lines that, that although the situation was indeed desperate, the monastery was defensible.

A little more than thirteen hundred soldiers had been collected, and the four thousand resident monks had been ordered to construct fortifications and otherwise prepare to defend the place. Bootai noted, however, that there were rumors that the treasurer of the monastery, the Drungpa *kūtuktu*, Lozang Jinpa (who was also a brother of the deceased Sixth Panchen Lama and the Tenth Zhamarpa), was preparing to flee. Therefore he had sent a letter to the lama ordering him to stay put and sustain the morale of the monks.[32] Unfortunately, after returning to Lhasa, Bootai was informed by the *kalön* that just three days after he had departed with the Panchen Lama, Drungpa slipped away, taking with him as much valuable treasure and he could carry and the morale of the remaining monks as well. The monastery fell into the hands of the Gurkhas the next day.[33]

At first the wrath of the court fell squarely on the Drungpa *kūtuktu*. When on November 5, 1791 (QL 56/10/10), the assistant *amban*, Yamantai, suggested permitting him to return to the monastery to assist in reorganizing the scattered monks, Qianlong ordered the lama sent to Beijing for trial and imprisonment. His indictment read as follows:

> The Drungpa *kūtuktu* is truly the chief villain in this case. . . . He has forgotten his principles, betrayed his teachings, and merely pursues whatever suits him. How could we have entrusted the Panchen Erdeni to him? From the standpoint of the laws of the Buddha, one should not value life any more than death. [One] should think nothing of laying down one's life for that which benefits Buddhism. Moreover, how can he so treasure these trifling objects? Truly the Drungpa *kūtuktu* is motivated by selfish desires, craves life, and turned his back on what was right. The nature of his offense is obvious. I have already instructed that in principle he should be executed for his crimes. Yet out of consideration for the fact that he is the cousin of the previous Panchen Lama, just have him brought to the capital to be confined in a temple.[34]

Qianlong's indictment was based on the principle that all able-bodied monks have the obligation to protect Buddhism by whatever means necessary. At the height of the crisis in early October 1791, when the Gurkhas were rumored to be approaching Lhasa from three directions and Qing reinforcements were still clambering their way across the mountains of Sichuan and Kham, a Manchu-language court letter was delivered to the regent, the Tatsak *kūtuktu*, ordering him to spread word among the high clergy of Lhasa that it would be necessary to take up arms. According to the edict, the Tatsak *kūtuktu* was to explain that "Although the Buddhist law prohibits killing, if the bandits arrive and we have not lent our energy to the defense, then everything will be harmed. Moreover, in the Buddhist texts there is the tradition of 'Taming the demons.' If the Gurkhas unleash their violence, then they have become your demons. At this urgent juncture, become their subjugators."[35] The vengeance of the emperor, however, would not end with the retroactive application of this principle to the Drungpa *kūtuktu*.

As the investigation into the collapse of Trashi Lhünpo evolved over the following month, so did the Qing court's interpretation of the crime. When Qing reinforcements under Cengde finally arrived in the region of Tsang, Qianlong ordered them to arrest the new "chief villain," *jedrung lama* Lozang Tenpé, and four other monks and escort them to Lhasa to be punished for the crime of "using divination to mislead the people."[36] On December 23, 1791, under the supervision of the chief *amban*, Ohūi, the convicts were tortured and confessed to the charges that Qianlong had leveled against them. They had made a divination before the image of Tara and recklessly claimed that it would be impossible to defeat the Gurkhas, thus confusing the morale of the people and causing the monks to flee. Specifically, the *jedrung lama* Lozang Tenpé described how they had conducted a tsampa dough-ball divination. Having encased the answers, "Yes, fight!" and "No, don't fight!" in small balls of tsampa dough, they posed the question to the deity and rolled the balls about on a pan until the answer, due to centrifugal force (or the intervention of the deity), rolled off. Having received the answer in the negative, they then asked whether they should attempt to parley with the Gurkhas. The ritual was repeated. In this case, the deity indicated in the affirmative. Unfortunately, the monk sent to locate the Gurkha forces ran away. At the conclusion of his confession the *jedrung* stated that despite this turn of events, he had remained in the monastery after the others had fled and attempted to do what he could to preserve its treasures.[37] As a reward for his troubles, the *jedrung* claimed that the Gurkhas had beaten him. Ohūi, "having gathered together a crowd including the *kalön* and the leading lamas of all the monasteries, had him defrocked and brought under guard to the market, where, before their eyes, he was beheaded."[38]

Both Ohūi and subsequently the Qianlong emperor made extensive justifications for what they acknowledged was an unprecedented punishment.[39]

Three weeks later the regent, Tatsak *kūtuktu*, was asked to confirm that the confessions were true. He then "requested that cases of those who mislead the people be handled with severity." Ohūi explained that the punishments were an expression of the dynasty's desire to protect the Buddhist teachings, which the lamas had violated. He reported to Qianlong that he had subsequently explained in private to the Dalai and Panchen lamas that *jedrung* Lozang Tenpé had "under the pretext of having made a divination betrayed the teaching and mislead the people. Not only was this difficult for the king's law (Ch. *wangfa* 王法) to forgive, but also it is something that the law of Buddhism cannot tolerate. In principle all five men should be executed, yet out of respect for the recent edict, only the leader has been punished. The emperor's desire to protect the Yellow Teachings spares no detail."[40]

Ohūi's justification before the Dalai Lama reveals, however, one major innovation that sets it apart, even from the indictment of the Drungpa *kūtuktu* a month earlier. The monk's "rash presumption to speak for the deities" was no longer merely a crime against Buddhism, it was now a crime against the "king's law," the temporal, universal law of the dynasty that was only now being extended to the Geluk elite. In a separate edict approving Ohūi's actions, Qianlong succinctly restated this change: "These lamas have rebelled against their teaching, which is difficult for the law of the king to forgive let alone for laws of the Buddha to tolerate."[41] In other words, the emperor was expressing the will to use the laws—and punishments—of the secular code to enforce the Buddhist law. At the conclusion of his edict, Qianlong emphasizes the novelty of this situation by contrasting it with the state of affairs during the Mongol Yuan Dynasty:

I lovingly protect the Yellow Doctrines and treat with special kindness those lamas who hold fast to the laws of the religion they revere. However, if there are those who cannot be pardoned for their failures and sins against the teachings, then they definitely will not be shielded from being promptly punished according to the law. Consider the manner in which the Yuan patronized lamas: They singlemindedly worshiped the lamas and differentiated not [between right and wrong]. It reached the point where someone who insulted [a lama] would lose their tongue and someone who hit [a lama] would lose their arm, causing the lamas to know absolutely no restraint. How then could they recover their government system? I intend that this judgment concerning Lozang Tenpé's use of divination to mislead the people serve the purpose of clarifying the intent of the law with regard to our protection of the Yellow Doctrines.[42]

In this statement Qianlong was careful to justify the extension of the emperor's legal authority over Tibetan Buddhists not on the basis of imperial prerogative alone, but rather because it was necessary to ensure that monks keep their faith and act selflessly. The emperor reserved the right to judge who had violated Buddhist law on the basis of his position as a Buddhist who wished to see the faith flourish. Thus he felt he was fully within his rights to determine that the *jedrung* Lozang Tenpé's divination was nothing more than a false prophecy designed to obscure the truth about his own cowardice. Moreover, Qianlong argued that it was the right of the ruler to enforce Buddhist law and pass judgment on the Buddhist community that maintained the overall stability of the government.

Qianlong was satisfied with this formulation, because he incorporated it into his *Discourse on Lamas* a year later. He evidently considered the execution of the *jedrung* a watershed moment, not only for his reign but also for the history of the dynasty. The forceful handling of this matter was proof that the achievements of the Qing would endure longer than those of the Mongol Yuan.[43] The case established two important precedents: first, lamas could be subjected to the full force of the "king's law"—in this instance a statute straight from the law code of the Qing interior. Second the court had the right to supervise and authenticate indigenous divination practices. In practice, the extent of the "king's law" would remain ambiguous. The fact that Qianlong stayed the axe when it came to the Drungpa Kūtuktu, the high-ranking reincarnation, demonstrated a continued deference to the Buddhist hierarchy. In the year following the collapse of Trashi Lhünpo, among the Qing and Tibetan officials who fell under the scrutiny of the court, including those Manchu officials discovered as complicit in making secret arrangements with the Gurkhas in defiance of the court, only the *jedrung lama* Lozang Tenpé was executed.[44]

Heliyen and the Oracles of Central Tibet

In late March of 1792, a little over a month after Fuk'anggan had arrived in Lhasa, Qianlong dispatched Heliyen to Tibet, first in the capacity of assistant to Ohūi and then as the senior *amban*.[45] This move not only reflected the gravity with which Qianlong viewed the situation but also indicated that the emperor desired an unusual degree of frankness, oversight, and discretion in dealing with Tibetan internal affairs. Subsequently many communications between the Heliyen and the emperor were conveyed within Manchu-language letters between the *amban* and his elder brother, the chief grand councilor Hešen. In fact, it appears that these brothers made use of the palace memorial system to exchange numerous private messages concerning Tibetan affairs' thus to some degree, Tibet policy for the next several years would become a family affair.[46] Heliyen's arrival in Lhasa corresponded with a shift in tone in the communications between Fuk'anggan and Qianlong. Even before arriving, Heliyen had seconded reports that the Dalai Lama was unfit for rule and had been secretly involved in negotiations with the Gurkhas. A messenger dispatched by Ohūi had reported directly to the emperor, for instance, that, "even among the people in Tibet, there are none who would claim that the Dalai Lama is intelligent."[47] Fuk'anggan, however, had repeatedly defended the Dalai Lama from these accusations.[48]

When Heliyen arrived in Lhasa in early June 1792, Fuk'anggan had already departed and was in the Tibetan border district of Kyirong preparing to launch the punitive expedition into Gurkha territory.[49] If Manchu-language reports are credible, Heliyen immediately struck a different pose from his colleague—literally—and declined to prostrate before the Dalai Lama. This was a radical and not entirely authorized act. As mentioned above, Qing rulers—the Qianlong emperor included—had promoted considerable deference to the Dalai Lama and Panchen Lama as a matter of state policy. Kim Hanung has recently pointed out that the Qianlong emperor even went as far as forcing Korean emissaries to prostrate before the Panchen Lama on the occasion of his visit to Chengde and Beijing in 1780. Officials from the Board of Rites informed the emissaries that as a buddha and "teacher," the lama deserved respect.[50]

The emperor revised this policy in an edict concerning Tibetan affairs dated to June 13, 1792. Qianlong maintained that "rules of the Buddha" dictated that when "worshiping a buddha" it was appropriate to prostrate. Henceforth, however, imperial officials were to desist from such acts in the context of handling temporal affairs. The emperor was trying to draw a line between Buddhism and governance as well as between the personal faith of his servants and their role as his representatives. Previous *ambans* who had routinely genuflected before the Geluk hierarchs, he wrote, had confused the relationship between the *ambans* and the Dalai Lama, making it appear as though the *ambans* were subordinate to the monks, not their equals when it came to administrative issues. The result, according to Qianlong, was that the *kalön* and other Tibetan officials had largely ignored the *ambans*, seeing them as peers and not superiors, and cut them out of the decision-making process when the Gurkhas threatened invasion. Qianlong continued:

> Ohūi and Heliyen are both imperially commissioned *ambans*. Except for prostrating when worshiping the Buddha, when handling all other matters they should be considered the equals of the Dalai Lama and Panchen Erdeni and superior to the *kalön*, who must refer all matters to the imperial *ambans*. This is like the manner in which the Ili general governs Ili and the way the Kashgar *amban* governs the Muslim region. Only this disposition will uphold our system and rectify discipline. Ohūi and Heliyen must together take advantage of this moment and conscientiously reform, forcefully eradicating the inveterate habits so that the *kalön* and the others truly know the dynasty's might and do not dare trifle with us. With authority over all matters thus united, we can nurture the Tibetan people and permanently pacify Ü-Tsang.[51]

The emperor thus hoped that an adjustment of ritual would establish the appropriate hierarchy of political relations in Lhasa. By this move, Qianlong and his ministers were attempting to convey a new message, or at very least one that they had not felt like pushing in the past. The emperor and his officials were aware of the format of previous encounters between *ambans* and the Dalai or Panchen Lamas and the mixed signals that could be sent by encouraging officials to prostrate in any fashion before Geluk hierarchs.[52] These instructions, however, were issued too late for Heliyen to receive them before his audience with the Dalai Lama.[53] As is indicated in the later Manchu-language report filed by Sungyun, Heliyen's decision not to prostrate *in any context* had been his own initiative. In early June 1792, the court was still deliberating their position in Tibet. It is most likely that if he received instructions about how to present himself to the Dalai Lama, they were along the lines of those received by Fuk'anggan, who had been allowed to use his own discretion.

Heliyen's investigations, his chasing of whispers across Lhasa, and his overall suspicions of the Tibetan elites and their governing capabilities led to an aggressive effort to limit and constrain the power of the Tibetan nobility and even began to undermine the legitimacy of the Dalai Lama himself. At the same time as Heliyen was getting a handle on affairs in Tibet, the Drungpa *kūtuktu* had arrived in Beijing for questioning. Qianlong's evolving pronouncements on Tibet are probably attributable to the arrival of new information that both confirmed old suspicions (that he probably had initially shared with Heliyen) and planted new ones.[54] In a pronouncement dated June 18, 1792, the emperor rebuffed requests to have the Drungpa *kūtuktu* sent back to Tibet. Instead, he criticized Tibetans for their reliance on divination and castigated their cowardice as behavior unbecoming of a Buddhist, noting that "true Buddhists do not begrudge their own lives for the sake of other living creatures."[55]

It was Heliyen's early reports on the activities of the family of the *kalön* Doring Tendzin Peljor (Ma. Danjin Banjur) that led to the emperor's first condemnation of the oracles of central Tibet. In August 1791, in a brazen raid that marked the renewed outbreak of hostilities between Tibet and the Gurkhas, the latter captured both Doring Tendzin Peljor and a second *kalön*, Yutok Trashi Döndrup, in the Tibetan border market of Nyanang and took them as hostages back to Katmandu. The court found the circumstances of the ministers' abduction highly suspicious, not only because Tibetan officials had provided conflicting accounts of why the minister had been traveling in the border region but also because the Zhamarpa Lama himself had originally claimed to have been abducted and now appeared to have taken the Gurkhas' side.[56] Upon arriving in Lhasa, Heliyen investigated and found that the recently deceased father of Doring Tendzin Peljor had been arranging a secret ransom to secure the release of his son.[57] Of even greater concern to the court, however, was the news that the second son of Doring Tendzin Peljor had been identified as the Eighth Lo Sempa *trülku* (Ma. Samba *kūtuktu*).[58] In his response composed on July 9, 1792 (QL 57/05/21), the emperor drew a line of causality between the oracles of central Tibet, most importantly the Lamo Chökyong, and the trend of identifying reincarnations among the scions of Tibetan noble households. Qianlong wrote to Heliyen:

It is said that [Doring] Tendzin Peljor's second son is the [Lo Sempa]. The Lo Sempa *kūtuktu* is a major *kūtuktu* of Tibet. Now this emergence within their family is like the selection of the *kalön* from the household of the *drungkhor*.[59] Pandita[60] is an aristocratic family of Tibet. Tendzin Peljor is already the husband of the younger sister of the Dalai Lama and nephew by marriage of the Zhamarpa. If the son of Tendzin Peljor is also the Lo Sempa *kūtuktu*, then it will be that a single household has taken possession of all of the major posts of Tibet. This matter cannot be true! This is definitely a case in which when it came time to identify the emergence of the *trülku*, preconceived notions had been planted in the minds of the Lamo Chökyong and the other [oracles], and their divinations clearly pointed out the sons of noble families. If this were not the case, then how is it possible that the reincarnations of all the major *kūtuktus* of Tibet have come to appear only in the noble households? Nowadays the Panchen Erdeni, Jebtsundamba *kūtuktu*, and even the Dalai Lama are all from one family.[61]

The emperor was not exaggerating. Aristocratic clans and prominent *trülku* increasingly overlapped in Lhasa: the Sixth Panchen Lama, Drungpa *kūtuktu*, and Tenth Zhamarpa were brothers or stepbrothers; the Fourth Jebstundamba (1775–1813) and Seventh Panchen Lama (1782–1853) were, respectively, brother and nephew of the Eighth Dalai Lama; and for good measure, Tendzin Peljor was married to a woman who was the sister of the Dalai Lama and niece of the Tenth Zhamarpa. This cocktail of siblings, cousins, and religious authority was unprecedented, especially since the family at the heart of it, the Lhalu clan, had only obtained noble status and bestowals of hereditary estates from the Ganden Podrang in the 1760s. But none of this should have come as a surprise the Qianlong emperor, since he had approved the designation of these reincarnations as *kūtuktu* and showered their parents with imperial titles.[62] The exception appears to have been the recent identification of Tendzin Peljor's son as the Lo Sempa *trülku*.

The fact that the son of a potentially traitorous Tibetan noble still held hostage in Gurkha territory had been recognized as a major reincarnation without the Qing court's knowledge clearly rankled. It led to the emperor's first articulation of doubt in the existing process of recognizing rebirths, in particular the practice of seeking final confirmation by soliciting prophecies (Tib. *lungden*, Ma. *lungdan*) from the oracles. It also sparked the first efforts of the court to modify the process of certifying reincarnations: "Therefore, henceforth whenever any *kūtuktu* passes into nirvana, when identifying the re-emergence of the rebirth, there certainly must be a true sign, or [the candidate] must be able to recognize objects owned by the previous generation. As for the Lamo Chökyong, it is not acceptable for him to identify reincarnations from among sons of the gentry families or the great clans (Ma. *mukūn*), or from among the cousins or brothers of the Dalai Lama or Panchen Erdeni, according to their own whim and on the pretext of their prophecies."[63] Heliyen dutifully responded a month later, "I will strictly see to it that, in accord with the imperial instructions, the existence of reincarnations (*hūbilgan*) will not be determined according to the writ of the self-motivated prophecies of the Lamo Chökyong. Furthermore, having entered this edict into the archives, I will ensure that this will become the precedent for subsequent generations of *ambans*."[64]

This measure, however, was still limited in both scope and impact. It reflects an intermediate moment between the emperor's previous support for the oracles (as in seeking the judgment of the Lamo Chökyong in the case of the Changkya *kūtuktu* just four years earlier) and the attempt to radically replace these practices that would soon transpire. In this decree Qianlong was still content to promote certain indigenous divination technologies over others. Thus instead of seeking confirmation from the oracles, Tibetans were limited to interpreting portents and conducting trials of the candidate children. Still, the chief *amban* and the emperor were clearly building a rationale for further intervention. From Heliyen's perspective the prevailing practices of recognizing rebirths and their resulting failures were manifestations of the fact that "the affairs of Tibet are entirely without fixed laws!"[65] This specific exclamation, with its implicit dismissal of indigenous legal structures and traditions, reverberates throughout the subsequent archival record. The emperor, Hešen, Fuk'anggan, and Agūi all deployed the phrase in later communications as they made the case for various programs of law making in Tibet.[66]

A Crisis of Faith

The emperor first broached the idea of establishing a lottery in a letter to the Grand Councilor Agūi dated August 17, 1792 (QL 57/06/30). It is clear that Qianlong's suspicion of the oracles of Tibet, in particular the Lamo Chökyong, had evolved significantly since his previous letter to Heliyen.

Here, for the first time Qianlong fully articulated his belief that the corruption of the oracles had led to a general crisis of faith in the *kūtuktus* of Tibet and that the Dalai Lama himself was complicit:

> Previously, the identity of the reincarnations of the Dalai Lama, Panchen Erdeni, and all other *kūtuktus* has been determined by observing the prophecies made in person by the Lamo Chökyong. As for this, it is impossible that the [oracle's] decisions have not been corrupted by having accepted goods in advance, from being willfully partial to his relatives, or due to ideas that have been planted in his head by the Dalai Lama. Not only has this made it impossible for the people to be convinced [about the authenticity of the *kūtuktus*], it is also not the way to ensure that the doctrines flourish. As a result the Gurkha bandits fearlessly invaded and ran amok in Tibet. It is my intention that henceforth, when determining the reincarnation of the Dalai Lama, Panchen Erdeni, and all other major *kūtuktus*, observation of the divinations of the Lamo Chökyong will completely cease. Instead a golden vase will be dispatched to [Tibet] and set before the Buddha in the Jokhang Temple. Having placed the names of the *trülku* that have appeared inside, the resident *ambans* together with the Dalai Lama will observe as sutras are read and one [name] is selected from the urn. Only then will the true reincarnation have been identified.[67]

Qianlong's line of reasoning in this letter—that the root cause of the Gurkha invasion was the corruption of the oracles—was unprecedented. His diagnosis was very different from that of Fuk'anggan, who just six months earlier had divided the blame for the fiasco between the Tibetan lay officials and the Gurkhas and praised the resolute decisions of the Dalai Lama and other Geluk prelates.[68]

As Qianlong's rescripts on Fuk'anggan's report indicate, the emperor had initially concurred with his general's conclusions.[69] Fuk'anggan's analysis not only influenced the program of reform of Tibetan administration and especially the Kashag meetings that would get under way seven months later in October, it also constitutes the foundation of most late nineteenth-century and twentieth-century Western interpretations of the war.[70] Yet in his Manchu-language letters to his closest advisors, Hešen and Agūi, Qianlong probed beyond Fuk'anggan's analysis, ultimately deciding that the crucial factor was the corruption of the oracles and the moral decay of the Geluk establishment itself.

Qianlong's reasoning in this matter is perhaps best understood when placed in the context of his prior history of dealing with matters involving clergy, divination, and other magical arts in China proper. In particular, his suspicions of the oracles and the Dalai Lama, as well as the extremely harsh punishment meted out to the *jedrung lama* Lozang Tenpé, recall two aspects of his response to the soul-stealing crisis of 1768 as described by Philip Kuhn.[71] First, by the midpoint in his reign Qianlong had already expressed on multiple occasions his distaste for the clergy of China proper. Kuhn writes that "monk-bashing was a source of moral satisfaction for rulers who considered clergy to be mostly hypocrites and corrupters of the community."[72] Kuhn places this hostility in the context of concerns shared by both society and the throne for the increasing numbers of mendicant monks thronging the roads and markets of the country. Qianlong was unsympathetic to the growing numbers of Buddhist clergy both on Confucian grounds, as these men had abandoned their filial obligations to be productive members of both family and society, and because their numbers had long since surpassed the abilities of the state to license them and the state-sanctioned temples to house them. The impossibility of knowing exactly who these people were and what they were doing especially troubled the emperor.[73]

Among the behaviors the court worried about was the potential for these individuals to engage in communication with the spirit world and conduct divinations, thus usurping a role that the Qing Code, like those of previous dynasties, had reserved for the emperor and his authorized representatives. Statutes in the sections of the Qing code on sacrifices and ceremonies forbade shamanism and prognostication, particularly when the latter touched on the future of the dynasty. Limiting knowledge about the future to the emperor and officialdom more generally was essential to social stability lest unauthorized fortune-tellers delude the people with false tales of dynastic decline and collapse.[74] This brings us to the second aspect of the situation in 1792 that resembles that of 1768: what Kuhn labels the "panic factor," the "imperial belief that the credulous masses were ever on the brink of violent panicky reactions to hints of political crisis or cosmic disorder."[75] In 1768, this belief underlay the emperor's fear that rumors of sorcerers wandering the land stealing souls would trigger public disturbances—events that would surely be read as signs of the dynasty's frailty. This belief also explains why in 1768 the emperor made debunking the authenticity of claims of "soul stealing," divining, and other black arts a priority for his officials.

In light of proscriptions against unauthorized divination in the Qing Code, Qianlong's desire to restrict the activities of the state oracles of Tibet does not seem unprecedented. The events of the Gurkha war served as an unwelcome reminder that the court's monopoly over forecasting the future was still incomplete. Moreover, a crisis of faith in the sanctity of *kūtuktu*hood, the lynchpin of governance throughout Tibetan regions, might easily set off the kind of panic that the throne had feared in 1768. The Gurkha war, which was still very much under way when Qianlong first floated the idea of the urn among his confidants in August 1792, had already provided evidence of Tibetan susceptibility to "panicky" reactions to "false" divinations, the evaporation of defenses at Trashi Lhünpo being the case in point.

Other recent events in the Qing border regions had also carried warnings about the dangers of divisions within state-tolerated religious groups. In 1781 and again in 1784, Sufi Muslims in Gansu province had launched attacks on Qing officials, resulting in protracted and costly pacification campaigns. In the aftermath of the first campaign, the Qing court determined that the root of the violence lay in theological feuds within Muslim communities over what constituted Islamic orthodoxy. Agūi, Hešen, and Fuk'anggan were at different times all directly involved in enforcing the emperor's decision to preserve the "orthodox" "Old Teachings" and suppress the "heterodox" "New Teachings." Although Fuk'anggan later expressed qualms about executing heterodox Muslims and doubts about the capacity of the state to actually eliminate the New Teachings, the lessons of the violence were clear: the dynasty needed to carefully manage and if possible prevent debates about religious faith and ritual, regardless of whether the teachings were Islamic or Buddhist.[76] In the privacy of the imperial palace's inner quarters, Qing rulers engaged in an idiosyncratic assortment of Buddhist practices derived from the teachings of both the Geluk church and its competitors. Qianlong patronized lamas such as the Third Tukwan *kūtuktu*, Lozang Chökyi Nyima, took an "inclusivist" approach to the diverse doctrinal traditions of Tibet.[77] However, such ecumenical thinking had its firm limits when the throne encountered argumentative monks or "local traditions" such as the practices of divination that threatened the integrity of core governing institutions like the Geluk church.

Neither Tibet policy nor policy for the rest of the empire's Inner Asian domains was made in a vacuum. Previous accounts of the Golden Urn have interpreted the law primarily as a tool for limiting the influence of the Mongol and Tibetan nobility.[78] Yet it is clear from the private correspondence of the emperor and his agents in the field that they did not feel directly threatened by these families. Quarrels among the Tibetan elite could result, as they had with the Gurkha wars, in foreign invasion and the outlay of considerable imperial resources. The Qing state, quite reasonably, saw the Gurkhas as a local irritant, not a strategic threat. Moreover, there is no evidence in this correspondence that the throne worried about a military threat germinating within the Tibetan aristocracy. Even in Mongolia it had been thirty years since a significant revolt against Qing rule. The era of conquest was over and the process of consolidating Qing governance well under way. The misbehavior and avarice of the Inner Asian nobility posed a threat to the church first and the state second. In both the original mention of the urn in the confidential letter to Agūi in August and the *Discourse on Lamas*, the emperor's overriding rationale was the desire to stamp out doubts in reincarnate lamas and shore up faith in the Geluk church.

The emperor's intervention in the identification process was thus not simply an attempt to bring resolution to an old and thorny political problem unique to the court's management of Inner Asia. Rather, it was an attempt to eliminate the danger that unsupervised communication with the spirit world posed to faith in the Geluk teachings and the political order that the court believed hinged on that faith. The Geluk arts of divination were no longer any less dangerous than those of the sorcerers of the interior. Worries that preoccupied the court in sustaining its rule over China were beginning to bleed into the way it thought about Inner Asia. Seen in this light, the Golden Urn lottery is a perfect symbol of this moment: a Ming ritual brought out to solve an Inner Asian crisis. The Golden Urn was not a new solution to an old problem, it was an old solution to a new problem.

Interpretations of the Golden Urn

Among the Tibetan arts of divination, the Golden Urn lottery most closely resembled a category of practices generally referred to as *zentak* or *zengyur*, meaning respectively "investigation with dough balls" or "dough ball transformation." We have already been introduced to a version of this practice in the case of the *jedrung lama* Lozang Tenpé, who had encased various possible outcomes from the expected Gurkha attack within balls of barley dough (*tsampa*), balanced them on a special plate, then gradually spun the plate until the correct answer fell off. This technology was widely known throughout Tibet and employed to assist with making a variety of decisions. The *Oceanic Book*, a large Tibetan-language history composed in the first half of the nineteenth century, describes numerous usages of the ritual, most frequently in the context of identifying the rebirths of *trülku* or assigning posts within the monastic bureaucracy. For example, the *Oceanic Book* records that in 1707 the first Jamyang Zhepa (1648–1721) supervised the search for the Mindröl *trülku* and that this involved conducting a dough ball investigation at Drepung monastery.[79] In this, as in most other cases, the dough ball investigation was but the last in a series of divinations. Only when the outcome of the *zentak* and the divinations of the Lamo and Nechung oracles was known and concurred with the advice of the Dalai and Panchen lamas was the reincarnation conclusively confirmed. In another case, when asked to assign a lama as regent to the domain of the Mongol *qinwang* of Kökenuur in the mid 1700s, the abbot of Labrang resorted to a *zentak*. The abbot had first asked a certain qualified monk to take up the position. When the monk refused, the abbot performed a dough ball investigation. The divination confirmed that indeed the task should fall to that monk, yet he again rejected the appointment. Ultimately the abbot went in his stead. Shortly thereafter, the obstinate monk died, thus sending a warning that the results of the ritual were not to be taken lightly.[80] *Zentak/zengyur* divinations do not appear to have been commonly used, however, for the identification of *trülku*. A dough ball divination was used to verify the identity of the Fifth Dalai Lama in 1622. Tibetan accounts of this incident, including that of the Fifth Dalai Lama himself, considered the resort to a *zentak* ritual exceptional, and it was not replicated in other searches during the seventeenth and eighteenth centuries.[81]

Although Tibetan authors would later refer to the Golden Urn lottery as a kind of *zentak*, the structure of the ritual was in significant ways qualitatively different from indigenous methods of performing dough ball investigations. As we will see in act 3, for this reason and others Tibetan authors clearly saw the ritual as a novel imposition on their own methods of divination. This is not to say that Tibetans rejected the ritual outright as a foreign institution, but it is a bridge too far to claim, as recent Chinese historians have, that because both the new ritual and indigenous tradition involved "lots" (Ch. *qian* 簽), it was easily accepted and assimilated.[82] Just because China and Tibet both possess divination traditions (Ch. *shenpan* 神判) does not mean that they constitute a *shared* tradition. Moreover, the archival record makes clear that neither Qianlong nor his associates took into consideration the indigenous Tibetan traditions when casting the Golden Urn. Their inspiration lay elsewhere.

Qianlong himself stated quite clearly that the idea for a lottery was borrowed from the Board of Civil Appointments, where drawing lots (Ch. *cheqian* 掣簽 or *nianjiu* 拈鬮) had been a standard method of appointing officials to open posts in the field administration of China since the late Ming.[83] Given that Qianlong believed that personal greed and influence peddling by the high lamas of Tibet had corrupted the recognition process, it is no surprise that he would turn to this administrative lottery—a measure expressly designed to foil these sorts of human machinations. The holistic and generalizing train of thought that led to this decision is remarkable given that Qianlong is better known for policies that attempted to compartmentalize and segregate the various parts and peoples of his domain. Yet it is striking that the emperor made no analogy to the procedures of the Board of Civil Appointments when he first presented the idea of a lottery for *kūtuktu* in August 1792. Not until March 1793 did the emperor acknowledge the connection. Moreover, there appears to be no record of any mention of the urn in any other court document before the letter from the emperor to Agūi. This suggests that the idea was either the emperor's personal inspiration (as he claimed) or arose in the course of oral consultations that could have taken place among officials with only the most intimate connections to the emperor—the Grand Councilor Hešen being the most likely candidate. Furthermore, just a day after sharing the plan with Agūi (and perhaps by default the rest of the Grand Council), the emperor ordered the imperial workshops to commence work on the urn itself—a display of supreme confidence that his new measure for regulating reincarnation would be implemented.

But what was the metaphysical underpinning of the procedure, and how did the court expect the ritual to be understood in Tibet? In February 1793, four months after he had first been informed about the new ritual, Fuk'anggan submitted a memorial to the throne in which he recounted the reasoning he had used to justify the use of the Golden Urn to the Dalai Lama and other leading Tibetans. Fuk'anggan reported that he had discussed with the Tibetans the use of a lottery to make civil appointments in China proper and analogized it to the use of the Golden Urn. The memorial is significant also because it marks the first time that the connection between the two rituals was explicitly stated in a Qing government document. Fuk'anggan's opinions on the importation of the ritual to Tibet contain a rich metaphysical exegesis of the ritual and thus deserve to be quoted at length:

> Your servants respectfully translated your edict. We compared the identification of reincarnations to the practice of drawing lots in the Board of Civil Appointments, which is truly an appropriate analogy. We observe that in the lotteries held by the Board of Civil Appointments the [expectant] officials personally draw the lots, and although the clerks may attempt to indicate the post and cheat, only occasionally does this work, and usually someone else gets the post. In fact the clerks really have little influence, and one can see that a man's glory or obscurity depends on his fate [*mingshu* 命數]. This should all the more hold true for the Dalai Lama and Panchen Erdeni, who as the leaders of the Yellow Teaching have jurisdiction over Tibet, and having received the emperor's munificent kindness from above and the faith of the Mongols and Tibetans from below, already possess an exceptional fate [*fuming* 福命] regardless of whether they truly possess that innate endowment [*genqi* 根氣] [of being reincarnated buddhas].[84]

According to Fuk'anggan, there was little difference between a *trülku* and a magistrate who drew a fat post in a prosperous corner of the empire—they were both lucky. One's "allotment" or "fate" (both possible translations of *mingshu*) was something externally determined, either at birth or perhaps over time, according to the patterns of Heaven. The lottery then was understood as a mechanism for forcibly stripping humans of their will and unmasking what fate had in store for them.[85] In the last sentence the general was remarkably frank: the Dalai Lama and Panchen Lamas might well be charlatans, but they had still received a boon from destiny. To the degree that the lottery appeared to make determinations that were unrelated to the innate moral qualities of the candidates—whether for office or for rebirth—it seemed at least somewhat arbitrary, if not completely random.

Fuk'anggan's explanation of the lottery reveals the degree to which the underlying Qing official understanding could be at odds with the purpose the ritual had to serve in a Tibetan Buddhist context. The Tibetan divination tradition did possess rituals that could double as games of chance. Since the era of the Tibetan empire, lotteries or dice (Tib. *mo*) were often used to resolve legal conflicts or assist government officials in making judgments with the appearance of impartiality.[86] Drawing lots could also be employed as a means of avoiding the centralization of political authority in particular individuals or families. Many communities across the Himalayas and the Tibetan plateau, both settled and nomadic, had historically made appointments to positions of leadership in this way. Participants often viewed the outcome as random and assumed no direct intervention by gods or other cosmic forces.[87] This political tradition may have made it easier for Tibetans and Mongols to accept the Golden Urn, which the Qing court publicly promoted as a means of weakening the influence of elite families over *trülku* lineages. However, in most divination procedures, and especially in the use of *zentak/zengyur*, the outcome was understood as a revelation that exposed a preexisting condition, one that had "arisen dependent"[88] on the chains of cause and effect that linked all things and all generations of things. Tibetan divination rituals were designed to provide beings possessed of omniscience and keen foresight—either adept lamas and *trülkus* or deities and gods—with the opportunity to communicate otherwise hidden truths.

The Golden Urn would have to identify which child among several possessed the attributes of a bodhisattva, not dispense an office or reveal a man's "fate," as Fuk'anggan argued. The difference between these two understandings is apparent in the language used in Manchu and Tibetan texts: the Manchu-language discussions of the urn often conflate all the candidates as *hūbilgan* (*trülku*);[89] Tibetan texts refer to them as "suspects" (Tib. *dokné*, literally meaning "point of doubt"), among whom the "unmistaken" (Tib. *trülmé*) reincarnation had already taken rebirth.[90]

Qing officials were not unaware of Tibetan understandings of reincarnation. Hening (1741–1821), the Mongol bannerman from the lower Yangtze region of China who replaced Cengde as assistant *amban* in 1793 and resided in Lhasa until 1800, personally picked several lots from the urn. He was also a prolific writer. His literary corpus, *Collected Poems from the Yijian Studio*, published shortly after his death, contains the following poem that illuminates the experience of participating in the urn ritual:

DRAWING LOTS FROM THEΔ GOLDEN URN TO LOCATE THE *TRÜLKU*

In ancient hall a golden vessel rests,
Propitious morn, let the search for the buddha commence!
Where art thou bright and timely child,
Who entered the world as an infant through enlightenment's door?
Never having suffered the torments of Hell,
Thou relied only on the vehicle of the Six Virtues.
Blessed Karma has preordained thy birth,
Now trust my hand to pluck thee out![91]

《金本巴瓶籤掣呼畢勒罕》

古殿金瓶設，祥晨選佛開。
誰家聰齡子，出世法門胎。
未受三塗戒，先憑六度媒。
善緣生已定，信我手拈來。

In the *amban*'s poem, his grasp of reincarnation was simplistic, but not entirely discordant with that of his Tibetan contemporaries. Hening recognized that well before the ritual commenced the bodhisattva had transmigrated and taken rebirth in the shape of a small child. The last line of the poem, however, creates a powerful tension between that knowledge and the act of drawing a lot and thus reads like a riddle. Here at the end of a profound chain of supernatural events lies the action of a very human, very mundane hand that leaves the reader wondering, Why trust the hand? What guides it? Hening is silent on this issue, attributing the selection neither to fate nor to the intervention of the protector deities of Tibet. However, the challenge of reconciling the Golden Urn *lottery* with the indigenous tradition of *divination*—in other words, reconciling conceptions of fate with karma—would have to be surmounted by the court's agents if they wanted to see Qianlong's new measure accepted in Tibet.

Advice and Consent from the Resident Lamas
of the Capital

Let us return to the discussion that Qianlong had initiated with his officials when he first introduced the Golden Urn to Grand Councilor Agūi in late August 1792. When the emperor wrote to Agūi, the proposal for a lottery was more than tentative, yet still not fully formed. The throne was still looking for confirmation that its suspicions were correct and that the measure stood some chance of acceptance. In his letter, Qianlong directed Agūi to submit his opinion about whether the proposal had either "not gone far enough" or, to the contrary, was ill suited to the moment. He also ordered Agūi to solicit opinions from among the *kūtuktus* and other ranking *jasak lamas* of the capital.[92] Specifically, he was asked to make inquiries of the Gomang *kūtuktu*, the second-highest ranking lama residing in Beijing during the spring and summer of 1792.[93] The lama's opinion on the "matter of determining things by drawing wooden name-cards[94] from a golden urn" was attached to Agūi's memorial detailing his own thoughts on the issue.

The *kūtuktu* reported to the grand councilor that, "while making inquiries [I] have heard that it is indeed the case that there exists corruption when observing the prophecies of the Lamo *chökyong*."[95] Although the Gomang *kūtuktu* provided no examples, with this statement the lama added a key voice from within the Geluk church confirming Qianlong's suspicions. It is perhaps ironic that this lama called on to testify about the corruption of the selection process had himself been the subject of Qianlong's suspicions just a few years prior when he had been involved in the search for the reincarnation of his teacher, Changkya Rolpé Dorjé.[96] Moreover, the lama continued to bring credibility to the new ritual by reporting that he had also heard that previously the Panchen Lama had drawn lots to determine the rebirth of the Dalai Lama. Finally, the Gomang *kūtuktu* expressed confidence that once the "Great Holy Lord Manjusri" (i.e., Qianlong) had dispatched the Golden Urn to Tibet, "all sorts of corruptions would be completely eliminated."[97]

To this resounding endorsement, Agūi added his own, more nuanced assessment of the proposal in a separate memorial. The grand councilor raised the thorny question of what would happen if upon reaching adulthood, the child identified by the lottery proved to be "lacking in grandeur." "It cannot be predicted," Agūi wrote, "if it will be possible to convince people."[98] As he went through the implications of such a scenario, he warned that it would be "unbecoming" for the dynasty to backtrack on the results of the lottery. Therefore the court had to be prepared to remind the people that the original candidates had been their choice and that multiple investigations had revealed that all the children were "endowed with the fortune of intelligence and wisdom."[99] Yet despite these reservations, Agūi concurred that the time to act had arrived. In fact, his diagnosis of the problem went much further back in time and higher up the hierarchy of the Geluk church.

Agūi placed before the emperor the argument that the Dalai Lama was more than just a weak ruler inclined to nepotism. Even worse, the grand councilor reported that his inquiries revealed that the Eighth Dalai Lama was in fact a false incarnation and the morally bankrupt core of an administration and religion in crisis. He wrote:

> The comportment and speech of the present Dalai Lama are incapable of inspiring feelings of respect among the people. This is because he possesses but meager fortune. When he was selected, the matter was not handled seriously and cautiously.[100] Thus, the Gurkha bandits out of disrespect encroached on the borders of Tibet like madmen. The Dalai Lama and Panchen Erdeni are great lamas to whom all the Mongols and Tibetans sacrifice. Surely if [they] possessed a perfected fortune [consisting of] wisdom, perception, and virtue, these events would not have occurred and they would have been able to work for the benefit of the Yellow Doctrines.[101]

Here Agūi turned back the clock to the conflict surrounding the recognition of the Eighth Dalai Lama in 1760, and, in an oblique criticism of Changkya *kūtuktu* Rolpé Dorjé, who oversaw the recognition process together with the Sixth Panchen Lama, argued that the traditional methods located the wrong man. The grand councilor also agreed with the emperor that the crisis of faith in reincarnation represented an opportunity for reform. He wrote, "At this moment the Dalai Lama can no longer rely on the support of all Tibetans. If we pursue this opportunity and convincingly explain [things to the Tibetans], we can rectify [matters]. How can the Dalai Lama do anything but obey?"[102] Agūi was suggesting that,

Agūi
Detail from *Yubi pingding Taiwan ershi gongchen xiangzan*, 1788

with the Dalai Lama's political influence at its nadir, his political *and* religious authority could be seized by the dynasty.

During the same month that Agūi submitted his opinion, Qianlong began to receive advice from other quarters via the efforts of the chief grand councilor, Hešen. Among the early reports forwarded to the throne was a letter from the Galdan Siretu *kūtuktu*, who had just arrived at the emperor's summer retreat in Chengde from Dolonuur. This lama's advice was evidently deemed significant, as it was copied into the Manchu-language court letter that first brought the proposal for a Golden Urn to the attention of the court's chief officers in Tibet and Fuk'anggan, who at the time was still campaigning in Nepal. The Galdan Siretu *kūtuktu* provided both a clarification for the emperor on the nature of the state oracles of Tibet and a larger ritual context for the Golden Urn. Hešen's court letter quoted the lama as follows:

> "The Lamo *chökyong* is a protector deity[103] and not at all human. In addition to the Lamo *chökyong*, there are also three other *chökyong*: the Nechung, Gadong, and Samyé. Whenever a *trülku* emerges, a prophecy will certainly be sought to determine his location. After the direction [in which the rebirth will be found] has been indicated, it is appropriate to conduct a detailed search. Henceforth, the matter of investigating and verifying where a *trülku* has been born, having been assigned to the Dalai Lama and Panchen Lama, good and virtuous mediums[104] having been selected, prophecies shall be sought successively from the *chökyong*. When the instructions of the oracles are all in accord, people shall be commissioned to search in those places. Once several places where *trülku* [may] have emerged have been located and investigated, if the true year and month of their birth are suitably auspicious and lucky, then their names should be written down and placed in a vase to be selected."[105]

In this letter the Galdan Siretu *kūtuktu* sanctioned the new ritual, yet avoided mentioning any culpability or corruption on the part of the oracles. On the contrary, his argument that the *chökyong* are in fact powerful deities reveals no loss of faith and provides a counterpoint to Qianlong's argument that the oracles were merely self-interested humans. Moreover, although he consented to the urn as the penultimate step in the recognition process, he argued that the oracles and the involvement of the Dalai and Panchen lamas remained unavoidable and necessary aspects of the search. In this respect, the *kūtuktu*'s letter posed an obstacle to the emperor's desire to see the oracles eliminated. Yet the fact that Qianlong allowed this scenario to be incorporated into a court letter explaining the new procedure to his field officials in Lhasa reveals that the lama's letter was seen first and foremost as legitimizing the Golden Urn ritual and offering a way to incorporate it into a search process that met the emperor's basic requirement: that mechanisms to check the willful exercise of power and influence by the oracles and prelates of the Geluk school be established. These are the first indications of the essential role that Tibetan Buddhist authorities themselves would play in transforming the lottery into a legitimate divination ritual.

A Doctrine for Governing the World

By early September 1792, the throne had amassed what seemed to be damning reports from its own officials as well as prelates of the Geluk church attesting to the corruption of the Dalai Lama and the oracles and the spreading suspicions about the authenticity of major *kūtuktu*. In a bilingual Manchu and Mongol edict that was widely distributed across Inner Asia, Qianlong opined that "nobody is completely convinced."[106] A crisis of faith was undermining Geluk teachings all across Mongolia and Tibet. The emperor had, however, it seemed to him, gained support for a possible remedy—the Golden Urn. In a draft court letter that circulated within the Grand Council, the emperor paused to take stock of the underlying significance of the reform measure he was about to circulate to his officials. In the following quotation, I have underlined the sections that the emperor crossed out and placed his amendments to Hešen's draft in brackets.

> Previously when identifying the *hūbilgan* of the Dalai Lama, Panchen Erdeni, and all other *kūtuktu*, only the prophecies of the Lamo Chökyong were considered. The <u>Buddhist</u> [Edit: Ü-Tsang's old] way was deliberately established and [Edit: for a long time until now] the Buddha's way alone was paramount [Edit: therefore the teaching declined and corruption arose]: everything is emptiness, nothing exists, and there is nothing else. If one does good, that is good. If one does evil, that is also okay. As for people's personal behavior, it will of its own accord lead to rebirth. The Buddha does not restrain people at all.
>
> The way of the emperor is different. He who does good will certainly be encouraged. He who does evil will be handled with punishments. [Edit: However] According to the way of the Buddha, one merely waits upon karma to of its own accord mete out punishment or reward. This is improper. [Edit: Truly, not only did this give rise only to evil but also, despite their best intentions, neither virtue nor sin ever received its just reward.] Therefore, due to the raids committed by the Gurkha bandits, a large army had to be quickly

dispatched, which defeated and destroyed them. Similarly, it would not have been appropriate to, in the manner of the Buddha, do nothing to restrain them, and just wait for karma to act of its own accord [Edit: which would have been just like saying "Let's just wait and see what happens to everyone's virtue and sins"]. This matter was handled according to the way of ruling the world. If it was the case that the Buddha took care of everything, then how was it that the Zhamarpa was not killed and the Gurkha bandits were not stopped?[107]

Unfortunately, the draft court letter is a fragment and cuts off shortly after the last sentence above. Yet the drift of the emperor's thinking is quite clear: one cannot expect to govern the temporal world by Buddhist principles alone. As a governing philosophy, the "way of the Buddha" seemed little more than a recipe for inaction. The "old way of Ü-Tsang," which Qianlong reduced to a parody, was so enthralled with the theory of karma that the rulers had failed to establish laws and codes. Lacking immediate inducements or punishments, the people existed "untamed" (Ma. *darkū*), without moral guidance. Here then, Qianlong explained to his officials why "Tibet is entirely without fixed laws," as Heliyen had put it just a month earlier.[108] Ecclesiastic governments, Qianlong argued, by their very nature do not produce laws. In contrast, the "way of the emperor" is a practical and tested "doctrine for ruling the world."[109] Thus, Qianlong explicitly rejected and delegitimized the underlying rationale behind the Buddhist government of the Dalai Lamas, paving the way for not only greater supervision of reincarnation but also the appropriation of the authority of the Ganden Podrang, as had been suggested by Agūi. The corruption of divination among Tibetan Buddhists and the preservation of the Geluk doctrines necessitated the extension of direct imperial rule to Tibet.

Within a month of this letter, Fuk'anggan had been informed of the proposal for the lottery and been given a firm mandate for drafting new regulations to establish the authority of the two *ambans* resident in Lhasa over the Tibetan council of ministers.[110] Fuk'anggan's response to the emperor's proposals strongly contrasted with his earlier portrayals of the Dalai Lama. Adopting the emperor's logic, Fuk'anggan for the first time joined the court in impugning the authenticity of the Dalai Lama. Both the ruler and the general recognized the importance of locating "genuine rebirths."

How to do so, however, was still subject to discussion. At this point the idea for a "lottery of *trülku*" was merely a sketch. Who would draw the lots? Where would it occur? How were names to be located? What role were the oracles and the protectors to play? Which *trülku* would fall under the jurisdiction of this new statute? The fact that over the next several years the ritual would be performed in several different ways and in different locations demonstrates the degree to which its basic procedure and metaphysical meanings were subject to negotiation, debate, and reinterpretation by the court, its field officials, and Tibetan elites. The emperor had instructed Fuk'anggan to not only discuss the proposal for the Golden Urn with the two other officials resident in Lhasa, Heliyen and Ohūi, but also consult with Tibetan elites. Qianlong wrote, "If after discussions with the Dalai Lama and Tatsak *kūtuktu*, it will be appropriate to handle things in this manner, then immediately promulgate the edict. If there are any aspects of this measure that are not suitable, then please compose a memorial informing me of the complete truth."[111]

Qianlong did not wait for further advice from his general or the Tibetan elite before beginning the process of formalizing and promulgating his new ritual. On October 14, 1792 (QL 57/08/29), he issued a formal decree in Manchu to the Mongol aristocracy apprising them of the new stance on the legitimacy of the major *kūtuktus* of the Geluk school, the prohibition against locating reincarnations within aristocratic households, and the establishment of the Golden Urn lottery as the final step in the recognition process. This was the earliest public promulgation of the new ritual and pre-dated the earliest Chinese-language proclamation, the *Discourse on Lamas*, by over two months. In this edict, Qianlong articulated in no uncertain terms both the importance he placed on the elimination of doubt in the authenticity of reincarnations and his conviction that the current generation of *kūtuktus* were false:

Only if all the people are convinced that the rebirths of the Dalai Lama and Panchen Erdeni are definitively true will the Yellow Doctrines flourish and spread. From the beginning, when identifying [possible] *hūbilgan*, only the prophecies of the oracles have been sought and those whom they have indicated have become *hūbilgan*. For the past several years, it has been impossible for the divine to descend because the mediums possess only ordinary abilities. The Dalai Lama, Panchen Erdeni, and Jebtsundamba *kūtuktu* are all from one clan perhaps because, having accepted requests from various people, [the oracles] falsely identify [*hūbilgan*]. In my opinion, because [they] have all appeared among close relatives, I cannot consider them to be genuine. [. . .] Truly [this] joke has reached the point of destroying the Yellow Doctrines. In my opinion this is greatly unbearable.[112]

Already these comments stand in stark contrast to official pronouncements made just a year earlier, when the emperor praised the fortitude of the Dalai Lama and his closest advisors for their organization of the defense of Lhasa.[113] Yet Qianlong went further still, questioning the doctrine of reincarnation:

I have zealously examined the Buddha's sutras and thoroughly understand the way of the Buddha. The Buddha has neither going nor coming. Moreover, the existence of the oracles has never been proclaimed in the sutras. It has been written that even the Buddha is without achievements and that the root is emptiness and nothingness. It has been said [by the Buddha] that all exploits are but the deceits of dreams. Even though the oracles are meritorious, the mediums then, on the pretext of channeling the instructions of the Protector [deity], act corruptly. None of this is the way of the Buddha. However, there is nothing we can do but carry on their old customs. We can only plan on suppressing their private corruptions. Similarly, it is naturally their private and public opinion that if there were no *trülku* there would be no one to protect and govern the disciples of the Yellow Doctrines.[114]

Qianlong incorporated these ideas into the tetraglot edict *Discourse on Lamas*. In the *Discourse* he continued to argue that despite the court's reservations, it would continue to patronize the Geluk church: "As for [our] high esteem for the Yellow Hat teaching, it is in accordance with the desires of the Mongols and is therefore not only important but also necessary."[115]

It is this tone of political expediency that has made the *Discourse on Lamas* so familiar to Qing historians.[116] Few scholars have failed to comment on the significance of Qing patronage of the Geluk with regard to the dynasty's rule in Mongolia. Yet the singular focus of these early pronouncements on the Mongols deserves further consideration. It should not be surprising that the first public edicts on the Golden Urn were addressed primarily to the Mongol aristocracy and the court officials charged with their supervision, not to the Tibetans. The degree to which the Geluk church, and Tibet more generally, were important only as they related to the court's strategic interests in Mongolia is readily apparent. In the earlier of the two edicts, the Tibetans (Ma. *Fandze*) are only mentioned once, whereas the Mongols are mentioned five times. Similarly, despite the fact that the *Discourse* is "about lamas," the most significant of whom reside in Tibet, the essay is primarily concerned with the faith of the "Mongols," not the "Tibetans (Tib. *Böpa*)." The emperor justified his new measures by explaining that they were "in harmony with the wishes of both the outer and inner Mongols."[117] For Qianlong, the primary strategic challenge the dynasty faced in 1791 was the potential political instability *in Mongolia* that would be the inevitable fallout from the spread of doubts in the authenticity of reincarnation. The predicament at hand seemed to the court to be primarily due to the moral failings of its governing elite in Inner Asia, both lay and ecclesiastic. Thus the Gurkha invasion of Tibet was understood first as a symptom of failure of *personnel* and only second as violation of imperial sovereignty. From Qianlong's own writing it appears that the military campaign against the Gurkhas was motivated neither by the cant of conquest nor by any fear that the Gurkhas represented a serious competitor to Qing interests in Tibet, as had the Junghar Mongols a generation earlier. Tibet, Tibetans, and their neighbors to the south remained ancillary to the perennial concerns of the northwest.

The fact that directly controlling Tibet was not initially an end in itself explains why Qianlong's pledge to extend the application of the "king's law" to the Geluk church and the confiscation of their sovereignty (Ma. *toose*) in 1792 was so novel, a situation that he himself recognized. The *Discourse*, as well as several other major imperially sanctioned pronouncements issued in the immediate aftermath of the Qing intervention, trace the relationship between the dynasty and Tibet back to the arrival of emissaries from the Fifth Dalai Lama at the court of Hong Taiji (r. 1626–1643), even before the Qing conquest of China. The Qing attempts to reform Tibetan governance in the 1790s coincided with a veritable explosion of writing including gazetteers, saga-length prose poems, and especially stelae, which sought to inscribe the unprecedented Qing achievement permanently on the landscape of Lhasa.[118] On the Smallpox Stele erected outside the Jokhang in 1794, the chief *amban* Heliyen gushed in Chinese, "From the Tang and Song [dynasties] on, although [Tibet] had contact with

China it was not part of the latter's territory. During the time of Emperor Taizong Wenhuangdi (Hong Taiji) they sincerely returned, and over the past hundred-odd years, due to the influence of the imperial instruction, have gradually been transformed."[119] But lest we misinterpret what were evidently overenthusiastic reinterpretations of the historical scope of the Qing domain, Qianlong himself provided an important corrective. Among the annotations to his poetry, the emperor offered the following information on Tibet: "Although [Tibet] came to an imperial audience during the Chongde reign (Chongde seven, 1642), their territory still was not ours. . . . Even during the early Shunzhi reign when the Dalai Lama arrived for an audience and received his original golden seal [of office], their territory was still not possessed by China."[120] Full control of Tibet had not been realized, Qianlong argued, until after the Gurkha war, when "everything is handled by [my] ministers and I have but to command and it will be obeyed."[121] He contrasted this new state of affairs to the situation just two years earlier, when the "resident *ambans* entrusted everything [to the *kalöns*] and took responsibility for nothing."[122]

Conclusion: Sovereignty and Divination

What, then, did it mean to be possessed by "China"? From his discussion of the "doctrine for ruling the world" to the *Discourse on Lamas*, the emperor argued that imperial sovereignty was primarily a legal enterprise. In exchange for submission, Qianlong promised to deliver a more just system of rewards and punishments. Concerned primarily with tracing the history of Qing imperial patronage of the Gelukpa, prior examinations of Qing–Tibetan relations have missed the degree to which Qing rulers and their representatives also attempted to legitimize their rule through the promise of a superior legal order. The institution of the Golden Urn was not merely about subordinating the political and religious authority of the hierarchs of the Gelukpa church to the emperor, but also an argument for the superior justice of the imperial legal order. The new Qing statutes for Tibet drafted between 1792 and 1793 promised authentic reincarnations and the amelioration of what the court perceived to be widespread corruption in Tibet and Mongolia.

Although the year 1792 had witnessed the application of aspects of the Qing Code to Tibet, the emperor was clear that this entailed not the expansion of "China," but rather the authority of the ruling house—the "king's law." In the *Discourse on Lamas*, Qianlong wrote exclusively of the subordination and loyalty of his Inner Asian subjects—Mongol aristocrats, lamas, and to a lesser extent Tibetans—to the state (Tib. *gur*, Ma. *gurun*, Ch. *chao* 朝). "China" was not mentioned. Qianlong furthermore recognized the delicate balance between imposing his laws and imposing an alien culture. As noted in the introduction, the ruler urged his colonial officials to observe the ancient dictum that when governing strangers, one should "improve their teachings, not replace their teachings; improve their laws, not replace their traditions."[123] Two years later, when the emperor commissioned the engraving of the *Discourse on Lamas* onto stelae at Yonghegong and the Jokhang Temple, he boiled his philosophy for governing the frontiers down to an even more pithy slogan: "Follow the [local] customs, promote the common good."[124]

Still, one cannot underestimate the difficulty Qing frontier officials faced in interpreting this slogan in practice and communicating it to the Inner Asian elite. How were the emperor's officials to explain to the ruling elite of Tibet, both lay and clerical, that the dynasty's goal was to reform their traditions without in the same breath insulting them? How would subsequent Qing rulers and officials persuade Tibetan and Mongol elites that their "reform" measures were not simply "Chinese" practices? How would Geluk elites interpret the Qing state's increasingly emphatic claims of sovereignty?

The Tibetan reception of the Golden Urn policy did not rely on the *Discourse on Lamas*, which was not translated into Tibetan until June 1794. Instead, the new policies were initially conveyed to the Tibetan elite by court-affiliated lamas such as the Galdan Siretu *kūtuktu* or in the form of oral instructions from officials such as Fuk'anggan and Heliyen on the basis of Manchu- or Mongol-language edicts such as that of October 14, 1792 (QL 57/08/29). Unlike the *Discourse on Lamas*, in this edict the emperor seemed to make a more sympathetic attempt to relate to the Inner Asian elite. In the unique conclusion, Qianlong humbly noted that he too obeyed what he preached. "My handling of things in this manner was expressly for the protection of the Yellow Teachings. It is my desire that true *trülku* be located. It is definitely not my intention to bring them grief. If I were to appoint one of my own sons a *trülku*, I fear that as a matter of course this would be greatly derided by everyone and surely could not be carried out."[125] What was absurd for the Mongol princes was equally so for the emperor.

The *Discourse on Lamas* also made no mention of the issue that would soon preoccupy the emperor and the *ambans* in Lhasa: the purported corruption of the oracles, and the Lamo *chökyong* in particular. When this essay was first composed in the winter of 1792, the court appears to have resigned itself to the idea that the traditional divination arts would have to be included in the process of locating *trülku*. However, in the spring of 1793, the Qing ruler came to believe more strongly than ever that his sovereignty over the Geluk church and Tibet could only be made secure if he dominated the technologies of divination. As long as the oracles of Tibet remained active, the emperor perceived a threat to his decision-making power and the stability of the realm. It is to the Qing campaign to stamp out the oracles that we now turn.

ACT II

Shamanic Colonialism

In the late fall of 1791, the monk Nawangdasi arrived in Lhasa from Mongolia to commence the search for the reincarnation of his master, the Erdeni Pandita *kütuktu*, the ecclesiastic ruler of a network of monasteries and herding communities in the alpine grasslands of western Outer Mongolia. As treasurer of his master's estate, Nawangdasi was responsible for supervising the search.

The treasurer would later explain to his interrogators in Beijing that the search had been complicated from the outset by the fact .that his master had passed away without providing a clear testament describing where he would be reborn. In such cases, he stated, it was the custom to first travel to Tibet and request a divination from the Lamo oracle concerning the location of the rebirth. Once the location was ascertained, candidate children could be selected and tested. Finally, the searchers would return to central Tibet to confirm their identification with the Dalai Lama and the Lamo oracle. "Only at this point," stated the treasurer, "will everyone believe [in the reincarnation]."[1] Yet, as Qing investigators would later observe, Nawangdasi had not followed his own prescriptions.

After arriving in Lhasa and attending a brief audience with the Eighth Dalai Lama, Nawangdasi proceeded to the monastery of the Lamo oracle. There, he presented various gifts and then began making inquiries about the reincarnation of his master. According to Nawangdasi, the initial instructions were not very satisfying. The Lamo oracle merely told him to "recite the appropriate sutras" and that news would be forthcoming. Several months later, shortly after the start of the Tibetan new year (late January–early February, 1792) the treasurer visited the oracle again, presented gifts, and received a divination instructing him to seek out the rebirth of his master among commoner households in the eastern area of the Sain Noyan league. According to Nawangdasi, this advice was also disappointing. He later told his interrogators that, having "squandered" over ten thousand silver taels[2] on a long journey to Tibet, he was disinclined to believe that his master had reincarnated among a non-noble family.[3]

Nawangdasi resolved, therefore, to approach the Lamo oracle a third time with the names of two candidate children who, although from noble families, had at least been born within the eastern districts of his tribe. He wrote the two names on separate slips of paper and presented them to the oracle. While possessed by the Lamo protector deity, the medium immediately placed a mark on the name of the son of Cedendorji, the Tüsiyetü Khan.[4] The Dalai Lama would later testify that, "having always found the speech of the Lamo oracle to be reliable," he personally confirmed the authenticity of this divination.[5] Thus, considering the matter successfully and "truthfully" resolved, the treasurer returned to the Khalkha lands and reported the results of the search to his league captain.[6] The latter subsequently ordered Nawangdasi to submit a final report to the Court of Colonial Affairs in Beijing.[7]

A year later, in the winter of 1792–93, when Nawangdasi's report eventually reached the Court of Colonial Affairs, it encountered an environment that, as we have seen in act 1, had not only grown hostile to the oracles of central Tibet but also proscribed the identification of *kūtuktu* among the sons of Mongol aristocrats such as Cedendorji. In his own defense, the treasurer claimed that he was unaware of the new law concerning the use of the Golden Urn—an edict that had been promulgated well after he had departed central Tibet. Considering that Qing officials in Outer Mongolia first began to report receipt of the *Discourse on Lamas* edict only in March 1793, approximately five months after the first urn was dispatched from Beijing to Lhasa on October 25, 1792, it is easy to believe that Nawangdasi knew nothing of the statute when he filed his report.[8] Yet the investigators were unswayed and found even the act of filing the report suspicious. They wrote, "After you returned from Tibet, in principle you could have not reported [to the Court of Colonial Affairs]. Instead, feigning ignorance, you wrote requesting that the old customs be [observed]. How can you say that [you] were not seeking your own advantage?"[9]

Upon receiving word of the treasurer's request from the officials of the Court of Colonial Affairs, the emperor was immediately suspicious. In his first pronouncement on the case, enclosed in a letter to the Grand Council on March 16, 1793, he opined that the Dalai Lama's identification of the khan's son as a *kūtuktu* was "clearly the result of the bribery and corrupt actions of the khan Cedendorji and the treasurer Nawangdasi."[10] These suspicions were exacerbated by the unfortunate coincidence that in the edict promulgating the new Golden Urn lottery, the Qianlong emperor had singled out the father of the current Tüsiyetü Khan for ridicule. The *Discourse on Lamas* presented the failed attempt of the previous Tüsiyetü Khan to have his yet unborn child recognized as the Jebtsundamba *kūtuktu* in 1758 as the case in point for how Mongol nobility had corrupted the recognition process.[11] Although the emperor was convinced of the corruption, he could not definitively identify its source. He queried:

> Previously, when the treasurer arrived in Tibet, he repeatedly presented various gifts to the Dalai Lama. Was it Cedendorji who planted the idea of seeking out the Dalai Lama and spoke to [the treasurer] of how to approach him? Or was it the treasurer who sought to pass on his requests via the servants or close family members of the Dalai Lama? Or was it the Dalai Lama himself, who, because he wished to receive the usual alms from Cedendorji and had come to see the benefit in considering this [request], signaled that it was his son?[12]

Just three days later, the emperor received a transcript of the interrogation of Nawangdasi. On that basis, the emperor concluded that the idea to identify the Tüsiyetü Khan's son as the reincarnation of Erdeni Pandita originated with the khan himself. Yet the testimony of Nawangdasi not only confirmed his preexisting suspicions that Mongol aristocrats had corrupted the search process but also revealed that Inner Asian elites possessed certain fixed notions that stood in the way of the successful implementation of his reform measures, most importantly the statute on the Golden Urn. Furthermore, the testimony revealed, to the consternation of the throne, that faith in the efficacy of the oracles and the divination skills of the Dalai Lama and Panchen Lama remained strong and that the repeated reincarnation of *kūtuktu* and other influential lamas among the households of the Mongol or Tibetan aristocracy was not necessarily considered corrupt.[13] On the contrary, nobility, wealth, power, and religious attainment went hand in hand: if the wealth and status of the Inner Asian nobility could be attributed to the karma they had accrued by means of their meritorious activities on behalf of Buddhism, then it was but the natural order of things that they also produced miraculous offspring. In the course of his interrogation, the treasurer was brought to admit that indeed there was corruption among the Mongol nobles as a result of "struggles for profit and fortune" and that the Golden Urn might eradicate it, but he did not budge on the authenticity of his choice.[14]

When asked why he had followed neither his own original plan nor the prophecy of the Lamo oracle, the treasurer replied that it would be a waste of money to search for a child among commoners because the majority of the people would not believe in such a candidate. Nawangdasi testified:

> The children of the common ranks are not as good as children from the lineages of the nobility. Among their children there are many who are intelligent and handsome. And after they become *trülku*, every khan, prince, and so forth will prostrate before them. [However,] if the [child] is from the lineage of an ordinary family, it is impossible to predict whether everyone will be convinced and have faith in his authenticity.[15]

In response, Qianlong wrote:

> Nawangdasi has stated in his deposition that, "the Mongols' nature is such that they reverently believe that the emergence and identification of all reincarnations of *kūtuktu* in the households of great families is simply [a sign] of their innate endowment of genius and good fortune." Observing this, it would appear that the Dalai Lama must also hold similar opinions. Moreover, since Nawangdasi only reported the sons Cedendorji and Erincindorji, the Dalai Lama's selection of the son of Cedendorji was merely a matter of calculating whose rank was higher.[16]

The Qianlong emperor rejected the treasurer Nawangdasi's petition and launched an investigation of the case. The importance placed on this matter was underscored by the dispatch of several high-ranking officials with expertise in Mongol affairs. No less a personage than Sungyun, a vice-minister of the Board of Revenue recently appointed to the Grand Council, was ordered to personally travel to the pastures of the Tüsiyetü Khan to probe the origins of the relationship among the khan, the treasurer, and the Dalai Lama. Another Mongol bannerman, Kūišu (奎舒 d. 1809), a vice-minister of the Court of Colonial Affairs who had previously served as Qinghai *amban*, and a senior monk from the Gelukpa establishment in Beijing, Gelek Namk'a,[17] were commissioned to lead a new search for the reincarnation of the Erdeni Pandita *kūtuktu*. This time the emperor ordered that the child be recognized in accordance with his decree on the Golden Urn:[18] candidate children were to be identified among non-noble households and, because the estate of the *kūtuktu* was located in Mongolia, the final lottery would be conducted not in Lhasa but at the Geluk monastery at Yonghegong in Beijing.

Yet even though the search for the Erdeni Pandita *kūtuktu* involved Mongols and was to be resolved in Beijing, the emperor coordinated the prosecution of the affair closely with Heliyen, his chief representative in Lhasa. The emperor justified this in a Manchu-language letter to Heliyen, one of several he posted to Lhasa just days after the treasurer's petition reached Beijing:

I have dispatched Kūišu and Gelek Namk'a and ordered them to locate several children in the vicinity of Erdeni Pandita *kūtuktu* and select one by drawing lots. [You] must devote great attention to this first case and resolutely uphold the law, punish these people, and identify this one reincarnation in exactly this [manner]. Afterward, only when the corrupt habits of the Lamo oracle have been rectified and the Dalai Lama's independent authority over identification [of rebirths] removed, and we have elucidated the stupid and muddleheaded Mongols, will it be possible to consistently carry out this edict [i.e., the Golden Urn lottery].

Once an identification of a [*kūtuktu*] of a rank such as this has been successfully accomplished, in the future the Dalai Lama, Panchen Erdeni, and other major *trülku* will have no need to seek divinations from the Lamo oracle. Because I have entrusted [matters] to the *ambans* resident in Tibet, the names of all auspicious and miraculous children shall be collected from across Tibet and subjected to a lottery in the Jokhang. *Thus at this point authority over all the affairs of Tibet will be consolidated in us.*[19]

Even at this early stage in the investigation of the Tüsiyetü Khan case, it was apparent to the Qing court that introducing the new recognition procedure and finding acceptance for the law among Mongols and Tibetans would be much harder than initially thought. As the quote from Qianlong's letter to Heliyen reveals, the emperor recognized that the act of promulgating the new statute was insufficient on its own. Moreover, the Golden Urn ritual could not merely be appended to the recognition process. The emerging details concerning the involvement of the Lamo oracle and the Dalai Lama in the identification of the khan's son as a *kūtuktu* persuaded the emperor that the Golden Urn could not complement or otherwise coexist with the existing tradition. As long as the oracles and the Dalai Lama remained credible prognosticators, the possibility remained that the indigenous leadership could settle on a final candidate without reference to Qianlong's new law. If the emperor were to truly have the last word, control over divination would have to be enforced. The Ganden Podrang's tradition of "oracular governance" in which Dharma protectors and divination played a central role in the decision-making process would have to be dismantled.

Therefore, to paraphrase Qianlong, if the dynasty was to have any success in meeting its goals of instituting the new law and reversing the loss of faith in the authenticity of the reincarnate lamas of the Geluk church, it would have to dislodge the indigenous tradition first. This would require an aggressive campaign to discredit the oracles and the Dalai Lama and persuade Tibetans and Mongolians that the Golden Urn was a more effective method. Moreover, the campaign would have to be carefully coordinated between Mongolia and Tibet.

In this light, it should come as no surprise that the first article of the *Imperially Sanctioned Twenty-Nine Articles of Reconstruction*—the Tibetan-language omnibus proclamation of all the reform measures approved by the emperor and delivered to the Dalai Lama by Fuk'anggan on April 4, 1793 (QL 58/02/24)—mandated the use of the Golden Urn. Planning for the implementation of the lottery began nearly two months before Fuk'anggan was asked to draft the other reforms of the Tibetan administration. Subsequent discussion of these twenty-eight measures was nearly nonexistent in the months and years following Fuk'anggan's departure from

Lhasa. In contrast, the Golden Urn and divination more generally remained the dominant topic of conversation between officials in Lhasa and the court in Beijing throughout the remaining days of the Qianlong emperor's life and into the first several years of the Jiaqing reign. With the notable exception of Fuk'anggan's memorials on the subject, the discussion of divination was conducted in Manchu and considered separately from other issues pertaining to the reform of the Tibetan administration. Moreover, the numerous imperial rescripts on these documents attest to the fact that this issue remained a priority concern of the emperor despite his advancing years and gradual withdrawal from the daily oversight of other issues. Thus, the records constitute a distinctive deliberative process that was accessible only to a select number of Manchu-speaking officials. Previous scholarship on the aftermath of the Gurkha war that has not made use of Manchu sources has overlooked both the importance of divination in Qianlong's thinking on sovereignty and the significance of the emperor's belief that the effort to impose the Golden Urn ritual was incumbent on stamping out the oracles of central Tibet.

This act examines the court-orchestrated campaign to persuade Tibetan Buddhists to abandon the oracles in exchange for a new method drawn from the practices of the bureaucracy of China proper. The campaign was conducted over the spring and summer of 1793 and consisted of two critical components: first, the emperor ordered the careful management of the search for the reincarnation of the Erdeni Pandita in Khalkha Mongolia and the dissemination of incriminating evidence concerning the Tüsiyetü Khan's attempt to have his son recognized as a *kūtuktu*. The emperor hoped that exposure of the Tüsiyetü Khan's collusion with the treasurer as well as the influence of money and gifts on the decisions of the Dalai Lama and the oracles would persuade Tibetans and Mongols that the existing procedures were in need of reform. The eventual dissemination of news of the "successful" identification of the Erdeni Pandita *kūtuktu* would establish the legitimacy of the new law. Second, the emperor ordered his agents in Lhasa to organize a series of public tests and trials intended to discredit the claims of the oracles and undermine their reputation for accuracy.

Both elements of this campaign were built on a particular conception of "faith" and were overtly concerned with the arts of persuasion, or more specifically, a desire to achieve compliance not through force but by changing Tibetans' personal conviction. In Manchu-language documents, the Qing court discussed faith in two ways. Officials spoke of "service to the

Buddha" (Ma. *fucihi be uilembi*) as axiomatic or innate to the Mongols and Tibetans. They also operated as if faith was something that arose from subjective observation and thus was inherently malleable. In this latter sense—faith understood as "trust" (Ma. *akdambi*)—Qing authorities believed that it was possible not only for followers of the Geluk to lose their faith but also for the dynasty to "change the minds" (Ma. *gūnin dahambi*) of their Tibetan Buddhist subjects.[20] Public spectacles might cause witnesses to "be persuaded" (Ma. *gūnin dahabumbi*) of the virtue of the dynasty's laws. Similarly, the emperor hoped that the influence of the oracles would naturally fade away or "self-defeat" (Ma. *ini cisui nakambi*, Ch. *zibai* 自敗) once the Tibetans and Mongols had a chance to test the accuracy of the oracles against the Qing court's divination technologies.[21]

What is significant about the deep interest in persuasion is that it was premised on the assumption that there were shared standards of evidence and understandings of divination, and that Manchus, Mongols, and Tibetans could arrive at similar conclusions through a process of empirical investigation. In some respects the Qing officials were not wrong. The Manchu connotations of *akdambi* are similar to those of the word they chose when translating the term into Tibetan: *depa*. According to Buswell and Lopez's definition of *depa*, "faith" or "confidence" in Buddhism similarly arises from experience with the Dharma or Buddha, or at least is "a tacit acceptance of the soteriological value of specific beliefs, until such time as those beliefs are verified through practice and understood through one's own insight."[22] This and the subsequent act explore the points of overlap and divergence between Qing official and Tibetan Buddhist notions of faith as the dynasty campaigned for the urn in the 1790s.

"Legislating the Possible"

From the very moment when the idea for the Golden Urn began to circulate among Qianlong's inner court advisors, he intended for it to completely replace the custom of seeking prophecies from the oracles, especially the Lamo oracle.[23] Yet the emperor was initially forced to compromise, and the first edicts promulgating the Golden Urn in 1792 all included the oracles in the recognition process. Two individuals in particular seem to have been instrumental in negotiating the initial configuration of the new statute: the Galdan Siretu *kūtuktu* and military commander Fuk'anggan.

The emperor had sought out the Galdan Siretu *kūtuktu*, the highest-ranking Gelukpa monk to pass through the emperor's summer retreat at Chengde in 1792, to provide an explanation of the nature of the oracles of central Tibet as well as an assessment of the feasibility of the new procedure. The Galdan Siretu *kūtuktu*'s advice was subsequently included in the first letter concerning the new ritual dispatched to Fuk'anggan in Tibet.[24] As noted in act 1, the *kūtuktu* sanctioned the Golden Urn yet also advised the emperor to retain the oracles in the process. A later document, however, reveals more clearly the role of this monk in both legitimizing the ritual within the Tibetan Buddhist tradition and also forcefully rejecting the emperor's wish to proscribe the use of the oracles.

Labeled "A draft letter from the Galdan Siretu *kūtuktu* to the Dalai Lama and Panchen Lama translated into Manchu," this document recounts how the monk traveled from Dolonuur to the emperor's summer retreat at Chengde and subsequently learned of the new "process for drawing lots." The monk wrote to the Dalai Lama and Panchen Lama that upon hearing the news he was "deeply persuaded and appreciative," and confident that the new measure would "eliminate the corruption of the mediums."[25] He also added the following observation: "Having thus established this change, it is exactly in accord with the manner in which the *hūbilgan* of the Fifth Dalai Lama and previous Panchen Lama were identified. . . . Truly the edict of Manjusri, the Great Holy Lord of the East, resplendent like the sun and moon, has reached the point of clearly perceiving the state of affairs of our western land and the feelings of the people."[26] The Fifth Dalai Lama had actually been identified using a *zentak* divination, a process qualitatively different from the Golden Urn lottery.[27] Yet this bold comparison would have major repercussions for the subsequent reception of the ritual among Tibetans, and later commentators would make a similar comparison. Placing the Golden Urn ritual within the same category of practices that had located the Great Fifth Dalai Lama had a powerful effect on legitimizing the new ritual.

However, the Galdan Siretu *kūtuktu* did not offer unreserved support. He informed the Dalai Lama and Panchen Lama that he had told the grand councilor (most likely Hešen[28]) and assembled Qing officials that he disagreed with the recommendation to prohibit the use of the oracles. He wrote, "If the prophecies are not consulted concerning the place where the reincarnation is located and children's names are submitted according to people's desires to be selected from the urn, petty quarrels will arise and it will be impossible to convince the clergy and laypeople [of the authenticity of the child]."[29] The monk then continued that he had advised that once "good and virtuous mediums" had been located, the four protector deities (i.e., the Lamo, Nechung, Gadong, and Samyé oracles) could be invoked to provide information on the location of the rebirth. As noted in act 1, the grand councilor relayed to the emperor the *kūtuktu*'s proposal for continued use of the oracles but dropped mention of the underlying rationale for the disagreement.[30]

This letter from the Galdan Siretu *kūtuktu* is but one of a large body of Manchu-language translations of letters that passed between Tibetan elites between 1791 and 1793.[31] These letters were collected and translated by the Grand Council in Beijing. The flattering tone and formal organization of the letter, in addition to the indication that this was a "draft," suggests that either the monk was well aware of the possibility that the court would inspect the contents of his letter or it was actually drafted under the supervision of the court. Regardless of the impetus behind its creation, its existence and content indicate the degree to which the Qing court officials were able to use monks based at imperially sponsored institutions such as Yonghegong or the monasteries at Chengde to convey imperial policy to local elites in Tibet and Mongolia. The term "degree" is crucial here because, as this letter demonstrates, Geluk elites could be counted on to support imperial initiatives, but not in an unqualified manner. The letter exposes not only the power of the emperor but also the advisory authority of the Galdan Siretu *kūtuktu*.

The Galdan Siretu *kūtuktu*'s sketch of the ritual was included in Qianlong's court letter to Fuk'anggan that first informed the commander, then still in Nepal, of the idea for the lottery. As a result, this *kūtuktu*'s draft configuration of the Golden Urn ritual would influence both Fuk'anggan's understanding of the statute and all subsequent public edicts concerning the Golden Urn until Qianlong categorically outlawed the use of the oracles in a major decree issued eight months later.[32] The *Discourse on Lamas* proclamation of December 1792, for instance, accorded the oracles a major role. Ironically, *Discourse on Lamas* had only just begun to circulate widely in Mongolia when the Tüsiyetü Khan case broke and the emperor began to push more forcefully for the eradication of the oracles. In light of this, it is perhaps understandable that Qing field officials in Mongolia and Tibet, as well as local Mongols and Tibetans, would not yet have understood the establishment of the Golden Urn as an attempt to supplant the oracles.

Of additional significance is the fact that the Galdan Siretu *kūtuktu*'s blueprint for the lottery interpreted the emperor's edict as implying that it would be either the Dalai Lama or the Panchen Lama who drew the lot from the urn.[33] In his early formulations of the ritual, Qianlong had not explicitly addressed the issue of who would physically draw the lot. Major imperial pronouncements concerning the Golden Urn that were handed down in the first month after the idea was floated stated ambiguously that the lots would be "selected jointly by the Dalai Lama and the resident *ambans*."[34] Fuk'anggan's own first blueprint of the ritual, submitted to the throne in December 1792, just a week after his first meetings with the Dalai Lama and other Tibetan elites upon returning from Nepal, recommended that the Dalai Lama and Panchen Lama personally draw the lots. In the event that there was a search for a Dalai Lama or Panchen Lama, the living member of the pair would identify the reincarnation of his colleague, "in the spirit of the master–disciple relationship."[35] In all cases, the *ambans* resident in Tibet would observe the ritual. Fuk'anggan's advice probably reflects the influence of local Tibetans, if not also the original input of the Galdan Siretu *kūtuktu*.

It seems, however, that Fuk'anggan felt obliged to modify the proposed statute on the Golden Urn in one significant way. Although he evidently concurred with the Galdan Siretu *kūtuktu* that a role for the oracles was necessary, he seems to have anticipated a potential problem: if the oracles were permitted to arrive at a set of unified instructions for where and how to search for candidates, what was to prevent them from unifying around the candidacy of a single child, thus preempting the need for a lottery? To solve this problem, Fuk'anggan proposed a control test in which a lot bearing the single candidate's name would be placed in the urn along with a blank lot. If the blank lot was drawn, he wrote, the candidacy of the child would be thrown out and the search would have to start anew.[36] Although this amendment to the statute did not arrive in Beijing in time to be included in the emperor's formal proclamation of the ritual in the *Discourse on Lamas*, it was established as a precedent the next year after Fuk'anggan himself oversaw just such a test in March 1793 (QL 58/02/11).[37]

Colonial Discourses on Shamanism, East and West

It was in direct response to Fuk'anggan's plan for the lottery that the emperor first broached the idea of testing the oracles more closely. Noting that Fuk'anggan had advocated the consultation of the oracles as the first stage in the search process, Qianlong was still resigned to their inclusion, stating, "At the present we can only do like this."[38] Although suspicious of the oracles, he seems to have been open to their continued use, especially if it could be ascertained that they were effective and credible before the wider audience. He ordered Fuk'anggan and the other Qing officials resident in Lhasa to "examine the Lamo and other oracles. If what they [divine] is not found trustworthy before the people, it merely becomes a joke, and thus we will be unable to use them in the future." A separate court letter from the emperor to his field officials was more strongly worded:

> The protectors all use various heterodox methods to mislead the people. When the deity descends to them, they use a knife to stab themselves, yet their bodies are unharmed. These arts of illusion make their method appear true. Among the teachings of the Buddha these [arts] are the most inferior. If [these arts] are fraudulent, then they are not even worth a laugh! How could anyone believe in them as before? Fuk'anggan and the rest should promptly put the methods of those four protectors to the test. Have them stab themselves! And if their methods are not efficacious, then immediately point out their absurd and unbelievable claims to the people to educate them. The monks and laity will then know of their presumption and shall not act in accordance with their foolishness. Thus in the future when an incarnation appears the use of oracles can be forbidden. [Instead,] the names of several candidates with similar dates of birth shall be [placed] in the golden urn, and the Dalai Lama will by drawing a lot come to a decision, and by means of this promulgate what is equitable and fair.[39]

Although in this command the emperor communicated more strongly his distaste for the oracles and expectation that they would be found false, it is important to distinguish this request to investigate the oracles from subsequent tests conducted by Heliyen. At this stage, the emperor was still only conditionally disdainful of the oracles—wary of the authority they might wield on the basis of certain abilities, base as they might be. The emperor not only was willing to countenance some role for them but also still positioned the Dalai Lama front and center in the lottery as the man who would draw the lot.

A month later, Fuk'anggan, Sun Shiyi, Heliyen, and several other officers submitted a joint memorial detailing the results of their investigations in Lhasa. The document deserves to be examined in detail because the results of the investigation forced the authors to walk a delicate line between affirming the ideas of the emperor but also conveying to the throne the enduring influence of the oracles.

The officials began by confirming the emperor's impression that recent reincarnations had been poorly verified and were of dubious authenticity:

> We find that during the early period following the founding of the teaching, when the Dalai Lama, Panchen Lama, and other great *kūtuktu* reincarnated, they did not lose their fundamental natures. Yet with regard to whether or not later reincarnations truly possessed the root essence, this matter has been vague from the beginning. There has not necessarily been irrefutable evidence or tests and [we] have not heard that there were any who truly could recall matters from their past lives or recognize objects from their previous generations.[40]

Fuk'anggan and his fellow officials then observed that despite a purported lack of confidence in the identifications, faith in these *kūtuktus* had been shored up because ultimately the emperor himself had sanctioned the selections:

> As it is the intention of the Holy Lord to promote the Yellow Doc-trines, and because all the Mongol tribes and Tibetans customarily worship the Buddhist teachings, they are therefore guided according to their situation and we facilitate their customs and pacify these for-eigners. This [is the principle behind how,] in the past, whenever the *chökyong* pointed out a person, after the details were reported, an edict would be passed down recognizing them as a *trülku* and thus all the millions of Mongols and Tibetans would have faith in [the child] as a true [reincarnation] and wholeheartedly worship them.[41]

In other words, the officials were pointing out that even before Qianlong introduced the Golden Urn, the actions of Qing rulers had been key in preserving Tibetan Buddhists' faith in the reincarnations. And the court had already been doing this despite reservations about the authenticity of the reincarnations—reservations that the authors imply were shared by Tibetans. The influence of the indigenous tradition on sustaining peace in Mongolia and Tibet led the dynasty to add its authority to the decisions of the oracles. Fuk'anggan et al. then turned to recounting their own personal observations of the activities of the oracles:

> Since your servants have arrived in Tibet, we have personally witnessed how a deity descended to *chökyong*[42] in order to exorcise demons and the streets became crowded with tens of thousands who pressed in to watch. Long lines formed of those who wished to present *kadak* and others who wished to be touched on the head while they prostrated themselves bareheaded. They proceeded in an orderly line and galloped out like crazy people! Their absurdity reaches such a degree that there are even those who, having been accidentally cut by the knife of an oracle in the midst of their mad dancing, promptly recite a mantra and then happily look to the future thinking that all those who receive such an injury will never suffer misfortune or illness! When your servants brought this excessive faith to the attention of important lamas and Tibetan headmen and carefully explained to them the ridiculous aspects of such oracles, they looked at each other in astonishment and dared not reply, as they feared their excessive guilt. When we consider such sincere faith, there are ultimately no words that will change their minds.[43]

With regard to why the oracles held such widespread authority, Fuk'anggan provided the following reasons:

> As for the methods of the *chökyong*, regardless of whether they dress up as deities, read sutras or pray, dishonestly claim that the deity has possessed their body, dance with knives, shake their heads and spit out hot air, make prognostications about the future of the harvest or smallpox epidemics; no matter what kind of test they are subjected to, after the spirit has left them they abruptly wake up. And if you ask them about what they just said, they look dumbfounded and can remember nothing. Thus there is not a Tibetan who doesn't believe them. Rumors about what they do while under the influence are not at all reliable. Even claims that they can stab themselves with knives are all myths and unreliable hearsay. In fact, nothing of the sort happens. Speaking of their skill, it really is not worth a laugh. But although it is inferior to that of the sorcerers of the interior, it can be eye-catching and will fool the stupid.[44]

The comparison with the shamans of the interior in this memorial introduced a theme that would become prominent in later trials of the oracles. Qing colonial officials placed the Tibetan mediums who spoke for the protector deities within their own familiar category of "shamans" and "sorcerers."[45] But if the oracles were shamans, they were at best degenerate shamans whose abilities paled in comparison with those of the superior tradition of the Manchus and the "interior." Fuk'anggan argued that if the Tibetans could be brought to understand that their shamans were less efficacious than those of the interior, they could be persuaded to support the Qing emperor's efforts to stamp out the oracles. This aspect of official thinking recalls Homi Bhahba's theory of "colonial mimicry," the idea that colonial discourses find ways to portray the subordinate Other as similar yet not quite the same, and that their claim to authority lies in the conviction that the Other is fundamentally incapable of rising to the status of being fully the same and thus equal.[46] The colonizer notices or establishes some sort of similarity, yet then continually "disavows" it.[47] The subject can "mimic" or "ape" the colonizer but never fully become assimilated. While Bhabha was primarily thinking of English colonialism in India, the Qianlong court's "shamanic imperialism" was very much a variation on this phenomenon. The similarity of the oracles to the "shamans of the interior" (Ma. *dorgi ba i saman*)[48] meant that the court naturally had a certain expertise in the oracles; this translated into an obligation to test, rectify, and transform. Moreover, Bhabha notes that what seemed similar could also seem "menacing."[49] As we have seen in act 1, the threat that oracles and unregulated divination posed to the stability of the Qing order and the credibility of the Geluk served as justification for the imposition of Qing sovereignty.

What seems unique in the Qing case is that the officials not only portrayed Tibetan shamans as charlatans but also took an ambiguous position on the underlying value and identity of the superior category, the "shamans of the interior." By the end of the Qianlong reign, successive Qing rulers had established and codified an elaborate set of shamanic rituals and ritual sites dedicated to the state and banner elite as well as individual clans, including the Aisin Gioro, the imperial clan.[50] As Rawski notes, over the course of this codification process, the Qing court had consciously "removed the ecstatic element from all the rituals except the palace evening services."[51] These were witnessed only by the imperial family and their personal attendants. The court had eliminated rituals involving trance from the formal liturgies for court shamanic rituals.[52] The Qing Code also proscribed most of these activities among the Han of China proper. According to Donald Sutton, during the early Qing, shamanism and specifically spirit possession had come under increasing attack from Neo-Confucian literati in China proper. From the perspective first of literati and subsequently of Qing officials, shamanic practices transgressed proper social boundaries and threatened the position of educated Confucian men at the top of the social and ritual hierarchy. Spirit mediums were often female, frequently worked at night, and were generally of low status yet capable of providing ritual services across social classes. Literati attempts to suppress shamanism were infused with the argument that spirit mediums were avaricious charlatans who preyed on the naïve and impressionable.[53] As Qing officials in Tibet and at court homed in on the state oracles of Tibet, their critiques borrowed from this discourse. Fuk'anggan et al. were therefore comparing the activities of Tibetan oracles to activities of shamans in the "interior" that were forbidden, or at least looked upon with increasing suspicion. It is unclear if Fuk'anggan had the Manchu shamanic tradition or the activities of Chinese "sorcerers" in mind. But regardless, both had been the focus of a kind of shamanic imperialism—regimentation, rectification, and often eradication, since the early years of the dynasty.[54]

The Qianlong court's assessment of the oracles as examples of the "low tradition" (Ch. *xiacheng* 下乘)[55] of Tibetan Buddhism would find an echo in the Western Orientalist scholarship of the late nineteenth century. Their studies of Tibetan religion attributed what they perceived as the degeneration of high, classical Buddhism to the influence of Tibet's indigenous "shamanist" beliefs.[56] Since the 1960s, the association of the pre-Buddhist tradition, and Bon in particular, with shamanism has been the subject of much contumely. In a recent critique of the application of the label "shamanism" to the religious traditions of Tibet, Zeff Bjerken has argued that the concept of "shamanism" as understood by Western Orientalists and later social scientists had no direct equivalent in Tibetan thought.[57] Bjerken also makes the argument that although the application of the term "shamanism" to Tibetan religious culture was a novel, outside imposition by Western Tibetologists, their analysis (alternatively pejorative and glowing) has been strongly influenced by polemical arguments *within* the Tibetan tradition.[58] For instance, the nineteenth-century scholar Sarat Chandra Das dismissed Bon as "shamanism," but his critique was largely based on a reading of the Third Tukwan *kūtuktu*, Lozang Chökyi Nyima's, *Crystal Mirror of Doctrinal Systems*, a Qianlong-period work that was critical of Bon.[59] The Manchu-language sources permit us to modify Bjerken's argument: Western Orientalists were not the first to apply the label "shaman" to Tibetan religious culture and to do so pejoratively in a colonial context.

Testing the Oracles

After dismissing the oracles as but a shadow of the their peers elsewhere in the empire, Fuk'anggan and his associates turned to the actual test they had conducted:

> Then your servants, in accordance with your instructions, gathered the oracles together and ordered them to perform their conjuring arts in the Jokhang. They all stated that up until the present they had only practiced possession and transmission of the words of deities and that there were no other arts. [We] tested them, ordering them to become possessed. What we observed resembled what we had seen and heard previously. We examined them by posing one or two questions about what kind of woes Tibet might soon face. Each oracle, speaking for their deity, said nothing more than that there will be an outbreak of smallpox as a result of the incoming spring winds. Given that the Tibetans fear smallpox more than anything else, at first we did not take [the oracles] seriously. Yet just a little more than ten days after the prophecy, over two hundred Tibetans came down with the pox. This was thus a small proof of their abilities.
>
> In conclusion, these sorts of absurd and preposterous matters are in principle impossible to believe in. Unfortunately, the inborn nature of both the Tibetan clergy and the laypeople is extraordinarily stupid. To the end of their days they will worship the Buddha and recite their sutras, thinking of nothing but what benefits the Buddha realm. Although one can appeal to them to consider the higher tradition[60] and not follow those who speak empty gibberish, this can ultimately not be achieved, and, as if cast in iron, their habits will continue on. It is difficult to quickly break through their muddled perplexity.[61]

The forceful official boilerplate about the "preposterous" claims of the oracles, however, rings hollow in this letter. The test seems to have left

Fuk'anggan and his fellow officials not fully persuaded that they were without abilities, and if anything may have had the opposite effect. Seen in this light, much of the letter seems like a carefully calibrated attempt to convey the importance of a continued role for the oracles. Fuk'anggan's comment about the previous widespread credibility of imperially licensed *kūtuktu* seems intended to persuade the emperor that the pre-Gurkha war status quo had been working well enough to justify its continuation. Moreover, the commander ultimately concurred with the Galdan Siretu *kūtuktu* that the oracles were essential to the process of locating candidate children:

> Now our Enlightened Holy Lord promotes the Yellow Doctrines and has issued a Golden Urn to be held at the Jokhang. All those incarnations identified by the *chökyong* shall ultimately, as a rule, be selected using the urn lottery. Thus [we] will not only shore up the faith of the Tibetans but also be able to covertly eliminate the evils of the existing practice of collaborating to selfishly transmit [*trülku*hood] among themselves. This is a good law with a profound intent. Although reincarnations recognized by the *chökyong* are not in the slightest believable, if some [candidates] are not identified by the *chökyong*, not only will there be no basis for writing names on the lots and no way of putting the lots into the urn, but also, [we] fear, the many disciples and followers of the reincarnation will individually presume to make identifications, abuses will flourish, and the results will be even more unreliable. There are, after all, only four *chökyong*, and the [candidates] whom they identify are not numerous. . . .
>
> Now the exclusive use of the imperially decreed Golden Urn means that not only will [those candidates] indicated by the oracles be credible, but when lots are pulled from the urn and the robes and bowl are inherited [i.e., the child is enthroned as the lama reincarnate], the clergy and laity will be naturally persuaded and in agreement, and the abuses of the past will be eliminated.[62]

Just a week after submitting this memorial, Fuk'anggan dispatched a second report about the oracles, evidently in respose to yet more impatient requests for information from the emperor. For a second time, Fuk'anggan attempted to dispel imperial misunderstandings. He argued that although all kinds of rumors circulated about the abilities of the human mediums, they were largely untrue and had not originated with the mediums themselves. For instance, he wrote, the oracles had not claimed the ability to stab themselves or swallow knives—an assertion that the throne had fixated on previously. He explained that the mediums were also reincarnations who had been carefully vetted by traditional means before being recognized.[63] Fuk'anggan's strategy seems to have been to distract the emperor from the oracles by downplaying their strangeness or purported magical powers: "They are no match for the shamans of the interior. Do not exaggerate the mysteriousness of what they say, because in fact there is no such thing."[64] The emperor, however, was less than satisfied. Next to Fuk'anggan's closing statement that only the continued inclusion of the oracles would satisfy the local people, Qianlong penned in the margins with evident exasperation, "This too is little more than an expedient!"[65]

The emperor had also asked about the feasibility of requiring *kūtuktus* in the Chamdo area of Kham to submit to the Golden Urn. Fuk'anggan cautioned against subjecting them to the new law. He noted that in the history of these lineages there existed no indigenous precedent for seeking out divinations from the oracles, the Dalai Lama, or other authorities in Ü and Tsang. Thus, he argued that forcing the names of the candidates to be dispatched to Lhasa to be subject to the urn lottery would, "I fear, be more than what the Tibetan mood can accept."[66] Fuk'anggan seems to have been more aware of the diversity of traditional strategies for locating reincarnations and of the historical tensions between outlying Tibetan regions and the Dalai Lama's administration in Lhasa. Still, he noted that if disciples of the *kūtuktu* in question heard about the Golden Urn and wished to have their candidates confirmed using the lottery, they would not be refused.[67]

Setting Precedents

The urn arrived in Lhasa on January 2, 1793 (QL 57/11/20) and was immediately installed in the Jokhang Temple under the supervision of the Dalai Lama.[68] Having promised on March 15, 1793 (QL58/02/04), to "test the lottery" on some "insignificant reincarnations" at the earliest possible opportunity, on March 24, 1793 (QL 58/02/13), Fuk'anggan reported that no fewer than five different searches had been subjected to the Golden Urn lottery in a single day.[69] The event established a number of important precedents, the least of which was a cast and format for conducting the ritual. The lotteries were held in the Jokhang and preceded by a ceremony of sutra recitation led by the regent, Tatsak *kūtuktu*, before the image of Tsongkhapa. "On the twenty-first day of the second month, the Dalai Lama descended from the [Potala Palace] to the Jokhang. Your servants went in person to supervise as the lots were written and placed in the urn. The lots were drawn jointly."[70] Although the last sentence does not state explicitly who drew the lots, it was most likely the Dalai Lama, as Fuk'anggan had previously advised.[71] When in later editions of the Golden Urn ritual the *ambans* personally drew the lots, this was always explicitly stated in the follow-up report.[72]

A second precedent set by these lotteries was the application of the Golden Urn statute to relatively minor reincarnation lineages. Furthermore, these were all lineages that had never previously had an obligation to report their reincarnations to the Court of Colonial Affairs. Only one of the five reincarnations had the status of *kūtuktu*, and even this lineage, according to Fuk'anggan, had historically been outside the purview of the Court of Colonial Affairs. The implication of this precedent was profound: tt demonstrated that the Golden Urn could be used to extend imperial oversight over a category of local elites that had historically eluded the dynasty. Observing that the "mood of the audience was deeply moved and heartily enamored with this edict, which their hearts are inclined to embrace," Fuk'anggan wrote, "from now on all reincarnations large and small shall be identified by lottery according to the manner of this [trial]."[73]

The first test runs were pivotal for two further reasons. First, all five of the reincarnation lineages in question had traditionally sought the counsel of the Dalai Lama or Panchen Lama in making the final identification, yet none of them had a history of seeking divinations from the oracles.[74] The use of the Golden Urn in these five cases thus conveyed the message that the court intended the lottery to supersede not only the oracles but also the divination authority of the Dalai Lama and Panchen Lama. Second, the native places of the five reincarnations subjected to the Golden Urn were not without consequence.

The first reincarnate lineage on Fuk'anggan's list was the Sumpa *kūtuktu*, who hailed from the jurisdiction of the Xining *amban*. Coincidentally, on the same day that Fuk'anggan submitted his memorial reporting the selections, the emperor dispatched a court letter to Tekšin, the Xining *amban*, requesting advice on whether it would be "more frugal" to have the *kūtuktus* of that jurisdiction identified in Lhasa or Beijing.[75] Of course, this decision was about more than just frugality. The statute on the Golden Urn had ethnic undertones with geopolitical implications. In the *Discourse on Lamas*,

Qianlong had legislated that the urn at Yonghegong was intended for use by *kūtuktus* from Mongolia while the urn in Lhasa was for *kūtuktus* of Tibetan regions. But he had not considered the status of *kūtuktus* from the jurisdiction of the Xining *amban*. This area was home to a mixed population of Mongols and Tibetans and could be conceived of from the perspective of indigenous historical memories both as the heartland of the Khoshud khanate of Güüshi Khan and as the northeastern province of "Greater Tibet"—Amdo. Fuk'anggan's decision, therefore, to include the Sumpa *kūtuktu* in the ritual set a precedent that not only preempted any decision the Xining *amban* might come to but also made a de facto claim about the inclusion of the Kökenuur Mongols within the sphere of influence of the Dalai Lama's government in Lhasa. The identification of the Sumpa *kūtuktu*'s reincarnation using the Golden Urn could thus be understood as simultaneously setting a precedent for both the emperor's control over Tibet and Lhasa's authority over Amdo.

The other four lineages identified on day one of the Golden Urn lottery hailed from the Khorchin of Inner Mongolia. In contrast to the case of the Sumpa *kūtuktu*, the identification of the reincarnations of the lamas from Khorchin was a kind of anti-precedent. As subsequent generations of Mongolian reincarnations would be confirmed using the urn at Yonghegong, this moment was also symbolic of the gradual diminishment of the Dalai Lama's authority to personally supervise his fellow Gelukpa lamas in Mongolia.

Less than two weeks after overseeing the trial run of the Golden Urn statute, Fuk'anggan took his final leave of the Eighth Dalai Lama and departed Lhasa on the road to Sichuan. In his last report from Lhasa, Fuk'anggan informed the emperor that during his final meeting with the Dalai Lama and a large assembly of Tibetan officials both lay and clergy, he had presented the complete set of new regulations for the reform of the Tibetan administration in a Tibetan translation and explained them point by point. Most likely this reference is to a version of the *Imperially Sanctioned Twenty-Nine Articles of Reconstruction*, perhaps the copy that was subsequently stored in the Jokhang Temple.[76] The commander and his associate officials assessed their accomplishments as follows:

> [Your servants] observe that the inborn nature of the Tibetans of Tibet has never in the slightest been regulated. . . . Respectfully obeying the imperial instructions, [your servants] observed the state of the

Tibetans, promulgated statutes, and gradually displaced their entrenched habits. Our reforms were instituted without aggravating or worrying [the Tibetans], and *we legislated only what was possible to implement*. . . . Recently the Tibetans have absolutely changed their minds concerning their degenerate customs. There is now no major administrative issue about which the Dalai Lama will not inform your servant Heliyen, and officials from the *kalön* on down all acknowledge and respect the law.[77]

Their stated concern with legislating within a limit of what they perceived would be tolerated by their Tibetan counterparts seems well borne out by the record of communications concerning the early implementation of the Golden Urn statute. The Galdan Siretu *kūtuktu* and Fuk'anggan took actions that deflected early efforts by Qianlong (and perhaps other officials in Beijing) to fully eliminate the oracles from the process of identifying reincarnations. The Tibetan-language version of the ritual Fuk'anggan presented to the Dalai Lama and assembled Tibetan dignitaries included, therefore, notification that the oracles would continue to play an essential part in the search and recognition process.[78] Furthermore, the Qing officials' descriptions of their investigations of the Tibetan oracles remind us that Qing skepticism of and hostility to Tibetan divination technologies should be understood as an expression not of a blanket disbelief in divination, but of a prejudice against indigenous technologies that existed in a seemingly unregulated and corrupt system.

Fuk'anggan recorded the Dalai Lama as responding to the presentation of the new regulations as follows:

As for the regions of Ü and Tsang that are united under me, I shall not handle matters by myself. [Instead] I will trouble the Heaven heart of the great emperor and belabor the great ministers who are his representatives to provide advice. The other clergy and laity and I all share unsurpassable gratitude for the [emperor's] grace. Henceforth we will assiduously preserve the regulations, and manage every matter together with the resident *ambans*.[79]

Recall, however, from act I that the Demo *kūtuktu*, author of the *Biography of the Eighth Dalai Lama*, who witnessed these events, mentioned no such power-sharing arrangement or even the *Twenty-Nine Articles* in his account of Fuk'anggan's departure. But both accounts share an atmosphere of congeniality that perhaps attests to the abilities of Fuk'anggan and Tibetan elites to diffuse tensions that may have arisen from imperial imperatives to assert authority over the Tibetan government. Moreover, just days after Fuk'anggan's departure, the Dalai Lama's chronicler noted how the lama had, "in accordance with custom, propitiated the Lamo *chökyong*, presenting him with many offerings of the faith. The protector, with unsurpassed sincerity, again agreed to promote the success of all affairs."[80] The remaining Qing officials in Lhasa, most importantly Heliyen, the chief *amban*, would soon have a very different agenda.

Heliyen and the Prosecution of the Oracles

Fuk'anggan's report concerning the investigation of the oracles arrived at court at the same time as the Tüsiyetü Khan scandal broke. The emperor was greatly disappointed with both the outcome of the investigation and the manner in which it had been conducted. Qianlong expressed his displeasure by adding caustic interlinear comments directly on Fuk'anggan's memorial. Next to the description of having asked the oracles to make general predictions about potential afflictions that might affect the Tibetan people, the emperor scribbled, "You shouldn't have asked about this matter!"[81] Asking open-ended questions was clearly not the way to entrap the oracles. As for the prediction concerning the smallpox epidemic, the emperor observed that since such incidents occurred every year when the weather turned from winter to spring, "How can this possibly constitute an unusual prediction?"[82] In a separate letter he continued to dress down Fuk'anggan:

> The way you have handled things is really not suitable. Your knowledge of these matters is still rather crude. With regard to the matter of the oracles, the Tibetans have governed themselves for a long time and therefore it is difficult to break through [their accumulated malpractices] in just one go. . . . Having brought everyone together, how could you not test [the oracles] by requiring them to swallow swords or cut their own flesh? . . . You should present difficult tests![83]

In contrast to his initial instructions in January 1793 (QL 57/11/29), by March the emperor was interested in testing the oracles not out of curiosity about their potential utility, but in order to demonstrate to the Tibetans and Mongols that their abilities and claims were completely fraudulent.

Fuk'anggan defended himself from these critiques, protesting that the tests had been conducted before large audiences and that the "wild talk" of the oracles had been exposed when the lottery returned results different from their predictions. But the matter was now largely out of his hands. Fuk'anggan was already on the road back to Beijing when he received the emperor's criticisms. A successful military commander, he seems to have had little patience for Qianlong's increasingly myopic focus on the oracles and again pointed out that he doubted faith in the oracles could be overcome. In response, the emperor wrote darkly, "There are yet other methods by which to deal with this matter. No need for worry."[84]

The renewed effort was now Heliyen's responsibility. The emperor's letter to Heliyen on March 16, 1793 (QL 58/02/05), ordering him to get to the bottom of the "mistaken" identification of the Tüsiyetü Khan's son as the Erdeni Pandita *kūtuktu* marked the turning point in the throne's willingness to tolerate the oracles and the opening of a concerted campaign to discredit both the oracles and the Dalai Lama.[85] Heliyen concurred with the emperor's focus on the oracles, noting how the dynasty had largely overlooked their significance in Tibetan political and religious affairs. He memorialized, "It is well known that the Dalai Lama is a leading person of the Yellow Doctrines. But the Lamo *chökyong* also reincarnates and has done many corrupt deeds that are revealed when people are asked straight on. Yet people not only do not consider him a leading figure but also ignore his crimes."[86] The importance of this policy shift was made evident by the fact that the emperor demanded the transmission of the instructions to Tibet at the extraordinary speed of 600 *li* (approximately 160 kilometers) per day. These letters also marked the shift of communications concerning implementation of the Golden Urn statute and other matters concerning the investigation of the Dalai Lama back to being solely in the Manchu language.

Heliyen submitted the results of his investigations to the court on April 25, 1793. In contrast to Fuk'anggan's reports, which were usually dry, succinct summaries of events, Heliyen's reports read like theatrical transcripts. Heliyen's memorials, and the "testaments" and "confessions" attached to them, re-created the dialogue between the *ambans*, the Dalai Lama, and the oracles, as well as the spontaneous responses of onlookers, establishing an atmosphere of verisimilitude that Qianlong and his capital officials evidently appreciated. In fact, Heliyen's memorials often enacted scripts that the Qianlong emperor provided him in advance and were designed by the ruler to entrap the Dalai Lama and the oracles.[87] Considering that none of Heliyen's subsequent efforts to embarrass the Dalai Lama and the Lamo oracle has yet been corroborated by contemporaneous Tibetan sources, it is important to qualify the following discussion by noting that these components of the campaign to suppress the oracles may have existed primarily in the imagination of the Qing court. The possibility that the events did not occur as described should not, however, blind us to their potential influence, since the Qing court ensured that accounts of them circulated widely in edicts and other imperially sanctioned histories and literary projects in multiple languages.

Heliyen began his reports by providing a revisionist account of the first trial, conducted jointly with Fuk'anggan. This time Heliyen was careful to point out that before "a mass of monks and laypeople that had been gathered in the Jokhang Temple,"[88] they had in fact demanded that the four oracles stab themselves. When the oracles refused, the Qing officials rhetorically entrapped them: "If the deities really descend into your body, then naturally you should invisibly be receiving their support. Why then do you still fear the blade of the sword?"[89] This point had the desired effect on both the oracles and the onlookers: "The oracles were thus obstructed and fell silent, their expression disordered. And the surrounding monks and laypeople were now only half believing."[90] Thus, Heliyen presented the prior test as having had a greater impact than Fuk'anggan originally had suggested.

Shortly after receiving instructions to conduct further tests and just a day after Fuk'anggan had departed, Heliyen again gathered all four oracles in the Jokhang and asked them to "perform their arts" before an audience that included the Dalai Lama, the Tatsak *kūtuktu*, the Demo *kūtuktu*, and a crowd of other prominent lamas and lay Tibetan leaders. He informed the mediums that:

The interior also has people similar to you who are able to serve as mediums and make predictions about the future trials and tribulations of the people. They are all able to swallow knives and cut off pieces of flesh and in doing so demonstrate their magical powers. Of course these are nothing more than small tricks of illusion. Yet even so, officials forbid these activities. And these [oracles] are without a doubt deluding the people in a similar fashion. Their crimes must be heavily punished![91]

Having concluded his speech, Heliyen wrote, he promptly handed out knives to the oracles. Whereas Fuk'anggan had primarily been testing them against prior claims about the abilities of Tibetan oracles, Heliyen was more explicitly testing them against a catalogue of skills possessed by shamans from the interior of the empire and making a justification for the extension of imperial law. Given the way Heliyen framed his challenge by pointing out that even shamans in the interior, skilled as they might be, faced punishment, it should come as no surprise that the oracles "threw themselves to the ground in fear, pleading that 'the knives and swords are merely tools for attracting people. We do not dare make a game of our lives!'" Having "truly frightened them," Heliyen continued to needle the oracles: "I have heard that previously, when speaking on behalf of the deity that has descended [to you], you wildly slash with your knives at onlookers. Why are you able to stab others when you cannot stab yourselves?" The oracles fell into the *amban*'s trap: "We have heard that among previous generations of oracles there were those who could stab themselves, and perhaps some, when they were truly possessed, were able to act like that. However, we are truly not able to do this." Heliyen then sprung the rhetorical trap: "Then you not only possess no [magical] arts but cannot even accomplish spirit possession! How then can you make such rash predictions?"[92]

Heliyen reported to the emperor that by the end of this exchange, not only had the oracles provided a public admission that they "truly possessed no methods or arts and that everything relied on empty words," but also the onlookers "were laughing behind their hands."[2] With the indigenous technology thus thoroughly discredited, Heliyen reported that "the fairness and credibility of the imperially sanctioned Golden Urn" would be widely accepted. He placed the Dalai Lama on record as having been convinced by the trial. He quoted the Dalai Lama as stating, "I have always believed in the truth of the oracles, yet today I have finally learned that they are not trustworthy."[94] Heliyen requested that the Eighth Dalai Lama prepare a proclamation on this matter.[95] The *amban* then optimistically concluded his memorial with the opinion that although Tibetans should be permitted to continue to seek out the oracles for divinations concerning other issues, the use of the oracles to identify reincarnations could be permanently forbidden without much opposition.

Imperial Theater from Tibet to Mongolia

With regard to the Erdeni Pandita, the emperor provided Heliyen with an even more detailed script to follow should the Dalai Lama prove less recalcitrant. The fact that one of the emperor's first official utterances regarding this case took the form of a court letter to Heliyen (dated QL 58/02/05, March 16, 1793), demonstrates not only the emperor's interest in getting to the bottom of how the son of the khan had been identified as one of the leading reincarnations of Outer Mongolia, but also his expectation that the prosecution of the case and resolution of the search using the Golden Urn at Yonghegong would help persuade Tibetan Buddhists of the advantages of the new procedure and the underlying fairness of the new law.

Tibetan Buddhists in Tibet and Mongolia were not, however, the only audience. The documentation of both the trials of the oracles and subsequent interrogations of the treasurer, Nawangdasi, the Tüsiyetü Khan, the Dalai Lama, and the medium of the Lamo *chökyong* first circulated privately among Qing officials in Lhasa and at court. The production of these documents played an even more important role in persuading Qing officials and the throne that their suspicions were justified and that their reforms were legitimate and would be broadly supported by both Tibetan and Mongol elites and their subjects. As we shall see in the following examination of the exchange of letters between Heliyen, the Grand Council, and the emperor, the court's constant concern with assessing the mood of the public and the sentiments of leading Tibetans such as the Dalai Lama and the Tatsak *kūtuktu* is evidence of how their own feelings about the legitimacy of their efforts hinged on the Tibetan response. Moreover, the intensive concern with understanding the oracles and local sentiments reflected how little the late Qianlong court still knew about Tibetan affairs in general, and especially those of central Tibet. Elliot Sperling's short study of the visit to the Qianlong court in late 1792 by a lay official of the Tibetan government, the former *kalön* Doring Tendzin Peljor, amplifies this point. In his autobiography, Tendzin Peljor observed that Qing officials in Beijing had never seen Tibetan aristocrats before and expressed great curiosity about his costume and jewelry.[96] The presence of Tibetan laypeople at court and their status as subjects of the Qing were still novel in 1792 despite a relationship with Tibetan monks that stretched back to the early years of the dynasty, prior to its conquest of the Ming. In this light,

Qianlong's early requests to Fuk'anggan and Heliyen to test the oracles can be understood as expressions of not only hostility but also a genuine need to acquire more credible information about their abilities, their influence on Tibetan affairs, and their potential to remain part of the recognition process.

In addition to contrasting Tibetan divination technologies unfavorably with Manchu ones, another key strategy employed by Qing officials to undermine Geluk hierarchs and the oracles was to insinuate that these monks were fundamentally motivated by avarice and that the maintenance of their institutions—monasteries, hermitages, and the corporate estates of their reincarnate lineages—had led them to immoral or at the very least problematic entanglements with noble patrons and lay support communities. The interrogation of the treasurer of the Erdeni Pandita's estate, Nawangdasi, highlighted the manner in which the treasurer had seemingly compromised his principles in the interest of financial expediency. Qing interrogators lingered on the accounts of gift exchange and alms seeking in order to insinuate corruption or bribery. That bureaucrats of the Hešen-dominated late Qianlong court, an administration already infamous for its opulent gift culture and dogged by scandal and accusations of venality and bribery, would raise similar accusations against the Geluk establishment in Tibet and Mongolia is hardly remarkable. The hunt for corruption within the Geluk church was yet another reflection of the degree to which the perceived crisis of official malfeasance had become the overriding concern of the Qing officials in the 1790s.[97]

The *amban* Heliyen's reconstruction of his interviews with the Dalai Lama and the oracle of the Lamo *chökyong*, as well as the transcripts of the testimony of these figures appended to his memorial, focused on the trail of gifts (Ma. *belek*, Ch. *baileke* 伯勒克) presented by the treasurer. Ultimately Heliyen seems to have decided that the lists of gifts received by the Lamo oracle and the Dalai Lama provided the clearest evidence of corruption, since neither the Dalai Lama nor the oracle could ever be brought to state directly that the treasurer had told them to sanction the child of the Tüsiy-etü Khan as the next Erdeni Pandita *kūtuktu*. Qianlong himself had demanded such an explicit statement when he first wrote about the case to Heliyen: "Only after the Dalai Lama himself has definitively said that it was the idea of Nawangdasi will it be possible to punish the treasurer."[98] In order to arrive at such a statement, Qianlong provided Heliyen with the following script for the cross-examination:

Heliyen must meet in person with the Dalai Lama and ask him what is true. If the Dalai Lama spits out the truth, immediately and speedily memorialize what he hears. If the Dalai Lama does not report the truth, Heliyen should elucidate the Dalai Lama by inquiring, "This matter was definitely the idea of the treasurer Nawangdasi and since it has absolutely no connection to the Dalai Lama, certainly no harm can come to the Dalai Lama if he reports the truth. Besides, how can this be disguised with lies if the treasurer is currently being interrogated in the capital? After the treasurer has spoken, there will be even greater obstacles before the Dalai Lama!"

If the Dalai Lama is still not forthcoming with the truth, Heliyen should, according to my words, thoroughly interrogate the Dalai Lama, saying, "Among the Buddhist sutras there is the teaching called, "*jeodun barihū ubadis*. When one recites with conviction this *dharani*, the air will certainly change, and by the power of the *dharani* a trance will occur. Ordinary people will understand nothing of their visions. [Those] capable of understanding visions when using a *dharani* to enter a trance are able to clearly know the matters of other people. In this there are three levels of "*hūmhatu breath* attainment." (The superior level is that of those who are able to know things [in advance]). In my opinion, does the Dalai Lama's talent rises to this superior level? If his capabilities do not rise to this level, how could he know that the son of Cedendorji is the only reincarnation of the Erdeni Pandita *kūtuktu*?" After he hears this, the Dalai Lama will certainly reveal the truth.[99]

In addition to advising Heliyen to adopt the classic interrogation technique of threatening the subject with the incriminating testimony of an accomplice (in this case, the treasurer Nawangdasi), the emperor was also prepared to reach for a highly technical argument based on a reading of a specific Tibetan Buddhist text. He believed that such a move would force the Dalai Lama to admit that he possessed no ability to make the kind of difficult divination required to identify the rebirth of a powerful Buddhist adept.

Heliyen's report to the emperor notes no such recourse to technical discussions of divination abilities. To the contrary, the *amban* smugly reported that he had called on the Dalai Lama in the Potala Palace and taken advantage of a "casual conversation to discuss the [Dalai Lama's] livelihood and the amount of gifts received from the various [Mongol] leagues."[100] He then made circuitous inquiries about the specifics of the Erdeni Pandita case. The *amban* reported that on three different occasions the treasurer and the chamberlain presented gifts to the Dalai Lama and that the latter freely admitted that he had instructed Nawangdasi to seek out divinations from the Lamo oracle. But in neither his primary, Manchu-language memorial recounting the interview nor the Chinese-language transcript of the interview attached to the memorial did Heliyen record the Dalai Lama as admitting to having received any specific request to identify the son of the Tüsiyetü khan.[101] After detailing for the *amban* a long list of gifts he had received from Nawangdasi when he approved the Lamo oracle's identification of the Tüsiyetü Khan's son, the Dalai Lama stated, "We have always accepted all the gifts offered without regard to amount. When we receive things we make bestowals in return that reflect the value of the original gifts. The Tüsiyetü Khan never made any entreaties, nor did Nawangdasi ever beg for my help."[102] Despite this denial, Heliyen and the emperor seized on the record of gifts received as evidence that the Dalai Lama had been bribed.

The interrogation of the Lamo oracle presented further complications. First the medium refused outright to answer questions, claiming, "When possessed by the deity, I cannot clearly remember anything that I say. I beg, therefore, that you ask my assistant Döndrup Dorjé."[103] Next, Heliyen reported that the assistant also repeatedly refused to talk and only did so when he was "frightened by the prospect of being tortured."[104] Despite the initial intransigence, the account of the treasurer Nawangdasi's visit to central Tibet in Döndrup Dorjé's deposition corresponds closely with the presentation of events provided by the Dalai Lama *and* the original deposition of Nawangdasi taken in Beijing and forwarded to Heliyen in Lhasa. The similarities should not be surprising given that it was in the *amban*'s interest to provide the throne with a clean case shorn of any conflicting details. Beyond adding some new information about where the divinations occurred, Heliyen's transcript devotes similar attention to cataloging the multiple gifts the treasurer distributed to the oracle and his assistant on the three different occasions when they sought divinations. In total, the assistant stated that the oracle had received four hundred *liang* of silver in return for his divinations in addition to other gifts.[105] Yet the deposition also records that despite what appeared to the *amban* as overwhelming evidence of corruption at multiple stages of the divination process, the assistant continued to insist that he was innocent and refused to describe Nawangdasi's actions as bribery.[106]

On April 25, 1793 (QL 58/03/15), Heliyen submitted his complete report about the Tüsiyetü Khan case to the court. The *amban* determined that the treasurer had colluded with the Tüsiyetü Khan to bribe the Dalai Lama and the Lamo oracle. The Dalai Lama and the medium of the Lamo *chökyong* emerge stained in this report—intentionally so, but at least Heliyen declined to identify the Dalai Lama as the originator of the plot, as the Qianlong emperor had previously suggested.[107] Yet even before the emperor received Heliyen's report, the Qing court had moved to resolve the case.

Just two days after Heliyen had dispatched his report from Lhasa, the emperor, clearly frustrated by what seemed like a delayed response (it had been 42 days since Qianlong had dispatched the first court letter to Lhasa), wrote again, updating him on events at court.[108] Qianlong informed him of several decisions. First, reports from Sungyun and Kūišu in Mongolia had pinpointed the origins of the plot in a chance meeting of the treasurer Nawangdasi and the Tüsiyetü Khan at Erdeni Jui monastery in Outer Mongolia. Second, Mongols would henceforth be permanently forbidden from seeking divinations regarding reincarnations in Lhasa. And third, preparations were already under way to recognize the reincarnation of the Erdeni Pandita from among three new candidates using the Golden Urn at Yonghegong.[109]

That identification was finally confirmed using the Golden Urn at Yonghegong on May 10, 1793 (QL 58/04/01).[110] This event marked not only the first instance in which a Mongol *kūtuktu* was identified in Beijing but also a departure from the recommendations of the Galdan Siretu *kūtuktu* and Fuk'anggan that leading lamas draw the lots from the vase. Although the Gomang and Tongkhor *kūtuktus* had been commissioned to lead three days of recitations before the ritual took place and were present for the selection, it was an imperial prince and officials of the Court of Colonial Affairs who played the penultimate role.[111] This seems to have set an important precedent because subsequently, in Lhasa as well as Yonghegong, it would be Qing officials instead of Tibetan lamas who drew the lots.

Yet the court hesitated before widely circulating a formal account of the Golden Urn lottery at Yonghegong. News of the event spread first only in Manchu- and Mongol-language court letters and edicts that were disseminated to inner court officials, officials of the Court of Colonial Affairs, Qing resident officials in Inner Asia, and select Tibetan and Mongol elites. Not until July 1, 1793 (QL 58/05/25), when the court had fully assessed the mood of the Khalkha Mongols, did the throne issue a broadly distributed public announcement of the "successful" conclusion of the Erdeni Pandita case.[112] The court was sensitive to the fact that because the recognition of the Erdeni Pandita was unprecedented, it would take continued careful management to ensure that this particular event became an established legal precedent. The following section will explore the tenuous process of transforming *precedent* into repeated *practice*.

Managing the Identification of the Erdeni Pandita

The identification of the Mongol child Ciwangjab as the reincarnation of the Erdeni Pandita *kūtuktu* was momentous for several reasons. First, as Qianlong had ordered, the child hailed from a non-noble family. Second, the recognition of this child using the Golden Urn at Yonghegong marked the explicit rejection and replacement of another child whose authenticity had already been vouchsafed by the Dalai Lama. The emperor's decision also overruled the local aristocracy of Khalkha Mongolia, most obviously the sanction of the captain of the Sain Noyan League, not to mention the wishes of the neighboring Tüsiyetü Khan.[113] Moreover, as interrogations of the treasurer Nawangdasi and the Tüsiyetü Khan revealed, the birth of the khan's son had been attended by a variety of auspicious signs that had also bespoken the child's legitimate candidacy.[114] That reincarnations of the *kūtuktu* should emerge in noble families was also not unusual: the First and Second Erdeni Pandita *kūtuktu* had both been identified in princely families—a junior line of the Tüsiyetü Khan lineage—and shouldered responsibilities for the administration of both monasteries and lay herding communities. The Qing court formally recognized this when it incorporated the Second Erdeni Pandita (1703–1788) and his domain into its administrative system in 1737 by granting him official status as the commander (Ma. *jasak*) of an autonomous "ecclesiastical banner" (Ma. *lama gūsa*, Ch. *lama qi* 喇嘛旗) within the Sain Noyan League.[115] The appointment of a child of "common rank" to a position that had historically been the fief of the local nobility therefore carried inherent risks.[116] These reasons help explain why the court made careful preparations for the ritual and carefully managed the reception of the result.

Well before the final identification of the Erdeni Pandita's reincarnation was held at Yonghegong, the court began making public efforts to justify its intervention in this process. On April 25, 1793, a bilingual edict in Manchu and Mongol, intended for widespread promulgation, was issued to officials in both Lhasa and Mongolia. This edict offered an extensive justification for the use of the Golden Urn. In a major departure from the previous year's *Discourse on Lamas*, the emperor elaborated his "crisis of faith" argument to the public for the first time. The "Yellow Teachings," the emperor wrote, were being undermined because "nobody is completely convinced" by the recent generation of reincarnations.[117] Turning to the details from the investigation of the Tüsiyetü Khan and the treasurer of the Erdeni Pandita, the emperor elaborated on the ways the oracles had been corrupted, concluding that: "In the past several years, whenever it was time to identify a *hūbilgan*, because the mediums have attained no special talent, they are incapable of possession by the gods and simply affirm whatever is requested of them by other people."[118] The emperor then announced comprehensive punishments for the Tüsiyetü Khan and Nawangdasi.[119]

The final third of the edict offered an extensive moralistic critique of the Geluk teachings based on the emperor's claim to unrivaled expertise in Buddhism. In a passage that recalled his earlier advice to Heliyen on how to interrogate the Dalai Lama, the emperor for the first time publicly stated that the Dalai Lama lacked the ability to perform divinations and interpret visions because he had not yet mastered the teachings concerning the *dharani* of the "*jeodun* or *sukdun barihū ubadis*" tantra.[120] Moreover, he continued to cast aspersions on the whole notion of directed rebirth when he noted caustically that neither Sakyamuni nor Tsongkhapa had reincarnated.[121] Yet this critique was also expressed in terms characteristic of an emperor who held an abiding concern with the preservation of traits he felt were crucial markers of Manchu—as well as Mongol and Tibetan—superiority vis-à-vis the Chinese. Behind the corruption of the oracles and the "rot of the old, pure, and simple manners of the Mongols and Tibetans,"[122] Qianlong ultimately described a Geluk establishment that had become debased as it grew accustomed to ever more lavish donations from the faithful. Among these gifts, the emperor even included standard offerings of support for the sangha such as food, butter, and tea. In closing, the emperor offered the Golden Urn as a means of halting the stream of corrupting gifts and an opportunity to return to a more "frugal" existence.[123]

Just two days later, Qianlong dispatched a court letter to Heliyen. In it he reiterated the new prohibitions introduced in his edict but was also clearly concerned about whether his extensive justifications had been persuasive. The emperor wrote, "Since there will definitely be no seeking out the Lamo oracle when searching for rebirths [of reincarnate lamas] from the Mongol lands, there will also be no necessity for travel to Tibet. [Therefore] I write to Heliyen, ordering him to investigate and exhaustively memorialize on whether, due to their loss of authority and decrease in alms, the Dalai Lama and Tatsak *kūtuktu* are truly obedient or are not very pleased."[124] The emperor also provided Heliyen with a new blueprint for the conduct of the ritual, which he expected the *amban* to follow in the future. Qianlong proposed that in the same manner as Kūišu, the vice-minister of the Court of Colonial Affairs who had personally traveled to Mongolia to collect the names of candidate children, the two Lhasa *ambans* should take over the task of personally locating candidates. The emperor then directed the *ambans* to supervise, as "the Dalai Lama together with the Galdan Siretu *kūtuktu* and other throne-holding great *kūtuktus* well versed in the prayers jointly observe and make an identification by drawing lots."[125]

This latter instruction is remarkable because it breaks the throne's prior reticence to spell out explicitly *who* would draw the lot. Yet less than a week later, the emperor prevaricated again in his final instructions about how to conduct the ritual to identify the Erdeni Pandita *kūtuktu*. Whereas in the Lhasa version he decided that responsibility for drawing the lot should fall to Geluk prelates, the instructions for the Yonghegong ritual were still unclear: "After their names have been written on lots and placed in the vase that has been installed at Yonghegong, the Gomang *kūtuktu* and Tongkhor *kūtuktu*, both seal-holding great *jasak* lamas, will be specially commissioned to gather together the lamas and from the twenty-seventh through the twenty-ninth earnestly and sincerely recite scriptures for three days. On the first [of the fourth month] the Eighth Prince, Liobooju, and Delek will be delegated to jointly observe as one name is drawn to be confirmed as the rebirth of the Erdeni Pandita *kūtuktu*."[126]

The lack of specificity should not be taken as a sign that the court was taking this detail casually. To the contrary, maintaining the ambiguity of the crucial moment in the ritual had several important implications. First, even if the court wished to have Qing officials draw the lot, as would ultimately be the case, the lack of clear directive on the issue left field officials with the leeway to negotiate a configuration of the ritual that would be acceptable to the Tibetan or Mongol audience. Second, the lack of specificity even well after the selection of the Erdeni Pandita *kūtuktu* had been determined indicates that the court purposely left room for both sides to flexibly interpret the official account, especially in the immediate aftermath of the event when the court was still unsure whether the selection would be welcomed in Tibet and Mongolia.

This interpretation is borne out by an examination of how the court managed information in the aftermath of the selection of the Erdeni Pandita reincarnation. In a private letter to Heliyen composed on the day of the ritual, the emperor's description of the event left out all mention of the Gomang and Tongkhor *kūtuktus*, signaling that it was either the imperial prince or the officials of the Court of Colonial Affairs who had drawn the lot.[127] Yet in the first mass dissemination of news of the ritual in Inner and Outer Mongolia on July 2, 1793, the edict did not state clearly who had drawn the lot. Consistent with prior announcements, it ambiguously stated that the lot had been drawn and that both court officials and Geluk monks were present.[128]

The Qing court chose its words with great circumspection, and nearly two months passed between the identification of Ciwangjab on May 10, 1793, and the dissemination of the news on July 2. The emperor was reluctant to issue a full account to the broader public until his field officials had fully assessed the impact this news would have on indigenous elites in Mongolia and Tibet. On the day the ritual had been held, Qianlong wrote privately to Heliyen that he believed the event had been "good and propitious"—the "selection was exceedingly fair and the weather . . . was clear and free of wind."[129] He ordered the *amban* to describe and explain the ritual to the Dalai Lama, Panchen Lama, Tatsak *kūtuktu*, and other major lamas. Yet he was wary of their reaction:

> With regard to the matter of this rebirth, we did not use the boy selected by the Dalai Lama and instead made a determination by drawing lots. It is difficult to predict if we can do this without offending him. Heliyen must therefore with great care observe the mood and manner of the Dalai Lama and all the lamas and *kūtuktus* and with haste and secrecy report what he hears.[130]

The court had also asked Kūišu to make another trip to the seat of the Erdeni Pandita *kūtuktu* and assess not only the character of the child whose name had emerged from the Golden Urn but also the attitudes of the leadership of the monastery and the local nobility. Kūišu's memorial, which arrived in court on June 15, 1793 (QL 58/05/08), and subsequent follow-up audience with the emperor two weeks later (July 2, 1793; QL 58/05/25), surpassed imperial expectations, leaving Qianlong ebullient. Upon returning to the monastery Kūišu learned that, of the five children who had originally been brought there as candidates, the fifth child, Ciwangjab—the boy ultimately chosen in the Golden Urn—had performed a number of acts that had left the monastic community persuaded that this was the genuine reincarnation. First, when the parents had returned to the monastery to collect their children after the initial round of tests, Ciwangjab, unlike the other children, refused to return home with his mother and father. As he was adamant that he wished to remain in the monastery, his parents eventually acceded to his demand and left him in the care of an uncle. Over the next several weeks the small child won the affection of the community for his diligence and helpfulness around the monastery. After it was learned that he had been identified as the reincarnation, further auspicious acts were witnessed. Kūišu and later Qianlong would seize on one detail in particular: while preparing for his enthronement, the child had refused to don the robes that the now disgraced treasurer had prepared for the occasion and would not take his seat until he had been offered an alternate costume. Kūišu confessed that when first presented with these "kinds of miraculous matters" he "hesitated in disbelief." Therefore, he "secretly dispatched" investigators to Chinese merchants residing in the vicinity of the monastery. After the merchants immediately confirmed that child's brief history of residence in the monastery had indeed been "miraculous," Kūišu posted his memorial and then rushed in person to the court.[131]

Kūišu's testimony resulted in the immediate and widespread dissemination of news of the identification of the Erdeni Pandita *kūtuktu* using the Golden Urn. This occurred despite the fact that Qianlong had yet to hear from Heliyen in Tibet (although the *amban* had already penned his response on June 16). The discovery of a child who exhibited signs of being a genuine reincarnation resulted not only in a surge of confidence in the legitimacy of the Golden Urn but also in the addition of an entirely new explanation for the efficacy of the ritual to the public discourse. The emperor summarized his understanding of the ritual as follows:

> After receiving Kūišu's memorial reporting that he had identified five boys, I immediately commissioned the Eighth Prince to supervise together with Liobooju and Delek the reading of sutras by lamas, after which, the lot of the fifth candidate named Ciwangjab was selected and emerged without prejudice from among the lots that had been placed in the golden urn. The revelation of such a miraculous situation wherein Ciwangjab was already residing in that monastery [makes] the principles of the Buddha especially clear and manifest. It must be said that what occurred as a result of having invoked the protector Amitāyus Buddha and received his invisible blessing is truly miraculous. My efforts to rectify the declining teaching of the Yellow Dharma were undertaken for the benefit of the Buddha's Dharma. That the Buddha has found this proper is evidenced by occurrences such as this that are genuinely miraculous. Henceforth, as the various corruptions are eliminated, may the true traditions of the Buddha's Dharma come to be restored![132]

Here we learn for the first time that it was not human but supernatural agency that orchestrated the successful outcome of the lottery. The emperor is referring specifically to Amitāyus,[133] a manifestation of Amitābha Buddha, who is associated in Tantric practice with the promotion of long life. It is perhaps not coincidental that the Yonghegong complex housed multiple images of Amitāyus, several of which were located in the Tantric Hall just to the east of the spot where Qianlong's tetraglot *Discourse on Lamas* stele stood.[134]

The attribution of the successful selection to Amitāyus may also explain the disinclination of the emperor to state explicitly who had drawn the lot. The ambiguity and passive-voice construction (literally, "the lot was selected and emerged," Ma. *tatami tucibuhe*) of official pronouncements such as the edict to the Inner and Outer Mongol aristocracy quoted above enabled readers to envision the intervention of an unseen supernatural actor. Such a linguistic strategy complements indigenous Tibetan Buddhist understandings of divination, particularly the practice of dough-ball investigation with which the Golden Urn was occasionally compared. Just as the fall of a ball from a rotating plate needed no direct human agency and could be explained as a divine intervention, so too could the emergence of a lot from an urn—if the sentence was constructed with subtlety.

The Golden Urn, Rendered Into Tibetan

The arrival of the Golden Urn in Tibet in late 1792 and its installation in the Jokhang is perhaps the main reason the temple became a focal point for formal encounters between Tibetan and Qing officials in 1793.[135] By the end of the year, the Jokhang also possessed a register of Tibetan-language translations of Qing official proclamations that had been issued over the course of the year. Known simply as the *Record of Royal Pronouncements from the Water-Ox Year*, it can serve as a rough guide to what Tibetan lay and ecclesiastical officials of the Ganden Podrang government might have known about Qing policy as it evolved from 1792 through 1793.[136] This register contained a full copy of Fuk'anggan's *Twenty-Nine Articles* as well as Tibetan-language translations of imperial edicts mandating the Golden Urn and describing the case against the Erdeni Pandita *kūtuktu*.

Among the first of these is the "Water-Ox Year Edict" (Tib. *chu glung wang zhu*).[137] The document begins with a brief history of its long journey from Manchu to Tibetan and from Beijing to Lhasa. Passed from the throne to the Grand Council on May 28 (QL 58/04/19), the edict then languished for four months until on September 24 (QL 58/08/20) the Court of Colonial Affairs produced a Chinese translation of the Manchu original. This was forwarded to Tibet via the office of the Sichuan governor-general and arrived in Lhasa on October 19 (QL 58/09/15), whereupon a Tibetan-language translation was finally produced.[138]

This edict marked the throne's fourth attempt to broadcast its (evolving) justification for the Golden Urn to a broader audience beyond the imperial bureaucracy and its field agents.[139] It is the first, however, for which there is a contemporaneous Tibetan translation extant in the archives. The "Water-Ox Year Edict" is therefore the earliest imperially sanctioned, written, Tibetan-language statement of the underlying rationale for the law on the Golden Urn known to have circulated in Tibet.[140] In fact, the promulgation of this edict coincided with the first appearance of the *Discourse on Lamas* in the Qing *Veritable Records*.[141] Contemporaries evidently recognized the import of this edict as well. It was included in the Tibetan compilation of key official documents from 1793 held at the Jokhang and reproduced in the influential *Comprehensive Gazetteer of Ü-Tsang*.[142] As will be discussed below, the Eighth Dalai Lama also issued a decree in response.[143] Long before the "Water-Ox Year Edict" arrived in Lhasa, Heliyen, like Fuk'anggan before him, had been ordered to explain the Golden Urn and the related prohibitions to the Dalai Lama and other Tibetan elites.[144] Yet this edict is the earliest record that reveals the exact wording by which the court attempted to communicate its policy and therefore provides a basis for beginning to think about how Tibetans might have understood the new policy. The edict is also significant because it contained the first public declaration of the emperor's intention to outlaw the solicitation of the oracles during the search for reincarnations.

The production of this formal, public, and textual justification for the Golden Urn narrowed and limited the ways field officials such as Heliyen and indigenous interlocutors could talk about the law. Committing the emperor's message to paper committed the messengers to a single message, thus restricting the officials' ability to rephrase or otherwise reconfigure the message in a form that might better accommodate indigenous sensibilities. And Qianlong was not unaware of these dangers. As illustrated in the preceding section, the deliberate pace at which the throne revealed information about the selection of the Erdeni Pandita's reincarnation, the preference for personal, private communications, and even his reluctance to spell out all the details of the Golden Urn ritual are all evidence of the degree to which the Qianlong emperor appreciated the utility of ambiguity. Having just received Heliyen's report on his final test of the oracles and the transcripts of the interrogations of the Dalai Lama and the Lamo oracle, as well as Sungyun's and Kūišu's earlier reports on Nawangdasi and the Tüsiyetü Khan, the emperor felt he now had sufficient evidence from both Mongolia and Tibet to mount a renewed effort to forbid Mongol and Tibetan nobility from seeking reincarnations among their kin and ban the use of the oracles in the recognition process.[145] The edict did not, however, mention the results of the search for the Erdeni Pandita *kūtuktu* (the emperor had still not received Kūišu's report on the mood of the Mongols).

Although the *ambans* in Lhasa and the staff of the Grand Council would have found little new in the emperor's edict of May 28, from the perspective of Tibetan officials and the Eighth Dalai Lama, the message must have been galling. The edict began with a succinct announcement that the steward Nawangdasi's attempt to have the Tüsiyetü Khan's son identified as a *kütuktu* was "wrongdoing" and that the Dalai Lama's sanction of the Lamo *chökyong*'s decision constituted complicity in the crime.[146] In the subsequent exposition of the Tüsiyetü Khan scandal, the edict construed the Dalai Lama's statements into admissions of, if not quite guilt, certainly gross ignorance. Quoting directly from the depositions of the Dalai Lama and the Lamo oracle, the edict undermined the authority and integrity of the Dalai Lama. Although it allowed him to protest that he had "always found the Lamo *chökyong* to be credible," the subsequent presentation of evidence contradicted his account.[147] Translated back into Tibetan, the testimony of the assistant to the Lamo oracle asserted that the medium was bribed with goods and that the questions put to the oracle were contrived in such a manner that he could not but point to the son of the Tüsiyetü Khan.[148] If the Dalai Lama actually read this text (which I suspect he did), he would have been reading his own words after they had passed through a minimum of four stages of translation (Tibetan > Chinese, Chinese > Manchu, Manchu > Chinese, Chinese > Tibetan).[149] One can only speculate about how familiar they sounded. Yet at least between the original Manchu-language edict and the final Tibetan-language translation the content of the proclamation underwent very little change.

Qianlong's message in the edict can be summarized as follows: first the emperor arrogated to himself the roles of both patron *and* priest. He made this claim on the basis of the Dalai Lama's relative youth and ignorance, expressed in the following terms: "Since this Dalai Lama is still young, he is still in the early stages of study, and it is impossible that he has acquired higher forms of perception. Thus when asked to identify a *kütuktu*, he is only able to call upon the prophecies of the Lamo *chökyong*."[150] In contrast, the emperor claimed a long personal history of Buddhist study as well as a tradition of patronage by his "royal state":[151] "Since I ascended the throne, fifty-eight years have passed. I have sought out the learning of Mongolia and Tibet and, although I have studied for only fifty-plus years, my dynasty has always protected the teachings of the Buddha."[152] Such knowledge also provided him with the following perspective: "Nowadays, not only has the behavior of the clergy fallen into wickedness, but also the craving of the Mongols and Tibetans for material things bears no resemblance to before. They no longer possess single-minded devotion to the religious laws of the Buddha."[153]

Faced therefore with a crisis in the Geluk church, the emperor argued that it was his obligation to subject Mongols and Tibetans to his law. Moreover, he felt that his recent success against the Gurkhas had proven the benefits of such control. Qianlong stated, "Recently there arose great discussion because of the conflict over property involving the Zhamarpa. Due to the vast strength of my dynasty,[154] peace was established. Similarly, the distant land of Tibet and all the Mongol *jasaks* must necessarily be placed under the Court of Mongol Affairs (i.e., the Court of Colonial Affairs), which will render fair justice if conflicts again arise."[155] However, the translator of this passage made a significant adjustment between this text and the Manchu- and Chinese-language versions. Where the original edict states that "all the Mongol *jasaks* should be placed under the governance of the Court of Colonial Affairs," the Tibetan text has "Tibet and the Mongol *jasaks*," thus clarifying that now Tibet would also fall under the jurisdiction of an institution that, from its Tibetan-language name at least, would seem to have only supervised Mongol affairs. This specificity is important because at several points in the text, the emperor's attention seems focused on Mongols and not Tibetans. For instance, the injunction against seeking reincarnations among aristocrats explicitly pertains to Mongol nobility.[156] The Tibetan aristocracy is not mentioned, potentially raising questions about whether this restriction would apply in practice in Tibetan regions.[157]

Having asserted the sovereignty of the Qing dynastic house over Tibet, the edict culminated with an exhibition of how the emperor's representative had exposed the oracles as charlatans:

As for the *chökyong*'s mediums, they are the equivalent of the spirit possession that occurs in China. In China, people who are possessed by gods and ghosts build faith among the people by means of magical displays involving stabbing with knives, swallowing swords, and hatchets. Recently, when the resident amban in Tibet, Heliyen, gave the mediums knives to see what they would do, they all went into a state of panic. Since they could not match the skills of those possessed by gods and ghosts in China, they obviously have no ability to recognize *trülku*.[158]

Thus the throne restaged the contest between the shamans of the interior and the oracles of Tibet in written form for widespread distribution.

On the basis of this test, the emperor rested his case for why "It will never again be acceptable to make identifications using the *chökyong*." As the Manchu-language original makes clear, the emperor envisioned the elimination of the oracles from this process as a "victory by means of legislating" (Ma. *eteme fafulaha*).[159] Yet he also hoped that such tests would eventually accomplish what lawmaking alone could not—thorough change and transformation of Tibetan and Mongol customs.[160] While the edict firmly decreed that oracles could no longer be consulted in the process of locating reincarnations, it recognized that the government's ability to enforce its will through the law was limited. He was confident, however, on the basis of Heliyen's report that when presented with the failures of the oracles, the the people would arrive on their own at the intended conclusion: that the mediums were frauds. Thus the emperor, noting that it was "provisionally impossible to change" widespread belief in the oracles, offered the following concession in the Tibetan-language edict:

> However, the Tibetans [Tib. *böd mi*] universally find [the oracles] credible and for many years have never tested them. Because when asked about trifling matters they may make accurate [predictions], it is unnecessary to issue a command instantly outlawing their prophecies. Naturally, it is not necessary to prohibit Tibetans from making inquiries of the *chökyong* [with regard to minor, personal matters]. . . . As for the *chökyong*, they will gradually weaken and over time will definitely disappear of their own accord.[161]

The Qing strategy for the elimination of the oracles hinged on two assumptions: first, that Tibetans would recognize the shamans of the interior and the *chökyong* as comparable; and second, that Tibetans would also accept the method—public tests of the oracles by Qing officials—as an acceptable way of disproving the oracles. Both of these assumptions reflect hierarchical systems of knowledge anchored in the purported intellectual authority of the emperor. The first operated from an implied hierarchy of divination technologies in which shamans were superior to mediums. The second assumption reflected the imposition of a particular method for generating and interpreting empirical information. The vision of a future Tibet free of oracles was a peculiar and paradoxical expression of Qianlong-era Qing colonialism.[162]

Qualified Support from the Dalai Lama

The depositions of both the Dalai Lama and the oracle of the Lamo *chö-kyong* indicate that, although Tibetans may have seen the shamans and mediums as both speaking on behalf of deities and spirits, they had different expectations for the use of the oracles and different standards for evaluating the accuracy of their prophecies or actions more generally.

As mentioned above, the Dalai Lama and the Lamo oracle engaged in several strategies to deflect Qing interrogations. They also asserted a vigorous defense of the oracles. First, both the medium and his assistant insisted upon the complex and often indeterminate nature of seeking prophecies. The following exchange between Heliyen and the medium of the Lamo *chökyong* illustrates these differing expectations:

[Heliyen] asked: "If you are truly able make requests of the gods, why did you not spontaneously and immediately point out the name of the rebirth when Nawangdasi had asked you to become possessed by the deity? Why was it that even after several attempts you still had not made an identification? You obstinately prevaricated, saying that you had to wait for Nawangdasi to provide a letter stating the ages and year of birth of Cedendorji and his wife along with those of their son. Then, only after they delivered silver and satins did you identify the son of Cedendorji! How can you recognize the son of the Tüsiyetü Khan if you originally said that the [reincarnation] would emerge in an average household? It is obvious that the son of the khan received special consideration. Nawangdasi bribed you. You most definitely have no innate ability with spirit possession! Moreover, it is obvious that on a daily basis you fake possession in order to trick the stupid Tibetans out of their money and goods! Today the truth has finally been exposed. Do you still dare make a false confession?"

The oracle prostrated and responded: "I have been an oracle for generations. It is commonplace for people to come to Tibet to seek reincarnations. Some ask, 'In what place?' Others ask, 'Which of these one or two, or even of these three or five, names is the one?' Frequently there are identifications that are not correct and they are asked to renew the search. The first two times he approached us,

Nawangdasi did not tell us the number of candidates or their names, he only asked where the incarnation had taken rebirth. Therefore, the prophecy told him to search in his home region. Without having returned to his home, he persistently asked us to see if it was either of the names that he delivered to us on the basis of previous answers. [I] could not refuse to make an identification for him. Therefore [I] again checked and [the protector] indicated that it was Ceden-dorji's son. The stamp of the *chökyong* placed above his name is authentic. This and similar types of matters have always been handled in this manner. Moreover, as for the relationship between myself and the Tüsiyetü Khan, there were no dealings between us. Nawangdasi never insisted that [the protector] choose between these two people. He only wanted to know if the [reincarnation] was one of those two people."[163]

In his response, the medium provided Heliyen with an outline of a divination technology that delivered results not by means of singular or sudden revelations, but rather through an accumulative process. According to the medium, an accurate decision required multiple stages of inquiry by both he protector deity and the supplicant. Moreover, there was no expectation that the process was infallible, especially if the deity was not provided with accurate or complete information.

Other contemporaneous Tibetan-language commentaries about oracles make the same point. In his description of the search for the reincarnation of the Second Jamyang Zhepa in 1797 (the focus of act 3), Drakgönpa recorded how the protector deities themselves, speaking through the mediums, expressed uncertainty about which candidate was the genuine article. In this case, the search party sought multiple prophecies from multiple deities, who all offered different assessments of the candidates. The author presented this as a sign not of the inaccuracy of the oracles but rather of the complexity of the task. Moreover, in this specific case, the deities not only hedged their predictions but also recommended the utility of subjecting the candidates to further tests such as a *zentak*.[164] Thus from an indigenous perspective, oracles delivered the best results when used responsibly in combination with other divination technologies and tests.

The Dalai Lama and the medium of the Lamo *chökyong* both also attempted to defend the indigenous tradition by making more modest claims about the abilities of the oracles. In a sense their responses under interrogation seem strategically designed to lower imperial expectations. In this regard, the Lamo oracle is reported as stating, "All Tibetans come to inquire about the harvest and whether or not there will be smallpox. However, we respond in accordance with the statutes of the classics. Some of these [predictions] occasionally hit the mark. The Tibetans then disseminate [these predictions] as evidence of our powers."[165] Yet in the same breath the medium also situated the technology firmly within a written legal tradition. In the transcript of his deposition, the Dalai Lama made a similar move, pointing out that the use of oracles in the Tüsiyetü Khan case was "in accordance with the ancient statutes."[166] Moreover, in these statements, both the Dalai Lama and the Lamo *chökyong* medium pinned the blame for misconceptions about the abilities of the oracles firmly on the common people, thus distinguishing the text- and law-based *civilization* of the Geluk church from the rumor mongering of the illiterate hoi polloi. Given the degree to which Qing officials overtly spoke of indigenous practices of divination as a "low tradition" and Tibet more generally as a land without law, it is difficult not to view the Dalai Lama's and the oracle's statements as intentional moves to reassert the high status of their tradition according to what they perceived were the standards of the Qing emperor and his representatives.[167]

The Eighth Dalai Lama's personal decree issued in response to the Qianlong emperor's "Water-Ox Year Edict" offers a further glimpse of how Tibetan elites might have understood the Golden Urn. The decree conveys the Dalai Lama's strong support for the new measure, yet also describes a configuration of the ritual that departed in crucial respects from the emperor's instructions. Thus, much like the letter from the Galdan Siretu *kūtuktu* to the Dalai Lama analyzed earlier, the Dalai Lama's decree hints at the range of strategies the court employed to express its will in a Tibetan voice. It is impossible not to suspect that the Qing officials resident in Lhasa had a hand in either drafting the document, vetting its contents, or at the very least encouraging its production. Yet the final product is perhaps a testament to the limits of Qing influence and the dangers the imperial message faced during the translation process.

The Dalai Lama began the edict by thanking the emperor—"The Heavenly Deity Manjusri and Great Sovereign Emperor"—for his support of both the "doctrine of those who wear yellow" and Tibet more generally.[168] Echoing the structure of the edict, the Dalai Lama then turned to the emperor's claim to have studied the Gelukpa teachings yet then significantly embellished it: "The Manjusri emperor especially cherishes the monks who follow the doctrine of Tsongkhapa, zealously studies, and has personally and assiduously strived to achieve the goal of taking the vows of a renunciate."[169] From this passage it is unclear if the Dalai Lama believed that the emperor had already become a monk or was working toward such a goal by observing the vows. The Demo *kūtuktu*'s biography of the Eighth Dalai Lama describes the lama as leading a ceremony of offerings to an image of Qianlong as a "Vajra-holding monk." The Demo reports that on the occasion of the ritual, because "there were those who were not enthusiastic," the Dalai Lama offered a passionate defense of the emperor.[170] Thus, although it would seem that such veneration was not universally supported, it was promoted by the Eighth Dalai Lama (or his assistants, such as the Demo *kūtuktu*) as justification for implementation of imperially sanctioned measures such as the Golden Urn lottery.

The Dalai Lama then seconded the emperor's observation that the recent crop of reincarnations had not elicited the deep faith of the past. He wrote:

Nowadays, because the majority of reincarnated lamas do not study the Dharma, when it comes time to identify a rebirth they are unable to make a clear, convincing decision. Therefore they do not receive unanimous faith and respect, even from the sangha. Similarly, when requests are made to the protectors, whatever is revealed in the prophecies becomes a pretext for making an identification. In reality, in accordance with their greed they merely recognize the children of those who possess material wealth, giving rise to debates among the people over whether or not they are really [rebirths].[171]

Although the Dalai Lama ostensibly shared the emperor's sense that there was a crisis of faith in the reincarnations and his diagnosis that the oracles had been corrupted, his analysis in this passage is different in key respects. First, unlike Qianlong, he did not point to specific lineages as corrupt. The tone of this statement is thus greatly softened by the lack of direct accusations against leading monks. Second, the Dalai Lama did not single out particular clans or Mongol aristocrats for attempting to influence the selection process. There is no mention of the Tüsiyetü Khan's attempt to have his son recognized as the Erdeni Pandita *kūtuktu*. In searching for the roots of the crisis, the Dalai Lama's analysis led him not outward to the Mongol aristocracy but rather inward to the purported laxity of the contemporary training regime for monks.

The most striking departures from Qianlong's edict are contained in the concluding section of the decree, where the Dalai Lama laid out a blue-print of the Golden Urn ceremony. First, where the emperor had limited the law to major *kūtuktus*, the Dalai Lama broadened the scope of the rit-ual to apply to "all reincarnations of lamas born in the land of Tibet."[172] Second, the Dalai Lama described the Qing *ambans* as drawing the lots.[173] And finally, despite the emperor's forceful prohibition of the use of the ora-cles, the Dalai Lama still reserved a role for the oracles in the recognition process. Much as the Galdan Siretu *kūtuktu* and Fuk'anggan had advised a year earlier, the Dalai Lama positioned the oracles as playing a role in the nomination of candidates for the final identification using the Golden Urn.[174] Given the fact that his articulation of the Golden Urn ritual ignored the key injunction of the emperor's public edict as well as private instruc-tions ostensibly passed to him via the *ambans*, it is not difficult to under-stand the degree to which the successful implementation of the new law remained a consistent concern of the Qianlong emperor through the remainder of his reign and into the first years of his son's reign. In his decree, the Dalai Lama in certain respects accorded the emperor a greater role than the court had anticipated. Yet the continued reliance on the oracles reveals the indelible stamp of the Dalai Lama's will on the ritual.

The Golden Urn as "Law" and "Omen"

April and May of 1793 found the emperor vacillating—much as he had in 1789 and again in 1791–92—over what to do about the temporal powers of the Dalai Lama. Behind the bluster of his public utterances, the limits and uncertainties of imperial influence on Tibet and the Geluk are revealed in his instruction to his advisors to consider recalling the regent, the Tatsak *kūtuktu*, to Beijing and allowing the Eighth Dalai Lama to resume greater control. In contrast to previous advice, during these delib-erations it was Fuk'anggan who cautioned against taking this step:

> The Dalai Lama appears to have truly understood the perfection of the emperor's loving grace and be genuinely overjoyed and sincerely appreciative. Since your servants Fuk'anggan and Heliyen arrived in

Tibet last year, we have observed that although the Dalai Lama is a good judge of people and exceedingly zealous in his study of the sutras, he does not understand [worldly] affairs. . . . [Although] he has heard the emperor's edicts with their various instructions, only after your servants have elucidated the main principles numerous times will the Dalai Lama come to grasp what he previously [didn't understand], genuinely appreciate the emperor's perfect and loving grace, and comprehend the many ways of handling affairs.[175]

In summary, Fuk'anggan argued that the Dalai Lama was loyal, but not a reliable vehicle for the execution of imperial policy. He needed constant tutoring from officials both Qing and Tibetan in the realm of temporal administration. According to Heliyen, the difficulty the Dalai Lama had in comprehending Qing policy was shared by Tibetans more generally. In the aftermath of the public tests of the oracles, Heliyen cautioned the emperor that the "muddleheaded Tibetans" seemed unable to comprehend the "true way": "Having been thoroughly deceived, they firmly believe . . . thus false actions become ever more true."[176]

A month later, Heliyen arrived at a more positive assessment. Having been asked by the emperor to secretly assess the mood of the Dalai Lama and other Tibetan elites in the aftermath of the selection of the next Erdeni Pandita *kūtuktu*, he reported that among the "*kūtuktu* and important lamas" he had gathered for a meeting at the Potala Palace, "there was none who was not pleased."[177] Heliyen reported that the lack of dissent extended to the Dalai Lama, whom he quoted as offering his approval of the (re-) identification of the Erdeni Pandita and promising to spread word of the new statute through the entirety of Tibet.[178] According to Heliyen, the emperor's fears that the Dalai Lama would react with hostility to the rejection of his original candidate and the potential loss of donations from Mongolia were groundless. Heliyen also put the Dalai Lama on record as referring to the new method as "fair and measured," phrasing key to the court's self-perception of its legitimacy.[179] Heliyen furthermore implied that the Dalai Lama had concurred with the imperial law prohibiting the use of the oracles.[180]

Upon receiving Heliyen's report, Qianlong seized on the news that indigenous Tibetans had found Qing law "fair" and had, in the aftermath of the public tests and promulgation of the Erdeni Pandita case, begun to reject the "old laws."[181] Heliyen's report implied that there had been a

crucial shift in the way that both Tibetan elites and comm
about reincarnation. In a court letter to Heliyen composed
received the *amban*'s memorial, the emperor wrote:

> Since Heliyen has explained things to the Dalai Lama an
> ers, not only is the Dalai Lama overjoyed and thankful, bu
> ular people as well discussed among themselves in a grea
> that, "It is also possible for a reincarnation to emerge amon
> folk!" Observing this, it is revealed how, because all the r
> tions had only emerged among the households of nobles a
> among those of the common people, the common people w
> pletely unconvinced.[182]

Having been persuaded that the selection of the Erdeni Pand
only not been opposed but also been embraced by the comm
the emperor approved Heliyen's request that the new statute "
into the records to become a permanent law."[183]

Yet despite these optimistic reports from the field, the emper
to have been deeply concerned about the future implementation
Over the summer and late fall, as Qianlong's mood swung from
(that the oracles would "vanish of their own accord") to pessimisti
tinued to badger the resident officials in Lhasa for any news, inc
suspicious that the rebirth and identification of reincarnate lamas v
hidden from him. Upon receipt of a report from Heliyen that in f
were no "suppressed reports" of rebirths, the emperor remained
suaded that the "foolish Tibetans" had accepted the new law. He
Heliyen to warn the Dalai Lama and the oracles that they would be
no leniency if caught violating the law.[184]

During the winter of 1793–94, the Lhasa *ambans* dispatched mes
across Tibet and to "all three [Buddhist orders]—the Yellow, Re
Black" to gather news of any ongoing or future searches regardless
status of the lineage. The court was also anxious to apply the new
dure to a reincarnate lineage that hailed from a Tibetan region. I
ticular, the Qing government was particularly vigilant for the emer
of rebirths of *trülku* in several districts of Kham—Chamdo, Riwoch
Drakyab—that fell within the territory accorded to the administrati
the Ganden Podrang. On February 25, 1794 (QL 59/01/26), He
reported that he had received news that searches might commence for t

fferent reincarnation lineages in those regions.[185] This news prompted the throne to insist that these rebirths be confirmed using the Golden Urn, a decision that went against Fuk'anggan's advice from a year earlier that searches in the Chamdo region continue to be conducted according to local customs.[186] This reversal can be attributed to the emperor's stated desire to establish a *Tibetan* precedent for the use of the Golden Urn, and perhaps also to the strategic location of this region at the intersection of trade and communication routes between Sichuan and central Tibet. The Lhasa *ambans* would have to wait another five months, however, to finally receive word via a Qing logistics official stationed in Chamdo that a *kūtuktu* had actually died—the Seventh Pakpalha *kūtuktu*, Jigme Tenpai Gonpo (1755–1794).[187]

In order to subject the search to final confirmation using the Golden Urn, the emperor and his field officials realized they faced an extremely delicate task. As Fuk'anggan had previously pointed out, the estate of the Pakpalha *kūtuktu* had never accepted outside interference in the search process.[188] For this reason Heliyen traveled in person to Chamdo and initiated negotiations with the estate of the Pakpalha *kūtuktu* and other local elites well before the search for the *kūtuktu*'s reincarnation had even begun. Heliyen and the assistant *amban*, Hening, were both aware of the stakes: they wrote to the emperor that selection of the Pakpalha would be the ultimate test of "over two years of continuous efforts to promote the use of the Golden Urn among Tibetans."[189]

Deliberations about how to handle the Pakpalha *kūtuktu* case had begun in private among Qing officials long before they had received news of the monk's death. Although the need to establish a Tibetan precedent for the use of the Golden Urn clearly outweighed Fuk'anggan's concern for local sensibilities, the emperor still granted broad discretion to his officials to implement the new law flexibly. Qianlong's instructions in this regard marked a rejection of several strict interpretations of the Golden Urn statute that Heliyen had floated in the winter of 1793–94. For instance, on February 25, arguing that even if the urn was used there was nothing to stop the treasurers of the *kūtuktus*' corporate estates from choosing candidates from among their relatives or disciples, Heliyen advised that the entire search process be turned over to local "Han officials."[190] He furthermore proposed a blanket rule that all search parties be limited to searching within one to two hundred *li* of the place where the lama in question had passed away and restricted from searching within the same clan as the man who had just died.

The emperor approved of these latter two measures, yet in the same breath offered an exemption in the case of the Pakpalha *kūtuktu* and the other leading *kūtuktu* of Riwoché, Drakyab, and Markham. In court letters to Heliyen, Qianlong observed that these kūtuktus deserved special attention because they were not just influential monks but also temporal administrators. Out of apparent deference to the historical autonomy of these communities, especially vis-à-vis the administration of the Dalai Lama, the emperor advised Heliyen to allow them to locate their own candidates. He wrote:

> I observe that the *kūtuktu* of the places of Chamdo, Riwoché, Zhaya, and Markham . . . administer common people. And moreover, the Dalai Lama has never administered any of their affairs. Therefore, it will be beneficial if identifications of rebirths are made in accordance with the wishes of their subordinates. Do not obstinately enforce the new laws. Handle matters by observing their old customs and taking into consideration what the people will find persuasive.[191]

That the search for the reincarnation of the Pakpalha *kūtuktu* would have special significance for the Qing is especially evident if one considers briefly the biography of the Seventh Pakpalha, Jigme Tenpai Gonpo. The Seventh Pakpalha was born into a noble family of Litang and recognized as a rebirth of an august and wealthy *trülku* lineage that traced its roots to the generation of monks who founded the Geluk order and promoted its teachings after the death of Tsongkhapa in 1419. During his lifetime, the Seventh Pakpalha had been responsible for the construction of a massive palace in Chamdo, had participated in the enthronement of the Eighth Dalai Lama, and had even founded a temple in Lhasa in honor of the Qianlong emperor's eightieth birthday.[192] The Qing had reciprocated by conferring on him the title *nomunhan* in recognition of his temporal authority.[193] Thus, given the Pakpalha lineage's ties to the dynasty as well as noble families located in Litang, well beyond the two-hundred-*li* boundary proposed by Heliyen, the emperor had good reasons to consider an exemption from key provisions of the Golden Urn law.

However, Qianlong was firm on the importance of subjecting the final candidates to the Golden Urn lottery and preventing any recourse to the prophecies of the oracles of central Tibet. In this respect, the emperor's instructions concerning the Pakpalha search signaled to his officials that the fundamental purpose of the new statute had become the elimination of the oracles. The eradication of reincarnations among the Inner Asian nobility was now relegated to only secondary significance. Yet this shift in priorities resulted in a thorny problem: if the Pakpalha lineage's historical ties to aristocratic households were now acceptable and the estate of the lama possessed no tradition of consulting the oracles of central Tibet, what then was the rationale for insisting that the final identification be made in Lhasa using the urn? What improvement did the new method offer over the existing traditions?

Perhaps fortuitously for the Qing emperor, into this conundrum stepped the newly appointed Lhasa *amban*, Sungyun. Although modern Chinese scholarship on Sungyun's tenure in Lhasa tends to view his appointment as the outcome of factional battles between Hešen and his detractors (among whom Sungyun purportedly considered himself), the arrival of an official who was contemporaneously recognized as an expert in frontier regions and who had just successfully managed the investigation of the Tüsiyetü Khan case at such a critical juncture hardly seems like the unintentional result of banishment from court.[194] Sungyun's appointment was made a month before the court learned of the death of the Pakpalha *kūtuktu*, but probably reflected the emperor's desire to have someone competent in Tibet to implement the new statute.[195]

Before Sungyun departed from Beijing, the emperor issued instructions on how to handle the search for the Pakpalha *kūtuktu*. Sungyun was to do his best to follow the letter of the new law. Ideally, the emperor wrote, the *ambans* were to identify appropriate candidates and make sure they did not hail from noble families or other households associated with the prior incarnation. However, Qianlong also ordered Sungyun to gauge local sentiments and, if necessary, use the candidates the locals had nominated, regardless of background:

> In the event that this is impossible, instead, in accordance with what they find persuasive, select several [candidates] from among the boys who are reported to have emerged among his subjects and have their names placed into the urn. It will also be acceptable if [the rebirth] is identified in this manner. But it will surely be unacceptable if they are able to select one as they wish according to the previous ways.
>
> Because Sungyun will be passing through Chamdo, he should definitely probe deeply the [local] opinions and after arriving in Tibet,

discuss with Heliyen how to handle this matter. Overall, since it will be unacceptable for them to identify [a rebirth] in accordance with their previous customs as they wish from among the [children] of their own clan, you must handle the selection in a fashion that takes into consideration what will both be advantageous and probably cause them to be convinced.[196]

On the one hand, the emperor repeatedly expressed his desire to control the entire search process. Ideally the candidates could be vetted to ensure that they hailed from particular locations and common households unrelated to the established aristocracy. On the other hand was the larger strategic picture: candidates, regardless of origin, had to be persuasive, which at least from the throne's perspective required at a minimum the use of the Golden Urn. Thus the passage above demonstrates the degree to which a genuine concern for the believability of reincarnations drove the deliberative process behind the creation and implementation of the Golden Urn law.

Sungyun's task was to balance the emperor's desire to see all aspects of the law implemented with the need to ensure that the outcome was considered legitimate and would not upset the political status quo in Chamdo. Qianlong's appointee appreciated this subtlety. The following day he advised the emperor to lower his expectations that the identification could be resolved quickly. He noted that if they immediately held a lottery, the Tibetans would complain that the candidates were too young, as it was the custom to wait until the children were at least able to speak. Yet if they waited three or four years, there might be "no point in conducting a lottery." Thus, he proposed that names be gathered in a little over a year.[197] He also indirectly warned the emperor that the relationship between the Pakpalha *kūtuktu* and the central Tibetan government was more complicated than the emperor had previously stated. Sungyun wrote that, although the Pakpalha administered his own vast territory, he had also historically been a "close assistant to the Dalai Lama and Panchen Lama."[198] As a result, the court would have to take into consideration the sentiments of Tibetans outside of Chamdo. Still, despite these complications, Sungyun concluded his memorial with the opinion that "without resorting to coercion, I will handle things properly and arrange things such that everyone will definitely be convinced."[199]

A little more than a month later, Sungyun reported that he had arrived in Chamdo and reached an agreement to subject the future candidates to the Golden Urn lottery. Sungyun met with the treasurer of the Pakpalha estate and the Zhiwala *kūtuktu*, whom the *amban* described as "seventy-seven years old but still lucid."[200] The Fourth Zhiwala Pakpa, Gelek Gyelt-sen (1720–1799), had received the title *kūtuktu* from the Qianlong court in 1754 and overseen the search for the Seventh Pakpalha shortly thereafter. This monk's assent was therefore essential, and Sungyun secured it. In fact, Sungyun characterized the Zhiwala *kūtuktu* as being highly supportive of the new measure and advocating on its behalf among the other disciples of the Pakpalha. Perhaps even more significantly, Sungyun quoted the Zhi-wala as presenting his own novel justification for the ritual: "The Great Holy Lord on High is the Manjusri Buddha. If, after sutras have been recited, a decision is made by drawing lots, I will consider it appropriate. One can say that this is the true *trülku* that has just been indicated by Tsong-khapa."[201] The attribution of agency in the ritual to Tsongkhapa was orig-inal in this document and a theme that Sungyun and Tibetan elites would return to in subsequent communications. Moreover, Sungyun reported that the Zhiwala *kūtuktu* had been "thoroughly convinced" (Ma. *umesi gūnin dahame*) that it would be "unprincipled" if the reincarnation was recog-nized within the same clan as that of the Seventh Pakpalha.[202] In return for what Sungyun admitted was unprecedented outside interference, del-egates from Chamdo were invited to travel to Lhasa the following year to observe the actual lottery.[203]

Although Sungyun had informed the emperor that he had arranged to return to Chamdo in the summer of the following year to gather the names of candidates, by August 1795, he still had reported no further progress on the identification of the Pakpalha *kūtuktu*. Much as he had a year earlier with Heliyen, Qianlong began to voice suspicions that searches were being undertaken in secrecy. He wrote to Sungyun asking, "At this time, although everyone has come to realize the spuriousness of the Lamo *chökyong*, have there been any cases of identification of *hūbilgan* according to the divina-tions of the Lamo *chökyong* by lowly, muddleheaded people who still trust in the oracles?"[204]

In his letter to Sungyun, the emperor had also identified the Golden Urn lottery for the first time explicitly as a "law."[205] Sungyun's detailed response to the emperor's concerns revealed the extent to which the grad-ual establishment of the lottery as law had entailed the construction of an enforcement apparatus within both the *ambans'* office in Lhasa and the administration of the Ganden Podrang. This supportive scaffolding had apparently been erected in the two years since Heliyen had first requested that the measure be "committed to the records."[206] Sungyun reported:

> Since the establishment of the Golden Urn, there has not been a single case of the Tibetan people recognizing a reincarnation on the basis of secretly observing divinations. The reason for this is that since establishing the Golden Urn, Heliyen et al. have respectfully obeyed the imperial decree and together with the Tatsak *kūtuktu* have collected the names and numbers of the major and minor *kūtuktu* and *zhapdrung* and reported them to the board as well as placed them in our office of seals for safekeeping. Moreover, whenever it is time to recognize the reincarnation of a *kūtuktu* or *zhapdrung*, having received the name of the small child that has emerged from each respective monastery's investigations, we can make accurate reports.[207]

It is evident that the reification of the Golden Urn as *law* also involved the cooperation of Tibetans. The regent of the Eighth Dalai Lama, the Tatsak *kūtuktu*, and the *ambans* had jointly established an inventory of reincarnate lamas, laying the groundwork for what Sungyun envisioned as the comprehensive management of *trülku*. Further classified as "major *kūtuktus*" and "minor *kūtuktus* and *zhapdrung*," the different ranks of reincarnations would receive different bureaucratic treatments, with the former being handled via the palace memorial system and the latter being supervised via routine communications with the Court of Colonial Affairs.[208]

Sungyun offered a striking assessment of the success of the new law:

> Previously the Tibetans had trusted the *chökyong* and observed their divinations. And nothing could be done about the way they squandered wealth on the *chökyong*. Since the urn was established in accordance with the edict, once [the names of candidates] are reported, the selection of lots is immediately carried out. Their wealth is now spent much more frugally and they rejoice together, all having been convinced that the Great Holy Lord Manjusri's identification [method] is very proper.
>
> I observe that the Tibetans are no longer deceived by the *chökyong*. Originally they found the *chökyong* credible, even in the matter of identifying *hūbilgan,* despite there being nothing reliable about it, and their arbitrary words were taken as omens. Now, the Tibetans believe

the determination of *hübilgan* made according to the imperial decree by selecting lots from a golden urn after reciting prayers before the Buddha Tsongkhapa to be an unusual omen and are persuaded. Therefore the divinations [of the oracles] are not secretly observed by anyone anymore.[209]

Sungyun's interpretation of the Golden Urn lottery as an "omen" (Ma. *temgetu*) casts light on the *amban*'s strategy for implementing the law. According to Sungyun, the believability of the event hinged on transforming it into a spectacle more impressive than that of the oracles. The key to the success of the law was its reinterpretation by Tibetans as an "omen," and Sungyun was a consummate stage manager of the Golden Urn ritual. He adapted and modified the configuration of the lottery such that the agency of unseen forces (deities, buddhas, emperors, etc.) could be imagined and appreciated. Moreover, this attention to the staging of the Golden Urn lottery carried over both to his advance planning—the cultivation of the search party members in the lead up to the drawing—and to his later representations of the event in subsequent celebrations and reports to Beijing. Thus Sungyun, more than any other Qing official who served in Lhasa during the 1790s, appears to have influenced the organization and interpretation of the lottery during the nineteenth century.

It was not until another year had passed that the reincarnation of the Seventh Pakpalha *kūtuktu* was identified in the form of a one-year-old child from a "commoner Tibetan" household in the Litang region. Sungyun's subsequent report to the throne detailed a ritual that departed significantly from previous ones. His arrangement of the ritual offered an innovative interpretation of the Golden Urn statute. First he shifted the venue from the Jokhang Temple to the Potala Palace. As Sungyun described the event, the Dalai Lama, Tatsak *kūtuktu*, Démo *kūtuktu*, several other monks with the rank of abbot, and two chamberlains of the Pakpalha estate brought the Golden Urn, along with various possessions of the previous Pakpalha *kūtuktu*, to the Potala and arranged them before a painted image (Ma. *enduringge nirugan*; Tib. *tangka*) of the Qianlong emperor. This marks the second innovation: in contrast to early blueprints that positioned the urn and the prayer service in the presence of either the Jowo Sakyamuni or Tsongkhapa, Sungyun brought the ritual into the presence of the emperor. After these monks had led seven days of prayers the final lottery was conducted. Here too was a difference: whereas the Erdeni Pandita lottery at

Yonghegong had lasted only three days, the preparatory prayer service for the Pakpalha *kūtuktu* was stretched over a week. Finally, Sungyun offered the first unambiguous account of how the lottery was conducted. He personally made up the lots and placed them in the urn. Then, following another round of prayers, "both *ambans* genuflected before the urn and images and in a manner such that the audience could observe, the assistant *amban* respectfully drew the [name] of the Tibetan child from Litang."[210] This involvement of both *ambans* in the physical work of conducting the lottery subsequently became the model for all future Golden Urn lotteries.

The structure of Sungyun's written announcement of the lottery results was also influential. As he would do in later memorials that announced the results of other Golden Urn lotteries, Sungyun concluded this report with personal reflections on the meaning of the ritual and its reception among the Tibetan witnesses. In this case he first presented evidence of how the Tibetans had appreciated the ceremony, noting that they had immediately prostrated before the image of Qianlong and exclaimed, "The Great Holy Lord on High is truly the Manjusri Buddha!" He followed this observation by stating that the "*trülku* had definitely been indicated by Tsongkhapa," an opinion he then conveyed in letters to the Zhiwala *kūtuktu* and other disciples of the Pakpalha in Chamdo.[211] As a result of this careful framing, the presentation of the ritual itself served as a kind of public exchange of agency: the Qing officials attributed the accuracy of the lottery to Tsongkhapa, and the Tibetans credited Qianlong. Finally, Sungyun reflected on his own personal satisfaction with the ritual. He was very pleased: the first test of the Golden Urn in the case of a major Tibetan reincarnation had been successful. There was no evidence that Tibetan nobility had corrupted the process. And the oracles were absent from his account.

Conclusion: Faith Through Law

The first mention of the Golden Urn in the *Biography of the Eighth Dalai Lama* is in the context of the search for the reincarnation of the Pakpalha *kūtuktu*. The author, the Demo *kūtuktu*, whom Sungyun recorded as having witnessed the event, arrived at a similar observation about the synthesis of forces that had come together to make this a successful identification. The idea for the method had originated in the "perfect wisdom of the emperor," who had perceived that "corruptions stemming from human beings' desire for status and power" had led to "ever greater disputes and quarrels." But the correct result ultimately relied on the intercession of Tsongkhapa who had to be carefully propitiated before and during the ritual. The Demo *kūtuktu*'s account noted that the emperor's original edict had also listed two specific texts dedicated to Tsongkhapa that should be recited before conducting the lottery.[212]

The Demo *kūtuktu*'s account differed from Sungyun's in a handful of ways. The text reported the specific location of the ritual, the Chapel of Victory Over the Three Realms in the Potala Palace. Although the mention of this site might have implied the presence of the Qianlong emperor to individuals familiar with the room's association with the propitiation of Qing rulers, the *Biography* did not reference the painting of Qianlong as playing a role in the ritual, as Sungyun had. Nor did the text mention the direct involvement of the *ambans* in selecting the lot. To the contrary, after names had been written on "golden cards" and the prayers to Tsongkhapa had been completed, they "entrusted the veracity [of the ritual] to the Dharma protectors of the previous incarnations of the lama." The subsequent description diverged even further:

> Having mixed the lots, because the one that was pulled out was the Litang [candidate], a child who had already been greatly favored by all the people—from aristocrats to commoners—of Chamdo and had also been identified by the testimony of the protectors, he was [celebrated] as a true Jewel and [people] swore that the emperor's measures to avoid conflicts [over the identification of reincarnations] were in fact good. Among those witnesses [from Chamdo], the faith derived from conviction increased very greatly.[213]

In a sense, the Demo *kūtuktu*'s description is a testament to the success with which the Qianlong emperor and his field officials in Inner Asia had integrated a Ming bureaucratic practice into the process of locating reincarnate lamas. Moreover, the metaphysical understanding of the ritual had evidently undergone a transformation. Qianlong's ritual had worked as Sungyun (and the Zhiwala *kūtuktu*, perhaps) intended: the urn had become a venue for the unseen powers of Tsongkhapa and the deities to act, and the winning lot had become an omen (Tib. *tsenté*) of their wishes. But far from displacing the oracles, from an indigenous perspective the urn had become a complementary technology. The oracles were back. And despite Sungyun's bluster, they had probably never left. The Demo *kūtuktu* was willing to concur with the throne that "mistakes" (Tib. *dzölga zhik*) had been made in the identification of reincarnate *trülkus*.[214] Yet at no point did the Demo *kūtuktu* cite the oracles as the source of the corruption and lack of accord over the authenticity of candidates.

Evidence from Tibetan sources casts doubt on Sungyun's claim to have completely eliminated the oracles. Prior scholarship has argued that the Tibetans never shared the Qing ruler's sense of crisis or doubt about the incarnations and that Qianlong's interest in reforming the system was either a pretext for asserting political supremacy over the Geluk church or simply an expression of his ignorance of Tibetan understandings of reincarnation (or perhaps both). However, accounts such as that of the Demo *kūtuktu* suggest that some Tibetan elites from the Geluk church did concur with the throne that faith in the authenticity of the *trülkus* had been compromised.

Writing in the 1790s, no less an authority than the Third Tukwan *kūtuktu*, the Qianlong emperor's principal advisor on the Geluk teachings following the deaths of Changkya Rolpé Dorjé and the Galdan Samadi Bakshi Ngawang Tsultrim, complained that "all sorts of corruption and decadence" had become commonplace during the search for the rebirths of prominent lamas. Without identifying specific cases, the Third Tukwan accused wealthy and powerful families of banding together with venal estate managers to bribe monks and the human mediums of various oracles to identify their children and kinsmen. "In light of this," the monk wrote, "not only is it now impossible to speak of finding a genuine rebirth, but conscientious and strict monks like those who conducted the search for the Changkya *trülku* are rarer than lotus flowers."[215]

The reports of both the Demo *kūtuktu* and Sungyun focused attention on whether the identification process inspired a very specific type of faith. The emperor, and subsequently Sungyun, spoke explicitly of achieving obedience to the law on the Golden Urn not through force but as a result of "having become convinced" (Ma. *gūnin dahabumbi*). Similarly, the Demo *kūtuktu* wrote that the use of the Golden Urn in the case of the identification of the Pakpalha had instilled in observers a particularly strong form of faith: "faith from conviction" or "faith from trust."[216] The use of these phrases in the documents above suggests that in both Manchu and Tibetan they express a form of faith based on the kind of conviction or trust that one acquires from personal observation.

It is striking that in the Manchu language the concepts of persuasion and obedience are intimately linked by the same root verb (*günin dahabumbi* and *dahambi*, respectively). In the context of the court's attempts to implement the statute on the Golden Urn, the link hardly seems coincidental. The gradual establishment of the Golden Urn as law and the concomitant reification of certain elements from the management of the Erdeni Pandita and Pakpalha cases into precedents were attended by a constant concern with not merely whether the court's directives were obeyed, but if they were obeyed out of personal conviction. As a result, the dynasty directed its field officials in Mongolia and Tibet to orchestrate public tests of the oracles and criminal proceedings against the Tüsiyetü Khan and the steward of the Erdeni Pandita estate. These proceedings were staged not merely to expose the corruption of the Geluk church but also to demonstrate the superiority of Qing laws and administration. As Qianlong himself frequently stated, Qing success was a "victory of lawmaking." The court's strategy for the eradication of the oracles, therefore, hinged on the belief that when exposed to the Qing system, Tibetans would choose it over their own system on account of its fairness and frugality. This explains the emperor's pleasure in receiving the news that common folk had purportedly reacted with astonishment at the news that *kūtuktu* could emerge within their families. This extended as well to the notion that the Qing was rule-based and systematized and therefore more just. Unlike the "way of the Buddha," Qianlong's "way of the emperor" promised not only equality before the law but justice in the here and now, without having to wait for karmic retribution.

The degree to which the argument for the replacement of the oracles and the imposition of Qing sovereignty (Ma. *toose*) in Tibet was legitimized in terms of extending legal justice to Tibetans should not only give us pause to reconsider the importance of law and legal discourse in the expansion of Qing colonialism but also draw our attention to the ways Qing expansion paralleled other contemporaneous empire building. As Elizabeth Kolsky argues with regard to colonial India, the belief that the British could deliver impartial justice and stronger legal protections to Indians than the indigenous legal traditions was the most important device for legitimating colonial rule, both in the home country and abroad.[217] Qing official discourse in 1790s Tibet was little different.

Yet how far, ultimately, was the late Qianlong court willing to go to delegitimize the indigenous legal system? What kind of role did it envision for Qing administrators in local jurisprudence? As a concluding vignette, a case handled by Sungyun at the same time as he was dealing with the Pakpalha search paints an extreme picture. On August 13, 1795, Sungyun reported that he had been approached by a group of Tibetans who filed a lawsuit against the Nechung oracle. They claimed that the oracle had, on the authority of a decree from the Dalai Lama, occupied their land and claimed their produce for three full years. Sungyun investigated the case and, finding the medium guilty, had him caned thirty times. Sungyun summarized the case as follows:

> In Tibet there are only four major *chökyong*, the Lamo, Nechung, Samye, and Gadung. In accordance with their faith, the Tibetans in a muddled manner inquire after the fortunes of their petty matters. Their divinations not being at all clear, their credibility is accordingly also minimal. Among the four protectors, the Nechung protector has willfully taken possession of the people's fields. Because of this, our servants have frightfully punished and imprisoned him. The Nechung *chökyong* is the object of faith and worship by the Dalai Lama and all the monks of Drepung monastery. The Dalai Lama only knows how to read sutras. He understands nothing of the ways of things. Thus when we explain to him what we have done, he just approves and thanks us and states that he will not again issue decrees. The Tibetan people fearlessly point out how [the Dalai Lama] has wronged them and raise their grievances against the oracles. Indeed these are clear signs that they no longer have faith in the protectors.[218]

In this case the *amban*, in an unprecedented fashion, not only involved himself in a local property dispute but also reversed the decision of the Dalai Lama. Sungyun also seized on the complaint as a further opportunity to discredit the oracles. Yet the additional pressure the *amban* reports having placed on the Dalai Lama to recuse himself from making further judgments on property issues, and the insinuation that he was complicit in the crime, suggests that agents of the court were growing more comfortable in presenting to the broader public what previously had only been an internal discourse challenging the fitness of the Dalai Lama and other religious figures for temporal administration.

Just three months after the successful identification of the Pakpalha *kūtuktu*, the dynasty received word that the monks of Labrang monastery in Amdo had already identified the reincarnation of the Second Jamyang Zhepa, preempting the Qing emperor. This case was to prove much more complicated than the Pakpalha case: the Xining *amban* had had been caught flatfooted, having conducted none of the advance work that Heliyen and Sungyun had carried out in Kham. This recognition generated significant friction, both between the Qing state and Tibetan Buddhists and among Tibetan Buddhists. However, despite divergent ideas about divination and reincarnation, all sides strategically engaged one another in the shared pursuit of "convincing" identifications.

ACT III

Amdowas Speaking in Code

The identification of the Third Jamyang Zhepa was by all accounts tremendously successful. From the perspective of the Qing court, it was the most significant test to date of its ability to enforce the law on the Golden Urn among Tibetan Buddhists. In September 1797, the Lhasa *amban* Sungyun reported to the now (ostensibly) retired "Supreme Emperor" Qianlong that he and the assistant Lhasa *amban*, Hening, had used the Golden Urn to confirm the identity of the reincarnation of the Second Jamyang Zhepa (1728–1791). The procedure followed the format developed by Sungyun a year earlier: Tibetan dignitaries including the Eighth Dalai Lama, the regent, Tatsak *kūtuktu*, and representatives of the Jamyang Zhepa's estate were brought together before the image of Qianlong in the Potala Palace, and, as the "scriptures of Tsongkhapa were recited," Sungyun inscribed the names of three candidate children on lots. Hening drew the winning lot, that of candidate number two, a three-year-old child named Kelzang Bum (Ma. *G'aldzangbum*), "the son of the Tibetan Rinchen Gyatso [Ma. *fandze Rincinjamseo*], from Xunhua subprefecture."[1]

Sungyun concluded his report by noting that the outcome had received the acclamation of the witnesses. In particular, he recorded that Belmang Pandita Könchok Gyeltsen (Ma. *Kaimong surulku*, 1764–1853), the chief representative from Labrang monastery, the seat of the Jamyang Zhepa *kūtuktus*, had prostrated himself before the painting of Qianlong and exclaimed, "The Great Holy Emperor on high is truly the Manjusri

Buddha! The determination that has been made while reciting the sutras and drawing a lot appears to me to be completely proper. This cannot be considered to be anything but Tsongkhapa's indication of the genuine reincarnation. I myself am truly and joyously convinced."[2] The chosen child was duly enthroned the following spring at Labrang as the Third Jamyang Zhepa, Lozang Tupten Jikmé Gyatso (1792–1855).

Sungyun's Manchu-language palace memorial reporting this matter circulated not only within the court in Beijing but also among the disciples of the Jamyang Zhepa, who quoted it in subsequent Tibetan-language accounts. The biographer of the Third Jamyang Zhepa accorded the Golden Urn lottery a prominent place in the account of the search process and included Sungyun's memorial, translated in its entirety from Manchu into Tibetan.[3] This biography, composed between 1859 and 1889, as well as four other nineteenth-century Tibetan-language narratives, portrayed the urn as a complementary component of a complex search process. The chroniclers argued, however, that the Golden Urn confirmed the authenticity of a child whom the Labrang community had already identified as the leading candidate.

Not without justification, therefore, modern scholarship on Labrang monastery and the lineage of the Jamyang Zhepas has pointed to the "fact" that the lottery ultimately identified the candidate favored by the Tibetans as evidence that the Qing court exercised little more than ceremonial authority. On the basis of the description of the search in the *Life of the Third Jamyang Zhepa*, Paul Nietupski has written that "The Tibetans carried out their own selection procedure but at least went through the motions of the Qing policy. At once Tibetan tradition and authority were preserved and the Qing voice was heard."[4] The unstated implication is that the leaders of the Jamyang Zhepa's estate had the power and authority to guarantee that the results of the lottery could be fixed in their favor. Thus the use of the urn was but one of several gestures made by Tibetans from Labrang during the nineteenth century as a "diplomatic courtesy" to uphold the fiction of Qing authority.[5] However, discoveries in the Manchu-language archives of the Grand Council force a revision of this assessment. The formal, public accounts of the search produced by Geluk and Qing officials were misleading, and purposely so.

In the days following the identification of Kelzang Bum as the Third Jamyang Zhepa, Sungyun had submitted not one, but two reports to the court—the formal memorial that appears to have been composed from the outset for the consumption of officialdom and the broader reading elites across Inner Asia and a second, secret note intended only for the Qianlong emperor and his inner circle of advisors.[6] In this second letter Sungyun informed the emperor that he had successfully ensured the "correct" outcome of the lottery. Seven months earlier, Qianlong had decided that among the three candidates whose names had been brought to the attention of the Qing court, the child listed first was unacceptable. Therefore, he ordered Sungyun to arrange the lottery so as to ensure that the name of the first child was not drawn.[7]

Sungyun's mission was doubly complicated, however, because according to a Manchu-language report from the Xining *amban*, it was the first child listed, Wangchen Bum (Ma. *wangcinbum*), *not* Kelzang Bum, whom the Labrang community had identified as the most promising candidate and wished to see confirmed as the Jamyang Zhepa.[8] In Lhasa, Sungyun and Hening would have to not only fix the lottery but also manage what, from the perspective of the delegation from Labrang, might be an unexpected and disappointing outcome.

In his secret communiqué, penned just two days after the lottery had been conducted, Sungyun was confident that he had pulled the matter off: "Nothing has been divulged. We have ensured that their first-ranked child, the son of the Tibetan headman[9] Dülagyel, was not selected. Having seen to it that the name of the second-ranked child, the son of a Tibetan with no official status, was drawn, we explained the benefits of this [selection] to the Belmang *trülku* and the other of the disciples [of the Jamyang Zhepa], who were all completely thankful and convinced."[10]

Sungyun's confidence does not appear to have been misplaced. Starting in 1798 with the completion of the *Life of the Second Jamyang Zhepa*[11] and culminating in the late nineteenth century with the composition of the *Life of the Third Jamyang Zhepa*,[12] members of the Labrang community composed a series of written accounts of the search for the reincarnation of the Second Jamyang Zhepa that legitimized the candidacy of Kelzang Bum. A direct witness to the events in Lhasa, Belmang Pandita provided several brief descriptions of the search in his *Labrang Monastery Gazetteer*, completed in 1800. His student, Drakgönpa Könchok Tenpa Rapgyé, edited and printed the gazetteer in 1821. Drakgönpa also incorporated Belmang's reminiscences about his trip to Lhasa into both his history of the Amdo region, the *Oceanic Book* (first printed in 1849, expanded edition 1865), and his *Life of the Second Belmang Pandita* (1864).[13]

Although the composition and printing of these books spanned nine decades, they presented a unified narrative of the events of 1796 through 1798 that recalled the search for the rebirth of the Second Jamyang Zhepa as uncontroversial. These books in turn influenced subsequent generations of historians of Labrang and the Jamyang Zhepa lineage and anchored a widely accepted historical narrative within the Labrang community and the Amdo region that, well into the early twenty-first century, still memorializes the Third Jamyang Zhepa as a legitimate *trülku* and an effective spiritual guide for all his disciples and subjects. Even PRC-era authors, many of whom are employed by state-run universities and publishing houses and therefore may not believe in the *trülku* institution, make no mention of any disputes surrounding the identification of the Third Jamyang Zhepa.[14] This is a stark contrast to the divisive search for the reincarnation of the First Jamyang Zhepa in the 1720s, which resulted in two candidates, a division of the original Labrang community into irreconcilable camps, and simmering feuds that continued to generate bloodshed well into the late nineteenth century—conflicts well attested to in works such as *The Life of the Second Jamyang Zhepa* and Drakgönpa's *Oceanic Book*.[15] The historical record contains no trace of comparable conflicts in the aftermath of the identification of the Third Jamyang Zhepa. Why was this the case? How did Tibetan authors bury the promising candidacy of the child who was ultimately passed over?

Qing officials such as Sungyun made great efforts to cultivate indigenous authorities and make the lottery and its outcome palatable to Tibetan Buddhists. However, the key work of managing the reception of Kelzang Bum as the reincarnation of the Second Jamyang Zhepa fell to Tibetan Buddhist elites in both Lhasa and Amdo. The case of the Third Jamyang Zhepa—the "truth" of which appears never to have leaked beyond Sungyun, Hening, (retired) emperor Qianlong, and perhaps the Grand Council and the new emperor, Jiaqing—demonstrates that the Qing could rig the lottery. The success of their intrigue hinged on the actions of a wide range of Gelukpa hierarchs, witnesses, and later chroniclers. These Tibetan Buddhists harmonized two seemingly incompatible systems for locating reincarnations and naturalized the result of a highly contentious and unexpected identification.

Without recourse to Manchu-language communiqués, the viability of the alternate candidate remains largely hidden behind a screen of hagiographic camouflage. The biographers of the Jamyang Zhepa communicated their initial suspicions of the Golden Urn and knowledge of the contested identity of the reincarnation to a limited audience of their immediate peers and contemporaries through heavily "coded" language and subtle hints, but for later nineteenth and twentieth-century readers with no direct memory of Labrang in the 1790s, the full scope of the conflict became invisible.

Sons of the Geluk, Servants of Empire

Manchu- and Tibetan-language materials from 1797 raise questions about the nature of service to the Qing state and Qing authority in Tibetan Buddhist contexts. Several of the Gelukpa hierarchs portrayed in these texts as playing key roles in the search for the Third Jamyang Zhepa also possessed strong ties to the Qing court. In particular, Tukwan Lozang Chökyi Nyima (1737–1802), Gungtang Könchok Tenpé Drönmé (1762–1823), and Tatsak Tenpé Gönpo (1760–1810) had not only received the title of *kūtuktu* but also been elevated to the status of "*kūtuktus* resident in the capital" (Ch. *zhu jing zhi hutuketu* 駐京之呼圖克圖).[16]

The cultivation of certain lineages of reincarnate lamas by successive Qing rulers was a key component of the empire's strategy for managing relations with Tibetan Buddhists in Inner Asia. The Qing tradition of inviting Tibetan Buddhist monks to reside at court began well before they had conquered the Ming and accelerated during the Kangxi reign as the empire turned from the pacification of China proper to the growing strategic threat posed by the Junghars.[17] Yet these efforts were highly fraught. For instance, starting in the mid-1650s the Shunzhi and Kangxi emperors successively maintained the Ilaɣuɣsan *kūtuktu* in Beijing to serve as the leading representative of the Geluk church and intermediary between the court and the Dalai Lama. However, when this lama was dispatched to Lhasa in 1689 with instructions to aid the court in working out a peace accord with Galdan's Junghar khanate, he ultimately joined the Junghar cause.[18] During the Qianlong reign efforts were made to establish a more permanent legal framework for hosting Geluk hierarchs and assigning responsibilities. Internally circulated draft *Statutes of the Court of Colonial Affairs* (c. 1756) record that following the establishment of the Yonghegong temple (1744) and the Office of Lama Seals and Service (Ch. *Lama yinwuchu* 喇嘛印務處, 1745) within the Court of Colonial Affairs, the court legislated the presence of three *kūtuktu* in the capital—the Changkya, Galdan Siretu, and Tatsak lineages.[19] Thirty-three years later, after the death of Changkya Rolpé Dorjé, Qianlong undertook another major reevaluation of the situation and expanded the formal list of *kūtuktus* resident in the capital to include twelve *kūtuktu* divided into left and right wings.[20] Chen Xiaomin has suggested that the practice of inviting prominent lamas to Beijing; granting them titles, stipends, and residences; and delegating to them a range of formal administrative and religious responsibilities constituted by the late Qianlong period a full-fledged "system."[21] Yet considering that this institution was only formally articulated in 1786 (at the beginning of Qianlong's final decade of rule) and that many of the *kūtuktus* living at the time would never visit Beijing, it is perhaps appropriate to think of the "*kūtuktu* resident in the capital" not as a fixed system but rather as a discursive resource that could be used strategically by both rulers and lamas. Thus in the nineteenth century, the legacy of the "Beijing *kūtuktus*" remained to be shaped and debated by contemporaries.

The complexity of these institutions and their continuous adaptation during both the Qianlong and subsequent reigns suggest that what it meant to be a Beijing *kūtuktu* was open to a range of interpretations. It is perhaps not a coincidence that Qianlong proclaimed a revised and expanded system of resident lamas in the year that Changkya Rolpé Dorjé (1717–1786), the longest serving and most influential "state preceptor," passed away. Because he is understood by both contemporaries and modern historians to be *the* paradigmatic "Resident Lama in the Capital," Rolpé Dorjé's career has been exhaustively studied for information on the nature of this role. However, preoccupied with the question of whether Changkya was an agent of Qianlong's empire building or an advocate of "Tibetan" concerns, modern scholarship has left unanswered the question of how contemporaneous understandings of his career, expressed in widely read biographies such as those by his disciple Tukwan Lozang Chökyi Nyima (1737–1802) and Chuzang *kūtuktu* Ngawang Tubten Wangchuk (1725–1796), influenced the subsequent development of Qing–Geluk relations and the careers of later monks who traveled to court and undertook various tasks at the dynasty's request.[22] Furthermore, Yonghegong- and Changkya-focused studies of Qianlong's relationship with Tibetan Buddhist hierarchs have rarely addressed the question of what these monks actually did in their home communities and how their affiliation with the court was perceived. Rolpé Dorjé's court-centered career, which stretched from childhood to death, was an outlier from the experience of most "Beijing *kūtuktus*," who spent the majority of their time away from court.

One of the few scholars to address these questions is Paul Nietupski, whose study of Labrang monastery has cataloged the relationships of numerous local reincarnate lineages with the Qing state. Tibetan-language sources from Labrang identified monks who taught in neighboring Chinese communities or ministered at court as "Chinese lamas" (Tib. *gyanakpa lama*).[23] Nietupski depicts them primarily as "emissaries" who periodically traveled to Beijing to take up translation or teaching tasks on behalf of the Qianlong court, but whose fundamental orientation was toward the interests of their home institutions and perhaps the Geluk school more generally: they "worked on behalf of Labrang monastery."[24] Nietupski's case in point is Lozang Tenpé Nyima (1689–1762), the reincarnation of the Forty-fourth Ganden Tripa (Lubum Ngawang Lodrö Gyatso, 1635–1688). He was invited to Beijing during the last year of the Yongzheng reign and under Qianlong was instrumental in the translation of the Tengyur into Mongol and the conversion of the Yonghegong princely residence into a monastery.[25] He was known at court as the "Galdan Siretu *kūtuktu*," and his was one of the first three estates to be permanently established in Beijing by the Qianlong emperor early in his reign.[26] His exceptionally esteemed status and long residency in Beijing suggest that this lama, like Rolpé Dorjé, was much more than just an emissary from Amdo; he was also a servant of the emperor.

Rather than approaching interpretation of Labrang's Beijing-affiliated lamas as a case of sorting out whether they were acting on behalf of the Qing emperor or Labrang, it might be helpful to interpret their project to legitimize the influence of Qing laws and officials as a product of what Johan Elverskog has referred to as the "Qing cosmopolitan culture" of Inner Asia.[27] Elverskog defines this cosmopolitanism as "the ability of the various peoples within the Manchu state to see, think, and act beyond the local, be they Mongol, Tibetan, Manchu, or Chinese."[28] Elverskog elaborates this picture of Qing cosmopolitanism primarily by describing several examples of Qing literature composed in Inner Asia that not only combined literary traditions from China, Mongolia and/or Tibet but also synthesized these components into a novel yet coherent product.

Similarly, during the search for the Third Jamyang Zhepa, a host of Gelukpa hierarchs from both Amdo and central Tibet fabricated an original Qing ritual out of Tibetan and Chinese components. In the aftermath, Tibetan-language chroniclers would over the span of eighty years engage in an ongoing revisionist project to produce a narrative of these events that posited a legitimate place for the Qing emperor and imperial law in the search process. It should come as little surprise that court-affiliated hierarchs such as the Tukwan *kūtuktu* proved instrumental in the legitimation of the Golden Urn. The Tukwan *kūtuktu* was not intervening on the side of the "Tibetans"; nor would he have conceptualized himself as an "ally" of the dynasty—for it is unlikely that he saw himself as an "enemy" of Tibetan Buddhists. To employ such terms implies an anachronistic dichotomy dividing Geluk Buddhists from the Qing. The resistance that had to be overcome in the case of the urn should not be understood as "Tibetan." It is also based on modern, twentieth-century assumptions concerning the coherence and stability of "Tibetan" as a category of meaning during the Qing period. This is not to say that there was not a strong sense of local identity vis-à-vis "China" and perhaps even other regions of Tibet. Cultural identity was a factor in what was very real resistance to the notion of using the urn. Building on Elverskog, I would add that Qing cosmopolitanism did not necessarily hide the traces of its creation. Much as Tukwan had been willing to confess in his writings that elements of non-Geluk religious traditions had shaped his own teachings,[29] in the case of the identification of the Third Jamyang Zhepa, commentators did not hide the disparate origins of different elements of the search process and the Golden Urn ritual.

The search for the Jamyang Zhepa fell at a unique moment. It was preceded by a burst of legal reforms of Tibetan administration that intensified Qing imperial involvement in central Tibet and, as we have seen in acts 1 and 2, divination technologies. Yet it was followed shortly afterward by the death of the Qianlong emperor and the first imperial succession in sixty-four years—the end of an epoch that had begun well before any of the major characters in the search had been born. The Tibetan-language narratives produced by this encounter between Tibetan Buddhist elites and the Qing colonial bureaucracy thus had the potential to not only define the Qianlong legacy but also shape local understandings of the Geluk–Qing and local–center relationships more broadly. The proper management of the search for the Jamyang Zhepa was thus essential to the survival of the institutional innovations of the Qianlong reign and setting the right tone for the uncertain times that lay ahead. In the following section we will begin our examination of this event from the perspective of the Manchu-language sources.

The Manchu-Language Record

In the early winter of 1796–97, the Xining *amban* Tsebak[30] reported to the throne that he had personally examined three children whom preliminary tests had indicated might be the reincarnation of the Second Jamyang Zhepa. During the winter months it was not unusual for the *amban* to head out to the pastures south of the Yellow River beyond the subprefectures of Guide and Xunhua to check the border posts that marked the Gansu–Qinghai frontier. Early winter, when the earth firmed up and the rivers froze over, and the animals were still fat and healthy, was the perfect time for "tribal Tibetans" (Ma. *aiman i fandze*) from the nomadic regions beyond the frontier to launch raids on the Mongol banners of Qinghai or other communities in Guide and Xunhua. And the frequency of these raids had been increasing of late.[31] The *amban* claimed that since he was in the area, it was "convenient" to drop by the households of the candidate children to make a personal inspection. His subsequent reports suggest that he may have been motivated by more than curiosity, but regardless, what he perhaps hoped would be perceived as conscientiousness landed him in very hot water.

Tsebak's memorial began by quoting the treasurer of the Jamyang *kūtuktu*'s estate, Lozang Dargyé (Ma. *Lobdzangdarji*).[32] The treasurer reported that since the death of his master in 1791, he had traveled frequently in the places of the "Mongols and Tibetans" near the monastery and after much investigation identified three children: 1) Wangchen Bum, the son of Dülagyel (Ma. *Dula*), a headman from Rangen (Ma. *Ranggan*) in Guide subprefecture; 2) Kelzang, the son of Rinchin Gyatso, a "Tibetan subject of the Rongwo Nomunhan of Xunhua subprefecture"; and 3) Bomandorji, the son of Nyima (Ma. *Nima*), a "nomadic Tibetan from Nangra in Guide." After stating that he thought the first two candidates displayed the most potential, the treasurer requested, "Please send these names to Tibet and subject them to the lottery in the Golden Urn!"[33] The depiction of the treasurer's request to use the urn as voluntary is significant. The Labrang leadership was presented as not merely obeying the law but rather actively seeking out the intercession of the Qing. During the nineteenth century, this leitmotif appeared in numerous memorials from Xining legitimating the use of the urn.[34]

Tsebak also filed a secret note that accompanied the memorial. This memo raised a thorny problem: he worried that the son of Dülagyel might be disqualified on account of his father's status as headman.[35] According to Tsebak, the law stated that "When rebirths arise, they cannot be recognized among the sons of Mongol *han, wang, beile, beise, gung, jasak,* or *taijis.*[36] Recognize them only from among the sons of *taiji* with no official post or subjects of common status." Tsebak wondered if this statute applied to Dülagyel's son, even though the father was not a Mongol and, although an "indigenous official of the sixth rank," did not obviously hold one of the aristocratic ranks the Qing doled out to Mongol nobles. Yet the problem was even more complicated:

> Although it is not permitted to enter his child [as a candidate], however, the birth of this child was auspicious and impressive. The treasurer Lozang Dargyé and everyone else collectively acclaims this marvelous child as the reincarnation of the *kūtuktu.* This year Dülagyel, in obedience to your servant Tsebak's orders, delivered and promulgated [official] instructions among the raw tribal Tibetans. In the course of recovering goods that had been stolen by bandits, he zealously made a great effort. Since Dülagyel is after all merely a sixth-rank indigenous official, he should not be compared to the Mongol khans, princes, dukes, and so forth. In violation of the statutes, your servant has rashly not withdrawn the name of his child. . . . I politely request an edict indicating whether it is appropriate to enter the son of Dülagyel into the determination of the Jamyang *kūtuktu* by drawing lots.[37]

Tsebak's hope that his "rash" petition would find a sympathetic ear was not unprecedented. Just a year earlier the emperor had granted a special dispensation to the community of the Cagan Nomunhan, a prominent reincarnation lineage that administered a Mongol banner in the pastures south of the Yellow River. In that case, the edict permitted the monk's disciples to identify candidates as they saw fit because the lineage was "important" and had recently assisted in rounding up bandits (much like Dülagyel purportedly had).[38] Unfortunately for Tsebak, he had misjudged the underlying purpose of the law.

According to the emperor, the problem lay not with the family background of Dülagyel but with the fact that the treasurer had already begun to promote the child as the authentic reincarnation. He dispatched the following orders to Sungyun in Lhasa:

> Tsebak has memorialized concerning the matter of identifying the rebirth of the Jamyang *kūtuktu*. The name of the child of Dülagyel, the headman of Rangan, has been placed at the head of the list. Moreover, he reports that the treasurer Lozang Dargyé has spoken with awe about how this child is probably the rebirth of their *kūtuktu* because the child's birth was auspicious and magnificent. I observe that the subordinate treasurer's earnest opinion reflects only his selfish intentions. [He] obviously desires that the son of the headman will be selected. Yet honestly, if things are done in this manner, for a long time afterward it will be impossible to eliminate widespread skepticism. Therefore, I have passed down a secret order to Sungyun et al. At the time [of the ritual], regardless of which children's names Tsebak sends to Tibet, discreetly and without revealing anything, handle the selection in such a way that the name of the candidate who has been listed first, the son of the Tibetan headman Dülagyel, definitely does not emerge. Regardless of the artifice and cunning you employ, ensure that you disclose nothing to anyone.[39]

Qianlong clearly explained his priority: the identification of persuasive reincarnations, free from what he perceived was the debilitating stain of self-interest and corruption of the Geluk establishment. In contrast, the status of Dülagyel was of perhaps only secondary concern and not even mentioned. Since Dülagyel's son's name was already circulating, it would be tactless to directly prohibit his candidacy. It would be up to Sungyun to identify a "convincing" rebirth by fixing the lottery.

Sungyun and Hening responded to the imperial instructions as follows:

> The [emperor's] continuous protection of the Yellow Doctrines is authoritatively handled with completely lofty intentions. It will not do for the suspect and evil customs of the treasurer to flourish. At this time I still have not received the names of the three children from Tsebak. After the treasurer Lozang Dargyé has arrived, your servants will promptly, in accordance with the existing [laws], take the Dalai Lama et al. before the image of the Holy One [i.e., the emperor] to recite sutras. There in the presence of the treasurer and the Dalai

Lama we will inscribe the names of the three children on the lots. Yet your servants will covertly remember [which is which]. Your servant Sungyun will himself place the lots in order into the Golden Urn. When the recitation of prayers concludes, your servant Hening will choose from between the second and third candidates only. It will remain a secret that only the son of the Tibetan headman Dülagyel will not be allowed to emerge. Therefore there will be no grounds for the old doubts to reemerge. Since the identification will have taken place according to the edict, the Dalai Lama will still be convinced and will not be persuaded by anything the treasurer Lozang Dargyé says. Additionally, here in Tibet there is the nephew of the former Jamyang *kūtuktu* and also a chamberlain lama [Ma. *jonir*, Tib. *drönyer*] named Sherab Kanjur [Ma. Šarab Coinjur]. Könchok Senggé [the nephew of Jamyang Zhepa 02] has been in Tibet for fourteen years; his knowledge of the virtuous teaching of the sutras is great, and he has attained the status of *lharampa*. The disciples of the Jamyang *kūtuktu* all respect this Könchok Senggé. After the treasurer Lozang Dargyé has arrived, we will gather Könchok Senggé and the chamberlain Sherab Kanjur and let them both also observe the selection of lots. After the reincarnation has been identified, these two [monks] will be sent back [to Amdo] to inform all the disciples. The new reincarnation will be entrusted to Könchok Senggé, who will oversee his education in the sutras. This will also be beneficial. Your servants have secretly conferred and personally written this memorial. We urgently dispatch this to inform Your Highness.[40]

Sungyun and Hening's strategy for manipulating the ritual reveals keen attention to the use of witnesses and more than passing knowledge of the biographies of the monastic population of Lhasa. The *ambans* appear to have undertaken at least a basic survey of Labrang's connections in central Tibet. Although the identity of the chamberlain Sherab Kanjur is difficult to verify in Tibetan sources,[41] Könchok Senggé (Ma. Gongcuk Sengge, 1768–1833) was indeed the nephew of the Second Jamyang Zhepa and had recently received the highest scholarly credentials (Ma. *jaramba*, Tib. *lharampa*) from Gomang College at Drepung monastery.[42] The *ambans* planned to affix the authority of this monk to the selection process by including him in the ritual and make him a stakeholder in the continuing legitimacy of the candidate by honoring him with the appointment of tutor to the next

Jamyang Zhepa. The role of the Dalai Lama, in contrast, appears to have been considered rather insignificant. The emperor was pleased with this plan. In the margins of the memorial he jotted, "Good! Do not divulge this to anyone!"[43]

The emperor issued a court letter to Tsebak and Lozang Dargyé, the treasurer, with a very different message. Here, he permitted all three original names to be sent to Tibet. He admonished the treasurer, however, writing that, "When identifying any *trülku*, [we] prayerfully seek a decision from the Buddha. This matter cannot be determined through the surmises of any human."[44] The emperor then encouraged Tsebak to send the treasurer to Tibet in accordance with his original plans: "Furthermore, having elucidated the treasurer, definitely have him sent to Tibet. If he observes things with his own eyes, perhaps regardless of which candidate is selected, his suspicions will disappear."[45] The Xining *amban* does not appear to have been informed about the plan to doctor the results of the Golden Urn.

While it might be easy at this point to portray the emperor's actions as cynical manipulations, one should not dismiss out of hand Qianlong's insistence that the Buddha alone could identify reincarnations. The fact that the emperor insisted on secrecy in this matter should not be confused with an admission of wrongdoing. The emperor saw himself as removing a false candidate from the competition, not manipulating the ritual. As emperor and Buddhist adept, his involvement was legitimate—it did not constitute biased human interference like the actions of the treasurer. Rather than narrowing the field, he could have seen himself as opening it up to candidates from less well-connected backgrounds, reminding his officials that in the implementation of the new statute, they should not take their cues from elite Geluk hierarchs.

Although the emperor claimed that he did not mind if Lozang Dargyé proceeded to Lhasa, the treasurer evidently came to understand that he had angered the ruler and resigned from the search. Labeling himself a "foolish Mongol slave" and "dizzy with fear," Lozang Dargyé now claimed that his advanced years made it unwise to travel to "distant lands."[46] The monk now requested permission for a new party, consisting of nineteen monks and led by Belmang Pandita and chamberlain Sherab Gyatso, to set off for Tibet in the spring.

According to Manchu-language reports filed later that year after the Labrang delegation arrived in Lhasa, Sungyun and Hening followed through on their plans and selected between only the second and third candidates. As intended, Könchok Senggé was in attendance and, together with the Dalai Lama and the regent, Tatsak *kūtuktu*, lent authority to the proceedings. Sungyun reported that Könchok Senggé had agreed to return to Labrang and take up the job of chief tutor to the young reincarnation and that the Dalai Lama had bestowed not only a formal name on the young child but also a new title on Könchok Senggé.[47] Three months later, upon receipt of the emperor's acknowledgment of the identification of the Third Jamyang Zhepa, Sungyun reported that he had translated the edict (essentially a reprint of his original memorial reporting the selection) into Tibetan and that Belmang and the other disciples of the Jamyang Zhepa remained persuaded and would return to Labrang the following year to enthrone the child.[48] Reflecting on the successful outcomes of both the Pakpalha and the Jamyang Zhepa cases, Sungyun speculated that in the future it would "be easy" to deal with other reincarnations and that "their past customs could be thoroughly eliminated."[49] He wrote confidently, "If your servants carefully handle each case of drawing the lots of *trülku*, [no one] will dare consult the oracles. If prior to drawing lots we explain to them that this is proper and beneficial and make them understand the foolish blunders of the oracles, they will believe that obeying the imperial decree and drawing lots to make a determination is proper."[50] Although Sungyun claimed to have established "a model" for future searches that excluded the oracles, the Tibetan-language sources reveal that the *amban*'s claims were false, if not intentionally misleading. Sungyun and Hening may have had their secrets, but so did the Tibetans.

The Tibetan-Language Record

By the 1880s, Tibetans and Mongols literate in Tibetan could have located an account of the search for the Third Jamyang Zhepa in at least five different block-printed books. In chronological order, these were: *The Life of the Second Jamyang Zhepa* by the Third Gungtang *kūtuktu*, Könchuk Tenpé Drönmé Pelzangpo (1762–1823); the Second Belmang Pandita's *Labrang Monastery Gazetteer*; *The Life of the Third Jamyang Zhepa* by Khenpo Ngawang Tupten Gyatso (1836–1889); and the biography of Belmang Pandita and the *Oceanic Book*, both by Drakgönpa.

The Third Gungtang *kūtuktu* composed the earliest of these works, the biography of the Second Jamyang Zhepa, in 1797 at the request of

Tukwan Chökyi Nyima.[51] Both of these monks were instrumental in the search process. Gungtang *kūtuktu* had been the chief abbot of Labrang monastery from 1792 to 1798, during which time the rebirth of the Jamyang Zhepa was located and enthroned, and also abbot of Gönlung monastery, the home residence of Tukwan, from 1797 to 1799.[52] Given their close personal relationship, Gungtang's account of the search for the third Jamyang Zhepa may also reflect the views of Tukwan *kūtuktu*. Although but a brief synopsis of these events—only five pages in the modern edition—Gungtang's description laid down a basic narrative that would be reproduced and elaborated on in subsequent accounts.

The next three works to appear all bear the stamp of either Belmang Pandita, Drakgönpa, or both of these authors. As noted earlier, the *Labrang Monastic Gazetteer* was first penned by Belmang in 1800, but subsequently enlarged and repeatedly blockprinted in the 1820s through 1840s. The *Oceanic Book*, a comprehensive history and geography of the Amdo region (part 1) and a history of Labrang and its abbots (part 2), probably achieved the widest contemporary readership of any of the texts that included an account of the search for the Third Jamyang Zhepa.[53] According to his own explanation, Drakgönpa commenced his history of the Amdo region in his youth at the urging of Belmang Pandita. Although early drafts of the history of the "northern lineages" (the monasteries to the north and west of Labrang, the section labeled "part 1" in modern editions) appeared first in 1833 and again in 1849, it was not until 1865 that this historical guide to Labrang, its abbots, and affiliated schools ("part 2") appeared in print.[54] Slightly before this date, in 1864, Drakgönpa completed his biography of his teacher, Belmang Pandita. It included an entire chapter devoted to Belmang's 1797 trip to central Tibet.

On the basis of this chapter's title, "A Description of [Belmang's] Journey to Lhasa, the Place of the Dharma, Where the All-seeing Victorious Pair Presided Harmoniously Over the Identification of the Supreme Incarnation According to the Prophecy of the Superior Deities and the Experience of the Festival of the Breadth of the Dharma," one might assume that the Qing had little role to play in the search for the Third Jamyang Zhepa. However, Drakgönpa argued that the search required the joint involvement of both central Tibet and "China," i.e., the Qing court. He wrote that at the very beginning, "The first sign indicated that this matter must be decided by means of the relationship between Ü [i.e., the Ganden Podrang government in central Tibet] and China [Gyanak]."[55] This sign, as we shall discuss below, was the fact that indigenous authorities in central Tibet and the emperor had directed the estate of the Jamyang Zhepa to seek a final decision using the Golden Urn.

Yet Drakgönpa is also clear that, especially in the early stages of the search, Belmang Pandita felt significant reservations about the imperial directive—based on a sense that this command and the monastery's initial plans for the search were discordant. This frank admission of doubt gives Drakgönpa's retelling of the search a compelling narrative arc that sets it apart from other accounts. Belmang's journey to Lhasa was a life-changing personal pilgrimage that simultaneously consolidated his faith and spread his own reputation as a competent administrator and learned Buddhist scholar. This was the only trip to central Tibet that he undertook during his life. Moreover, the confirmation of the Third Jamyang Zhepa by means of both the Golden Urn and other tests affirmed for him the legitimacy of an order in which the Qing state and the Geluk church were integrally linked. Whether intentional or not, Drakgönpa's construction of a narrative journey from skepticism to deeply held personal conviction makes a highly effective argument for the legitimacy of the child who was ultimately identified as the Third Jamyang Zhepa, as well as of the Golden Urn. And as a reincarnation who himself was confirmed by the Third Jamyang Zhepa in 1804, Drakgönpa had ample personal reasons for promoting his authenticity.

Khenpo Ngawang Tupten Gyatso began drafting the *Life of the Third Jamyang Zhepa* four years after his death in 1855, but the final work does not seem to have appeared in print until 1889, the year the author died.[56] This work was directly influenced by Belmang's account as transcribed by Drakgönpa, since several long and important passages are either quotations or paraphrases of Drakgönpa's biography of Belmang Pandita. As Belmang's student, Ngawang Tupten Gyatso also would have heard about the search first hand. Ngawang Tupten Gyatso's status as fifty-first abbot of Labrang gave this account—the most elaborate of the accounts studied here—the imprimatur of the Jamyang Zhepa's estate and the monastery leadership.

As is typical in eighteenth- and nineteenth-century hagiographies of Geluk *trülku*, the abbot Ngawang Tupten Gyatso preceded the chapter on the recognition of the reincarnation using the Golden Urn with a detailed history of the Third Jamyang Zhepa's family and birth. By testifying to the noble deeds of his ancestors, as well as the various auspicious occurrences and supernatural events that accompanied his mother's pregnancy, his birth, and his early childhood, Ngawang Tupten Gyatso immediately began the task of establishing the *trülku*'s authenticity.[57] Having described his recognition and enthronement, the remainder of the book offers a panoramic view of his miraculous achievements as an embodied bodhisattva, as well as his work as a Geluk scholar and temporal administrator. Confident throughout that Kelzang Bum really was the Third Jamyang Zhepa, Ngawang Tupten Gyatso nonetheless inserted several details that hint at the existence of an alternate story.

These five texts were themselves key components of an ongoing process of legitimation. Taken together, they narrate a single story with few contradictions or inconsistencies. However, each author also introduces some unique elements that reveal how Geluk elites with varying types of affiliation to Labrang monastery intervened to resolve concerns about the accuracy of the search. The following section will simultaneously narrate the history of the search for the Third Jamyang Zhepa and examine the different tactics employed to solve the problems posed by the Golden Urn and the actions of Qing field officials stationed in Xining and Lhasa.

The Power of Dreams

The emperor's insistence on the implementation of the Golden Urn law seems willfully ill conceived when considered in light of the plans already circulating at Labrang for the identification of the reincarnation of the Second Jamyang Zhepa. Unlike the case of the Pakpalha *kütuktu* in 1795, wherein Heliyen and Sungyun had already laid the groundwork for the use of the urn well before the search commenced, there is no record of advance work by Qing officials at Labrang in the aftermath of the death of the Second Jamyang Zhepa in 1792. Instead, prior to the visit of the Xining *amban*, Tsebak, the Labrang community had already begun to plan a recognition procedure modeled after the one that had identified the Great Fifth Dalai Lama. Not only did this seemingly preclude any use of the Golden Urn, but it also carried the sanction of a historical tradition independent of and prior to any Qing claims of authority over Tibetan Buddhists or reincarnation.

According to the *Life of the Third Jamyang Zhepa*, shortly after the death of the Second Jamyang Zhepa, a well-educated monk from Tongkhor monastery in Amdo traveled to "Tibet [Tib. *Böd*]" in order to offer a commemoration of his life and accomplishments.[58] This monk then requested a divination from the Longdöl Lama (1719–1794) on how to locate the reincarnation.[59] According to his biographers, in the 1790s the Longdöl Lama was one of the most august and popular teachers living in central Tibet, with a wide network of students and disciples across Inner Asia.[60] Although he hailed originally from Kham, he seems to have had many connections to Amdo and Labrang monastery. Among his students was the nephew of the Second Jamyang Zhepa, Könchok Senggé.[61] The Longdöl Lama advised the monk from Tongkhor monastery that the reincarnation of the Jamyang Zhepa should be identified by conducting a dough ball investigation (Tib. *zendril*) before the image of Manjuvajra at Reting monastery (Tib. Reting Jowo Jampé Dorjé), as had been done when the reincarnation of the Fourth Dalai Lama was determined in the early 1620s.[62] The Longdöl Lama also specified that the divination should be conducted only after the disciples of the Jamyang Zhepa had completed a *sadhana* ritual from the Kadampa tradition.[63] Finally, the biography of the Third Jamyang Zhepa reports that Longdöl warned that no other method would deliver an accurate result: "Neither a lama nor a Dharma protector [i.e., an oracle] is capable of making this decision. Only after one has completed the Kadam *sadhana* of the 'sixteen spheres' before the Manjuvajra of Reting will the correct [result] drop when one conducts the dough ball divination."[64] Both Gungtang *kūtuktu* and Drakgönpa record similar advice from Longdöl in their accounts of the search.[65] The biographer of the Third Jamyang Zhepa, however, adds a further detail, noting that when the delegation from Tongkhor monastery returned to Amdo and reported the Longdöl Lama's advice, the Tongkhor *kūtuktu* dreamt that he had seen the Jamyang Zhepa return to Labrang, providing further confirmation that the Longdöl Lama's divination was correct.[66]

Thus when the Labrang community received the imperial edict ordering them to use the Golden Urn in the spring of 1797, they already had alternate plans in place and had been warned by a highly respected Geluk hierarch that any deviation from the elaborate ritual procedure jeopardized the accuracy of the search. Moreover, the Longdöl Lama's placement of the Jamyang Zhepa lineage within a ritual tradition that evoked the "great wisdom, great auspiciousness, vast power, and immense generosity of the Great Fifth [Dalai Lama]"[67] meant that departure from this program would also threaten the historical association between the Jamyang Zhepas and the Fifth Dalai Lama. The Great Fifth had personally blessed the First Jamyang Zhepa (1648–1721/22) when he was a young child and, after the boy had arrived in Lhasa to continue his religious studies, initiated him as a novice and eventually granted him the full vows of ordination. Henceforth, both the First and Second Jamyang Zhepas had direct personal relations with successive Dalai Lamas, as both teachers and disciples. This relationship held profound significance for the Labrang community, as it quite literally embodied their intimacy with the center of the Geluk faith, despite the vast geographic distance between Lhasa and Labrang.

The imperial instructions were met with a mixture of concern and derision. Gungtang wrote that shortly after Labrang received the edict, they raised their concerns with the Tukwan *kūtuktu*, who had traveled to the monastery to examine the three candidates. "They insistently queried of the honorable Tukwan *rinpoché*, 'If the [Golden Urn divination] is performed using these three names, as a matter of course one will be drawn. It is very important that the root principle is not mistaken. Is it possible to hope that there is another method and that if the [ritual] is postponed the [true incarnation] will emerge?' "[68] Drakgönpa provided further details, noting how monks at Labrang made light of the controversy by pointing out the superficial similarity between the two sets of instructions: "At that time, the lamas of Labrang Tashi Khyil sarcastically joked, 'The dough ball divination is definitely required!' "[69] Belmang, however, upon learning of the emperor's edict, worried aloud, "In that case, other than follow [the emperor's] command, is there any other choice? But will it be possible to truly get the unmistaken reincarnation?"[70]

The Tukwan *kūtuktu* played the key role in allaying these concerns. According to the *Life of the Third Jamyang Zhepa*, after the names of the potential candidates had been collected, Tukwan was invited to Labrang to consult with the Gungtang and Hortsang *trülkus*, the two most senior of the four "Golden Throne holders"[71] of the monastery at that time. At the conclusion of this meeting, Tukwan announced, "Henceforth, the two Golden Throne holders and myself, having conducted the recognition tests, affirm that among the four [candidates] there is indeed the true incarnation. Thus it is necessary to hold a dough ball examination [*zentak*] in the chapel that holds the remains of the two previous incarnations."[72] While it would seem from this statement that Tukwan was advocating yet another method of identifying the reincarnation, he modified his advice on the basis of a dream that occurred to him that evening. The *Life of the Third Jamyang Zhepa* describes the dream as follows:

> That night in his dream, [Tukwan] found himself sitting together with the Great Sovereign Emperor at the summer retreat [in Chengde]. A man appeared who claimed to be from the holy estate of the Jamyang Zhepa. In his sash he had tucked four arrows. He then took three arrows into his hand. He shot the first, which missed the target. The second arrow, however, struck the target, and afterward he did not shoot again. [Later] when [Tukwan] stated that [this dream] was a sign that the unmistaken [reincarnation] was among the first two, all the monks were as ecstatic as magpies when they hear thunder.[73]

In contrast to the previous dream of the Tongkhor *kūtuktu* that sanctioned the Longdöl Lama's method, Tukwan appears to have introduced his own competing dream, one that clearly legitimized the participation of the Qing emperor and approved of the method dictated by the new statute on the Golden Urn. The dream also winnowed the four candidates that had been located by the search party down to three and sent a clear signal that most likely the second candidate would prove to be the genuine reincarnation. With the exception of the *Labrang Monastery Gazetteer*, all four of the other books mention this dream. However, their authors deployed it at slightly different moments in the chronology of events.

The author of the biography of the Third Jamyang Zhepa, Khenpo Ngawang Tupten Gyatso, wrote that Tukwan announced his dream at Labrang well before the community had received word that they would be required to use the Golden Urn. As noted above, after conducting their first round of visits to households of promising children in the spring and summer of 1796, the leaders of the search party brought four names back to Labrang and requested Tukwan's advice. Following this meeting and the promulgation of the dream, Tukwan traveled to Xining and informed the *amban* of the status of the search.[74] According to this account, it was only at this point that the *amban* personally traveled to the pastures between Xining and Labrang to visit the candidates. The biographer writes, "At that time, because it became clear for the son of Dülagyel of Rangan, it quickly became common opinion that this was the true and unmistaken incarnation."[75] Here we have evidence for the accuracy of the *amban*'s report that

Dülagyel's son was widely viewed as the most promising candidate. However, this biography records that when the *amban* submitted his memorial to the emperor, he wrote that the second candidate, not Dülagyel's son, was probably the actual reincarnation.[76] Since the Manchu documents reveal that this was not the case, it seems likely that either the author or his sources revised this detail in the aftermath of the search.[77] According to Khenpo Ngawang Tupten Gyatso, only after the *amban*'s visit did Labrang learned definitively that the Golden Urn would have to be consulted.[78] The structure of this narrative would suggest, therefore, that the imperial command was but the fulfillment of Tukwan's prophetic dream.

Of Drakgönpa's two relevant books, the *Oceanic Book* does not mention the Longdöl Lama's instructions at all and, in a fashion similar to the *Life of the Third Jamyang Zhepa*, presents Tukwan's visit to Labrang and his dream as occurring before the community learned of the imperial decree.[79] However, Drakgönpa added a small yet telling detail. He writes that although prior to his dream, Tukwan had instructed the disciples to conduct a dough ball divination (Tib. *zengyur*) at Labrang, after the dream he stated that "although representatives will be sent to Ü, the outcome will still be the same as in my dream."[80] In other words, Tukwan appears to have predicted that the site of the divination would be shifted to Lhasa. Thus this account not only minimizes the existence of competing instructions but also presents Tukwan's dream as a clear affirmation of the Golden Urn method.

Drakgönpa's other account of the search, contained in his biography of Belmang Pandita, as well as the Gungtang *kūtuktu*'s recollection of the events, both position the emperor's edict ordering the use of the urn as arriving shortly after the instructions from the Longdöl Lama. Tukwan's dream is introduced later.[81] Thus, in Gungtang's narrative, Tukwan's dream is more easily interpreted as reconciling two potentially conflicting sets of instructions. In fact, Gungtang records that Tukwan's dream was the direct result of the request for a divination made by those at Labrang who were troubled by the two sets of instructions.[82] Furthermore, Gungtang implies that it was only after Tukwan had approved the ritual that the emperor made the final decision to send the candidates' names to Lhasa to be tested in the urn.[83]

The temporal proximity of Gungtang's account, published in 1798, might support the argument that the utility of Tukwan's dream was such that later authors pushed it up in the chronology of events, granting him prophetic authority. Given the accuracy of the dream and its obvious sanction of Qing imperial involvement in the search, it is impossible not to take this argument a step further and speculate that the dream was a useful *ex post facto* fabrication of either the Tukwan *kūtuktu* himself or our authors. Regardless, the printing of Gungtang's account in 1798 indicates that information about the dream was circulating no later than late 1797 or early 1798, roughly the same time that news of the identification of the Third Jamyang Zhepa using the Golden Urn first arrived in Amdo. The consistent inclusion of Tukwan's dream in successive accounts written between 1798 until the 1880s demonstrates that it was understood as a key instrument for legitimating the candidacy of the second child.

Yet Gungtang also wrote that there were those who perceived a basic similarity between Longdöl's and Qianlong's instructions: both had ordered an "investigation by rolling" (Tib. *takdril*).[84] Drakgönpa also promoted this equivalency in his biography of Belmang Pandita. This seemingly coincidental agreement between two separately issued decrees, one from central Tibet and one from the Qing ruler, was for Belmang a "sign" or "omen" (Tib. *tsenté*) of the "connection" between Tibet and China.[85] According to Gungtang, the fact that the emperor had also ordered a *takdril* "increased [people's] trust and confidence in what the [Longdöl] lama had said."[86]

Gungtang and Drakgönpa's claim of similarity between the Golden Urn and the dough ball divination hinged on the semantic incorporation of the urn into the divination tradition. Drakgönpa, much like the other three authors of these works, rarely used the term "golden urn" (Tib. *ser gyi bum*). Instead, he almost always referred to the imperially sanctioned procedure as *zentak* (a "dough ball investigation"), *zendril* ("rolled-up dough balls"), *zengyur* (a "dough ball divination"), or *takdril* ("an investigation by rolling [things up]"), thus firmly placing it within an indigenous category of divination technologies. Even where the words "golden urn" are used, they are usually found within a phrase that presents the urn as a type of *takdril*, as in the following example from Gungtang's account: "Shortly thereafter, a golden edict arrived from the Manjusri emperor stating, 'With regard to the *trülku*, the identification must be made by conducting a *takdril* within the golden urn.'"[87] When describing the final ritual, Gungtang avoided direct reference to the golden urn, writing instead that a "name-card transformation" (Tib. *tsen jang gyurwa*) had been done, thus conveying the notion the cards had been "transformed" in the ritual in the same fashion as a dough ball might be in the *zengyur* ritual.[88] If the Tukwan *kūtuktu's* dream can be understood as a strategy for legitimating the urn, the semantic assimilation of the urn into an indigenous category was part of a related set of tactics that minimized the appearance of incongruity between the two traditions.

Such efforts to harmonize the two ritual prescriptions can be found in several places in these texts. For instance, Gungtang's account neglects to mention any of the specific details of the Longdöl Lama's instructions (such as location or accompanying offerings and prayers) other than that the ritual should occur "before *something like* the Jowo *rinpoché*" (emphasis added). Thus when he writes in the following sentence that the emperor has also ordered that ritual be held before a "Jowo," it appears that the Longdöl Lama and the emperor were talking about the same image.[89]

That Gungtang would downplay the differences between the instructions of Longdöl Lama and the emperor in his text is perhaps not surprising given that both Drakgönpa and Khenpo Ngawang Tupten Gyatso quote Gungtang as arguing that the venue of the ritual was of little significance. It appears that even as the search party prepared to depart Labrang for central Tibet there were still reservations about the imperial instructions. Just days before their departure, Belmang and the other leader of the search party, the estate chamberlain Shérap Gyatso,[90] met with the Gungtang *kūtuktu*, who pointedly instructed them to obey the imperial instructions. According to the *Life of the Third Jamyang Zhepa*, the Gungtang *kūtuktu* stated:

> Although it is not appropriate to perform the *zengyur* before the Manjuvajra at Reting monastery, having completed the basic conditions by offering the sixteen spheres there and reverently praying, is it really still necessary to roll up the dough balls at that place? While on the road, you should inquire in detail about this with the Tukwan *rinpoché*.[91]

Belmang's biography records this same statement, although modified slightly to suggest that Gungtang felt strongly that the ceremony of the "sixteen spheres" and the prayers were important prerequisites that should be completed even if they did not ultimately perform the *zengyur* at Reting monastery.[92] Gungtang's advice was significant. First of all, he was unequivocal in his support for the imperial command. Second, he authorized the Belmang Pandita to reconcile the conflicting methods by incorporating elements from the original plan into Qianlong's new ritual procedure. Whether the divination was held at Reting monastery or the Jokhang, the result would be accurate, provided that they sincerely completed the preliminary rituals as spelled out by Longdöl.

When Belmang Pandita and several assistants visited Tukwan near Kumbum monastery several weeks later, the latter affirmed Gungtang's advice:

> The Tukwan *rinpoché* clearly explained, "According to the words of Gungtang and the Qianlong emperor's prior edict, 'High-status monks from [places like] Kumbum must be recognized through a trial of the *zendril* before the Jowo [statue] in Lhasa, whereas lower-status *trülku* shall be tested before sandalwood Jowo.'[93] However, nowadays because many people regard the *zendril* as no different from simply tossing lots, there have arisen various controversies as to whether this actually makes accurate [identifications]. [For example] previously, the elder prince of Choné said sarcastically, 'If one performed a *zendril* to determine who was the [incarnation] of Tsongkhapa—either myself or Khyagé *pönlop*,[94] of course one of us would be selected!' Although some people understand things in this manner, due to our faith in the Jewel [i.e., the Dharma] we each have no qualms about the *zengyur*. It is a fundamental principle of the Dalai Lama that the most important matters of that honorable Government are decided before the Lhamo *sungjönma*.[95] Moreover, [this course of action] accords with my own previous dream. It resembles what will befall us."[96]

The quotation above is from Khenpo Ngawang Tupten Gyatso's biography of the Third Jamyang Zhepa. Drakgönpa's biography of Belmang Pandita also records this exchange but adds, however, that Tukwan also provided Belmang with several prayers dedicated to the deity Tara written by Changkya Rolpai Dorjé that he should recite en route for good luck.[97] Such actions further legitimized the journey and embellished this increasingly hybrid recognition process with a liturgical framework. Overall, Tukwan's statement accomplished several important tasks. First, he again reminded Belmang (and, of course, the readers of these narratives) of the overlapping endorsement of the imperial command by himself and Gungtang *kūtuktu*, as well as by supernatural authorities in the form of his dream. Second, he compared the imperially sanctioned divination ritual to the set of divination practices historically conducted before the Lhamo Sunjönma by the central Tibetan government. The point Tukwan appears to be making is that these things are fundamentally similar and therefore of little concern. Finally, Tukwan argues that the broader category of divination technologies labeled *zengyur* or *zendril* are legitimate *Buddhist* practices. Both Gungtang and Tukwan maintain that those who have faith in the dharma and conduct the ritual with sincerity need not fear the results.

This leads us to an interim conclusion: we should not assume, as modern scholarship does, that Tibetans from the outset viewed the establishment of the Golden Urn as foreign "interference."[98] From the perspective of Gungtang, Tukwan, and ultimately, Belmang and later disciples of the Third Jamyang Zhepa at Labrang monastery such as Drakgönpa and Khenpo Ngawang Tupten Gyatso, it was the apparent incongruity of the two ritual configurations that posed a problem, not the "Chinese" origins of the Golden Urn. Belmang and Drakgönpa did not shy away from characterizing Qianlong's instructions as symbolic of "China." Yet the foreignness or (perhaps more appropriately) strangeness of the ritual could be elided or obscured by discussing it in terms from a familiar indigenous tradition. Moreover, as the critique of the Choné prince reveals, the overall category of divinations known as *zengyur* were suspect, not the Golden Urn in particular. Tukwan's commentary suggests that he was aware of a strand of thinking circulating in Amdo that considered dough ball divinations in general to be nothing more than "lotteries" that could be easily twisted and warped by human self-interest. The problem the Qing court faced in implementing the Golden Urn policy was therefore a problem indigenous elites in Inner Asia also faced whenever they engaged in divination: they had to overcome the possibility that divinations could be mistaken for lotteries.

Divinations and Machinations in Lhasa

The search party peregrinated methodically across the Amdo region before departing for central Tibet. On September 3, 1797, the party crossed over the mountains into the territory of Nakchu, the first major outpost within the jurisdiction of the Ganden Podrang government. Before arriving at the town, they were met by two Tibetan lay officials[99] who delivered confidential letters from the senior Lhasa *amban*, Sungyun. Sungyun informed Belmang that although he had planned to travel to Tsang on an inspection tour, he had delayed his departure and urged the delegation from Labrang to hasten to Lhasa before September 20.[100] As it turned out, this was the date the *amban* had set to conduct the Golden Urn ritual, because it was "auspicious according to the Chinese calendar."[101] The sudden speed required of the delegation seems to have taken them by surprise. The accelerated schedule caused problems for Belmang because it forced him to circumscribe the ritual preparations for the Golden Urn and thus threatened his ability to blend the ritual demanded by the Longdöl Lama with the instructions of the Qing emperor and guarantee a result credible among the Labrang community.

Belmang and the chamberlain were provided with fresh mounts by Tibetan officials and traveled ahead of the rest of the delegation, arriving in Lhasa on September 12. Since the arduous journey had sickened the chamberlain, Belmang "had to shoulder the responsibilities alone."[102] He immediately met with Sungyun. Drakgönpa's and Khenpo Ngawang Tupten Gyatso's accounts leave the impression that the *amban* was kind and accommodating. On learning that the chamberlain had become ill, he offered to postpone their meeting. Belmang did not delay, however, and when he "met with the *amban* it elicited feelings of pleasure like the encounter between a mother and son."[103] Sungyun advised Belmang that they should promptly handle the matter. At this point, Belmang appears to have attempted to slow down the process, expressing concern that the date could not be set until he had met with the Dalai Lama and the regent, Tatsak *kūtuktu* Yeshé Lozang Tenpé Gönpo.[104]

Sungyun agreed to this request, but it is difficult not to suspect that *ambans'* seemingly sincere desire to "handle the matter expeditiously"[105] disguised ulterior motives. The less time that the delegates spent in Lhasa, the fewer opportunities there would be for them to settle on a final candidate by other means or raise objections to the procedure. The separation of Belmang and the chamberlain from the rest of the party also meant that there would be fewer witnesses when the ritual was conducted. Within two days of their arrival, Drakgönpa reports, the *ambans* had fixed the date and ordered the Golden Urn moved to the Potala to begin a week of preparatory services under the watch of the Dalai Lama. Although Belmang does not appear to have a problem with selecting a date based on a "Chinese calendar," at his second meeting with Sungyun, "He informed the *amban* that he had grave concerns about the upcoming identification of the *trülku* because they had not even had the slightest opportunity to request the advice of the Panchen Lama."[106] Sungyun agreed to settle this issue by sending a letter to the Panchen Lama on behalf of Belmang. There are hints in several of the sources that the lack of consultation and involvement by the Panchen Lama was considered problematic, both at the time and by later authors.[107]

While in Nakchu, Belmang had received a separate letter from the Tatsak *kūtuktu* in addition to those from the *ambans*. The contents of this letter and the conversations that subsequently transpired between Belmang and the regent reveal that both monks had other concerns that they did not share with the *ambans*. These concerns led to a series of activities that the *ambans* may not have known about. Drakgönpa, the primary source for this information, claims that the subject of the conversations was confidential and that the activities undertaken as a result were conducted in secret.

In his letter to Belmang, the regent asked, "How many candidates are there for the reincarnation? Among these candidates, who is the most promising? What did you report to the Xining *amban* and the emperor? How do you plan to report to the *amban* here?. . . The Jamyang Zhepa is more important to [me] than the Buddhas of the Three Epochs. Therefore, on account of his grace, I will diligently offer all assistance here to him."[108] Drakgönpa gives no comment on whether and how Belmang responded to this inquiry. If the tone of these questions seems to imply that the regent had already received news about the search and possibly a conflict between the estate of the Jamyang Zhepa and the Qing government, the conversation that transpired when Belmang first met the regent confirms this hunch:

> When the Tatsak *rinpoché* held a private audience with Belmang Pandita, he asked, "Among the three candidates, which is the most promising or preferred?"
>
> [Belmang] replied, "There is no difference."
>
> "Then why is the one from Rangan[109] more famous?"
>
> [Belmang] jokingly replied, "It is just like the saying, 'The Amdowas speak in code and the Khampas feign ignorance.' "[110]
>
> [Tatsak *rinpoché*] laughed at this.
>
> Belmang then recounted [for the regent] the advice that had been successively given by Longdöl Lama, Tukwan *rinpoché*, and Gungtang Jamyang. [Belmang Pandita] then made the following detailed request:

Tatsak rinpoché o8 Yeshé Lozang Tenpé Gönpo
Rubin Museum C2011.2.1 (HAR 65916)

"At Tashi Khyil [Monastery],[111] when we departed, it was widely known that the *zengyur* would be conducted before the Lhasa Jowo. But now it seems as though the ritual will take place in the Potala. Although [we realize] it makes no difference, because [they are people] of a remote place, it is possible that their expectations will not be satisfied. If things thus transpire, if someone like you were to conduct the ritual before the [Lhasa] Jowo *rinpoché*, the people would be satisfied. But who would dare ask such a thing?"

At this the [regent] replied, "I can do the ritual myself in front of the Jowo, but it must be kept as secret as possible." He then continued, "I plan on going before the Jo[wo] on the twenty-sixth and will conduct the *zengyur*. Furthermore, I will bring pieces from the *zentak* that was conducted before the Manjuvajra Jowo [of Reting monastery] and offer them before the naturally occurring Lokeshvara [image] in the Potala."[112]

The regent had already independently received information concerning the relative standings of the three candidates. However, Belmang was unwilling to divulge any further information or state his own preferences. Drakgönpa offers no explanation for his teacher's silence. Belmang might have been reluctant because he did not want to present any details that might bias Tatsak *kūtuktu* if and when the regent conducted additional *zengyur*. For Belmang, the overriding concern was that the format of the divination ritual had been changed yet again. They had not expected Sungyun to shift the venue to the Potala. The Tibetan-language accounts concur that the emperor's original edict positioned the ceremony in the Jokhang.[113] And on the basis of what Qing officials in Gansu and Qinghai claimed to have discussed with local people, it is not surprising that the Labrang community would have had this expectation. The Xining *amban*'s original Manchu-language reports from the time of his visit to Labrang state that the ritual was to be held in the Jokhang Temple.[114] It appears, however, that from the time when he first learned of the search for the Jamyang Zhepa and the need to fix it, Sungyun had intended to hold the ceremony in the Potala, "before the painting of the Holy One"—i.e., Qianlong.[115] This was where he had also conducted the ritual on behalf of the Pakpalha *kūtuktu*.

Sungyun had probably not intended to make the upcoming ceremony less credible to the delegation from Labrang. But from the latter's perspective, the shift in location had far-reaching implications because different sites were home to different combinations of tutelary deities, protectors, and buddhas. Different sites therefore required different ritual preparation, and the associated deities might look on the affair with unequal degrees of benevolence. The change in location thus called into question the carefully laid plans that Belmang, Tukwan, and Gungtang assembled before the delegation departed Amdo for central Tibet. That change and the accelerated schedule provoked a flurry of secret activity by Belmang and other Geluk hierarchs in Lhasa in the days leading up to the Golden Urn ceremony.

Some of these activities had already been planned well before Belmang Pandita arrived in Lhasa. Most importantly, the delegation sought the assistance and prophecies of the oracles (i.e., the *chökyong*/protectors) and the Eighth Dalai Lama—actions the Qing state had vigorously tried to proscribe following the introduction of the Golden Urn. The biography of the Third Jamyang Zhepa and the *Oceanic Book* describe in detail the results of these inquiries. Given the seemingly comprehensive solicitation of the oracles around Lhasa and the importance of the Jamyang Zhepa within the Geluk establishment, it is unlikely that the *ambans* did not know what was happening. Drakgönpa summarized the advice of the oracles as follows:

> Prophecies were sought from several protectors. The Nechung stated that, "For the time being, it appears that the first [child] is authentic. At the time of the *zentak*, [I] will indicate the authentic one by means of an invisible action." The Tenma[116] prophesied, "The second one, Kelzang, the son of Rinchen Gyatso, is the true emanation body. During the *zentak* he will be [identified] through an invisible action." The Gadong stated, "The first one has a beautiful appearance. However, you must still do prayer services for each one in accordance with the proper order of the recognition process."[117]

All three oracles qualified their predictions with tentative language, and the very diversity of their answers necessitated further tests. It is ironic that although the emperor was insistent that the oracles be stamped out, in this case, their prophecies were interpreted as reinforcing the need to conduct the *zentak* in the Golden Urn. Contrary to what Qianlong had hoped yet in line with advice offered to the emperor by the Galdan Siretu *kūtuktu* and other Gelukpa lamas in 1792, the oracles could indeed facilitate the use of the urn.

It was not until after the oracles had been consulted that Belmang finally had the opportunity to meet with the Eighth Dalai Lama. Belmang's biographer states that his teacher was "filled with happiness and inspiration," then quickly turns to other matters. In contrast to the detailed presentation of Belmang's more personal interactions with the *ambans*, the regent, and even other lamas in central Tibet, the impression given is that the Dalai Lama's influence on the proceedings was important, but not transformative. The Tibetan-language sources portray the Dalai Lama as being directed by the *ambans* to conduct various rites, as opposed to taking any initiatives of his own accord.

From the perspective of the commentators from Labrang, the final significant event that occurred before the urn ritual was the completion of the so-called "Sixteen Spheres" *sadhana* that had been ordered by the Longdöl Lama. According to Khenpo Ngawang Tupten Gyatso, this ritual was organized by the regent and conducted by monks at Reting monastery.[118] Gungtang also emphasized this event and noted that Könchok Senggé, the nephew of the Second Jamyang Zhepa, played a leading role.[119]

In the *Oceanic Book*, Drakgönpa described the ceremony involving the Golden Urn on September 20 (JQ 02/08/01) as follows:

Holding the same wish, everyone came on the first day of the Auspicious Month to the palace [at the top of the Potala]. The Supreme Victorious One arrived, treading on lotus, as did the pillars of the teaching of the Snowy Lands. Together with the two *ambans* who protect Tibet and in front of the likeness of the emperor, a determination was made by spinning the Golden Urn. At that time, the Supreme Victorious One extemporaneously chanted true words so that there would emerge from the urn the authentic name card. When the great lamas together with the chief cantor of Namgyel monastery[120] and its monks, together with the whole congregation, were chanting prayers, the *amban* witnessed that the name card of [the Jamyang Shepa] leaped up. Finally, the "Flame of the Teachings," "The Dharma King," and the "Self and Others" [prayers] were chanted rhythmically in unison; thus their pure intentions were conveyed.[121]

Overall, this depiction legitimates the Qing ritual by attributing the agency of the correct selection to the Dalai Lama, protectors, and overall sincerity of the congregation. The *ambans* were merely the instruments or "witnesses" of the unseen forces invoked by the Dalai Lama and the other participants. In Gungtang's account, the Qing elements are even further minimized. For instance, instead of being held before a *thangka* of Qianlong, he wrote that the ritual was conducted before the Jowo Lokeshvara image.[122] In the two biographies, Drakgönpa and Khenpo Ngawang Tupten Gyatso offered accounts of the ritual that are broadly similar to that in the *Oceanic Book*. Although they both provide a more extensive list of participants and witnesses, they place slightly more focus on the actions of the *ambans*. The *ambans* are reported to have prostrated twice, once before placing the lots in the urn and once before drawing the lot.[123] As in the accounts of the Pakpalha identification, the human agency of the Qing officials was downplayed: Khenpo Ngawang Tupten Gyatso quoted Hening as turning to the audience and exclaiming, "The name card of the Supreme Incarnation [the Jamyang Zhepa] leaped upward of its own accord!"[124]

According to the Third Jamyang Zhepa's biographer, the drawing of the winning lot was followed by a sudden and seemingly spontaneous outburst from Belmang's partner, the chamberlain, who had apparently roused himself from his sickbed to attend the ceremony. The statement provided a summary judgment on the proceedings and asserted in no uncertain terms the significance of the emperor's grace. As we have seen in the introduction to this chapter, the *ambans* were struck by it as well and reported it to the emperor. The biographer of the Third Jamyang Zhepa commented, "There arose amazement among all with regard to the splendor of the uncoerced speech and actions [of the chamberlain], whose health had not been good on account of not acclimating well to the unfamiliar environment due to his age."[125]

All three authors report that shortly after the ceremony using the Golden Urn, the regent, Tatsak *kūtuktu*, informed the Labrang delegation of the results of his own, secretly conducted tests. According to Drakgönpa, the regent told Belmang:

Since [I] had heard that the one from Rangan was better known, I myself made up two dough balls [concerning the question] of whether he was or was not the reincarnation and rolled them before the [Jokhang] Jowo. The "no" fell. [I then] took dough balls [representing] all three candidates and rolled them together. The name of the second candidate fell for the second time. Then before the Lokeshvara [I] again rolled the names of all three candidates at once, and it was the second candidate that again descended of its own accord. It is a fine thing that today's [winning] name card from the Golden Urn is in accord with my previous results.[126]

According to Drakgönpa, this news had a profound effect on Belmang. "When this was spoken, there arose feelings of great confidence and trust in the deities and lamas."[127] Khenpo Ngawang Tupten Gyatso's account contains the same statement from the regent, but then adds another significant detail. He reports that representatives of "the lineage" of the Jamyang Zhepa also conducted their own "covert investigation using dough balls" before the Manjuvajra at Reting monastery while en route home from Lhasa. As this trial also resulted in the identification of the second candidate, "it generated a faith of conviction in the deities and lamas that resulted in even greater confidence in the refuge [i.e., the candidate identified as the reincarnation]."[128] According to Gungtang *kūtuktu*, the result of the successive tests was that "among the superior and inferior, deep conviction and faith in the incontrovertible truth of the supreme incarnation was established."[129]

These three appraisals share a concern with the creation of a specific type of faith, *yiché*. As the third of the "four types of faith" in Tibetan Buddhist thought, *yiché* connotes a higher order of faith or trust that has been attained through a logical process of reasoning (valid cognition, *tsemé drangpa*).[130] In these three texts, the achievement of this particular type of faith seems to have hinged on a process that was explicitly empirical. Multiple tests and personal observation moved Belmang and the other participants beyond "blind faith" to a confidence in the outcome of the Golden Urn based on evidence. As we have seen in act 2, the establishment of this sort of evidence-based faith was also a goal expressed by the Qing court in Manchu-language documents. By stating that the process generated this type of faith, the participants and later commentators were intentionally making an even stronger claim of the legitimacy of the search.

Although Gungtang, Drakgönpa, and Khenpo Ngawang Tupten Gyatso all mention the other dough ball divinations, these *zengyur* tests were less significant than the Golden Urn. The regent claimed that his tests were conducted before the Golden Urn ceremony, but the three authors placed their discussion of the test results *after* the ceremony in their narratives. Moreover, these tests were presented in less detail. The Golden Urn ceremony is the central event, the culmination of the search process in these accounts. This common narrative structure suggests that far from being a symbolic, diplomatic courtesy that followed the "real" tests, the Golden Urn mattered and the dough ball investigations were props—although not insignificant ones. These additional tests provided the empirical evidence for the reliability of the Golden Urn, the deities that had been invoked, and the monks who had participated in the ceremony. And for Belmang personally, it appears that the Golden Urn ceremony and the confirmation of its results by other means was a transformative moment in the evolution of his personal faith.

Conclusion: The Fabrication of Qing Ritual

From the late 1790s through the nineteenth century, Tibetan-language authors employed multiple strategies to bury the controversial selection of the Third Jamyang Zhepa beyond the reach of the memory of the Labrang community. Tukwan *kūtuktu* promulgated a dream that sanctioned Qing supervision of the search process and identified the second candidate as the true reincarnation. Tukwan, Gungtang, Tatsak, and other Geluk hierarchs sanctioned a new configuration of the search process that combined elements from both indigenous and "Chinese" traditions of divination. The strangeness and incongruity of the imperial ritual was obscured by the semantic incorporation of the Golden Urn into the category of dough ball divinations. And by all accounts, the birth and youth of the second candidate were attended by so many miraculous events that his authenticity was beyond reproach.

The Manchu-language sources reveal, however, that at the time of the search, the opinions of leading figures at Labrang were significantly different than portrayed in the Tibetan-language biographies, even that of Gungtang, who composed his account within the year following the identification. From the treasurer of the Jamyang Zhepa's estate to the Xining *amban*, there was much support for the first candidate both at Labrang and in the wider Amdo region. Thus the authors of these later accounts were not merely writing hagiographies of the Third Jamyang Zhepa but *making the case for his legitimacy* against competing memories. Studies of

Qing-period Tibetan biographies have underappreciated the political implications of the genre. Drakgönpa, the abbot Ngawang Tupten Gyatso, the Third Gungtang *kūtuktu*, and the Third Tukwan *kūtuktu* were also arguing for the legitimacy of the Qing state and its rituals. This only becomes obvious, however, when we break the "Amdowas' code" with Manchu-language sources and learn that the biographers were not only allaying fears of using the Golden Urn but also obscuring the very viable candidacy of an alternate child.

The Labrang community's faith in the Third Jamyang Zhepa as an authentic *trülku* was not built in a day. It was an ongoing process that was taken up by several successive generations of authors at Labrang, stretching from the return of the original search party from Lhasa in 1798 until the printing of the Third Jamyang Zhepa's biography in the 1880s. Each book helped consolidate and sustain a particular historical memory of what had happened when Labrang's monks went in search of the reincarnation. The actions undertaken by these Geluk monks flip the standard narrative of Sino-Tibetan relations during the Qing: no longer a story of how Tibetans slyly and astutely got their way in the face of a weakening imperial authority, it becomes a testament to the lengths Tibetans might go to in service of the "Great Sovereign Emperor."

Elisions and inclusions in both the Manchu-language archives and Tibetan-language sources raise further questions about the circulation of information. The inclusion of complete Manchu-language palace memorials in published Tibetan-language texts suggests that Tibetan elites had access to official Manchu-language communications and understood how the imperial communications system functioned. Moreover, it appears that by the early nineteenth century at the latest, the palace memorial, originally a secret, inner court document, had already entered the public realm (albeit limited to literate Tibetan and Mongol elites). It seems that Qing officials wrote their memorials with the expectation that they would be read by Tibetans. However, as the case of the Third Jamyang Zhepa also demonstrates, the medium could still be used in secrecy.

But did Qing officials read Tibetan? As in the case of the biographies of Belmang Pandita and the Third Jamyang Zhepa, if they had, they would have found a list of proscribed and suspect activities. The Tibetan authors from Amdo do not appear to have been much concerned about Qing officials reading their writings, probably because the possibility was remote. The Court of Colonial Affairs periodically trained classes of bannermen in the "Tanggūt" (i.e., Tibetan) language in Beijing and would even dispatch them to Lhasa for further practice, but there is little indication that bannermen ever immersed themselves in the literary world of Tibetan biographies, geographies, and histories. The Tibetan case was exceptional. The Qianlong-period court did exercise varying degrees of censorship elsewhere—most famously during the "literary inquisition" that accompanied the creation of the emperor's comprehensive catalog of Chinese-language literature (the *Sikuquanshu*), but in Mongolia as well.[131]

Moreover, despite the best efforts of officials such as Sungyun and Tsebak, the court was able to amass only very incomplete information on local conditions and the backgrounds of the candidates. If their primary goal was to prevent successive rebirths within the same families, they failed. The child ultimately identified as the Third Jamyang Zhepa was the scion of a notable local family and the nephew of the Shar Nomunhan, the leading *trülku* of Labrang's chief rival in the Amdo region, Rongwo monastery.[132] Qianlong's rationale for rejecting the candidacy of the first child reminds us, however, that his overarching priority in instituting the statute was eliminating the appearance of self-interest in the identification process. The

The Jamyang Zhepa giving teachings. Detail from "Map of Labrang monastery" Rubin Museum, C2012.4.3 (HAR 1097)

throne feared for the future of the faith and the institution of reincarnation if people had the impression that the treasurer could cherry-pick his own candidates. In this respect, the emperor may have succeeded. One need only look to a circa 1859 letter from the treasurer of the Jamyang Zhepa's estate requesting the use of the Golden Urn to locate the next generation reincarnation.[133]

The case of the Third Jamyang Zhepa represents an impressive accomplishment for the Qianlong emperor: a Chinese bureaucratic practice, a lottery, had been transformed into a Tibetan Buddhist divination technology. But the court could not take full credit for the success of the Golden Urn. The work of repackaging the ritual for consumption by Tibetan Buddhists was undertaken primarily by indigenous elites. The result was a cosmopolitan, ritual amalgam invented in the context of Qing colonialism. Khenpo Ngawang Tupten Gyatso, for instance, described it as having closely "followed the legal system of the emperor." The successful result, however, could be interpreted alternately as the result of the agency of the protectors, the "deities and lamas," and Tsongkhapa, as well as of the emperor himself.[134] The agent was perhaps ambiguous, but the result was not random. Yet the Tibetan-language sources also document that the new divination technology did not succeed in displacing the oracles—the original target of Qianlong's ire when he first promoted the Golden Urn in 1792. Sungyun's claim that the oracles had been eradicated was therefore either grossly ignorant of the situation in Lhasa or purposely misleading.

CONCLUSION

Paradoxes of the Urn and the Limits of Empire

Exactly fifty years after the idea for the Golden Urn was first advanced, the empire's most eminent scholar of statecraft and foreign affairs, Wei Yuan (魏源 1794–1857), praised the Qianlong emperor's sublime inspiration. The Qing imperial house had managed to assert dominance over Tibet and much of Mongolia through patronage of the Geluk church. Alluding simultaneously to the *Book of Rites* and Qianlong's *Discourse on Lamas*, Wei Yuan wrote that the Qianlong emperor had "reformed their teachings, but not altered their customs," causing the followers of the Geluk "to obey, but not know why." In other words, the Mongols and Tibetans had been reduced to a position of subservience without ever realizing it. Mocking the credulity of the frontier peoples, Wei Yuan quipped that the success of the Golden Urn was evidence that the emperor "truly was Manjusri."[1]

The history of the legitimation of the Third Jamyang Zhepa suggests that in some respects Wei Yuan's assessment rings true: agents of the Qing state were able to manipulate the recognition process without arousing suspicion among the lama's followers in Amdo. Moreover, Geluk monks who held imperial titles and benefited from imperial stipends had labored both in person among their followers and in writing to ensure that the imperial law was obeyed. Wei Yuan was not unaware that loyalty to the Qing imperial house hinged on the efforts of local elites. But had the Qing really succeeded in the sense understood by Chinese literati like him? What did the continued use of the Golden Urn mean during the nineteenth century?

The Golden Urn in the Nineteenth Century

Things were not quite as Wei Yuan imagined them to be. As we have seen, the decision to intervene in the process of identifying reincarnations and to eradicate the oracles did not develop inexorably from a single moment of imperial inspiration, despite claims to the contrary. Nor was the court acting from long-held plans for the closer political incorporation of Tibet into the empire or presumptions about the sovereign status of the Dalai Lama or other Tibetan elites. From a perspective of no less an authority than the monarch himself—which at times differed quite starkly even from the views of his closest subordinates—the obligation of the Qing imperial house to publicly assert its final decision-making authority (sovereignty or *toose* in Manchu terminology) had arisen only in the context of the court's investigation of the Gurkha debacle. Moreover, prior to 1792, the emperor had certainly not drawn a connection among the authority of the oracles of central Tibet, the divination technologies of Geluk hierarchs, and the sovereignty of the Qing state in its Outer Regions. Much as the job of *huangdi* in the Chinese context had traditionally implied monopolizing communication between heaven and earth, the preservation of empire in Mongolia and Tibet now required that the Manjusri emperor also be the final divination-making authority.

However convinced Qianlong was of the importance of the urn, both for asserting sovereignty over the Ganden Podrang government and for reinstilling faith in the authenticity of reborn lamas, the implementation of the Golden Urn ritual was hesitant and fraught with doubts about the reach of imperial influence. The fact that the initial idea of using a Ming bureaucratic technology to rectify the Geluk church germinated within the innermost confines of the court and perhaps with the emperor himself makes the policy highly unusual (it is rare not to be able to trace an important imperial policy such as the Golden Urn to a suggestion initially advanced by the bureaucracy) and a seemingly perfect example of autocracy. Yet the rollout of the ritual was gradual. Initial discussions were limited to a handful of Geluk and banner officials who had gathered at the summer court in Chengde. The first imperial memorandum to circulate widely among the lay and monastic aristocracy of the Outer Regions was not issued until nearly two months had passed.[2] A formal proclamation did not occur for yet another seven months, and after the search for the reincarnation of the Erdeni Pandita *kūtuktu* had been resolved to the Qianlong emperor's satisfaction.[3] Even then, it took another month and a half for the ruler to elevate the Golden Urn ritual to the status of a "fixed law" of the dynasty.[4] At every stage in this process, he was concerned with ascertaining whether the procedure would be tolerated by the Dalai Lama and other Inner Asian elites.

Between 1792 and 1797, the structure of the ritual and the attendant regulations also changed as a result of input from Qing field officials, Geluk prelates, and the emperor's own evolving concerns. Fuk'anggan, for instance, proposed a unique trial in order to test the authenticity of a single candidate. At the initiative of Qing agents in Lhasa and local elites, the ritual moved from the Jokhang to the Potala Palace and the tutelary and other protector deities and buddhas invoked in the course of the ritual shifted. In 1802, for instance, representatives of the estates of the Shartsang *kūtuktu* of Rongwo monastery and the Tongkhor *kūtuktu* were not only given the option of witnessing the Golden Urn ritual in person—as was typical—but also presented with the choice of holding it in either Yonghegong or Lhasa.[5] The court also repeatedly adjusted and compromised on eligibility requirements for candidates. In the case of the Pakpalha *kūtuktu*, the Cagan Nomunhan *kūtuktu* of Kökenuur, and ultimately the Third Jamyang Zhepa, the court either relented or was prepared to relent on its insistence that incarnates not be sought within noble families or families within which other *trülku* had been identified. It appears that with a handful of exceptions (most importantly the Dalai Lama, Panchen Lama, and Jebtsundamba *kūtuktu* of Outer Mongolia), the greater the temporal authority of the lineage in question, the greater the likelihood that the court would allow the local community to identify candidates as it saw fit. The result was that during the nineteenth century, elite families, especially in Kham and Amdo, were able to either retain or establish a limited number of reincarnate lineages as proxies for hereditary rule.[6] And as the case of the Third Jamyang Zhepa also makes clear, notwithstanding the Qianlong emperor's insistence that the security of the empire hinged on regulating Tibet's tradition of oracular governance, Qing officials were never able to dissuade Tibetan elites from consulting oracles when searching for reborn lamas or making other significant decisions.[7]

Contemporary polemics on the Golden Urn have focused almost exclusively on whether it was historically used to identify the incarnations of the Dalai Lama and Panchen Lama—a reflection of the degree to which these monks became global symbols of Tibet and Tibetan sovereignty over the course of the twentieth century. However, because of their concentration on these "nation-bearing" lineages, scholars have missed the broader pattern of Qing–Geluk cooperation in the recognition of lesser-known yet locally prominent *trülku*.

From the outset, the Qianlong emperor and his advisors envisioned applying the law very broadly. For instance, the *Discourse on Lamas* decreed that all reincarnations of "important lamas of Ü and Tsang," i.e., central Tibet, should be confirmed using the lottery.[8] The earliest Tibetan-language versions of the regulation were even more ambitious, stating that it was to be used in searches for any incarnate lamas in Mongolia and Tibet.[9] Similarly, the first official manual of regulations of the Court of Colonial Affairs to be published after the reforms of the late Qianlong reign also advised that the procedure applied to all reincarnations.[10] In practice—and as later specified in the substatutes to the regulations of the Court of Colonial Affairs—the Golden Urn lottery was generally used for those lineages of reincarnate lamas enrolled in the registers of the Court of Colonial Affairs.

According to Qing official publications, by the early 1800s the Court of Colonial Affairs ostensibly tracked the affairs of 160 incarnate lamas. Thirty hailed from central Tibet (the regions of Ü and Tsang), seventy-six from among the Mongol leagues, thirty-five from Kökennur, five from Kham (eastern Tibet and western Sichuan Province), and fourteen more from the district of the capital.[11] Registration with the Court of Colonial Affairs came with certain privileges. Upon reaching the age of eighteen or in some cases earlier, these lamas received official status as *kūtuktu*, as well as seals of office that empowered them to act, instruct, and issue commands to their lay and monastic followers with the imprimatur of the emperor. Imperial recognition also entailed the receipt of imperial stipends and subsidized travel in person or by emissaries—often to Beijing for formal audiences with Qing rulers or long-term residence at Yonghegong or other monasteries in the capital, but also to Lhasa, Dolonuur in Inner Mongolia, Wutaishan in Shanxi Province, and other important Buddhist sites in Inner Asia.

At the turn of the nineteenth century, these monks represented a small but disproportionately influential portion of a much larger and ever-expanding number of locally recognized incarnate lamas. At the behest of the Qing court, the Tibetan government undertook a census of all incarnate lamas resident in the areas under its control. First compiled in 1814 and updated repeatedly until 1825, the final document chronicled 137 distinct lineages—and the authors admitted that their work was still incomplete. Among these lineages, twenty-six of the lamas had reincarnated only once, suggesting that since the 1750s, the overall number of incarnate lineages had increased by 23 percent. This census also noted that forty-five of the lineages were registered with the Court of Colonial Affairs, fifteen more than the number promulgated in official publications in Chinese.[12] This state of affairs was replicated in both Mongolia and the neighboring regions of Kham and Amdo, where local Qing colonial officers attempted to maintain tabs on perhaps a thousand or more monks who claimed status as incarnations.[13] In Mongolia, for instance, Walter Heissig reports the existence of approximately 243 incarnate lamas in 1900. The Collected Statutes of the Court of Colonial Affairs in Beijing formally recognized only seventy-six of these Mongol lineages. Throughout the nineteenth century, in response to both local demands for recognition and their own political considerations, and despite the precedents of the Court of Colonial Affairs, the Qing court continued to enroll new incarnate lamas and grant them official status as *kūtuktus*.[14]

The nineteenth-century survey from central Tibet claims that between 1793 and 1825 just over half of the incarnations (twenty-six out of forty-seven) were identified with the Golden Urn ritual. A more complete reckoning would necessarily consult the archives of the Court of Colonial Affairs. Since these archives are no longer extant in their entirety, it is necessary to comb the reports of Qing colonial officials in Lhasa, Xining, and Urga (Mongolia), who were required to submit reports of incarnations of imperially sponsored lamas directly to the emperor (via the Grand Council). My own review of these documents yields an additional fifty-three usages of the Golden Urn. All together, archival records suggest that the urn was used seventy-nine times to identify reincarnations from fifty-two different lineages.[15] The partial nature of the archive indicates that there were most likely far more uses of the ritual. Of the fifty-two different lineages that appear to have used it at least once between 1793 and 1911, the majority underwent multiple incarnations during this period. It is safe to assume that several of these rebirths were also confirmed using the Golden Urn. Furthermore, the handful of copybooks and registers of daily business that have survived from Yonghegong and the office of the

Qing authorities in Lhasa record usages of the urn that do not appear among the formal palace memorials. One rare logbook from the Court of Colonial Affairs that covers only the years 1901–1909, for example, lists four identifications of Mongol lamas using the Golden Urn that do not appear in other documents.[16]

Having been absorbed into local traditions of divination, the Golden Urn was, if not necessarily embraced by the Geluk, employed with little controversy for the next century.[17] Indeed, it appears that Tibetan elites actively sought out the ritual and the concomitant involvement of Qing authorities. For instance, in 1801 the *amban* Hening reported that disciples of the *trülku* who had been tutor to the Eighth Dalai Lama requested the use of the urn to resolve internal debates over the legitimacy of his reincarnation.[18] Similarly, in 1904 the *amban* Yotai forwarded to the court in Beijing a letter from the treasurer of the monastery of the Deju *kütuktu* stating that by consulting the Golden Urn, the monastery had finally been able to bring to a conclusion eight years of debate over the authenticity of their lama.[19] Of the twenty-six usages of the urn reported by the Tibetan government by 1825, six were to identify reincarnations of *trülku* who were under no requirement to report to the Court of Colonial Affairs and therefore under no obligation to use the urn.

Other than the case of the Third Jamyang Zhepa, I have found no evidence within the Manchu-language records that Qing officials doctored searches; nor is there evidence of overt attempts by local elites to influence the outcome of the Golden Urn ritual. For example, Manchu-language reports of the candidates' names and backgrounds never indicate preferences among candidates. Candidates who were listed first were not routinely selected. Although some were described as members of the deceased lama's home community or family, final results of the ritual reveal no consistent bias on the part of Qing authorities either for or against these candidates. As I will discuss shortly, in only a handful of instances—all of which involved reincarnations of either the Dalai Lama or Jebtsundamba *kütuktu*—is there evidence of strong resistance to the use of the urn.

A Golden Urn for a Greater Tibet

Why did Geluk elites adopt the urn? The answer lies in the fact that the fundamental interests of the Qing court and the Geluk church overlapped: both wanted the identification process to produce lamas who were widely credible. Although the Galdan Siretu *kūtuktu*, Tukwan Lozang Chökyi Nyima, and perhaps even the Eighth Dalai Lama (or perhaps more accurately, the Tatsak and Demo *kūtuktus* who advised him) did not share the emperor's hostility to the oracles, they are on record as concurring that numerous lamas were not the genuine article. Like the Qing court, they were well aware that disagreements over the authenticity of different candidates posed a serious threat to the peace of local communities and the overall credibility of the Geluk church. The adoption of reincarnation as a key strategy for reproducing political and religious authority had never been frictionless.

Before 1792, the Geluk church had few centralized or codified procedures for identifying rebirths. Reincarnation as a system of rule was in many respects more unpredictable than hereditary succession within aristocratic families: not only could children prove weak-minded or sickly, but also it was possible for multiple children from a range of locations and backgrounds to be simultaneously elevated as candidates. As discussed in act 3, for instance, the unity of the monastic community of the First Jamyang Zhepa had been badly undermined in the mid-1700s by controversy over his rebirth. Even more recently, disagreements over the rebirth of the Fifth Tongkhor *kūtuktu*, another prominent incarnation lineage from Amdo and a frequent visitor to Beijing, had led to two competing Tongkhor lamas, one based at the lineage's original monastery and one based in Kham. Compliance with the Qing statute endowed the winning candidate with political capital and even military protection, not to mention financial emoluments. Far from undermining indigenous authorities or weakening institutionalized reincarnation, the Qing attempt to impose the urn contributed to a homogenization of traditions for identifying rebirths and paradoxically recentralized authority within the Ganden Podrang government, even granting it renewed or unprecedented influence over *trülku* in peripheral regions such as Amdo and Kham.

Thus, Geluk elites were willing to construct a theological rationale for the urn that included Emperor Qianlong, Tsongkhapa, and other deities. Qing colonial authorities, in turn, were inclined to adjust aspects of the ritual in order to enhance its palatability and credibility for indigenous audiences. Even during the Guangxu period (1875–1908), in their reports back to the throne, the Lhasa *ambans* reported engaging in advance consultations with the Ganden Podrang government and were careful to document the various ways they had tried to make the ritual transparent and convey their own "sincere thoughts" (Ma. *unenggi günin*).[20] It is certainly possible that the apparent harmony of these highly staged events masked collusion behind the scenes. Local estate treasurers or Qing authorities may have secretly communicated their preferences to Lhasa, where the *ambans* acted quietly upon them. Yet it would be wrong to interpret this activity as a result of late Qing "weakness" or deference to indigenous authorities. The actors on both sides had a vested interest in orchestrating smooth transitions of temporal and spiritual authority.

In the cases where the Golden Urn was not used, such as in the search for the Ninth and Thirteenth Dalai Lamas in 1808 and 1877, respectively, representatives of the Ganden Podrang government expressed reluctance because the evidence supporting the authenticity of one particular candidate appeared so compelling as to obviate the need for a further test. In both cases, the emperor granted an exemption to the use of the urn once the resident officials in Lhasa had assured him that popular opinion had indeed coalesced around a single child. Although modern Tibetan scholars, such as Shakabpa, have interpreted these incidents as indications of successful Tibetan resistance to Qing authority, contemporaneous Qing and Tibetan accounts do not share this understanding. On the contrary, Manchu and Tibetan-language sources have an overriding goal of identifying indisputably authentic rebirths.[21] Early nineteenth-century visual accounts of the search for the Ninth Dalai Lama, for instance (reproduced in the figures in this chapter) depicted Qing authorities as an integral part of the identification and enthronement process, despite the fact that the urn was not used. Although most likely the product of Beijing workshops, the urns appear to have been commissioned by Mongol elites, not the Qing court.[22]

The historical record also makes clear that well until the early twentieth century, the Qing court had the power to enforce the law and impose the ritual—even over local objections. In one particularly spectacular case, the court even went so far as to annul the results of the Golden Urn ritual after it determined that the winning candidate was unsatisfactory. When informed in 1823 that the child identified by the urn as the Ninth Tongkhor Lama was the son of a Chinese "commoner (*minren* 民人)" from the interior, the Daoguang emperor (r. 1821–1850) refused to grant the title of *kūtuktu* and ordered the search to commence again. Although the emperor claimed that his decision was in accordance with the "old regulations," it

Album: The Finding of A Dalai Lama, 19th century after 1809. Auspicious visions.
Harvard University Art Museums/ Arthur M. Sackler Museum, Bequest of the Hofer Collection of the Arts of Asia, (1985.863.1–8)

Offering prayers to a deity.

Birth.

Investigators arrive to interview the child at his home.

Arrival in Lhasa and exchange of ceremonial scarves with the Qing *ambans*.

Testing the ability of the child to recognize the possessions of the previous Dalai Lama.

Observing festivities in Lhasa with the Qing *ambans* and other dignitaries.

Enthronement of the Ninth Dalai Lama.

was clear to contemporaneous observers that his refusal to countenance the identification of Han commoners as reincarnate lamas represented an important new restriction.[23] In another case, in 1842, the court was able to quash renewed efforts by the Khalkha nobles to avoid the urn and identify a leading Geluk lama—this time the Seventh Jebtsundamba *kūtuktu*—among their own kinsmen and subjects. Despite the distraction of a disastrous war against the British (the Opium War, 1839–42), the court was able to insist that the candidates be identified within Tibetan regions and confirmed using the urn.[24] Dozens of other Mongol *kūtuktu* were identified with little controversy over the nineteenth century. In this particular case the court acknowledged some of the Khalkha concerns and allowed the ritual to be held in Lhasa, not Yonghegong as per regulation.

Although both European observers and many Qing officials agreed by the 1860s that the Qing state was in crisis (with starkly different diagnoses), we should reconsider the degree to which narratives of decline or stagnation resonated in the Outer Regions. Few Tibetan elites would have been unaware of the fact that in the 1870s the Qing state came roaring back to its Eurasian backyard, definitively stamping out sophisticated and well-resourced Muslim statelets in Yunnan, Gansu, and Kökenuur—all areas that also contained significant populations of Tibetan Buddhists with historic ties to central Tibet and the Geluk church. Geluk lamas had even played a direct role in the military campaigns of the 1870s.[25] The subsequent destruction of the emirate of Yaqub Beg in Kashgaria and transformation of the far west into the new province of Xinjiang in 1882 sent a clear message that the dynasty's strategic priorities still lay in the western borderlands, not among the treaty ports of the eastern maritime frontier. It should not be surprising, therefore, that the use of the Golden Urn increased in the 1860s through 1890s.[26]

The details concerning the historical development of the Golden Urn law suggest an additional, yet counterintuitive hypothesis about why the Geluk elite accepted it. The law helped redefine the geographic boundaries of "Tibet" to the advantage of the Ganden Podrang government. Qianlong's decision to place the reincarnate lamas of Qinghai and Gansu under the purview of the Golden Urn based in Lhasa was in many respects a radical move of considerable symbolic importance. This is because from the perspective of most Qing officials well into the nineteenth century, Kökenuur was a "Mongol" space. Eighteenth-century imperially sanctioned compendiums of frontier affairs had never listed the pastures around

Kökenuur lake or the broader Amdo region as a constituent part of Tibet. The 1763 *Multilingual Gazetteer of the Western Regions*, perhaps the most basic reference tool in the library of a Qing frontier official, like most other contemporaneous Qing sources, described Tibet as constituted of four major regions, Ü, Tsang, Kham, and Ngari.[27] Neither Kökenuur nor the neighboring Tibetan-speaking areas of Gansu Province was included. With the exception of a handful of mountains with Tibetan names, Kökenuur was envisioned as a landscape of Mongol place names inhabited by Mongol aristocrats and their subjects.[28] Seventeenth-century Tibetan-language sources similarly did not uniformly consider Amdo (the area including Kökenuur and the Gansu borderlands) either a unique geographical region or a part of Tibet.[29] The Fifth Dalai Lama might have claimed various forms of jurisdiction over the Mongols of Kökenuur, but not their lands as an integral territory of Tibet. Instead, it was the "virtuous deeds" of the "King of the Dharma," Güüshi Khan, that had unified these territories.[30] In the late Qianlong period, however, it became increasingly common for Qing officials to enumerate Amdo (or Qinghai in Chinese sources) as one of the three (or sometimes four) fundamental divisions of Tibet.[31] The Qing decision to place the *kūtuktu* of Kham, the Gansu borderlands, and Kökenuur within the scope of Lhasa's authority most likely reflected the evolving geographical conceptions of Tibetan elites, who themselves were promoting the notion of both a distinctive region of "Amdo" and a "Greater Tibet."[32]

Instead of viewing the Golden Urn as an imposition that undermined Geluk claims to temporal and spiritual leadership, it is therefore possible to reinterpret the ritual as a vehicle for expanding Tibet and aggrandizing the position of Tibetans within the Geluk church. The Qianlong-era assertion of Qing sovereignty did little to diminish the dominion of monastic authorities over their own local communities. Moreover, the reforms of 1793 were as much about centralizing the authority of the Ganden Podrang government—and the Geluk church within that government—than about asserting imperial decision-making authority. In his private missives to his courtiers, the Qianlong emperor expressed a desire to do away with governance by Geluk hierarchs—"Buddhist government"—entirely. But in practice, the court proved more interested in reforming the existing Tibetan administrative system.

It is therefore not surprising that the Ganden Podrang government's most authoritative public account of the 1790s, the Eighth Demo *kūtuktu's* biography of the Eighth Dalai Lama, completed in 1811 just as the author assumed the position of regent to the Ninth Dalai Lama, depicted the activities of leading Qing officials in Lhasa as a confirmation of existing preceptor-donor relations, not a fundamental realignment of political authority.[33] In particular, the Demo *kūtuktu* portrayed the Qing commander Fuk'anggan as a deeply pious man who had sponsored a series of religious ceremonies in Lhasa and took the Dalai Lama as his teacher:

> [Fuk'anggan] insisted, his voice hoarse with earnestness, "You are the sole protector of all the sentient beings and in particular the thirteen myriarchies of Tibet. Although we ourselves dwell in a distant land, you, Dalai Lama, exist in the center of our heart through our meditation. Regard us with compassion as a father does his son. We offer service out of the gratitude we have held in our hearts for all you have done *in the cause of the two traditions*. Just as a master apportions [work] to his servants, command me [to take up] your happy affairs. In what remains of my life, I shall, by performing the Three Pleasing Actions, follow you appropriately as your student." [34]

This depiction of Fuk'anggan's personal devotion and sincerity was important to the Demo *kūtuktu* because it attested to the authenticity and enduring vitality of the patron-priest relationship. Here, finally, was a flesh-and-blood confirmation that the Qing court stood behind its expressions of faith in the Geluk teachings. Fuk'anggan was a "second emperor" who sat with the Dalai Lama "together in the private chamber [of the Dalai Lama] as priest and patron."[35] In addition, the Demo *kūtuktu* reported to his readers that Fuk'anggan had personally conveyed the *truth* to the Qianlong emperor:

> Later, in response to the emperor's questions during an audience, [Fuk'anggan] reported, "When seen clearly and in person the Dalai Lama is in fact a genuine buddha in human form. He was able to answer questions with unobstructed wisdom. When we approached him with major unresolved debates among our officers and troops, he immediately solved them."
>
> At this the emperor rejoiced, saying, "You have honestly reported the attainments of my Dalai Lama's body, speech, and mind without

concealment." He then ordered the Grand Secretary to offer a *khatak* and other gifts to the [Dalai Lama].[36]

Tibetan readers would learn, therefore, that Fuk'anggan had explicitly recognized the Dalai Lama's political authority over central Tibet and praised him for his mastery of both spiritual and temporal matters. Even the Qing military victory had apparently hinged on the efforts of the Dalai Lama and the Ganden Podrang government. Although the Demo *kūtuktu* devoted fifteen folio pages of the biography to describing the Gurkha war and the relationship between Fuk'anggan and the Dalai Lama, there is no mention of the Golden Urn or any of the other administrative reforms proposed by Qing officials. It is possible that the Demo *kūtuktu* wished to downplay Qing influence in Lhasa and thus preserve the ability of the Ninth Dalai Lama to rule unencumbered by interference from the *ambans* or the Qing government. More likely, however, the regent felt that Qing refom efforts had not qualitatively altered the nature of the relationship between the Ganden Podrang government, which he led, and the Qing ruling house. Whether the Demo *kūtuktu* was describing the reality of Qing–Geluk relations or had embellished accounts of events in Beijing, he wished to present the encounter between Fuk'anggan and the Eighth Dalai Lama as a template for future cooperation. And other contemporary Geluk elites shared the view that ties between the Geluk and the dynasty remained mutually beneficial. In 1798, the Tukwan *kūtuktu*, Lozang Chökyi Nyima, found nothing remarkable about other Geluk hierarchs referring to the Qing court as their "family."[37]

Qing Colonialism: Midwife to the Tibetan State and Nation

In the early twentieth century the Thirteenth Dalai Lama (1876–1933) legitimized his rule by asserting that he was taking up the mantle of the Great Fifth Dalai Lama and restoring to himself administrative powers that had been lost since the late seventeenth century to the machinations of the Qing court and corrupt regents. Yet the very fact that there was still a centralized Tibetan government in Lhasa in 1895—the year the Thirteenth Dalai Lama assumed governing responsibilities after more than a hundred years of regencies and the untimely deaths of four successive Dalai Lamas—should force us to think again about the Qing colonial context.

Peter Schwieger in particular has recently made a strong case for reconsidering the significance of the relationship between the Qing court and the regents. Three of the four reincarnate lineages that supplied the Ganden Podrang with successive regents had received ongoing and direct support from Qing rulers since the Qianlong reign. The Seventh Demo *kūtuktu* (regent, 1757–1777), the First Tsemönling Galdan Siretu Samadi Baksi *kūtuktu* (regent 1777–1786, and again in 1791), and the Eighth Tatsak *kūtuktu* (regent 1791–1810) all received strong backing from the Qianlong emperor, and their estates derived considerable wealth from imperial patronage. Kundeling monastery, the seat of the Tatsak *kūtuktu*, was established on the basis of donations from Fuk'anggan and Hailanca in 1792.[38] The regent lineages, with their close ties to the Qing court, formed the backbone of a government that in the nineteenth century required none of the major investments of men and material that Qing rulers had repeatedly been forced to make during the eighteenth century. Creating a more self-sufficient and centralized government in Lhasa had been a major objective of Qing colonial agents like Fuk'anggan and Heliyen in the 1790s and a goal that they did not see as necessarily conflicting with assertions of Qing sovereignty.

The regents were not the only institutions created or reformed under the supervision of Qing authorities in the 1790s and early nineteenth century. Qianlong's program also tackled the Tibetan government's finances, currency, tax administration, postal service, frontier defenses, and military, with reforms that in the context of any other early modern colonial empire would be seen as laying the groundwork for the consolidation of national identities and perhaps even the nation-state. However, since the 1988 publication of Luciano Petech's study of the regents, these figures and the other points of contact among the Qing court, its colonial administration, and Tibetans have been largely ignored.[39] The desire of most non-PRC scholars to trace the independent development of Tibetan society as a clean trajectory from the era of the Great Fifth to that of the Thirteenth Dalai Lama is understandable in light of the events of the twentieth century. But this risks overlooking the degree to which intense and sustained encounters between Tibetans and Qing officials and other agents of Qing colonialism reshaped communities across greater Tibet during the last century of Qing rule.

If, through the invention of rituals such as the Golden Urn, the Qing state became a partner of sorts to Tibetan elites in the expansion of the geographic idea of Tibet and the consolidation of the Ganden Podrang government, it probably also influenced ideas about what it meant to be *Tibetan*. In the eighteenth and early nineteenth centuries, Tibetan-language chronicles sent mixed signals about whether all the people of Greater Tibet were Tibetan. On the rare occasions that the term *böpa* ("Tibetan") was used, it usually referred solely to the residents of Ü and Tsang.[40] As we have seen, Manchu and Chinese sources often preserved these distinctions among people of central Tibet, Amdo, and Kham. But Qing official notions of Tibet and Tibetans could also be more expansive than indigenous ones. Over the course of the eighteenth and nineteenth centuries, the distinctions between the people of central Tibet and Amdo and Kham faded into more generalized categories of Fan and eventually Zangzu (藏族)—the modern Chinese-language term for "Tibetan people."[41] The assumptions about Fan made by Qing officials and Chinese literati had increasingly concrete ramifications for communities across the Tibetan plateau in the late nineteenth century, as contacts with Qing civil and military officials and Han commoners became more frequent and sustained— especially in regions such as Kham and Amdo. Assumptions about Fan culture, faith, and legal traditions, for instance, led to attempts to implement uniform policies across regions that had previously been approached by Qing authorities in highly particularistic ways.[42] Did this context shape the way Tibetan elites thought about nation, state, and people? Did this history shape the emergence of a twentieth-century Tibetan nationalism that closely linked the Dalai Lama and the Geluk to the independence of the (now singular) Tibetan people?

Answers to these questions will require further investigation of nineteenth-century Tibetan sources and closer attention to the local histories of the peripheral areas of Greater Tibet. But to the extent that the answers are affirmative, the implementation of the law on the Golden Urn may have been one of several factors that helped redefine and reify the Geluk church as an increasingly "Tibetan" institution over the course of the nineteenth century. The insistence of the Qing imperial house that the chief Mongol incarnations be identified among "Tanggut" or "Fan" people, as well as its subsequent amplification by the regulation that no incarnations were to be identified among Han commoners of the interior, surely contributed to the spread of the idea that to be Geluk was to be

"Tibetan," and that to be Tibetan meant to be born into a household of "Tibetan" descent.

According to Wei Yuan, the Golden Urn was emblematic of the unprecedented expansion of "China" (*Zhongguo*). In equating the Great Qing State with China in this way, Wei Yuan presaged the elisions of modern Chinese nationalists and the historians of the People's Republic of China, who have similarly reified the Golden Urn as a symbol of Chinese sovereignty.[43] Yet neither the Qianlong emperor nor contemporaneous Tibetan chroniclers saw it in such terms. On the contrary, it was a symbol of the Qing imperial house's vested interest in promoting the Geluk teachings. For this reason we should not leap to the conclusion that occasional Tibetan efforts to avoid use of the urn in the nineteenth century or the abrupt abandonment of the ritual when the dynasty collapsed in 1911 indicated a rejection of the urn on nationalist grounds. The Golden Urn was a uniquely *Qing* ritual whose animating principles could not outlive the Qing state. Since it was but one of many colonial institutions that connected the Geluk to the dynasty, Qing rulers could afford to dispense with the Golden Urn from time to time. Thus, the use or avoidance of the ritual should not be used as a barometer for measuring the legitimacy of the Qing state among Tibetan Buddhists. The overall loyalty of Tibetan and Mongol elites to the imperial household was not in serious question until the early twentieth century. When after 1904 a handful of Tibetan elites began to take the first steps to extract themselves from the Qing empire, a new generation of Qing colonial authorities also began preparations to dispense with the Ganden Podrang—and the system of imperial sponsorship of reincarnate lamas in its entirety.[44] From the perspective of late Qing Chinese nationalists, the Golden Urn had become a vestigial organ of the old empire, unsuited to expressions of "modern," national sovereignty that prioritized race over religion.

The Reservations of Belmang Pandita

The late Qing witnessed the birth of a unique articulation of the Tibetan nation, not the reemergence of a national idea that had been long suppressed by the Qing empire. In 1913 the Thirteenth Dalai Lama informed his subjects that they were now an "independent country" (Tib. *gyelkhab rangwang*). Included in his proclamation were injunctions to colonize peripheral areas of the new country and defend the borders, especially that between Kham and the Chinese interior. To the traditional rhetoric about the ruler as an instrument of both temporal administration and spiritual salvation, the Thirteenth Dalai Lama had added the unprecedented assertion that the territory ruled by his ecclesiastic state and the lands populated by the Tibetan people had to be one and the same. The people were not yet imagined as sovereign citizens—this was to be no secular republic— but they were now informed that *they* were the ultimate guarantors of the Ganden Podrang government and the security of Buddhism—not the Dalai Lama or the Qing emperor.[45] One of the basic observations of this book is that much about this new Tibetan nation was the product of long-term interactions between Tibetans and other peoples in the context of Qing colonialism, not deeply felt hostility to Qing or "Chinese" rule and rituals such as the Golden Urn. Diverse and even conflicting ideas about Tibet, its borders, its people, and the relative responsibilities of the Geluk administrators and Qing officials moved back and forth among Tibetan and non-Tibetan Qing elites. It was only after the failure of the Qing state to stop the British invasion of 1904 and during the subsequent Qing military operations and administrative reforms, first in Kham and then in central Tibet, that resentment of Qing rule began to spread widely across Tibetan society.[46]

The writings of one of our chief protagonists, Belmang Pandita, both support and complicate this picture. In act 3, Belmang and his disciples played an essential role in legitimating the authenticity of the Third Jamyang Zhepa and vouching for the accuracy of the Golden Urn ritual. After returning from Lhasa, he served in a succession of important posts within the Geluk administration in Amdo, most significantly as the abbot of Labrang monastery from 1804 to 1809. These jobs brought him into regular contact with Qing officials. He would seem, therefore, the quintessential Qing elite for whom service to the dynasty and Buddhism posed no inherent contradiction. Yet by the 1820s, Belmang's magnum opus, *The Ladder for Guiding the Youth, Lessons Summarizing the History of India, Tibet, Eastern and Western Mongolia*, expressed profound disillusionment with Qing rule.[47] The arguments of this book reveal the limits of the Qing state's persuasive powers and a resurgent confidence in the capacity of the Geluk hierarchs to govern an expanded Tibet.

Belmang's first critique of the Qing state was an indirect one. Between the late Qianlong reign and the early 1820s, the Amdo region had become a violent place. On an increasingly regular basis, herding communities were launching large-scale raids and occupations of each other's pastures. By 1822, the turbulence had triggered a major political crisis as the Mongol nobles and their subjects began to retreat en masse into Gansu Province, seeking refuge outside the gates of Xining and other border towns. In other incidents, banner subjects abandoned their Mongol lords and joined the raiders.[48] Whereas Qing authorities tended to see the violence in broad strokes as a conflict between Mongols and Tibetans (Fan) for control of Kökenuur, Belmang saw things differently. He placed primary responsibility for the mayhem on the Mongol elite, but the Qing rulers were a close second.

Parting ways with previous Tibetan-language historians from the Amdo region, Belmang argued that the troubles of the Mongol nobles stemmed directly from their misapprehension of their duties as "benefactors" (Tib. *jindak*) of the Gelukpa.[49] From Belmang's perspective, the preceptor-patron relationship (Tib. *chöyon gyi kadrin*) was an exclusive arrangement: once Güüshi Khan had bound himself to the Fifth Dalai Lama in the 1630s, both he and his descendants were obligated to patronize only the Geluk church. Recent support from descendants of Güüshi Khan such as Naqan-Darji (r. 1771–1808), the highest-ranking Mongol prince in Kökenuur, for the Nyingma teachings had undermined the stability of their domains—a development that had been predicted in the era of the Fifth Dalai Lama. Belmang quoted this prophecy: "Having mixed blood with gold dust [the teachings of the Nyingma and the Geluk respectively], the children of demons and hungry ghosts will run and jump about. The waves of the ocean [i.e., Kökenuur] will froth in turmoil."[50]

Although Belmang claimed that he was not in principle opposed to the teachings of other schools, he argued that their adoption by Mongol rulers created a dangerous and untenable compromise—a mode of rule that was "neither goat nor sheep."[51] Mixed teachings led to clouded moral judgment and weak rule that undermined the stability of Mongol banners. Absolute fealty was not Belmang's only requirement for would-be benefactors of the Geluk church. He sought to remind readers that participation in a preceptor-patron relationship also entailed promulgating and observing the laws of central Tibet. His accounts of Mongol conversions to the Geluk teachings stressed the attendant legal obligations. Belmang noted that after the Tümed Mongol ruler Altan Khan converted to the Geluk teachings in 1572, he established laws "in accordance with those of Ü-Tsang." Belmang then commented, "This is the unimaginable liberation that comes from the [encounter of] donor and preceptor."[52] The final section of Belmang's *History* is a short legal treatise that enumerates the fifteen laws that constituted Güüshi Khan's legal code and places them within a single stream of codes and moral precepts dating back to the arrival of Buddhism in Tibet during the rule of Songtsen Gampo (c. 605–650).[53] Belmang then spelled out the underlying moral principles of the laws—most importantly the avoidance of killing.[54] The Geluk, in this view, was not simply a school or specific teachings, but a civilization unified by a single tradition of jurisprudence.

The Qing rulers did not measure up to Belmang's exacting standards. First he presented them as largely disinterested in the fate of the Mongols. Belmang's account of the Qianlong reign painted a portrait of an emperor who had grown weary of the chronic violence of Kökenuur and who admonished the third-generation Khoshud *qinwang* (Tib. Wangdan Dorjé Phalam, 1747–1770) to become more "self-reliant."[55] Belmang described Qing, or "Chinese," military efforts during the early Jiaqing reign to suppress the internecine raiding as a failure.[56] Furthermore, while he granted that the Qianlong emperor and his predecessors had entered into preceptor-patron relations with various Geluk hierarchs, he presented their overall reputation as benefactors of the Geluk and sovereigns of Tibet negatively in contrast with the praise he heaped on the Qing's archenemies, the seventeenth- and eighteenth-century Junghar rulers Tsewang Rabtan and Galdan Tsering.[57]

According to Belmang, the Qing incorporation of Tibet was an unfortunate development. Although he identified the Qing rulers as "Manchu kings," their realm was indistinguishable from "China" and the sovereignty they exercised over Tibet was as "kings of China." Thus, the *History* describes Tibet as becoming a subject of "China" and not a component of a greater, all-inclusive Geluk "Qing" empire. Kökenuur, Jungharia, and finally Tibet successively "entered under the authority of China" but remained distinct, separate, and alienable entities, not constituent parts of a greater whole.[58] Moreover, Belmang clearly distinguished individual acts of patronage offered by Kangxi, Yongzheng, and Qianlong from the establishment of Qing control over Tibet, which he dated to the reorganization of the Ganden Podrang government that followed the assassination of Gyurmé Namgyel in 1750:

> Although [Polhané's] son Dalai Batur Gyurmé Namgyel ruled for four years, he was killed according to the law of China, after which the four *kalön* were established. After the death of the Victorious One Kelzang Gyatso [1757], it has been said, "Thereafter the tradition was destroyed and supplications were made to beings on the outside." According to this statement, the tradition of the joint residence of the regent and *ambans* was instituted. Oh my! The three worlds are impermanent like the autumn clouds. Birth and death is like attending a dance. Our passing lives resemble lightning in the sky, transmigrating with the speed of a waterfall pouring off a precipitous mountain. All those things you have gathered, discard them without exception! Having reached the highest point, you can only come down! Having been born, you can only die! At that time, since the noble Dharma is the only refuge, solemnly discriminate between the consequences of good and evil actions![59]

The establishment of Qing rule in Tibet, therefore, had little to do with the establishment of preceptor-donor relations. Instead, it was an abject lesson in the negative effects of bad karma. Belmang leaves the impression that the establishment of "China's" control over Tibet not only was a misfortune for Buddhism but also marked the end of Tibetan history more generally: the death of the Seventh Dalai Lama shortly thereafter is the last event discussed in his chronology of Tibetan history. The events of the Gurkha war are of little significance. For Belmang, Qing sovereignty was also inaugurated with a characteristically non-Buddhist act: capital punishment. Thus, Qing sovereignty is expressed primarily through the imposition of "the law of China."

Here we return once again to the three interlinked themes of this book: sovereignty, faith, and law. The Qianlong emperor and Belmang Pandita both embraced law as the key justification for legitimate sovereign authority over others. Yet they could not have diverged more starkly on what constituted legitimate law. Unlike the administration of Güüshi Khan, who according to Belmang was a paragon for adopting and enforcing Geluk jurisprudence, rule by the "Manchu" emperors of "China" remained irrevocably foreign. Whereas the Mongols of old had assiduously purged themselves of non-Buddhist habits and customs, the establishment of preceptor-patron relations with the Qing rulers as described by Belmang entailed no subsequent transformation of customs and laws among the Manchus or in China more generally.

Belmang's *History* is significant not only because it sheds light on the historical thought of a scholar who would educate several generations of Labrang-affiliated historians during his lifetime but also because it presents a vision of the Qing and the proper ordering of politics and religion that strongly contrasted with that of contemporaneous Geluk elites and the Qing colonial officials with whom he had contact. Blockprinted versions of the *History* circulated widely in Inner Asia, influencing Tibetan and Mongol readers well into the twentieth century.[60] In Belmang's text, there are no "Manjusri emperors" or "our Great Qing."[61] If the Third Tukwan *kūtuktu* or Changkya Rolpé Dorjé was at "home" in the Qing court, Belmang implied that he would have preferred life in the Junghar state. The Manchu rulers of China appear only tenuously Buddhist in contrast with the zeal of the Junghars or Güüshi Khan. Whereas in the hands of the Tukwan *kūtuktu* or even the Qianlong emperor and his agents, Geluk Buddhism first appears as the cosmopolitan glue that binds the Qing imperial house to the Outer Regions, in the hands of Belmang Pandita, it is the sectarian axe that threatens to chop them apart.

Had Belmang Pandita imagined an alternative to the Qing empire? The *History* does not directly say so, and I believe that this was highly unlikely. At several points in the book, however, Belmang suggested that at least at the local level it might be appropriate to begin substituting Geluk hierarchs for the failing Mongol princes of Kökenuur. The *History*, after all, was intended as a guide for both Güüshi Khan's descendants and the Geluk "princes" who "possessed the discernment and wisdom of the two traditions of Dharma and statecraft."[62] In a passage laden with prophetic undertones, Belmang related a story that in the 1770s Changkya Rolpé Dorjé had contemplated advising Qianlong to replace the ranking prince of Kökenuur with the Second Jamyang Zhepa.[63] Perhaps in light of the troubled circumstances of the 1820s, Belmang was suggesting that the time for such a political change had come. Moreover, in his later career he devoted much of his own energy and that of his most prominent disciple, Drakgönpa, to elaborating a vision of Amdo as a Geluk space, part of

Greater Tibet and ruled by *trülku*. The concrete manifestation of this argument was the aforementioned *Oceanic Book*, the encyclopedic history of Geluk monasteries in Amdo.[64]

As Gray Tuttle astutely points out, the *Oceanic Book* should not be read as a nationalist handbook.[65] This assessment applies to Belmang's *History* as well. Both books were written in a specific historical context still quite without the nationalism that began to circulate in the early twentieth century. Their authors were directly grappling with the strengths and weaknesses of Qing administration for their own communities in Amdo. To the extent that these monks found the Qing flawed, we can find in their writings indications that some Geluk elite were souring on Qing rule and even Chinese people (Tib. *gyami*) in the early 1800s. Drakgönpa wrote proudly that Belmang was responsible for banning the residency of Chinese monks at Labrang after the enthronement of the Third Jamyang Zhepa and limiting contact with Chinese merchants.[66] Among their arguments were new definitions of Tibetanness that privileged Geluk governance and jurisprudence and new boundaries for Tibet. The Thirteenth Dalai Lama's 1913 declaration built on these ideas.

The Golden Urn and the People's Republic

Historians have been quick to point out that despite the antifeudal and anti-Qing rhetoric that fueled much of the push to overthrow the Qing dynasty in 1911, Chinese politicians were quick to see the utility of maintaining some of the old institutions and strategies that had seemingly bound Tibetan and Mongol Buddhists to the Qing imperial household. Uradyn Bulag has memorably referred to this strategy as "going imperial." Even the Chinese Communist Party at least provisionally embraced this approach, especially in the late 1930s when, having been pushed out of eastern China, its members began to encounter minority peoples in large numbers.[67] Although the Soviet Union's approach to the "nationality question" gave the CCP certain ideological leeway to embrace Mongol and Tibetan elites and grant legal status to Buddhist institutions, the CCP's policies were also shaped by the strategies of the Chinese Nationalist Party. Despite profound differences on matters such as the distribution of wealth and property within society, Chiang Kai-shek and Mao Zedong shared the conviction that although the minority peoples would ultimately assimilate into the Han majority, it was necessary in the short term to formally grant legal status to the political and religious institutions to which these groups had been accustomed in the late imperial period. For some influential Chinese patriots and activists, the Buddhist faith of the Tibetans and Mongols was not an obstacle to integration, but rather a powerful axis of shared culture that could be used to bind the new Chinese nation.[68]

To this end, the Republic of China (1912–1949), through agencies such as the Mongol and Tibetan Affairs Committee (*Mengzang weiyuanhui* 蒙藏委員會, the successor to the Court of Colonial Affairs) attempted to bring into the fold of the Nationalist Party those incarnate lamas who appeared willing to work on behalf of the national government. It continued the Qing policy of granting titles, emoluments, and in some cases actual administrative authority to monks such as the Changkya *kūtuktu* and the Panchen Lama. The Ninth Panchen Lama (1883–1936) had proven particularly valuable to the Nationalist Party. Having fallen out with the Thirteenth Dalai Lama and taken refuge within China proper, he was both a useful symbol of the party's claims to sovereignty in Tibet and a helpful intermediary between the party and Buddhists of all orientations. In 1936, in anticipation of the impending conflict with the Ganden Podrang government over who would be able to have the final word on the identity of the future Panchen Lama, the Nationalist government issued the "Law on the Method of the Reincarnation of Lamas" (*lama zhuanshi banfa* 喇嘛轉世辦法). This law closely followed the last Qing-period articulation of the law on the Golden Urn in 1907. The only major differences between the 1907 and 1936 statutes (beyond changing the names of various government agents and offices) were that the latter mandated that all incarnate lamas, regardless of title or status, must undergo the ritual and that no additional monks were allowed to reincarnate and establish new *trülku* lineages. However, the Nanjing government was unable to enforce the law, and neither the Tenth Panchen Lama (1938–1989) nor any other *trülku* was identified using the urn during the remaining years of the Republic of China.

After founding the People's Republic of China in 1949, the Communist Party did not move quickly to formalize regulations of reincarnate monks or the search process.[69] Perhaps troubled by the ideological contradictions of appearing to become directly involved in identifying religious figures, and perhaps comforted by the fact that a number of prominent reincarnate monks were willing to cooperate with the new regime, the

PRC appears to have been content to essentially adopt the pre-1949 approach of including incarnate monks on various consultative bodies and United Front committees.

Coincidentally, it was the search for the reincarnation of the Fifth Jamyang Zhepa from 1949 through 1951 that forced the PRC to grapple with reincarnation for the first time. But in this case, despite historical precedent for employing the Golden Urn ritual (1797, 1861), neither provincial officials nor cadres from the National Committee on Minority Affairs or other national organs insisted on its use. Government officials appear to have kept abreast of the search, but it was conducted entirely according to local designs. Subsequent accounts of the final test labeled it the "Golden Urn," but their description indicates that it was a traditional *zentak* ritual involving dough balls and a broad platter.[70] Only at the enthronement ceremony in 1952 did government officials appear, the most prominent of whom was Wang Feng, a member of both of the Northwest Military Governing Committee and the Nationality Affairs Commission. At this time, the government offered no formal sanction of the monk's status other than a banner that read, "Strengthen Minzu Unity, Struggle for the Sake of Building Our Ancestral Country"—a radical break from the practices of the imperial period (and even the Republican period) when the government would pass down seals and titles to the monk and possibly enfeoffments to his relatives.[71]

Following the massive disruptions of the "Democratic Reform" campaign of 1958–59 and the Cultural Revolution, the CCP took a relatively hands-off policy to the management of reincarnate lamas during the period of "Reform and Opening" (late 1978–1980s). It neither sanctioned nor obstructed the searches for reincarnations, and official publications make little mention of the Golden Urn. Many *trülku* had died during the carnage of the 1950s through 1960s, but those who survived returned to their monasteries and, in some cases, were restored to positions in the various United Front organizations they had belonged to prior to the political upheavals of the late 1950s. In no cases, however, did they return to positions of direct administrative authority over local communities. According to Chen Qingying, the government offered very little in the way of funding, but did tolerate the collection of alms from the monks' traditional support communities.[72]

The PRC did not feel compelled to resurrect the Golden Urn until the crisis that followed the death of the Tenth Panchen Lama in 1989—a turn of events that the Communist Party perceived as the most serious test of its rule in Tibet since the uprising in 1959, when the Fourteenth Dalai Lama, Tenzin Gyatso, fled to India and established an exile government in Dharamsala. In the late 1980s, large-scale public protests for independence within Tibet and the growing international prestige of the Dalai Lama (a Nobel laureate after 1989), followed by the dissolution of the Soviet Union, left the CCP with the impression that its control over Tibet was becoming precarious. The death of the widely respected Tenth Panchen Lama (b. 1938)—who had, at least in public, repeatedly expressed support for the incorporation of Tibet into the People's Republic—further compounded these fears. The party had grown accustomed to a Panchen Lama through whom its claims could be communicated. The government therefore hoped to identify and indoctrinate a new Panchen Lama who would continue to play a similar role.

Initially, the PRC tacitly tolerated the Dalai Lama's involvement in the search and even appears to have considered a process by which both sides could arrive at a joint declaration of the identity of the reincarnation. For reasons that remain obscure, however, relations between the PRC and the Dalai Lama's representatives broke down in 1993, and the search slipped out of public view. Two years later, in May 1995, the Dalai Lama broke the silence with the unilateral announcement that he had identified the rebirth of the Panchen Lama. In response, the Chinese government took the child into "protective" custody and turned to the Golden Urn as a tool for limiting the Dalai Lama's influence and acquiring a degree of confidence about the political reliability of the candidates and their families.[73] On November 11, after apparently little to no consultation with the United Front agencies that had been handling the matter, or even with government-affiliated Tibetan lamas, the PRC publicly announced that the Golden Urn would be utilized to make the final selection and excluded the child named by the Dalai Lama from participating.[74]

The actions of both the Dalai Lama and the Chinese government should be considered hard-line. The CCP most likely had decided to exclude the Dalai Lama from any role in the process well before he made his announcement.[75] Yet regardless of whether the Dalai Lama was justified in issuing his decision, he had overtly challenged not only the broader claim of PRC sovereignty in Tibet but also the CCP's long-standing principle of subordinating all religious organizations to the state. For the same reason that the PRC had not tolerated Vatican appointments of Chinese bishops, it was not about to swallow independent appointments by the Dalai Lama. In the face of such a challenge, it is not surprising that the party acted quickly to impose its own candidates. It also could not afford to grant the Dalai Lama's candidate time to either accrue additional credibility or be spirited away to India. The decision to exclude that candidate, however, meant that the Golden Urn could no longer be understood as anything other than a blunt declaration of Chinese sovereignty. Even the Qianlong emperor realized the importance of including the names of undesireable children: without some nod to local preferences and customs, it would be difficult for Tibetan Buddhists to view the urn as a mutually constituted religious technology designed to identify true rebirths. In effect, the ritual had become a lottery once more.

In the case of the Eleventh Panchen Lama, the CCP prioritized the symbolic unity of modern China over the integrity of the identification process. As a result, despite any merits the winning candidate, Gyaincain Norbu (the standard PRC transliteration of his name), may have possessed, his status has been dogged with controversy. Geluk monks within China infrequently display his image and often attempt to avoid meeting with him when he visits Geluk monasteries. The PRC-sanctioned Eleventh Panchen Lama has consequently spent much of his life in Beijing, confined to a house wedged along the narrow lane that separates the Qing imperial palace from the leadership compound of the Chinese Communist Party at Zhongnanhai, unable to escape either the vigilance of China's current rulers or the long shadow of Qing lawmaking.

In the aftermath of the Panchen Lama crisis, the CCP became much more directly involved in overseeing the education and finances of reincarnate lamas, investing in the economic well-being of incarnate monks and considering more carefully the legal regime by which they would be regulated. Internal debates about how the party should handle reincarnation were evidently contentious, because it was not until 2007 that the State Bureau of Religious Affairs finally promulgated a law on reincarnation, the "Method for Managing the Reincarnation of Living Buddhas of Tibetan Buddhism" (*Zangchuan fojiao huofo zhuanshi guanli banfa* 藏傳佛教活佛轉世管理辦法). This new law mandated that "all reincarnate lamas who have historically been identified by drawing lots from the Golden Urn must continue to have their reincarnations confirmed by drawing lots from the Golden Urn."[76] The government was therefore amplifying the precedent set in 1995 to cover an additional forty to fifty prominent incarnation lineages in Tibetan and Mongol regions. In 2010, the government orchestrated the first use of the Golden Urn ritual since the identification of the Eleventh Panchen Lama in 1995. On this occasion, officials from the Religious Affairs Bureau of the Tibetan Autonomous Region witnessed local monks conduct the ritual to confirm Jamyang Sherab Paldan as the reincarnation of the Fifth Dejū *trülku*.

It is impossible not to observe (and the CCP would not have it otherwise) that the new law on reincarnation and the growing edifice of physical, financial, and propaganda structures for supervising reincarnate monks have been designed to ensure that the future reincarnation of the current Fourteenth Dalai Lama, Tenzin Gyatso, can be educated within China in a manner that will ensure his sympathy for both the ongoing rule of the CCP and the position of Tibet within the People's Republic. Despite his long exile abroad, the Fourteenth Dalai Lama has become emblematic of Tibetan aspirations to statehood and Buddhist faith in a way that has no historical precedent among Tibetans. Professions of allegiance to or respect for the Dalai Lama are now so ubiquitous that they can even be found among Tibetan communities that have been historically opposed to the Dalai Lama and the Gelukpa or had few religious or political affiliations with central Tibet. The CCP believes, therefore, that a compliant Fifteenth Dalai Lama would mean the elimination of the animating and unifying nucleus of modern Tibetan nationalism.

But the government has also grown attentive to the role that other *trülku* lineages can play in the ubiquitious efforts at "stability maintenance" (Ch. *weiwen* 維穩) among Tibetans and Mongols. Following the proclamation of the 2007 law, the PRC government began issuing certificates of reincarnation. The law, therefore, should not be understood simply as a tool for subordinating the Geluk church to state control—it also marked the moment when the PRC formally legalized reincarnation. The majority of its fourteen articles laid out procedures for certifying Geluk and non-Geluk *trülku*, including those who were not subject to the substatute on the Golden Urn. The law asserted that final decisions about reincarnation were the prerogative of religious affairs departments at the provincial and national levels of government.

Unsurprisingly, the current Dalai Lama and the Tibetan government in exile have viewed PRC policies with considerable consternation and have taken aggressive measures to delegitimize the Golden Urn. In September 2011, the Dalai Lama issued his own proclamation stating that only he himself or the managers of his estate had the right to choose his successor. The proclamation furthermore introduced a range of methods that would allow him to identify a successor well before his death, thus avoiding in its entirety a search process that could be manipulated by the PRC.[77] In 2015 the Dalai Lama even publicly speculated that he might not reincarnate at all. These ideas elicited a caustic response among PRC officials. Zhu Weiqun, a member of the standing committee of the People's Political Consultative Congress, argued that such ideas represented a "double betrayal" of both the "motherland" and the "Dalai Lama system of Tibetan Buddhism." No individual Dalai Lama, he stated, has the right to change the rules of reincarnation without the approval of the Chinese central government.[78] Foreign observers, who appear to be viewing this conflict with more bemusement than genuine concern, have generally concurred with the Dalai Lama that there is something inherently illegitimate about an explicitly atheist government demanding the final say over his reincarnation.[79]

With regard to the ongoing conflict between the Fourteenth Dalai Lama and the CCP, two final observations are in order. First, it is helpful to point out why the CCP's claims makes sense—at least from the perspective of its cadres in institutions such as the China Tibetology Research Center. The party's justification for the 2007 law does not emerge from any claim that the CCP is some sort of higher Buddhist authority, nor does it derive simply from the question of national security and territorial integrity. Instead it derives its legitimacy from its claim to be enforcing a *law*. Agents of the CCP see themselves as providing the only transparent legal framework by which credible incarnations can be found. Within this framework, they imagine Tibetan Buddhist experts—monks from the home community of the lama in question or other religious authorities affiliated with China's various provincial and national Buddhist associations—conducting the search along "traditional" lines until the final candidate can ultimately be shepherded into the educational system of the PRC. Moreover, since 2014 the law on reincarnation has dovetailed with CCP General Secretary Xi Jinping's broader inititive to clean up the governance of China by "ruling the country according to the law" (Ch. *yifa zhiguo* 依法治國)—an effort to make government decision making more transparent, regularized, and less susceptible to corruption. In an uncanny way, the CCP's understanding of the Golden Urn is remarkably similar to that of the Qianlong emperor.

Second, we assume at our peril that Tibetan Buddhists within the PRC axiomatically view the CCP's policies as illegitimate and that the party will therefore struggle to find well-respected lamas to help identify and educate the young incarnations. Much as during the Qing period, state certification has enabled reincarnate lamas to more easily reside within the provinces of the Chinese interior and minister to ever-growing flocks of Han Chinese devotees. And it would be crude to view this as mere financial opportunism: many of the monks and lamas who have been busily expanding their missions among Han Chinese have taken inspiration from the current Dalai Lama, who has urged his followers to spread the faith beyond the ethnic or geographic confines of Tibet. Therefore, despite the adamance of both the Chinese government and the Tibetan government in exile that they will be the one to have the last word on reincarnation, it is perhaps safer to predict a future of multiple Dalai Lamas and competing reincarnation lineages.

The best evidence for this prediction is recent developments in the career of the PRC's Panchen Lama, who, despite careful state management (or perhaps because of it), has begun to gather a considerable following among Han Buddhists, who have few doubts about his authenticity and the identification process.[80] Since 2007, the target audience for performances of the modern Golden Urn lottery has been the majority Han population of China, not the Tibetans of the Tibetan Autonomous Region or neighboring autonomous areas. And this constituency has embraced not only the lottery but also the Communist Party's claim that the national government has a role to play in overseeing the selection and education of reincarnate lamas. To put it bluntly, the acceptance of the Golden Urn among Tibetans or foreign publics is of secondary importance to its acceptance by the broader non-Tibetan Han citizenry of the PRC. The party's reluctant decision to revive the Golden Urn and formally legalize reincarnation coincided with a great surge in efforts to revive "traditional" religious culture across China and gave further encouragement to those Han who were curious about Tibetan Buddhism. It is now possible to observe a strange paradox: faith in reincarnation is declining among Tibetan Buddhists, but perhaps growing among Han Buddhists.[81] From the perspective of some urban Han in the sprawling metropolises of eastern China, the "pristine" ecology of Tibet, the esotericism of Tantric traditions, and the apparent traditionalism and almost inexplicable devotion of the Tibetan faithful have all buttressed the perceived authenticity and even superiority of Tibetan reincarnate lamas to Chinese monks. In the 1790s, the Golden Urn lottery was invented as a solution to a perceived crisis of faith in Inner Asia; its revival in the 1990s exposed reform-era China's anxieties about the nation's territorial integrity and spiritual well-being. The Golden Urn has subsequently become an object of nationalist devotion within China, where the mystique of the lottery speaks to the desire to recover the religious practices of a glorious imperial past.

The significance of local elites in translating and transforming the ideas of the metropole into new and legitimate forms of local religious culture during the nineteenth century reminds us that although the ideological worlds of the Great Qing State and the People's Republic are almost entirely foreign to each other, we should pay more attention to the range of intermediary figures—Geluk lamas, party cadres, United Front operatives, state-employed academics, et cetera—who bridge the gap between Beijing and indigenous communities. One need look no further than the Sixth Jamyang Zhepa, Lozang Jigmé Tubten Chökyi Nyima (b. 1948) of Labrang monastery, current deputy chairman of the National People's Congress committee on *minzu* affairs, for an example of a Geluk *trülku* who has leveraged his local authority to serve the CCP's state-building policies in Tibetan regions. If the CCP hopes to rely on future generations of *trülku* and insists on using the Golden Urn to find them, they will have to work with people like the Sixth Jamyang Zhepa to find a way of making the lottery acceptable again to Tibetan Buddhists.

The CCP officials, however, are reluctant pluralists. The former Qing domain in Inner Asia is like a valuable piece of real estate, but one littered with ungainly buildings and obstreperous tenants. Like other postimperial states, the People's Republic has inherited the diverse cultures of the former empire, and struggles to balance this heterogeneity against the demands of the majority of its citizens for cultural conformity (especially with regard to use of the Chinese language), legal uniformity, free movement, and economic development. The PRC's willingness to tolerate diversity in the form of autonomous regions and party-supervised religious and cultural associations has become increasingly constrained by the view that such institutions not only have become enclaves of ethnic nationalism and separatism but also privilege minorities at the expense of the majority.[82] Aggressive state policy to promote the "fusion" (*ronghe* 融合) of the fifty-six state-sanctioned *minzu* leaves little room for *trülku* like the Jamyang Zhepa to reinvent a narrative of state–Geluk partnership in the promotion of Buddhism.

The early history of the Golden Urn should not be read, though, as an edifying tale from which the modern Chinese state should learn. The Qianlong emperor, his field agents, and the hierarchs of the Geluk church were also—with some rare exceptions—not willing pluralists. Qing cosmopolitanism had its limits. Commonplace dictums to "follow the local customs" or "nurture each separately without altering their traditions" reflected strategic forbearance for the ignorance and irritability of the common folk, not boundless tolerance for diversity. Qing and Geluk officials made such gestures from a position of blistering confidence in the righteousness of their "high" doctrinal traditions. They made common cause because they saw mutual benefit in the preservation and promotion of their truths. The Qing state was an empire of orthodoxies, and, when capable of it, sought its full measure of justice against those who held contrary notions. Just ask the oracles.

Chronology of Key Events

1788 (Qianlong 53):

May: Lamo Chökyong oracle confirms identification of Fourth Changkya *kūtuktu*.

Summer: First Gurkha invasion of Tibet.

1791 (Qianlong 56):

January 13: Galdan Siretu Samadi Baksi arrives in Lhasa to serve as regent.

April 29: Death of regent, reappointment of Tatsak *kūtuktu*.

August 21: Lhasa *amban* Bootai reports abductions of Tibetan ministers (*kalön*) and invasion of Gurkha forces.

September 5: Tatsak *kūtuktu* returns to Lhasa.

September 17: Gurkha forces capture Shigatze and Trashi Lhünpo.

September 22: Dalai Lama refuses *ambans'* instructions to leave Lhasa.

October 20: Gurkha forces pull back from Trashi Lhünpo.

November 29: Fuk'anggan ordered to lead troops against Nepal.

December 23: Lhasa *amban* Ohūi reports investigation at Trashi Lhünpo and execution of Lozang Tenpa.

1792 (Qianlong 57):

January 26: Fuk'anggan arrives at outskirts of Lhasa.

February 14: Fuk'anggan meets with Dalai Lama.

March 6: Fuk'anggan departs for the front.

March 22: Heliyen dispatched to Tibet.

June 4: Heliyen arrives in Lhasa.

June 13: Emperor issues instructions to Heliyen about how to present himself before the Dalai Lama.

July 9: Emperor demands eradication of the oracles.

August 4: Heliyen reports on the Lamo Chökyong oracle.

August 17: Emperor orders Grand Councilor Agūi to deliberate on implementing a lottery. First mention of identifying reincarnations using urn (Manchu).

August 18: Imperial workshops instructed to begin forging the urn.

September 11: Imperial court letter dispatched from Grand Council to Fuk'anggan informing him of the urn.

October: Qing military reaches Katmandu; Gurkhas surrender.

October 12: Emperor orders Fuk'anggan et. al. to consider broader reforms of Tibetan administration. First mention of Golden Urn in Chinese. Qianlong departs the summer residence in Chengde for Beijing.

October 14: Emperor issues Manchu- and Mongol-language proclamation to Inner Asian elites introducing the Golden Urn, banning rebirth of *kūtuktus* among noble households.

October 17: Urn completed in imperial workshop; October 25, dispatched to Lhasa.

Mid-November: Qianlong composes the edict *Discourse on Lamas*.

November 29: Fuk'anggan arrives in Lhasa, meets again with Dalai Lama.

December 6: Fuk'anggan and Heliyen offer advice on how to implement the Golden Urn.

1793 (Qianlong 58)

January 2: Golden Urn arrives in Lhasa.

January 9: Emperor learns that disciples of the Galdan Siretu *kūtuktu* have been caught illegally seeking alms among Oirad Mongols in far western Mongolia. He orders greater scrutiny of Geluk monks in border regions.

January 10: Emperor informs the Grand Council that he is suspicious of the authenticity of the Fourth Changkya *kūtuktu*.

February 8: Grand Councilor Agūi evaluates Fuk'anggan's reform measures for central Tibet.

February 9: Fuk'anggan investigates oracles in Lhasa.

March 16: Emperor orders Heliyen to secretly investigate the Erdeni Pandita case and interrogate the Dalai Lama.

March 24: Fuk'anggan reports first use of Golden Urn, identifies minor reincarnations from Inner Mongolia.

April 3–4: Fuk'anggan presents the *Twenty-Nine Articles* for reforming the Ganden Podrang government to the Dalai Lama. Departs Lhasa.

April: Tüsiyetü Khan brought to Beijing and interrogated. Heliyen interrogates Dalai Lama and medium of Lamo *chökyong* oracle in Lhasa.

April 25: Heliyen conducts further public tests of oracles in Lhasa.

April 27: Emperor bans Mongols from traveling to Tibet to consult the oracles.

May 5: Identification of Erdeni Pandita reincarnation at Yonghegong.

May 28: Emperor issues court letter to Tibetan and Mongol elites on the identification of the Erdeni Pandita (in Manchu, Mongol, and Tibetan). *Discourse on Lamas* entered into the *Veritable Records*.

July 2: Having received confidential reports on the Dalai Lama's mood from Heliyen, emperor issues edict formally proclaiming the successful identification of Erdeni Pandita.

July 15: Emperor orders that the Golden Urn become a fixed law.

September 18: Emperor orders the Dalai Lama and oracles to stop conducting all divinations.

October 19: Tibetan version of edict of May 28 distributed to Lhasa.

1794 (Qianlong 59)

April: Emperor issues private instructions to Heliyen about adjusting the Golden Urn law. *Kūtuktu* from Chamdo must be identified using the urn in Lhasa, but can be identified among noble families.

June 22: Emperor orders stone stele inscribed with the *Discourse on Lamas* to be erected at the Jokhang Temple in Lhasa and Yonghegong in Beijing.

September 11: Heliyen reports death of Pakpalha *kūtuktu*.

October 27: Sungyun informs emperor of his strategy for employing the Golden Urn in the case of the Pakpalha *kūtuktu*.

December 3: Noyan *kūtuktu* of Mongolia found to have committed murder and stripped of status.

December 5: Sungyun reports arriving in Lhasa and meeting with Dalai Lama.

1796 (Jiaqing 01)

February 9 (The Lunar New Year): The Qianlong emperor abdicates to his son but continues to rule in practice.

June: Fuk'anggan dies of disease while supervising campaign against Miao rebels.

September 10: Sungyun reports identification of Pakpalha *kūtuktu* using the Golden Urn.

September: Heliyen dies of disease in the Miao campaign.

December 19: Xining *amban* Tsebak reports status of search for reincarnation of the Second Jamyang Zhepa.

1797 (Jiaqing 02)

February 2: Sungyun reports plans to manipulate the Golden Urn in the case of the search for the Third Jamyang Zhepa.

March 26: Delegation from Labrang monastery has left for Lhasa.

Septermber 22: Lhasa *amban* Sungyun reports identification of the Third Jamyang Zhepa.

1798 (Jiaqing 03)

January 6: Sungyun reports on the successful aftermath of identification of the Jamyang Zhepa.

List of Usages of the Golden Urn Ritual

Year	Name/Title	Location	Golden Urn?	Sources
1793	Sumpa *kūtuktu* 遜巴呼圖克圖/逊巴呼图克图	Lhasa	Yes	YHGSL
1793	Da Lama Lozang Tupten 達喇嘛羅卜藏多布丹	Lhasa	Yes	YHGSL
1793	Da Lama Lozang Tenzin 達喇嘛羅卜藏丹津	Lhasa	Yes	YHGSL
1793	Lama Lozang Da-bu-kai 達喇嘛羅布藏達布凱	Lhasa	Yes	YHGSL
1793	Lama Döndrub Peljor 喇嘛敦珠布班珠爾	Lhasa	Yes	YHGSL
1793	Erdeni Pandita *kūtuktu*	Beijing	Yes	MWJXD
1796	Pakpalha *kūtuktu* 08	Beijing	Yes	MWLF
1797	Jamyang Zhepa *kūtuktu* 03	Lhasa	Yes	MWLF
1800	Tsemonling *kūtuktu* 02 (Yonghegong Samadi Bakši)	Beijing	Yes	MWLF/YHGSL/ BGLYB
1802	Sumpa *kūtuktu*	Lhasa	Yes	MWLF
1802	Zhiwala *kūtuktu* 05	Lhasa	Yes	MWLF/BGLYB
1803	Rongwo Nomunhan	Beijing	Yes	MWLF
1803	Tongkhor *kūtuktu*	Beijing	Yes	MWLF/YHGSL

(continued)

Year	Name/Title	Location	Golden Urn?	Sources
1804	Chuzang *kūtuktu*	Lhasa	Yes	MWLF
1808	Yongdzin Pandita Yeshé Gyeltsen	Lhasa	Yes	MWLF/ BGLYB
1808	Dalai Lama 09	Lhasa	Exempted	MWLF
1808	Pandita Nomunhan Lozang Jampa 班第達諾們罕羅布藏嘉木巴勒	Beijing	Probably	MWLF/BGLYB
1808?	Nakshö Takpu *trülku* 06	Lhasa	Yes	BGLYB
1809?	Tukwan *kūtuktu* 04	Lhasa	Yes	MWLF
1809	Ölga Jedrung 05	Lhasa	Yes	BGLYB
1809	Taklung *trülku* 05	Lhasa	Yes	BGLYB
1810	Wanggya *kūtuktu* 旺嘉呼圖克圖	Lhasa	Yes	MWLF
1811	Dreprung Ling *trülku* 04	Lhasa	Yes	BGLYB
1812	Tsurpu Gyeltsap *trülku* 05	Lhasa	Yes	BGLYB
1812	Ditsa *trülku* 07	Lhasa	Yes	BGLYB
1813	Tatsak *kūtuktu* 09	Lhasa	Yes	MWLF/ BGLYB
1813	Öngyel Sé *trülku* 06	Lhasa	Yes	BGLYB
1813	Taksé Khülzimpa Tago *trülku* 05	Lhasa	Yes	BGLYB
1814?	Karmapa *trülku* 14	Lhasa	Yes	BGLYB
1814?	Jorra *trülku* 06	Lhasa	Yes	BGLYB
1814	Dalai *kūtuktu* (?)	Lhasa	Yes	MWLF
1814	Nyidé Lama Jewön *trülku* 06	Lhasa	Yes	BGLYB
1815	Tongkhor *kūtuktu* 08	Lhasa	Yes	MWLF/ BGLYB
1815	Markham Özer *trülku* 06	Lhasa	Yes	BGLYB
1816	Drakyap *trülku ché* 06	Lhasa	Yes	MWLF/ BGLYB
1816	Jebtsundamba 06	Beijing	Yes	MWLF/ BGLYB
1816	Tsabor *trülku* 10	Lhasa	Yes	BGLYB
1816	Tashi Jong *trülku* 08	Lhasa	Yes	BGLYB
1817?	Ganden Ritrö *trülku* 08	Lhasa	Yes	BGLYB
1819?	Dorjédrak Rindzin Chenmo 07	Lhasa	Yes	BGLYB
1820	Riwoché *kūtuktu* 04	Lhasa	Yes	BGLYB
1822	Dalai Lama 10	Lhasa	Yes	Multiple sources
1824	Demo *kūtuktu* 09	Lhasa	Yes	MWLF
1825	Tongkhor Lama 09	Lhasa	Yes	MWLF/ BGLYB
1832	Tukwan *kūtuktu* 05	Lhasa	Yes	MWLF
1837	Cagan Nomunhan 06	Lhasa	Yes	MWLF

Year	Name/Title	Location	Golden Urn?	Sources
1841	Dalai Lama 11	Lhasa	Yes	MWLF
1843	Tukwan *kūtuktu* 06	Lhasa	Yes	MWLF
1844	Jebstundamba 06	Lhasa	Yes	MWLF
1846	Mindröl *kūtuktu* 敏珠爾呼圖克圖	Lhasa	Yes	MWLF
1850	Jebtsundamba 07	Lhasa	Yes	MWLF
1850	Changkya *kūtuktu* 05	Beijing	Yes	Multiple sources
1852	Galdan Siretu *kūtuktu*	Lhasa	Yes	MWLF
1852	Pakpalha *kūtuktu* 09	Lhasa	Yes	MWLF
1853	Wanggya *kūtuktu*	Lhasa	Yes	MWLF
1856	Panchen Lama 08	Lhasa	Yes	MWLF
1858	Dalai Lama 12	Lhasa	Yes	MWLF
1858	Tatsak *kūtuktu* 10	Lhasa	Yes	MWLF
1858	Demo *kūtuktu* 10	Lhasa	Yes	MWLF
1860	Sumpa *kūtuktu*	Lhasa	Yes	MWLF
1861	Chuzang *kūtuktu*	Lhasa	Yes	MWLF
1861	Jamyang Zhepa 04	Lhasa	Yes	MWLF
1865	Zhaya *kūtuktu*	Lhasa	Yes	MWLF
1865	Zhiwala *kūtuktu*	Lhasa	Yes	MWLF
1871	Jebtsundamba 08	Lhasa	Yes	MWLF
1875	Arjia *kūtuktu* 阿嘉呼圖克圖	Lhasa	Yes	MWLF
1877	Dalai Lama 13	Lhasa	Exempted	Multiple sources
1877	Reting *kūtuktu* 04	Lhasa	Yes	MWLF
1879	Cagan Nomunhan 07	Lhasa	Yes	Lhasa Copybook I /MWLF
1882	Changkya *kūtuktu* 06	Beijing	Yes	MWLF/YHGSL
1883	Mindröl *kūtuktu*	?	Probably	MWLF
1886	Zhaya *kūtuktu*	Lhasa	Yes	MWLF
1888	Tonghkor *kūtuktu* 10	Lhasa	Probably	MWLF
1888	Panchen Lama 09	Lhasa	Yes	MWLF
1890	Tatsak *kūtuktu* 11	Lhasa	Yes	Taibei Palace Memorial doc. # 171082

(continued)

Year	Name/Title	Location	Golden Urn?	Sources
1894	Changkya *kūtuktu* 07	Lhasa	Yes	Lhasa Copybook II
1900	Tukwan *kūtuktu* 07	Lhasa	Yes	Copybook II
1901	Mo-luo mu-lan zhan-ba-han erdeni hūbilgan 莫羅木蘭占巴綽汗額爾德尼呼畢勒罕	Beijing	Yes	YHGSL
1901	Cagan Dayanci *kūtuktu* 查罕典齊呼圖克圖	Beijing	Yes	YHGSL
1904	Dejū *kūtuktu*	Lhasa	Yes	MWLF
1908	Galdan Siretu *kūtuktu*	Lhasa	Yes	MWLF
1908	Pakpa Lha *kūtuktu*	Lhasa	Yes	MWLF
1908	Zhaya Pandita *kūtuktu*	Beijing	Yes	YHGSL
1909	Erdeni Mergen Pandita Nomunhan 額爾德呢墨爾根班第達諾門罕	Beijing	Yes	YHGSL
1910	Demo *kūtuktu* 11	Beijing	Exempted	清實錄

Tibetan Orthographic Equivalents

Amdo = A mdo

Belmang Pandita 02 Könchok Gyeltsen = Dpal mang paN+Di ta 02 Dkon mchog rgyal mtshan

böpa drungkhor nyi = bod pa drung 'khor gnyis

chakdzö = phyag mdzod

Changkya *kūtuktu* = Lcang skya *ho thog thu*

chö = chos

Chödrup Gyatso = Chog grub rgya mtsho (the Tenth Zhamarpa)

chögyel ma = chos rgyal ma

chökyong = chos skyong

chöné = mchod gnas

chö-si zungdrel = chos srid zung 'brel

chötrim = chos khrims

chöyon gyi kadrin = mchod yon gyi bka' drin

Chuzang 03 Ngawang Tubten Wangchuk = Chu bzang 03 Ngag dbang thub bstan dbang phyug

dakzhen ma = bdag gzhan ma

Demo 08 Ngawang Tubten Jikmé Gyatso = De mo 08 Ngag dbang thub bstan 'jigs med rgya mtsho

depa = sde pa

Ditsa *trülku* = Rdi tsha *sprul sku*

dokné = dogs gnas

Doring Tendzin Peljor = Rdo ring bstan 'dzin dpal 'byor

Dorjédrak Rindzin Chenmo = Rdo rje brag rig 'dzin chen mo

Drakgönpa Könchok Tenpa Rapgyé = Brag dgon pa dkon mchog bstan pa rab rgyas

Drakyap *trülku ché* = Brag g.yab *sprul sku che*

Dreprung Ling *trülku* = 'Bras sbungs gling *sprul sku*

drongjuk = grong 'jug

drönyer = mgron snyer

Drungpa *rinpoché* Lozang Jinpa = Drung pa rin po che Blo bzang sbyin pa

Dülagyel = Bdud la rgyal

dzölga zhik = 'dzol 'ga' zhig

Erdeni Pandita *kūtuktu* = Er de ni paN+Di ta *ho thog thu*

Ganden Ritrö *trülku* = Dga' ldan ri khrod *sprul sku*

Gungtang *kūtuktu* = Gung thang *ho thog thu*

gur gyi loppön = gur gyi slob dpon

gyami = rgya mi

gyanakpa lama = rgya nag pa bla ma

gyayül gyelkhap chenpo = rgya yul rgyal khab chen po

gyelkhab rangwang = rgyal khab rang dbang

gyeltrim = rgyal khrims

Gyelwa Gyatso (Tongkhor 03) = Rgyal ba rgya mtsho

Gyurmé Namgyel = 'Gyur med rnam rgyal

Jampel Gyatso (Dalai Lama 08) = 'Jam dpal rgya mtsho

Jamyang Gyatso (Tongkhor 06) = 'Jam dbyangs bstan 'dzin rgya mtsho

Jamyang Sherab Paldan (Dejū 06) = 'Jam dbyangs she rab dpal ldan

jedrung = rje drung

Jigme Tenpai Gonpo (Pakpalha 07) = 'Jigs med bstan pa'i mgon po

jindak = sbyin bdag

Jorra *trülku* = Sbyor ra *sprul sku*

kachu = dka' bcu

Karma Kagyü = Karma Bka' brgyud

Karma Püntsok Namgyel = Karma Phun tshogs dbang phyug

Karma Tenkyong = Karma bstan skyong

Kelsang Gyatso (Dalai Lama 07) = Skal bzang rgya mtsho

Kelzang Bum = Skal bzang 'bum

Kham = Khams

Khenpo Ngawang Tupten Gyatso = Mkhan po ngag dbang thub bstan ryga mtsho

Könchok Senggé = Dkon mchog seng+ge

Könchok Tenpé Drönmé (Gungtang 03) = Dkon mchog bstan pa'i sgron me

Künga Gyeltsen = Kun dga' rgyal mtshan

kutenpa = sku rten pa

Kyirong = Skyid grong

Labrang Tashi Khyil = La brang bkra shi 'khyil

Lamo *chökyong* = La mo *chos skyong*

Lamo Zhabdrung Karpo = La mo zhabs drung dkar po

lharampa = Lha rams pa

Longdöl *rinpoché* Ngawang Lozang = Klong rdol bla ma Ngag dbang blo bzang

Lozang Chokyi Nyima (Tukwan 03) = Blo bzang cho kyi nyi ma

Lozang Dargyé = Blo bzang dar rgyas

Lozang Tupten Jikmé Gyatso (Jamyang Zhepa 03) = Blo bzang thub bstan 'jigs med rgya mtsho

luk nyi = *lugs gnyis*

lungden = *lung dan*

Markham Özer *trülku* = Smar khams 'Od zer *sprul sku*

Mindröl *kūtuktu* = Smin grol *ho thog thu*

Nakshö Takpu *trülku* = Nags shod stag phu *sprul sku*

Ngawang Lozang Chöden (Changkya 02) = Ngag dbang blo bzang chos ldan

Ngawang Lozang Gyatso (Dalai Lama 05) = Ngag dbang blo bzang rgya mtsho

Ngawang Tsultrim (Tsemonling 01) = Ngag dbang tshul khrims

Ngawang Tupten Trinlé Gyatso (Galdan Siretu 04) = Ngag dbang thub bstan 'phrin las rgya mtsho

nyerpa = *gnyer pa*

Nyidé Lama Jewön *trülku* = Nyi lde bla ma rje dbon gyi *sprul sku*

Nyima = nyi ma

Ölga *jedrung* = 'Ol dga' *rje drung*

Öngyel Sé *trülku* = 'On rgyal sras *sprul sku*

Pakpa Lama = 'Phags pa bla ma

Pakpalha = Phags pa lha

Polhané = Pho lha nas

Rangjung Dorjé (Karmapa 03) = Rang 'byung rdo rje

Reting Jowo Jampé Dorjé = Rwa sgreng jo wo 'jam pa'i rdo rje)

Rinchen Gyatso = Rin chen rgya mtsho

Rolpé Dorjé = Rol pa'i rdo rje

Rangen = rwa ngan

Reting *rinpoché* = Rwa sgreng *rin po che*

ser gyi bum = *gser gyi bum*

Sherab Gyatso = Shes rab rgya mtsho

Sherab Kanjur = Shes rab bka' 'gyur)

si = *srid*

Sumpa Khenpo Yeshé Peljor = Sum pa mkhan po ye shes dpal 'jor

takdril = *brtag sgril*

Taklung *trülku* = Stag lung *sprul sku*

Taksé Khülzimpa Tago *trülku* = Stag rtse khul gzims pa rta mgo sprul sku

tangka = *thang ka*

Tatsak *kūtuktu* = Rta tshag *ho thog thu*

ten bar ma = *bstan 'bar ma*

Tengyur = Bstan 'gyur

Tongkhor *kūtuktu* = Stong 'khor *ho thog thu*

Tashi Jong *trülku* = Bkra shis ljongs sprul sku

Trashi Lhünpo = Bkra shi lhun po

trim nyi = *khrims gnyis*

trülmé = *'khrul med*

Tsabor trülku = Rtsa 'bor *sprul sku*

Tsang = Gtsang

tsemé drangpa = tsad mas drang pa

Tsemonling *kūtuktu* = Tshe smon gling *ho thog thu*

tsen jang gyurwa = mtshan byang bsgyur ba

tsenté = mtshan ltas

Tsurpu Gyeltsap *trülku* = Mtshur phu rgyal tshab *sprul sku*

Tukwan *kūtuktu* = Th'u bkwan *ho thog thu*

Ü = Us

Wangchen Bum = Dbang chen 'bum

Wangdan Dorjé Phalam = Dbang ldan rdo rje pha lam

yangsi = yang srid

Yeshé Lozang Tenpé Gönpo (Tatsak 08) = Ye shes slo bzang bstan pa'i mgon po

yiché = yid ches

yöndak = yon bdag

Yönten Gyatso (Dalai Lama 04) = Yon ten gya mtsho

zendril = zan bsgril

zengyur = zan bsgyur

zentak = zan rtag

zha ser = zhwa ser

Zhamarpa *lama* = Zhwa dmar pa *bla ma*

Zhiwala Pakpa Gelek Gyeltsan = Zhi ba lha 'phags pa dge legs rgyal mtshan

Translation of the Qianlong Emperor's
Discourse on Lamas

Translated from the Tibetan text.[1]

An edict concerning the succession of lamas:

As for the Buddha's teaching, it arose in the land of India and spread eastward to Tibet[2] (also [known as] Tanggūt or Zang). It is the tradition that monks of Tibet are called *lama*. This term *lama* does not exist in the documents of China. In the Chinese-language books of the Yuan and Ming states there is the incorrect expression *la mu*. (According to the written record *Chuogenglu*[3] composed by Tao Zongyi,[4] during the time of the Yuan court the preceptor of the king was called *la mu'a*. In the book *Unofficial History of the Ming* [emperor] *Wu Zong*,[5] written by Mao Qiling,[6] there was written the word *la ma*. Because they all wrote according to their own ideas, there was not a uniform way of writing.) When I carefully consider this matter, in the Tibetan language, *bla* means superior and *ma* means not; thus *lama* means unsurpassed.

This is similar to the way monks [Tib. *hwa shang*] are called "honored men" [Tib. *shang zhin*] in the language of China. The lama's learning is called the teaching of the Yellow Hats. The Tibetan lama of sublime superior knowledge, 'Phags pa (also called Phas ba), from the time of the Yuan court until the Ming court was celebrated by all as both the "Preceptor of the King" and "Preceptor of the State."

(Shizu of the Yuan first presented the title "Preceptor of the State" to the Royal Preceptor, 'Phags pa Lama. Later, [he] titled ['Phags pa], "Preceptor of the King, Great Precious Dharma Lord," and another famous person named Bstan pa was also titled "Preceptor of the King." After that, the number of other so-called "State Preceptors" was innumerable. In just the first year of King Hongwu of the Ming court's reign, the titles of "State Preceptor" and "Great State Preceptor" were given to at least four or five Tibetan people. In the reign of the Yongle emperor, there were two Tibetan people who received the titles of "Dharma Lord" and "Son of the Buddha of India." There were an additional eighteen Tibetan people who were titled "State Preceptor Who Upholds the Teaching." Up through the reigns of Jingtai [1449–1457] and Chenghua [1464–1487] there again were an uncountable number [of titled monks].)

In my state,[7] only the Changkya *kūtuktu*, having been entitled "State Preceptor" during the time of King Kangxi,[8] has from then until now continuously [held this title].

(Although my state holds in high esteem the Yellow Hat teachings, as for establishing the title of the so-called "Preceptor of the King," this has not [been allowed]. In the forty-fifth year of the Kangxi reign, according to edict, Changkya *kūtuktu* was given the [title] "Holder of the Teaching, State Preceptor," and after his death, in the twelfth year of Yong-zheng [1734], it was [permitted] to pass the title to all his subsequent incarnations.)

As for the titles of the Dalai Lama and Panchen Erdeni, we have followed the old practices of bestowing titles [begun] by the Yuan and Ming courts, and, other than carving new seals, have not added additional honors.

(As for the origin of the flourishing of the teachings of the Yellow Hats, it arose from the lama Tsongkhapa of the Ming dynasty. Tsongkhapa was born in the fire-bird, fifteenth year of Yongle [1417] and attained nirvana in the fourteenth year of Chenghua [1478].[9] He had two main disciples: one is called the Dalai Lama and the other one is called the Panchen. The Dalai Lama is of higher status, named Monlam Gyatso, and his successive rebirths are the Holders of the Teaching of the Yellow Hats. The name of the first incarnation was Gendun Drupba. The second was Gendun Gyatso [1476–1542]. The third was Sonam Gyatso [1543–1588]. At the time of the Ming his name [was written as, *sic*] "gson po so nan gyin tshu." The fourth was Yonden Gyatso. The fifth was Ngawang Lozang Gyatso. In the seventh year of the reign of Wesihun Erdemungge [1643] of my state, the Dalai Lama and Panchen Erdeni both presented valuable goods from their country. In the eighth year, letters were sent to both of them, written according to the old practices of the Yuan and Ming states. After he took control of the central land,[10] seals of office were sent to them both, establishing them as the governing lamas of the entire Yellow Teaching.)

Those two have taken charge of the Yellow Hat teachings in the Outer and Inner, and obtained the veneration of the Mongols of many regions. As for [our] high esteem for the Yellow Hat teaching, it is in accordance with the desires of the Mongols and therefore not only important but also necessary. It is not like during the time of the Yuan state when the lamas were venerated by flattery and gifts.

(During the Yuan state, due to the high esteem for lamas, the royal laws were broken and great injury arose. At that time, the pronouncements of the preceptor to the king were obeyed as if they were edicts of the king. At the place of audiences, the ministers stood while the preceptor of the king knelt on one knee at the side of the hall. Among the preceptor's monks there were those offered positions as minister of the treasury, minister of the household, and court duke; and when they had obtained gifts of seals made from gold and jade, there was disorder on account of their pride, and following their desires they engaged in lewd acts. Thus in every direction problems arose. In their conceit they raised taxes on the resources of their subjects, they beat ministers, and even, after robbing a consort of a great lord, dragged her down from her carriage and beat her. All this was done without punishment. Moreover, there were laws that if a servant struck a lama, his arm would be cut off, and if a [lama] was insulted, the tongue would be cut out. There has been no such veneration of lamas by me. The Mongols hold high the Buddha and have faith in the lamas; [therefore] as one leads a horse, they must be taken care of.)

As for the title of *kūtuktu* by which they are praised: since the lamas have no children, they are given disciples like one provides a son, searching for a child with insight and auspiciousness. The *trülku* (in the language of China, this is called "a person who is born generation after generation") having filled that role, he is given the title of *kūtuktu* and gradually takes up the teaching. Over many years this practices continues, and it is difficult to cut off. Now it has become a frequent occurrence that after successive generations the *trülku* have all begun to emanate among their near relatives, which is like a son taking the office of his father, and this causes my thoughts to become alarmed. Not to mention, if the Buddha himself was never reborn, where do all these common *trülku* come from? They cannot be done away with, for if today there were no more reincarnations of *hutuktu*, the thousands of lamas would no longer have that which they rely on.

(An examination of the successive generations of the Dalai Lama: as for the first birth, he reincarnated at the place *Sha do da* in Tsang. As for the second, [he was reborn] at *Ta na do rdo rje* in Tsang. As for the third, [he was born] at *Rdo rengs* in Lhasa. The fourth was born in the household of the Mongol Altan Khan; the fifth was born at *Chung skya* in Lhasa; the sixth was born at a place in Litang, and the current seventh was reborn at *Li kang* in *Thob rgyal* in Tsang. Since the locations are all different, is there still any need to discuss further that they hailed from different families? As for the Panchen Erdeni, after the previous one passed away into nirvana, the reincarnations of the present Dalai Lama and Panchen Erdeni, as well as the Jebtsundamba *kūtuktu* of the four Khalkha, all have been reborn as relatives, sharing the relationships of uncle and nephew. If great Holders of the Teaching such as these all share familial relations, then it is no different from the inheritance of titles within a lineage. Nowadays, the *trülku* venerated by *jasaks* of the Outer and Inner [Mongols] have also begun to emanate as the sons of their princes and dukes! The *Shi re tu* [Ma. Siletu] *kūtuktu* is the uncle of the Khalkha *chen wang* [first-rank prince] *Gu run E ha pu lha dbang rdo rje*. The *Stag pa kūtuktu* is the son of the Alashan *chen wang Blo bzang rdo rje*. The *No yon chos rje kūtuktu* is the son of the *Dur pan He'u hed jun wang* [second-rank prince] *Bkra shis yar 'phel*. The reincarnation of the *Mkhan po no min han 'Jam dpal rdo rje* is the son of the Tüsiyetü Khan, *Tshe ldan rdo rje*. It is impossible to have such a [large] number of this type! After the death of the previous Jebtsundamba *kūtuktu*, the queen of the Tüsiyetü Khan became pregnant. It was proclaimed to all that this would be the reincarnation of the Jebstundamba. However, when the time arrived, a daughter was born. This affair was laughable. As a result the Mongols came to be disdained.

Moreover there is the arrogant behavior of the Zhamarpa lama, who coveted the treasures of Trashi Lhünpo. Because he was a brother of the Panchen Erdeni and Drungpa *kūtutku*, he claimed a share [of the former's wealth] and passed secrets on to the Gurkhas. As a result, bandits from a distant land assailed and plundered the land of Tsang. Recently an army was dispatched that, having frightened the Gurkhas, forced them to beg forgiveness for their transgressions. However, if the source of this evil is not rooted out, in the future such reciprocal relations based on self-interest will make it impossible to restore the teachings of the Yellow Hats. Once two minds [i.e., doubts] have arisen among the Tibetans and Mongols, it is possible that there will be trouble. Therefore [I] have commanded that when there is a search for an important lama of Ü-Tsang, in accordance with their tradition, the whereabouts of the [incarnation] shall be identified by the special means of reciting scriptures and receiving [oracles] when the Lamo *chökyong* and the other four [protectors] descend to the medium. Rolls of paper with the names of each of the children shall be placed in a golden urn that will have been sent from the palace. Then, having chanted before the Jowo Sakyamuni, the Dalai Lama and Panchen Erdeni, together with the appointed *ambans*, will jointly pick out a roll of paper. That will be the reincarnation. I have ordered that the identification occur in this manner. Although this may not entirely eliminate the evils of doing things according to their individual desires, [I] believe that this is better than letting them make a decision regarding the identification however they please. Additionally, in accordance with the proclamation issued by the Mongol Yamen [i.e., the Court of Colonial Affairs], and following the newly established tradition of Ü-Tsang, the important *trülku* of the Mongols must be identified by having their names placed in the Golden Urn before the image of the Buddha at Yonghegong jointly by the seal-holding minister of the capital and the seal-holding Great Lama. If it is done in that fashion, the true incarnation will have been identified and there will be no further dispute over the selection like there would be if it was made according to their own self-interests.)

Last year's raid on the region of Tsang by the Gurkhas who trusted in the words whispered by the Zhamarpa offers what lessons? Having been terrorized by [our] military, [the Gurkhas] sought forgiveness and Tsang was returned to peace. Furthermore, when a new *trülku* emerges and is reborn again within the same family, this is a decision [motivated by] their own desires. The Buddha had no concern for himself. The royal law is indispensable. Now that I have forged the Golden Urn and had it dispatched to Ü-Tsang, paper scrolls with the written names of those who are suspected of being *trülku* shall be placed in the urn. Although this measure will not completely eliminate the evils, [I] have ascertained that it will be superior to identifications that are the decision of individual people. When making a judgment about a matter, it is necessary to examine relevant traditions concerning the matter. If I had not previously studied the Tibetan Dharma,[11] I would be unable to discourse on this. When I first started studying, there were some Chinese who said that I placed excessive importance on the teachings of the Yellow Hats. If, according to the Chinese books, the [teachings of the Yellow Hats] were simply famous for nothing, how is it that today, the new and old Mongols have been subjugated and for several tens [of years] have lived in peace and contentment?

Nowadays, as for the recent execution, conducted according to law, of the lama responsible for the troubles in the region of Tsang, was any similar action ever taken during the Yuan? (Last year when the Gurkhas raided Tsang, after the Drungpa *kūtuktu* fled, the great monks and sangha also, having heard a mistaken divination that they would be forced to break their vows, all fled and the thieves [were therefore able to] pillage. Having been specially detained and brought to Ü, the *jedrung* was defrocked and punished according to the law. The Drungpa *kūtuktu* was dispossessed of his so-called palace. The Yuan state venerated its lamas and not only did not punish them but also allowed them to damage the royal law. Although I supported the teaching of the Yellow Hats, [I] have done so according to a passage that appears in the *Royal Regulations*: "One should improve their teachings, not replace their teachings. One should improve their laws, not replace their traditions." Those who incite turmoil will be punished according to the law in the same manner as subjects of the interior. In the five hundred years since Phagpa Lama became the holder of the teachings, and from the time of the Yuan and Ming states until now, have there been great lamas who have had been defrocked and punished according to the law? Slanderers cannot say to me that I have excessively honored the teaching of the Yellow Hats!)

When undertaking a great enterprise, one must [act] not only at the appropriate time and context but also in accord with what is just and brilliant. If opportunity presents itself, yet one is unable to make a just and brilliant decision, then it will not be accomplished. If one makes a just and brilliant decision but at an inopportune moment, then it has been made in vain and nothing will come of it.

As for the recent establishment of a new procedure for the identification of *trülku* in the aftermath of the subjugation of the Gurkhas, it was easily accomplished because the moment was fortuitous. Eradicating the selfish desire of *trülku* to emanate among their kinsmen is in harmony with the wishes of both the Outer and Inner Mongols. Now I am in my eightieth year and approach the end of my rule, yet I have accomplished this great undertaking and established peace in the region of Tsang. The restoration of the outer peoples and the happiness and welfare of both the state and each household—an enduring achievement—is the fulfillment of my desires, and I am glad of heart.

Written by the king during the waxing days of the first month of winter, water-mouse year, Qianlong fifty-seven [late December 1792].

Notes

Epigraphs

Modified from James Legge's translation of *Book of Rites* [1885], *Chinese Text Project*, accessed August 2, 2017, http://ctext.org/liji/wang-zhi#n59341.

From Edward Kolla, *Sovereignty, International Law, and the French Revolution*, 51.

Ju mi pham rgya mtsho, *Rgyal po lugs kyi bstan bcos sa gzhi skyong ba'i rgyan* (An Ornament for Worldly Kings, A Treatise on the Way of the King), 37ba, 38na.

Preface

1. Devin Fitzgerald, "Research Note: Between Paper and Wood, or the Manchu Invention of the *Dang'an*," *Saksaha* 13 (2015): 75–80; and Pierre-Étienne Will, "Checking Abuses of Power Under the Ming Dynasty," in *China, Democracy, and Law*, ed. Mireille Delmas-Marty et. al. (Leiden: Brill, 2011), 148, 152–154, 160–161, 166.

2. Beatrice S. Bartlett, *Monarchs and Ministers: The Grand Council in Mid-Ch'ing China, 1723–1820* (Berkeley: University of California Press, 1991); Mark C. Elliott, "The Manchu-language Archives of the Qing Dynasty and the Origins of the Palace Memorial System," *Late Imperial China* 22, no. 1 (June 2001): 1–70, Philip A. Kuhn, *Soulstealers: The Chinese Sorcery Scare of 1768* (Cambridge, MA: Harvard University Press, 1990).

3. A palace memorial from Heliyen sent from Tibet on June 16, 1793, for instance, arrived at court just twenty-nine days later, on July 15 (YHGSL, 15:281–283).

4. Elliott, "The Manchu-language Archives of the Qing Dynasty," 18 n. 23.

5. The best example is a secret attachment to a memorial dated JQ 02/08/03 (September 22, 1797), MWLF microfilm 164: 0387–0389.

6. Matthew Mosca, "The Literati Rewriting of China in The Qianlong-Jiaqing Transition," *Late Imperial China* 32, no. 2: 89–132.

Introduction

1. Arjia Rinpoche, *Surviving the Dragon* (New York: Rodale, 2010), 205–207.
2. See for recent examples Liao Zugui, Li Yongchang, and Li Pengnian, eds., *Qinding Zangnei shanhou zhangcheng ershijiutiao banben kaolüe* (Beijing: Zhongguo zangxue chubanshe, 2006); Zeng Guoqing, "Lun Qingting zhi zang yu jinping cheqian," *Zangxue yanjiu* 10 (March 2011): 1–8; Zeng Guoqing, ed., *Bainian zhuzang dachen yanjiu luncong* (Beijing: Zhongguo zangxue chubanshe, 2014), and Wu Yuncen, "Jinping cheqian de sheli ji qi yiyi," *Xizang yanjiu* 1 (1996): 34–50. For the catalogue of an exhibition on the Golden Urn held at the museum of the China Tibetology Research Center, see Xiong Wenbin and Zhang Chunyan, eds., *Huofo zhuanshi: 2014 nian zang chuan fojiao huofo zhuanshi zhuanti zhan* (Beijing: Zhongguo zangxue chubanshe, 2014).
3. For an extensive discussion of this dynamic, see Uradyn E. Bulag, "Going Imperial: Tibeto-Mongolian Buddhism and Nationalisms in China and Inner Asia," in *Empire to Nation: Historical Perspectives on the Making of the Modern World*, ed. Esherick et al. (Lanham, MD: Rowman & Littlefield, 2006), 260–295.
4. John Powers, *The Buddha Party* (Oxford: Oxford University Press, 2017), 92–129; Sam van Schaik, *Tibet: A History* (New Haven: Yale University Press, 2011), 159; John Powers and David Templeman, *Historical Dictionary of Tibet* (Lanham, MD: Scarecrow Press, 2012), 277. Paul Nietupski, *Labrang Monastery: A Tibetan Buddhist Community on the Inner Asian Borderlands, 1709–1958* (Lanham, MD: Lexington Books, 2011), 134.
5. See for instance, Wu Fengpei and Zeng Guoqing, *Qingchao zhu zang dachen zhidu de jianli yu yange* (Beijing: Zhongguo zangxue chubanshe, 1989), 76.
6. Luciano Petech, *Aristocracy and Government in Tibet: 1728–1959* (Serie Orientale Roma 35. Rome: Instituto Italiano Per Il Medio ed Estremo Oriente, 1973), 4. This view has dominated subsequent historiography. For example, Patricia Berger argues that the Vajrayāna Buddhist ritual institutions and practices developed during the Qianlong reign as part of his patronage of Tibetan Buddhist adepts such as Changkya Rolpé Dorjé "faded into politically advantageous, rote usage by the end of the dynasty" (*Empire of Emptiness* [Honolulu: University of Hawaii Press, 2003], 196–197). For decline and stagnation narratives of Qing rule in Tibetan regions (including Amdo), see also: Melvyn Goldstein, *A History of Modern Tibet, 1913–1951: The Demise of the Lamaist State* (Berkeley: University of California Press, 1989), 44; Tsepon W. D. Shakabpa, *Tibet: A Political History* (New Haven and London: Yale University Press, 1967), 170; Lin Hsiao-ting, *Tibet and Nationalist China's Frontier: Intrigues and Ethnopolitics, 1928–49* (Vancouver: University of British Columbia Press, 2006), 8.
7. For an example of a Tibetan-language Qing document using this label, see the Smallpox Stele of 1794, in Hugh Richardson, *Ch'ing Dynasty Inscriptions in Lhasa* (Rome: Serie Orientale Roma, vol. 47 [1974]), 56–58.
8. By "China proper" I mean the eighteen provinces of the former Ming state often referred to in Qing documents as the "interior" (Ch. *neidi* 内地, Ma. *dorgi ba*) or

simply "China" (Ch. *zhongguo* 中國, Ma. *dulimbai gurun*). "Inner Asia" refers hereinafter primarily to what late eighteenth-century Qing authorities called their "outer domains" (Ma. *tulergi golo*) or "frontier" areas (Ma. *jecen*) of Inner and Outer Mongolia, Xinjiang, Qinghai, and Tibet. I use "Inner Mongolia" and "Outer Mongolia" in this book as imperfect shorthands for Qing-era geopolitical conceptions. Eighteenth-century sources mapped the *Mongols*, not *Mongolia*, and did so primarily in reference to the Mongol nobility, the *jasaks* (Mongol: *zasag* or *jasag*). Qing documents consulted for this book discuss the "inner *jasaks*" and "outer *jasaks*," not "Inner" or "Outer Mongolia." The distinction originally reflected not geography but the date of submission to the Qing imperial house, and thus also expressed implicit assumptions about political loyalty.

9. Pierre Etienne Will, "Creation, Conflict, and Routinization: The Appointment of Officials by Drawing Lots, 1594–1700" (unpublished manuscript, June 2009), 2.

10. Cited in Will, "Creation, Conflict, and Routinization," 18.

11. Will, "Creation, Conflict, and Routinization," 16–17, 19, 21.

12. First Historical Archives (Beijing), *Yangxindian zaobanchu zuocheng zuohuo jiqingdang* 養心殿造辦處作成做活計清檔, register for QL 57/07/01.

13. First Historical Archives (Beijing), *Yangxindian zaobanchu zuocheng zuohuo jiqingdang*, register for QL 57/07/02, QL 57/07/18, QL 57/08/09, QL 57/08/10, and QL 57/09/02.

14. YHGSL, 14:352, edict of QL 57/08/29 (1792–10–14).

15. Gaozong [Qianlong emperor], *Yuzhi shiwen shiquanji* (Beijing: Zhongguo zangxue chubanshe, 1993), 642.

16. Qianlong, *Discourse on Lamas* (*Lama Shuo* 喇嘛說), lines 30–31. Unless otherwise indicated, all translations from the *Discourse* are based on the Tibetan-language translation. A rubbing of the Tibetan inscription at Yonghegong is in O. Franke and B. Laufer, *Lamaistische Kloster-Inschriften aus Peking, Jehol und Si-ngan; mit unterstützung der Hamburgischen Wissenschaftlichen Stiftung* (Berlin: Verlag von Dietrich Reimer, 1914), plate 4.

17. The identification of the Geluk as a "church" has a problematic history in Western scholarship. Donald S. Lopez Jr. has argued that the comparison of the Geluk to the papacy has been employed to demonstrate that the Geluk were either misguided (or perhaps demonically inspired) imitators of Catholicism or a kind of adulterated Buddhism (Lopez, *Prisoners of Shangri-la: Tibetan Buddhism and the West* [Chicago: University of Chicago Press, 1998], 23, 39–43). Despite these pitfalls, I choose to interpret the (Tib.) *Dge lugs chos lugs* as "Geluk church" in addition to "Geluk school" in order to draw attention to its complex institutional structure and because the history of its interactions with the Qing court can usefully be compared to the history of relations between church and state in Europe and the Americas.

18. For a detailed examination of these events, see Leo E. Rose, *Nepal Strategy for Survival* (Berkeley: University of California Press, 1971), 36–67.

19. MWLF, 154:0980, Agūi memorial, QL 57/08.

20. Johanna Waley-Cohen, "Religion, War, and Empire-Building in Eighteenth-Century China," *The International History Review* 20, no. 2 (June 1998): 336–352.

21. "Central Tibet" refers in this book to Lhasa, the surrounding province of Ü, and the neighboring province of Tsang—the core territories administered by the Ganden Podrang government of the Dalai Lamas. Usage of this label, which implies that Tibet

was a much larger geographic entity, does not necessarily reflect Qing-period geographic understandings. In both Qing documents and Tibetan-language sources of the eighteenth and nineteenth centuries, references to Tibet frequently meant nothing more than the regions of Ü and Tsang or the regions directly governed and taxed by the Ganden Podrang. See further discussion of variant geographical conceptions of Tibet in the conclusion, especially the section, "A Golden Urn for a Greater Tibet."

22. As Benjamin Elman has pointed out, this system largely guaranteed their loyalty to the state (although not necessarily their uncorrupted service). See Elman, "The Civil Examination System in Late Imperial China, 1400–1900," *Frontiers of History in China* 8, no. 1 (2014): 32–50; and "Political, Social and Cultural Reproduction via Civil Service Examinations in Late Imperial China," *Journal of Asian Studies* 50, no. 1 (February 1991): 7–28.

23. Vincent Goossaert, "Counting the Monks: The 1736–1739 Census of the Chinese Clergy," *Late Imperial China* 21, no. 2 (December 2000): 40–85, and "Taoists, 1644–1850," in *The Cambridge History of China Vol. 9 Part Two, The Ch'ing Dynasty to 1800*, ed. Willard J. Peterson (Cambridge: Cambridge University Press, 2016), 412–457.

24. The authors of the *Qingdai Menggu zhi* write that in the nineteenth century there were approximately 1,200 monasteries and 100,000 monks in Inner Mongolia alone. A 1958 report from Communist Mongolia claimed that slightly over 44 percent of the prerevolutionary population of Outer Mongolia lived in monasteries (or 105,557 monks). Jinhai et al., *Qingdai menggu zhi* (Huhehaote: Neimenggu renmin chubanshe, 2009), 398. For a region with an overall population of less than one million, this is a striking ratio, especially when compared with China proper. Between 1736 and 1739, the Qing state counted approximately 340,000 Buddhist and Daoist clergy in a population of perhaps 200 million (Goossaert, "Counting the Monks," 49).

25. Matthew Kapstein, *The Tibetans* (Malden, MA: Blackwell, 2006), 119, 121.

26. For representative narratives, see Sun Zhenping, *Qingdai Xizang fazhi yanjiu* (Beijing: Zhishi chanquan chubanshe, 2004), 192–197; Zeng Guoqing and Huang Weizhong, *Qingdai Zangzu lishi* (Beijing: Zhongguo zangxue, 2012).

27. For a comprehensive study of the *Zhonghua minzu* paradigm, see James Leibold, *Reconfiguring Chinese Nationalism* (New York: Palgrave, 2007). In the 1950s, PRC historians still frequently conceptualized the *zhonghua minzu* as inherently plural (consisting of many *minzus*). Since the 1990s, PRC historians have placed greater emphasis on the unity and singularity of the *zhonghua minzu*, seeing "Chinese" as being in essence Han.

28. I borrow here from Bruce Grant's account of gift giving in the construction of the Russian empire: *The Captive and the Gift: Cultural Histories of Sovereignty in Russia and the Caucasus* (Ithaca: Cornell University Press, 2009).

29. Leibold, *Reconfiguring Chinese Nationalism,* 17–47.

30. David Brophy, "The Junghar Mongol Legacy and the Language of Loyalty in Qing Xinjiang," *Harvard Journal of Asiatic Studies* 73, no. 2 (December 2013): 233.

31. See note 4 above. Kapstein, writes, for instance, "As an imperial intrusion penetrating the heart of Tibetan religious life, it was by far the most resented, so that every effort was made to circumvent its use" (*The Tibetans* 159).

32. Sarat Chandra Das, *Journey to Lhasa and Central Tibet* (London: John Murray, 1902), 50, 178–179.

33. Shakabpa, *Tibet*, 168–170, and *One Hundred Thousand Moons: An Advanced Political History of Tibet,* trans. Derek F. Maher (Boston: Brill, 2010), 562, 568–569, 588, 628.

34. For a critique of historical assumptions about pre-twentieth-century Tibetan ethnic and national identities, see Sara Shneiderman, "Barbarians at the Border and Civilizing Projects: Analyzing Ethnic and National Identities in the Tibetan Context," in *Tibetan Borderlands,* ed. Christiaan Klieger (Leiden: Brill, 2006), 9–34; and Max Oidtmann, "Overlapping Empires: Religion, Politics, and Ethnicity in 19th Century Qinghai," *Late Imperial China* 37, no. 2 (December 2016): 41–91. Donald Lopez has also highlighted disjunctures between traditional definitions of Tibetanness and contemporary ones in *Prisoners of Shangri-La,* 196–200.

35. For example, Liao Zugui et al., *Qinding Zangnei shanhou zhangcheng ershijiutiao banben kaolüe*; Wu Yuncen, "Jinping cheqian de sheli jiqi yiyi"; Fabienne Jagou, "The Use of Ritual Drawing of Lots for the Selection of the 11th Panchen Lama," in *Revisiting Rituals in a Changing Tibetan World: Proceedings of the Seminar La transformation des rituels dans l'aire tibétaine à l'époque contemporaine held in Paris on November 8th and 9th 2007,* ed. Katia Buffetrille (Leiden: Brill, 2011), 43–68.

36. Qianlong, *Discourse on Lamas,* line 28.

37. This would be the edict of QL 58/04/19 (1793–05–28) that is recorded in the *Chu glung wang shu* [archives of the TAR] register as being translated into Tibetan and passed on to Lhasa on QL 58/09/15 (1793–10–19). See BLRYP, 214–220. No record has yet been located in the First Historical Archives (FHA) that indicates that the Lhasa *ambans* received the *Discourse on Lamas* in 1792 or 1793. The Qing colonial agents in Mongolia, however, all filed reports acknowledging receipt of the edict beginning in March 1793 (YHGSL 15:14).

38. The Court of Colonial Affairs was also known colloquially in both Mongolia and Tibet as the Mongol Court or Mongol Yamen, which was the name of the institution when it was first established in 1637 (Ma. *Monggo jurgan*). The practice of translating the name of this institution as the Court of Colonial Affairs dates to the mid-nineteenth century, when European diplomats and scholars envisioned its purpose in terms similar to their own "colonial" agencies and offices. According to this view, the Qing was essentially a Chinese core that ruled its periphery as colonies. See, for example, H. S. Brunnert and V. V. Hagelstrom, *The Present Day Political Organization of China* (Shanghai: Kelly and Walsh, Limited, 1912), who popularized this interpretation and reported that Russian scholars had first used the term "Colonial Court" in 1828. Although more recent scholarship has challenged the notion that the Qing was a "Chinese" empire, especially during the seventeenth and eighteenth centuries, as I will argue below, the Qing government's relationships to its constituent parts can nonetheless be analogized to the colonial strategies and experiences of contemporaneous European empires. Thus, while recognizing that "Court of Colonial Affairs" is an imperfect *interpretation* of the institution's various names, I will use it throughout this book. The Court of Colonial Affairs also employed *Hanjun* (Chinese martial) bannermen in addition to Manchu and Mongol bannermen.

39. David M. Farquhar, "The Emperor as Bodhisattva in the Governance of the Ch'ing Empire," *Harvard Journal of Asiatic Studies* 38, no. 1 (June 1978): 5–34; Samuel M. Grupper, "Manchu Patronage and Tibetan Buddhism During the First Half of the Ch'ing Dynasty," *The Journal of the Tibet Society* 4 (1984): 47–74; Evelyn S. Rawski, *The Last*

Emperors (Berkeley: University of California Press, 1998), 244–273; Berger, *Empire of Emptiness*, 7, 33, passim.

40. For the classic study of the reification of Hinduism, see Bernard S. Cohn, *Colonialism and Its Forms of Knowledge* (Princeton: Princeton University Press, 1996), 57–75; cf. Lauren Benton, *Law and Colonial Cultures* (Cambridge: Cambridge University Press, 2002), 128.

41. Johan Elverskog, *Our Great Qing* (Honolulu: University of Hawai'i Press, 2006), 3–6, 8, passim.

42. For an examination of colonial justice in India: Elizabeth Kolsky, *Colonial Justice in British India: White Violence and the Rule of Law* (New York: Cambridge University Press, 2010), 13, 15. For the Russian attempt to imitate the British: Alexander Morrison, "Creating a Colonial Shariʿa for Russian Turkestan," in *Imperial Cooperation and Transfer, 1870–1930*, ed. Volker Barth and Roland Cvetkovski (London: Bloomsbury, 2015), 127–149. Jonathan Ocko and David Gilmartin have also pointed out that Qing legitimacy vis-à-vis the Han interior of the empire was also substantially premised on delivering justice: "State, Sovereignty, and the People: A Comparison of the 'Rule of Law' in China and India," *Journal of Asian Studies* 68, no. 1 (February 2009): 55–133.

43. For an account of the limits placed on Han literati knowledge of the "Outer Regions," see Matthew Mosca, "The Literati Rewriting of China in the Qianlong-Jiaqing Transition," *Late Imperial China* 32, no. 2 (December 2011): 89–132.

44. The earliest connotations of the term *šajin* in Manchu were legalistic: "regulation," "prohibition," or "stricture." For instance, in the preconquest archives of the early Qing rulers the word appears in the compound *šajin fafun*, "prohibitions and laws" (Kanda Nobuo et. al., *Manbun Rōtō* 滿文老檔, volume 3, fascicle 2:906). Ishihama Yumiko has noted that in 1636 the Manchu ruler Hong Taiji ordered that henceforth the term *šajin* refer solely to the "Buddha's doctrines" (*fucihi šajin*). See Ishihama, "The Notion of 'Buddhist Government' (*chos rsid*) Shared by Tibet, Mongol, and Manchu in the Early 17th Century," in *The Relationship Between Religion and State in Traditional Tibet*, ed. Christoph Cüppers (Lumbini: Lumbini International Research Institute, 2004), 22. In later multilingual official texts, *šajin* appears as the translation of the Tibetan, *chos* (Dharma), and the Chinese *jiao* 教 (teachings). Since Manchu authors did not choose to use their own term *tacin* (teachings) to translate *chos* or *jiao*, I prefer to translate *šajin* as "doctrine" or "precept" in order to preserve the legalistic sensibility of the original Manchu.

45. For representative uses of *tanggūt* and *tubet* by the preconquest Qing state, see the *Manwen laodang* records for the reigns of Nurhaci and Hong Taiji. *Manbun Rōtō*, vol. 1, fasc. 32:465; vol. 1, fasc. 66:987, 996; vol. 2, fasc. 5: 60; vol. 3, fasc. 2, 906.

46. In these texts, *tanggūt* and *tubet* are usually in phrases that denote culture: *tanggūt hergen* (Tanggut writing/language), *tanggūt i tacikū* (teachings of Tanggut), *tubet i tacikū* (teachings of Tibet). These usages are preserved in the mid-eighteenth- century pentaglot dictionary, the *Wuti Qingwen jian* 五體清文鑑 (Kyōto-shi: Kyōto Daigaku Bungakubu Nairiku Ajia Kenkyūjo, Shōwa 41–43 [1966–1968]), 603, 673. Li Fengzhen also asserts that *Xizang* and other Chinese terms were not used in Qing correspondence until the Qianlong period: *Qingdai Xizang junwangzhi chutan du qingshi zhaji* (Beijing: Zhongguo Zangxue chubanshe, 2012,) 208.

47. The Kangxi emperor was the first to employ the term *Xizang* in official writing. Fabienne Jagou, "Étude des toponymes choisis par les Mandchous pour définir le territoire tibétain," in *Etudes tibétaines en l'honneur d'Anne Chayet*, ed. J. L. Achard (Geneve: Droz, 2010), 127–146; cf. Chen Qingying, "Hanwen 'Xizang' yi ci lai li jianshuo," *Yanjing xuebao* 5 (1999).

48. During the late 1700s and early 1800s the Qing emperor and Qing officials evidently felt obliged to repeatedly explain that "Tanggūt," "Fan," and "Xifan" were synonyms. See Qianlong's *Discourse on Lamas*, and the Jiaqing emperor's proclamation of 1808, subsequently inscribed on a stele in Lhasa. For the text of the latter document, see Zhang Yuxin, *Qing zhengfu yu lama jiao: fu Qingdai lama jiao beikelu* (Lhasa: Xizang renmin chubanshe, 1988), 503–507. Similarly, the bilingual Manchu–Chinese illustrated gazetteer of tribute peoples (*Huang Qing zhigong tu*) labels all the people of Kham, Ali, Ü, and Tsang as (Ch.) *fan* or (Ma.) *fandze*. Here Tibet is also depicted as apolity constructed primarily by loyalty to the Dalai Lama. Yu Zhengxie's 1807 "Origins of the Amban System" (*Dachen yuanshi*), Zhong-fang's 1843 "Research on the Fan monks" (*Fanseng yuanliu kao*), and Wei Yuan's 1842 *Shenwu ji* all explain that *fan* and *tanggute* are synonyms. See Yu Zhengxie, in *Yu Zhengxie quanji* (Anhui: Huangshan shushe, date uncertain), vol. 1:381–382; Zhong-fang, reprinted in *Xizang zongjiao yuanliu kao, Fanseng yuanliu kao*, ed. Wu Fengpei (Lhasa: Xizang renmin chubanshe, 1982), 1–39; Wei Yuan, *Shengwu ji* (Beijing: Zhonghua shuju, 1984), 139, 141–142. Yu Zhengxie and Wei Yuan, however, also continue to use the terms *fan* or *xifan* to denote people living along the borders of Sichuan and Gansu, thus preserving an underlying sense of difference. The Jiaqing-era Collected Statutes (*Huidian*) distinguishes between monks from central Tibet ("*zang lama*") and monks in Qinghai and Gansu ("*Fan lama*"). See Zhao Yuntian, annotator, *Qianlongchao neifu chaoben "Lifanyuan zeli"* (Beijing: Zhongguo Zangxue chubanshe, 2006), 368–369.

49. The eighteenth-century *Chengde Gazetteer* (*Rehe zhi*) quotes the Qianlong emperor distinguishing between the "Tanggūt" language (Ch. *tanggute yu* 唐古忒語) and the "Fan" language (Ch. *fan yu* 番語). Quoted in Zhang Yuxin, *Qing zhengfu yu lama jiao*, 57.

50. The Manchu version of Nian Gengyao's regulations for newly incorporated Qinghai uses the expression "*tanggūt* [and] *fandze*" and "*fandze* [and] *tanggūt*" repeatedly, implying a degree of difference between the two (National Palace Museum, Taibei, doc. no. 125.411000059). The Xining *ambans* submitted regular reports about the arrival of traders from Tibet at the trade fairs at Dangar (outside Xining). These reports customarily distinguished Fan from Tanggūt. See, for example, the following phrase: "The merchant Tanggūts of western Dzang and the tribal Fan of Derge subordinate to Sichuan (*wargi dzang ni hūdašara tanggūt se, sichuan i harangga derge aiman i fandze*)" in a memorial from the Xining *amban* concerning different traders arriving at the markets outside of Xining (MWLF doc. no. 03–0197–3663–024). In other Manchu-language reports, *Tanggūt* refers to a geographical place and *Fandze* to the people who inhabit it: "*tanggūt ba i fandze*" (MWLF doc. no. 03–0196–3615–032). The lexical diversity of Manchu and Chinese-language texts is not present in the Tibetan translations of Qing official documents, where *tanggūt* and *fandze* are consistently translated as (Tib.) *bod*. See for instance Qianlong's *Discourse on Lamas* or a bilingual Mongol–Tibetan edict issued on QL 60/04/15 (1795–06–01) concerning the

identification of future incarnation of the Cagan Nomunhan *kūtuktu* of Kökenuur (Qinghai Provincial Museum collection).

51. See for instance the Xining *amban* Tsebak's memorial MWLF 163:0641, JQ 01/11/21 (1796–12–19); Manchu-language reports on "Fan" raids on Mongol communities in Kökenuur during the 1790s and early 1800s; and the Gansu governor-general Nayan-ceng's Chinese-language memorials about Kökenuur published in the 1820s (*Pingfan zouyi*, Lanyuan a gong ci, 1853). For a detailed discussion see Oidtmann, "Overlapping Empires."

52. When the Qing court began drafting a legal code for the residents of this newly incorporated territory in the 1730s, they similarly distinguished "Tanggut people" of central Tibet from "Mongols and Fanzi" of Qinghai and Gansu. See "Xining Qinghai fanyi cheng li" 西寧青海番夷成例, in *Zhongguo zhenxi falü dianji jicheng bingbian di'er ce* (Beijing: Kexue chubanshe, 1994), 379.

53. See for instance the description of "Wargi Dzang/Xizang" in the four-volume bilingual illustrated album of Qing tributaries, *Huang Qing zhigongtu* (Beijing: Workshops of the Qing Imperial Household department, 1751–1790), currently in the collection of the Bibliothèque nationale de France, accessed February 15, 2018, http://catalogue .bnf.fr/ark:/12148/cb444768402, volume 2, 4a–b. A nine-volume block-printed, Chinese-only version of this text circulated much more widely. See Fu-heng, ed., *Huang Qing Zhi gong tu: jiu juan* (Beijing: Imperial Household Department [Nei fu], 1761–1805), Harvard-Yenching Library, accessed February 14, 2018, https://iiif.lib.harvard .edu/manifests/view/drs:26986317$1i, 4a–5b. For highly derogatory depictions of the Oirats and the Junghars in particular see Peter Perdue, "Tea, Cloth, Gold, and Religion: Manchu Sources on Trade Missions from Mongolia to Tibet," *Late Imperial China* 36, no. 2 (December 2015): 9, passim. These views of the Tibetans also contrasted with impressions of the Hui, who were seen as inherently more unified. In 1807, the Xining *amban* Nayanceng wrote that "The Fan reside in dispersed tribes. Since their nature is greedy and suspicious, they frequently trespass against each other and cannot act in unison." Song Tingsheng, *Nayancheng Qinghai zouyi* (Xining: Qinghai renmin chubanshe, 1997), 67.

54. Heqiyeletu, "Zang chuan fojiao hutuketu zhixiang kaoshi," in *Huofo ji zhuanshi zhidu yanjiu*, ed. Chen Qingying et al. (Beijing: Zhongguo Zangxue zhongxin zongjiao-suo, 2006), 236–248.

55. Per K. Sørensen, "The Dalai Lama Institution: Its Origin and Genealogical Succession," *Orientations* (September 2005): 53–60.

56. Peter Schwieger, *The Dalai Lama and the Emperor of China: A Political History of the Tibetan Institution of Reincarnation* (New York: Columbia University Press, 2015), 18–20; and Turrell V. Wylie, "Reincarnation: A Political Innovation in Tibetan Buddhism," in *Proceedings of the Csoma de Koros Memorial Symposium*, ed. Louis Ligeti (Budapest: Akadémiai Kiadó, 1978), 581–586. Leonard W. J. van der Kuijp writes that it was the Second Karmapa, Karma Pakshi (1206–1283), not the Third Karmapa, who was the first to claim to be a *trülku*. "The Dalai Lamas and the Origin of Reincarnate Lamas," in *The Dalai Lamas: A Visual History*, ed. Martin Brauen (Chicago: Serindia, 2005), 28.

57. Cidan Lunzhu, "Huofo zhuanshi de chansheng ji lishi zuoyong," in *Huofo ji zhuanshi zhidu yanjiu*, ed. Chen Qingying and Ga Dawa Caireng (Beijing: Zhongguo Zangxue zhongxin zongjiaosuo, 2006), 9.

58. Huang Weizhong, "Zangchuan fojiao de huofo zhuanshi zhidu," in *Huofo ji zhuanshi zhidu yanjiu*, ed. Chen Qingying and Ga Dawa Caireng (Beijing: Zhongguo Zangxue zhongxin zongjiaosuo, 2006), 101.

59. Van der Kuijp, "The Dalai Lamas and the Origin of Reincarnate Lamas," 28–29.

60. Van der Kuijp, "The Dalai Lamas and the Origin of Reincarnate Lamas," 21, 24.

61. Van der Kuijp, "The Dalai Lamas and the Origin of Reincarnate Lamas," 17–18.

62. Cankanjia, "Zangchuan fojiao huofo doushe zhuanshifa," in *Anduo yanjiu zangxue lunwen*, vol. 2, ed. Gansu sheng zangxue yanjiu suo (Beijing: Minzu chubanshe, 2006), 182–190; Schwieger, *The Dalai Lama and the Emperor of China*, 12.

63. Chen Qingying and Chen Lijian, *Huofo zhuanshi: qiyuan, fazhan, lishi dingzhi* (Beijing: Zhongguo zangxue chubanshe, 2014), 40–41.

64. Schwieger, *The Dalai Lama and the Emperor of China*, 21.

65. Rachel M. McCleary and Leonard W.J. van der Kuijp, "A Market Approach to the Rise of the Geluk School," *Journal of Asian Studies* 69, no. 1 (2010): 149–180; Brenton Sullivan, "Monastic Customaries and the Promotion of Dge Lugs Scholasticism in A Mdo and Beyond," *Asian Highlands Perspectives* 36 (2015): 84–105.

66. MSCB, Brag dgon pa dkon mchog bstan pa rab rgyas, *Mdo smad chos 'byung* (alt. title, *Deb ther rgya mtsho* [The oceanic book], Zi ling: Mtsho sngon mi rigs dpe skrun khang, 1987 [1865]), 184.

67. Gser tog blo bzang tshul khrims rgya mtsho, *Sku 'bum byams pa gling gdan rabs don ldan tshangs pa'i dbyangs snyan* (Zi ling: Mtsho sngon mi rigs dpe khang, 1983 [1903]), 83.

68. Moreover, certain steps in the search process that seem ubiquitous now (such as seeking visions in Namtso lake) are rarely mentioned in eighteenth- or nineteenth-century sources. There is much greater homogeneity in search procedures now than in the 1700s.

69. Although the Great Fifth also used the case of the Tongkhor lama to gently mock the claims of other adepts, especially "Bonpo lamas," to have transferred consciousness. Quoted in Gser tog blo bzang tshul khrims rgya mtsho, *Sku 'bum byams pa gling gdan rabs don ldan tshangs pa'i dbyangs snyan*, 83.

70. Jerry Dennerline, "The Shun-chih Reign," in *The Cambridge History of China, Volume 9, The Ch'ing Dynasty to 1800, Part One*, ed. Willard J. Peterson (Cambridge: Cambridge University Press, 2002), 73–119; cf. Frederic Wakeman, Jr., *The Great Enterprise: The Manchu Reconsctruction of Imperial Order in Seventeenth-Century China*, 2 vols. (Berkeley: University of California Press, 1985).

71. Zahiruddin Ahmad, *Sino-Tibetan Relations in the Seventeenth Century* (Rome: Istituto Italiano per il Medio ed Estremo Oriente, 1970), 39–41, 166–191; Gray Tuttle, "A Tibetan Buddhist Mission to the East: The Fifth Dalai Lama's Journey to Beijing, 1652–1653," in *Tibetan Society and Religion: The Seventeenth and Eighteenth Centuries*, ed. Gray Tuttle, Bryan Cuevas, and Kurtis Schaeffer (Leiden: Brill. 2006), 65–87.

72. There are no reliable reports of overall numbers of monks belonging to the various churches and sects of Tibetan Buddhism in the late 1500s and early 1600s. McCleary and van der Kuijp's research ("A Market Approach to the Rise of the Geluk School") suggests that as a result of the Geluk's emphasis on mass monasticism and construction of large-scale monasteries in central Tibet, particularly around Lhasa, they were probably the largest church by numbers of monks in the early 1600s.

73. For a reappraisal of the period, see the essays in Karl Debreczeny and Gray Tuttle, eds., *The Tenth Karmapa and Tibet's Turbulent Seventeenth Century* (Chicago: Serindia, 2016).

74. Ahmad, *Sino-Tibetan Relations in the Seventeenth Century*, 99–118; Schwieger, *The Dalai Lama and the Emperor of China*, 36–48; for tensions surrounding his identification, see Samten G. Karmay, trans., *The Illusive Play: The Autobiography of the Fifth Dalai Lama* (Chicago: Serindia, 2014), 35–36; and Kurtis R. Schaeffer, "The Fifth Dalai Lama Ngawang Lopsang Gyatso, 1617–1682," in *The Dalai Lamas: A Visual History*, ed. Martin Brauen (Chicago: Serindia, 2005), 65–91.

75. Some sources identify the fourth Dalai Lama as the great-grandson of Altan Khan. For a discussion see, Schwieger, *The Dalai Lama and the Emperor of China*, 36.

76. Schaeffer, "The Fifth Dalai Lama Ngawang Lopsang Gyatso, 1617–1682," 68; Ahmad, *Sino-Tibetan Relations in the Seventeenth Century*, 130–139. The question of whether the nature of the Dalai Lama's authority—did he "reign" or "rule"—has been fiercely debated by both modern scholars and seventeenth-, eighteenth-, and nineteenth-century Tibetan scholars. Authors from Amdo, for instance, tend to suggest that the balance of decision-making power lay with Güüshi Khan. In his 1786 *Annals of Kökenuur*, Sumpa Khenpo strongly asserts the primacy of Güüshi Khan in political affairs (Sum pa Ye she dpal 'byor, *Mtsho sngon lo rgyus tshangs glug sar snyan* (Xining: Mtsho sngon mi rigs dpe sgrun khang, 1982 [1786]), 16). A later Amdo author, Dbal mang 02 Dkon mchog rgyal mtshan (Belmang Pandita), similarly portrays the Fifth Dalai Lama as wielding power only within the context of Güüshi Khan's sovereignty. For a longer discussion, see Max Oidtmann, "Between Patron and Priest: Amdo Tibet Under Qing Rule, 1792–1911," PhD diss., Harvard University, 2014, 311–313. Schwieger's analysis of documents from Lhasa suggests that the Dalai Lama did indeed act as the final decision-making authority in central Tibet (*The Dalai Lama and the Emperor of China*, 55–60). It has been pointed out, however, that circa 1600s understandings of the Pakpa–Qubilai relationship were quite different from the understandings of the 1300s. See van der Kuijp, "The Dalai Lamas and the Origin of Reincarnate Lamas," 16; Schwieger, *The Dalai Lama and the Emperor of China*, 32–33.

77. These threats can be found in the writings of Dbal mang 02 Dkon mchog rgyal mtshan, *Rgya bod hor sog gyi lo rgyus nyung brjod pa byis pa 'jug pa'i 'bab stegs*, in *The Collected Works of Dbal-man dkon-mchog-rgyal-mtshan*, reproduced by Gyaltan Gelek Namgyal (Delhi: New Laxmi Printers, 1974 [1809–1820]), vol. 4, 578–579, 624.

78. D. Seyfort Ruegg, *Ordre Spirituel et Ordre Temporel Dan la Pensée Bouddhique de l'Inde et du Tibet: Quatre Conférences au College de France* (Paris: College de France, 1995), 152. Cf. Schaeffer, "The Fifth Dalai Lama Ngawang Lopsang Gyatso, 1617–1682," 65–91; Schwieger, *The Dalai Lama and the Emperor of China*, 52–53. Dobis Tsering Gyal, on the basis of examination of archival documents held by the Tibetan government dating to the 1640s–1650s, argues that the government of the Great Fifth and Güüshi Khan was less radical than it appears, having been built much more gradually on the foundations of the Ringpung and Tsang rulers: Daowei Cairangjia, "Xizang gandan pozhang difang zhengfu jianli chuqi Gushihan banfa de zangwen tiejuan wenshu kaoshu," *Xizang dang'an*, no. 21 (2015): 24–31.

79. Ishihama, "The Notion of 'Buddhist Government'," 15–31. According to Johan Elverskog, this language appears to have been adopted among the eastern Mongols at least as early as the 1570s (*The Jewel Translucent Sūtra* [Leiden: Brill, 2003], 15).

80. For the apt use of the term "concordat," see David Seyfort Ruegg, "Introductory Remarks on the Spiritual and Temporal Orders," in *The Relationship Between Religion*

and *State in Traditional Tibet*, ed. Christoph Cüppers (Lumbini: Lumbini International Research institute, 2004), 9–13, and "*mchod yon, yon chod* and *mchod gnas/yon gnas*: On the Historiography and Semantics of a Tibetan Religio-Social and Religio-Political Concept," in *Tibetan History and Language: Studies Dedicated to Géza Uray on his Seventieth Birthday*, ed. Ernst Steinkellner (Wien, Austria, 1991), 441–454. Cf. Grupper, "Manchu Patronage and Tibetan Buddhism"; and Schwieger, *The Dalai Lama and the Emperor of China*, "salvation project," 35.

81. Schwieger, *The Dalai Lama and the Emperor of China*, 17–50, 52–53; Ahmad, *Sino-Tibetan Relations in the Seventeenth Century*, 139–144.

82. See for instance Brag dgon pa dkon mchog bstan pa rab rgyas (Drakgönpa's) account of the rise of the Khoshud polities in Amdo and especially the account of the "Lama-lords" of Lamo Dechen monastery, the Lamo Zhabdrung Karpo *trülku*, in MSCB, 15–53, 269–272.

83. For use of term "syzygy" see D. Seyfort Ruegg, "*mchod yon, yon chod* and *mchod gnas/ yon gnas*," 451.

84. Samten G. Karmay, "The Fifth Dalai Lama and His Reunification of Tibet," in *Lhasa in the Seventeenth Century*, ed. Francoise Pommaret (Leiden: Brill, 2003), 72–73; Schwieger, *The Dalai Lama and the Emperor of China*, 57.

85. My modified translation of original passage quoted in Ahmad, *Sino-Tibetan Relations in the Seventeenth Century*, 174–175.

86. Grupper, "Manchu Patronage and Tibetan Buddhism," 56.

87. Schwieger, *The Dalai Lama and the Emperor of China*, 33; Elverskog, *The Jewel Translucent Sūtra*, 26.

88. Elverskog, *The Jewel Translucent Sūtra*, 77, 144.

89. Natalie Köhle, "Why did the Kangxi Emperor go to Wutai Shan? Patronage, Pilgrimage, and the Place of Tibetan Buddhism at the Early Qing Court," in *Late Imperial China* 29, no. 1 (June 2008): 73–119; and Farquhar, "The Emperor as Bodhisattva in the Governance of the Ch'ing Empire."

90. Farquhar, "The Emperor as Bodhisattva in the Governance of the Ch'ing Empire," 19; Grupper, "Manchu Patronage and Tibetan Buddhism," 47–74; Ishihama, "The Notion of 'Buddhist Government'," 15–31.

91. Ishihama, "The Notion of 'Buddhist Government'," 24–27.

92. Ma. *doro šajin*; Mongol *törü šajin*. Alternately translated as "administration" and the religious "precepts."

93. Schwieger, *The Dalai Lama and the Emperor of China*, 64.

94. This seems especially important since our sources are entirely public documents (stele, diplomatic letters, etc.) and not materials that record internal deliberations. The significance of the discourse on Buddhist governance may also seem blown out of proportion when considered—as it has been here—without reference to variety of other legitimating strategies employed by early Qing rulers.

95. Schwieger, *The Dalai Lama and the Emperor of China*, 107.

96. Luciano Petech, *China and Tibet in the Early XVIIIth Century: History of the Establishment of the Chinese Protectorate in Tibet* (Leiden: Brill, 1972), 8–32; Schwieger, *The Dalai Lama and the Emperor of China*, 116–120.

97. Although Qing rulers referred to him as the "Sixth" Dalai Lama in official documents.

98. Petech, *China and Tibet in the Early XVIIIth Century*, 32–90; Schwieger, *The Dalai Lama and the Emperor of China*, 121–127, 134.

99. Petech, *China and Tibet in the Early XVIIIth Century*, 158–197; Schwieger, *The Dalai Lama and the Emperor of China*, 140–145.

100. Petech, *China and Tibet in the Early XVIIIth Century*, 232.

101. Petech, *China and Tibet in the Early XVIIIth Century*, 223, 29–232; Schwieger, *The Dalai Lama and the Emperor of China*, 157–158.

102. Katō Naoto, "Lobsang Danjin's Rebellion of 1723," in *The Tibetan History Reader*, ed. Gray Tuttle and Kurtis Schaeffer (New York: Columbia University Press, 2013), 411–436; and Peter Perdue, *China Marches West: The Qing Conquest of Central Eurasia* (Cambridge, MA: Harvard University Press, 2005), 192, 243–248.

103. Gong Jinghan, *Xunhua zhi* (Xining: Qinghai minzu chubanshe, 1981 [1792]), 25–26, citing memorials of Danai. That this event marked the formal inclusion of Qinghai into the empire remained the view of Qing officials in the Guangxu period. See report from Xunhua subprefect, Qinghai Provincial Archives, *Xunhua ting dang'an*, 7–YJ–2681, Guangxu 15/06/10 (1889–07–07).

104. The process of delimiting borders, however, between Qinghai, Sichuan, and central Tibet took some time, as a memorial from Danai dated to 1732 indicates. MWLF doc. 03–0170–0125–002.

105. The chief Lhasa *amban*, Lian-yu, made these comparisons in 1909 in a memorial that discussed the prospects for constitutional reforms in Tibet. Wu Fengpei, ed., *Lianyu zhu Zang zougao* (Lhasa: Xizang renmin chubanshe, 1979), 87–88.

106. For a comprehensive survey of this work and the phrase "politics of difference," see Jane Burbank and Frederick Cooper, *Empires in World History: Power and the Politics of Difference* (Princeton: Princeton University Press, 2010).

107. Jürgen Osterhammel, *Colonialism: A Theoretical Overview, Second Edition* (Princeton: Markus Wiener Publishers, 2005), 15–16.

108. Although in the places where it did pay off, it could do so spectacularly and with profound historical ramifications, it is difficult to imagine the dominance of England without the profits of the sugar plantations in the West Indies or the inter-Asian opium trade.

109. For Partha Chatterjee's "rule of colonial difference," see *The Nation and Its Fragments: Colonial and Post-Colonial Histories* (Princeton, NJ: Princeton University Press, 1993), 16–27.

110. Stevan Harrell, "Civilizing Projects and the Reaction to Them," in *Cultural Encounters on China's Ethnic Frontiers*, ed. Stevan Harrell (Seattle: Uniersity of Washington Press, 1995), 3–36; and Osterhammel, *Colonialism*, 16.

111. For key studies of identity formation and differentiation between Qing ruling elites and subject populations, see Pamela Crossley, *A Translucent Mirror: History and Identity in Qing Imperial Ideology* (Berkeley: University of California Press, 1999); and Mark C. Elliott, *The Manchu Way: The Eight Banners and Ethnic Identity in Late Imperial China* (Stanford: Stanford University Press, 2001). For the ongoing cultural production of difference, see Crossley, "Manzhou Yuanliu Kao and the Formalization of the Manchu Heritage," *The Journal of Asian Studies* 46, no. 4 (November 1987): 761–790; Joanna Waley-Cohen, *The Culture of War in China: Empire and the Military Under the Qing Dynasty* (London: I. B. Tauris, 2006); and Nicola Di Cosmo, "Manchu Shamanic

Ceremonies at the Qing Court," in *State and Court Ritual in China*, ed. Joseph McDermott (Cambridge: Cambridge University Press: 1999), 352–398.

112. For examinations of the ethnic undertones of Qing claims to sagely, Confucian rule, see Philip A. Kuhn, *Soulstealers* (Cambridge, MA: Harvard University Press, 1990), 60; Elliott, *The Manchu Way*, 4–5; and Michael G. Chang, *A Court on Horseback* (Cambridge, MA: Harvard University Asia Center, 2007), 7–9.

113. James Millward, *Beyond the Pass: Economy, Ethnicity, and Empire in Qing Central Asia, 1759–1864* (Stanford: Stanford University Press, 1998), 15–18; Peter Perdue, "Comparing Empires: Manchu Colonialism," *The International History Review* 20, no. 2 (1998): 255–262, and "China and Other Colonial Empires," *The Journal of American-East Asian Relations* 16, no. 1–2 (Spring–Summer 2009): 85–103; and Nicola Di Cosmo, "Qing Colonial Administration in Inner Asia," *The International History Review* 20, no. 2 (June 1998): 287–309.

114. Perdue, "China and Other Colonial Empires," 93.

115. Benton, *Law and Colonial Cultures*; Lisa Ford, *Settler Sovereignty: Jurisdiction and Indigenous People in America and Australia, 1788–1836* (Cambridge, MA: Harvard University Press, 2010); Kolsky, *Colonial Justice in British India*.

116. James Hevia, "Lamas, Emperors and Rituals: Political Implications in Qing Imperial Ceremonies." *Journal of the International Association of Buddhist Studies* 16 (1993): 247.

117. This tension could also be described as a tension between "orientalism" and "ornamentalism," in other words, legitimating their rule through assertions of cultural superiority and mastery of indigenous cultures (such as Confucianism and Buddhism) or through cultivating a common culture among elites from different backgrounds. Elverskog, *Our Great Qing*, was the first to apply David Cannedine's concept of "ornamentalism" to the Qing case.

118. Osterhammel, *Colonialism*, 15–17 (emphasis in original). Osterhammel's definition of colonialism places great agency and transformative power in the hands of the colonizer. He is quick to note, however, that no colonial rulers ever succeeded in making the colonized fully subservient (15).

119. Mark C. Elliott, *Emperor Qianlong: Son of Heaven, Man of the World* (New York: Longman, 2009), 160–161. I use Elliott's translation of Qianlong's Manchu-language reign name.

120. For a summary of Fuk'anggan's service in Tibet, see Fabienne Jagou, "Manzhou jiangjun Fukang'an: 1792 zhi 1793 nian Xizang zhengwu gaige de xianqu," in *Bianchen yu jiangli* [Les fonctionnaires des frontiers], ed. Li Guoqiang et al. (Beijing: Faguo hanxue & Zhonghua shuju, 2007), 147–167.

121. Elliott, *Emperor Qianlong,* 157; cf. David Nivison, "Ho-shen and His Accusers: Ideology and Political Behavior in the 18th Century," in *Confucianism in Action*, ed. David S. Nivison et al. (Stanford: Stanford University Press, 1959), 211. Wook Yoon has recently presented a much more sympathetic revisionist account of Hešen: "Prosperity with the Help of 'Villains,' 1776–1799: A Review of the Heshen Clique and its Era," *T'oung Pao* 98 (2012): 479–527. My calculation of Hešen's relative wealth is based on figures in Yoon, 517, 524.

122. According to Petech, this occurred in 1748 (*China and Tibet in the Early XVIIIth Century* 255). For a recent summary of scholarship on the *ambans*, see Sabine Dabringhaus, "The Ambans of Tibet—Imperial Rule at the Inner Asian Periphery," in *The Dynastic*

Center and the Provinces: Agents and Interactions, ed. Jeroen Duindam and Sabine Dab-ringhaus (Leiden: Brill, 2014), 114–126; and Zhang Fan, "Grass-root official in the ideological battlefield: reevaluation of the study of the amban in Tibet," in *Political Strategies of Identity Building in Non-Han Empires in China*, ed. Francesca Fiaschetti and Julia Schneider (Wiesbaden: Harrassowitz Verlag, 2014), 225–253. For a synthesis of PRC scholarship, see Zeng Guoqing, *Bainian zhu Zang dachen yanjiu luncong* (Beijing: Zhongguo zangxue chubanshe, 2014). For the first Han literati account of the *ambans* from 1807, see Yu Zhengxie, "Origins of the Amban System."

123. Schwieger, *The Dalai Lama and the Emperor of China*, 150.

124. Zhang Fan, "Grass-root official in the ideological battlefield," 230; Petech, *China and Tibet in the Early XVIIIth Century*, 257–258; also Wu Fengpei, "Qingdai zhuzang guanyuan de shezhi he zhiquan," in *Bainian zhu Zang dachen yanjiu luncong*, ed. Zeng Guoqing (Beijing: Zhongguo Zangxue chubanshe, 2014), 105–107; same volume, Qi Meiqin and Zhao Yang, "Guangyu Qingdai Zangshi ji zhu Zang dachen yanjiu de jidian kaolü," 569–592.

125. YYZDZZ, 803–808, Agūi memorial of QL 57/12/28.

126. Deng Ruiling, "1789–1790 nian Ehui deng Xizang shiyi zhangcheng, 1789–1790," *Zhongguo zangxue* 83, no. 3 (2008): 138–146.

127. For recent assessements of Sungyun: Liu Zhong, "Shilun Qingdai zhu Zang dachen Songyun dui Xizang de gaige," in *Bainian zhu Zang dachen yanjiu luncong*, ed. Zeng Guoqing (Beijing: Zhongguo Zangxue chubanshe, 2014), 154–166; also in same vol-ume, Feng Mingzhu, "Zouguo liuhen: Songyun zhu Zang de zhengji yu zhuoshu," 448–479; and Zhang Yun, "Helin zhu Zang: Qingchao zhu Zang dachen de yige dianxingxing fenxi," in *Bianchen yu jiangli*, ed. Li Guoqiang et al. (Beijing: Faguo hanxue Zhongghua shuju, 2007), 168–189. In the 1900s, the Han official Zhang Yin-tang famously referred to the *ambans* as the "tea-boiling *ambans*" (Ch. *aocha dachen* 熬茶大臣), mocking them yet again for their perceived lack of influence over the Gan-den Podrang. See Wu Fengpei, "Sheng-tai he You-tai," in *Bainian zhu Zang dachen yanjiu luncong*, ed. Zeng Guoqing (Beijing: Zhongguo Zangxue chubanshe, 2014), 281.

128. The title purposely echoed that used in the historical relations between the Qubilai and the Sakya. Pu Wencheng, *Qinghai fojiao shi* (Xining: Qinghai renmin chubanshe, 2001), 247.

129. The identification of this monk is problematic. "Galdan Siretu" (Ch. Ga'erdan xiletu 噶勒丹錫哷圖), meaning "golden-throne holder," was a generic title frequently attached to monks who had served as the chief throne holder at Ganden monastery in Lhasa (the Ganden Tripa), the highest position in the Geluk church. In the mid-late Qianlong reign it was customary for the government of the Dalai Lama to dispatch former "golden-throne holders" from Lhasa to serve as chief of the Geluk mission in Beijing and minister to the throne. For example, Ngawang Tsültrim, the regent who passed away in 1791, had been known in official documents as the Galdan Siretu. The title was also used for monks who had been abbots of other major monasteries. There-fore, in the 1790s there were several monks from different parts of the empire who could have been the Galden Siretu. One possibility was the Galdan Siretu *kūtuktu* or Serkhri Rinpoché (Tib: Gser khri rin po che), a major reincarnate lineage from Amdo affiliated with Lamo Dechen and Labrang monasteries. This *kūtuktu* maintained an estate in Beijing, and his portfolio previously included assisting with Buddhist

projects in the capital and providing diplomatic services for the court in Kökenuur. In the early 1790s, the Fourth Serkhri Ngawang Tupten Trinlé Gyatso (1773–1815) was just emerging from childhood (age 19) and therefore was unlikely to have been consulted by the emperor (Sangs rgyas rin chen, "Laa mo bde chen dgon pa'i sku phyag gser khri rin po che'i sku phreng rim byon gyi lo rgyus mdo bsdus ngo sprod," *Mdo smad zhib 'jug* 1 (1999): 108–118). It is more likely that the Galdan Siretu resident at court in 1792–94 was either the Siretu Kurun Jasak Lama (錫勒圖庫倫札薩克喇嘛), a monk based among the Kharachin Mongols of eastern Inner Mongolia, or the Siretu *kūtuktu* (錫呼圖呼圖克圖) of Hohhot (Jin Hai, Qimude Dao'erji, Huricha, and Hasibagen, *Qingdai menggu zhi* [Huhehaote: Neimenggu renmin chubanshe, 2009], 211, 388–392). The monk in question was probably from the latter lineage because the Siretu Kurun Jasak Lamas were usually selected from a single clan based in Amdo and the Qianlong emperor noted that the Galdan Siretu *kūtuktu* he was working with hailed from a Khalkha Mongol princely family (Qianlong, *Discourse on Lamas*, lines 20–21).

130. The identification of this lama is also problematic. According to Pu Wenchang, the Gomang *kūtuktu* (Tib. *Sgo mang*) was one of the "nine lesser incarnation lineages" of Gönlung monastery, northeast of Xining. This may be the Kharachin Lama, Toin Tutop Nyima (Tib. Har chin tho yon mthu stobs nyi ma), who would subsequently serve as abbot of Gomang College, Drepung monastery (1792–98) and then Gönlung monastery, 1799–1800. See Brenton Sullivan, "The Mother of All Monasteries" (PhD diss., University of Virginia, 2013), 30, 52, 397.

131. YHGSL, 14:348.

132. Luciano Petech, *The Dalai Lamas and Regents of Tibet: A Chronological Study* (Serie Orientale Roma 80. Rome: Instituto Italiano Per Il Medio ed Estremo Oriente, 1988), 137–139.

133. Ma. *Jirung kūtuktu*, Ch. *Jilong hutuketu* 濟嚨呼圖克圖 or *Daca huofo* 達擦活佛.

134. Schwieger, *The Dalai Lama and the Emperor of China*, 160, 171–172.

135. *Lifanyuan zeli* (1817), in Zhao Yuntian, *Qianlongchao neifu chaoben "Lifanyuan zeli,"* 368.

136. Petech, *The Dalai Lamas and Regents of Tibet,* 139–140.

137. Schwieger, *The Dalai Lama and the Emperor of China*, 180.

138. Daowei Cairangjia, "Gandan pozhang shiqi Xizang de zhengzhi zhidu wenhua yanjiu," PhD diss. (Zhongyang minzu daxue, 2007), 42. Cf. Ga Dawa Cairen, "Xizang difang zhengfu de sida hufashen," *Xizang dang'an* 20 (2001, vol. 1): 92–96.

139. Tib. *tsangs pa dung gi thor tshugs can.*

140. Ma. *Lamu cüijung*, Ch. *Lamu chuizhong* 拉模吹忠. Christopher Bell, "Nechung: The Ritual History and Institutionalization of a Tibetan Buddhist Protector Deity" (PhD diss., University of Virginia, 2013), 81; René de Nebesky-Wojkowitz, *Oracles and Demons of Tibet: The Cult and Iconography of the Tibetan Protective Deities* (Graz, Austria: Akademische Druck, 1975), 145–153.

141. The first being that of the Jebstundamba *kūtuktu*. Jin Hai et al., *Qingdai menggu zhi,* 221–225.

142. Schwieger, *The Dalai Lama and the Emperor of China*, 29; Samten Chhosphel, "The Seventh Pakpa Lha, Jigme Tenpai Gonpo," *Treasury of Lives,* http://www.treasuryoflives .org/biographies/view/Jigme-Tenpai-Gonpo/3783, accessed March 14, 2013.

143. Nietupski, *Labrang Monastery,* 17–21. Nietupski writes that the first two colleges of Labrang already had a population of a thousand monks in 1738. In 1823, the

governor-general of Gansu and Shaanxi provinces estimated there to be twenty to thirty thousand monks distributed among the monasteries of Xunhua subprefecture, the nineteenth-century administrative unit that included Labrang monastery (Na-yan-cheng, 2:12a–b).

144. Labrang was a large monastery, but just how "large" and "influential" is difficult to quantify, especially in the 1790s. Contemporaneous Tibetan-language sources list donations to the estate of the Jamyang Zhepa and other affiliated *trülku*, but do not provide population figures for the communities they governed. The *Xunhua Gazetteer* of 1792 states that in the area around Labrang monastery there were 4,214 Tibetan households spread across 21 communities (Ch. *zhai* 寨). According to the revised Xining prefectural gazetteer of 1878, there were 8,549 Tibetan households and 177,729 people in the Tibetan areas of Xunhua subprefecture—a district that included both Labrang and several other large monasteries and communities (Deng Chengwe, *Xiningfu xuzhi* [Xining: Qinghai renmin chubanshe, 1985 (1883)], 33). However, these numbers are unreliable because they did not count the "inner communities" (Tib. *nang sde*) or "ecclesiastical communities" (Tib. *lha sde*) directly subject to the Jamyang Zhepa because this population was not under the jurisdiction of the Xunhua subprefect. A Republican-era survey cited by Paul Nietupski counted 39,676 laypeople and 7,640 monks in the "Labrang district" (*Labrang Monastery*, 54). These numbers are problematic because they conflate proximity of residence to Labrang with political subordination to the monastic estates based there. Living near Labrang or offering donations to its monks did not mean that one had become their vassal (Tib. *mgo btags*, Ch. *shuan tou*). In 1792, the Xunhua subprefect counted 691 lay households at Tsö, a monastery perhaps a third the size of Labrang. He counted 2,435 lay households around Rongwo, a monastery of roughly similar size to Labrang that stood in a larger and more intensely cultivated valley. In comparison, I estimate that the Jamyang Zhepa's estate directly governed 1,200 to 2,400 households (with an average household size of five to ten people), with the true figure somewhere at the lower end of this range.

145. I will refer to the treasurer by the transliteration of his name in Manchu.

146. For an extensive account of the war based on Tibetan sources, see Tsepon Wangchuk Deden Shakabpa, *One Hundred Thousand Moons* (Boston: Brill, 2010), 489–556; cf. Chen Qingying and Chen Lijian, *Huofo zhuanshi*, 170–173; and Rose, *Nepal Strategy for Survival*, 23–74.

Act I: The Royal Regulations

1. Henrietta Harrison has pointed out, however, that from the perspective of the Qianlong emperor the chief problem posed by the British embassy were its requests for diplomatic and economic concessions, which could have undermined the political and financial security of the dynasty. Harrison, "The Qianlong Emperor's Letter to George III and the Early-Twentieth-Century Origins of Ideas about Traditional China's Foreign Relations," *The American Historical Review* 122, no. 3 (June 2017): 680–701.

2. MWLF, 159:1202–1203, QL 59/11/13 (December 5, 1794).

3. Qianlong, *Discourse on Lamas* (*Lama Shuo* 喇嘛說), lines 32–36.

4. Deng Ruiling, "1789–1790 nian Ehui deng Xizang shiyi zhangcheng," *Zhongguo zangxue* 83, no. 3 (2008): 138–146.

5. DLNT08, 198ka.3.

6. *Qinding Kuo'erke jilüe*, edict QL 56/09/20 (October 17, 1791), 103.

7. DLNT08, 198ka.1.

8. MWLF, 155:0243, court letter to Agūi, QL 57/04R/05 (May 25, 1792). This was not the first time the Qing court deployed the spiritual weaponry of the Geluk church. Joanna Waley-Cohen observes similar tactics during the second Jinchuan war (1771–76): "Religion, War, and Empire-Building in Eighteenth-Century China," *The International History Review* 20, no. 2 (June 1998): 336–352. Cf. Dan Martin, "Bonpo Canons and Jesuit Cannons: On Sectarian Factors Involved in the Ch'ien-lung Emperor's Second Goldstream Expedition of 1771–1776 Based Primarily on Some Tibetan Sources," *Tibet Journal* 15 (1990): 3–28.

9. MWLF, 155:0244. Qianlong also mentions the importance of assigning monks the task of reciting mantras (Ma. *k'or maktambi*). I am uncertain of the Tibetan-language equivalents of the (Ma.) *g'al mandal* and the *doksit nomun*.

10. Liu Limei, "Guanyu zhu Zang dachen yu Dalai lama xianjian liyi wenti," in *Bainian zhu Zang dachen yanjiu luncong*, ed. Zeng Guoqing (Beijing: Zhongguo Zangxue chubanshe, 2014), 352–353.

11. YYZDZZ, 705–708.

12. DLNT08, 201ka.06–201kha.04.

13. YYZDZZ, 707.

14. DLNT08, 201ka.01–03.

15. YYZDZZ, 708. In many respects, the Dalai Lama's unwillingness to accept the prostrations of Fuk'anggan appear in both of these materials as more a matter of indulgence of the Qing than forcefully imposed.

16. YYZDZZ, 708.

17. YYZDZZ, 710.

18. YYZDZZ, 707.

19. Samten G. Karmay, *The Illusive Play: The Autobiography of the Fifth Dalai Lama* (Chicago: Serindia, 2014), 17.

20. Per K. Sørensen, "The Sacred Junipers of Reting: The Arboreal Origins Behind the Dalai Lama Lineage," *Orientations* (September 2008): 76–77.

21. Ling-wei Kung provided an excellent overview of the Manchu, Mongol, and Tibetan versions of this document in his presentation, "The Secret History of Tibet: The Mindstream Transference from the Fifth to the Sixth Dalai Lamas and Its Manchu-Mongol Translations in the Qing Archives," at the conference "Beyond Empire and Borders," Columbia University, September 6, 2017.

22. Karmay, *The Illusive Play*, 35, 43.

23. See Wang Xiangyun, "The Qing Court's Tibet Connections: Lcang skya Rol pai'i rdo rje and the Qianlong Emperor," *Harvard Journal of Asiatic Studies* 60, no. 1 (2000): 125–163.

24. MWLF, 155:0244. Joanna Waley-Cohen observes a similar approach to enemy lamas during the Jinchuan campaigns ("Religion, War, and Empire-Building in Eighteenth-Century China," 345).

25. Peter Perdue, *China Marches West* (Cambridge, MA: Harvard University Press, 2005), 279.

26. Chen Qingying and Chen Lijian, *Huofo zhuanshi: Yuanqi, fazhan, lishi dingzhi* (Beijing: Zhongguo zangxue chubanshe, 2014), 168–169.

27. MWJXD, 03–138–3–050, QL 51/06/28 (July 23, 1786).

28. MWJXD, 03–139–2–078, QL 52/12/18 (January 25, 1788).

29. MWJXD, 03–139–3–032, QL 53/04/07 (May 12, 1788).

30. First Historical Archives (Beijing), *Yangxindian zaobanchu zuocheng zuohuo jiqingdang*, registers for QL 46/02/11, QL 57/01/?; cf. Wang Jiapeng, "Qing gong cang youguan jinping cheqian de wu," in *Huofo ji zhuanshi zhidu yanjiu*, ed. Chen Qingying and Ga Dawa Cairen (Beijing: Zhongguo zangxue yanjiu zhongxin zongjiaosuo neibufaxing, 2006), 417–418.

31. The precise identity or position of this monk is unclear. Peter Schwieger notes that Tibetan sources refer to this monk as a *rtse drung lama*, not a *rje drung lama* (*The Dalai Lama and the Emperor of China: A Political History of the Tibetan Institution of Reincarnation* [New York: Columbia University Press, 2015], 277 n. 95). "*Jedrung*" is a honorific form of address for nobles or respected monks. See Zhang Yisun, "*rje drung*," in *Bod rgya tshig mdzod chen mo* (Beijing: Minzu chubanshe, 1993), 910.

32. YYZDZZ, 667.

33. YYZDZZ, 672–673.

34. YYZDZZ, 677–678.

35. MWLF, doc. # 3–10–1757–5, court letter, QL 56/09/25 (October 22, 1791). For the contemporaneous Chinese-language version, see *Qinding Kuo'erke jilüe*, 107. For a history of the concept of "taming demons," in Tantric Buddhism, see Jacob Paul Dalton, *The Taming of the Demons: Violence and Liberation in Tibetan Buddhism* (New Haven: Yale University Press, 2011).

36. YYZDZZ, 685–688, 689. Also, *Hanwen lüfu* doc. # 157–7633–17, Ohūi QL 56/11/28 (December 23, 1791).

37. YYZDZZ, 689–690.

38. YYZDZZ, 690.

39. The last time agents of the Qing state had ordered a public execution in Lhasa had been forty years earlier, in January 1751, when fourteen Tibetans were executed for their role in the murder of the two *ambans* during the Gyurmé Namgyel affair. The execution of the *jedrung lama* of Trashi Lhünpo was qualitatively different, as it marked the execution of a monk and the punishment of a crime that had not involved any overt or intended violence against the Qing house or its agents. See Luciano Petech, *China and Tibet in the Early XVIIIth Century: History of the Establishment of the Chinese Protectorate in Tibet* (Leiden: Brill, 1972). 225.

40. YYZDZZ, 690.

41. YYZDZZ, 691, edict to Grand Secretariat, QL 56/12/25 (January 18, 1792).

42. YYZDZZ, 691.

43. *Discourse*, Tibetan text, lines 13–13, 29–30.

44. The Manchu official Bajung committed suicide when it became known in Beijing that he had not informed the emperor of the secret protocol that the Ganden Podrang government had reached with the Gurkhas in 1789.

45. YYZDZZ, 729. The appointment letter read in part, "Ohūi is a coward and Cengde is boorish; neither of these two can competently hold the office. Heliyen is careful and attentive, have him proceed posthaste to Tibet to coordinate matters with Ohūi." Upon arrival in Lhasa, Heliyen's status was upgraded to senior *amban* (QL 57/05/19, July 7, 1792). For much of 1792 there would, unusually, be three *ambans* in central Tibet: Heliyen, Ohūi, and Eldemboo (as junior *amban*). For a rather hagiographic account of Heliyen's service, see Zhang Yun, "He-lin zhu zang: Qingchao zhu zang dachen de yige dianxingxing fenxi," in *Bianchen yu jiangli* [Les fonctionnaires des frontiers], ed. Li Guoqiang et al. (Beijing: Faguo hanxue & Zhonghua shuju, 2007), 168–189.

46. Hešen's letters seem to have come to light and been placed in the Grand Council archives when the Jiaqing emperor ordered the investigation of the former grand councilor following the death of Qianlong. MWLF 167:0339, letter from Hešen to Heliyen, QL 56/6/? (July–August 1792) and neighboring documents on the microfilm roll are good examples, specifically relating to the grand councilor's potential mishandling of subsequent tribute missions from the Gurkhas. The archives even contain several letters from Tibetan nobles and major incarnations sent directly to Hešen. For instance, an early 1792 (QL57) letter from the young Panchen Lama requested that Hešen intercede to ensure that the Drungpa *kūtuktu*, who had just been dispatched to Beijing, be treated leniently and permitted to return to Tibet as soon as possible (MWLF, 155:0047).

47. *Qinding Kuo'erke jilüe, juan* 15, Yan Tingliang memorial, QL 57/01/02 (January 25, 1792).

48. See Fuk'anggan memorial, QL 57/01/26 (March 18, 1792). Also *Qinding Kuo'erke jilüe, juan* 20, QL 57/02/18 (March 10, 1792); *juan* 28, QL 57/04/28 (May 18, 1792).

49. MWLF, 153:2676, Heliyen memorial, QL 57/04R/15 (June 4, 1792). Heliyen met with the Dalai Lama for the first time on this date.

50. Kim Hanung, "Another Tibet at the Heart of Qing China: Location of Tibetan Buddhism in the Mentality of the Qing Chinese Mind at Jehol," in *Greater Tibet*, ed. P. Christiaan Klieger (Lanham, MD: Lexington Books, 2016), 39–40.

51. QSL QL, fasc. 1483, QL 57/04R/24 *renchen* 壬辰 ("04R" stands for the intercalary fourth month, June 13, 1792).

52. The Korean emissaries, for instance, "mistook" prostration before the Sixth Panchen Lama as a political act and refused to perform it. Despite being told that the specific form of the prostration was different when done for a spiritual "teacher," they saw no fundamental difference and protested that regardless, it should be reserved for the "son of Heaven." Kim, "Another Tibet at the Heart of Qing China," 40.

53. Heliyen received these instructions after he had arrived in Lhasa and passed on imperial gifts to the Dalai Lama. See MWLF 153:2676, Heliyen memorial QL 57/04R/15 (June 4, 1792).

54. According to Deng Ruiling, Qianlong had begun to voice suspicions of the Dalai Lama on QL 56/12/26 (January 19, 1792). Deng Ruiling, *Qing qianqi zhi Zang zengce tanze* (Beijing: Zhongguo zangxue chubanshe, 2012), 200–201.

55. MWLF, 154:0063, Heliyen memorial, QL 57/06/17 (August 4, 1792).

56. The original report from Bootai contains the initial report from the Kashag that the *kalön* were merely in the region to inspect the border and deliver a letter to the

Gurkhas. See MWLF, 152:2295, QL 56/07/22 (August 21, 1791). The Dalai Lama astutely dispatched two attendants to intercept Fuk'anggan several days outside Lhasa in order to greet him and convey their side of the story. This tactic worked well. Fuk'anggan's memorial is quite sympathetic to the Dalai Lama and the case laid before him by the two attendants. Blame falls squarely on the incompetence of the *kalöns*. See the Grand Council file copy of Fukanggan's Chinese-language memorial in YYZDZZ, 695–699.

57. MWLF, 155:0207, Heliyen memorial, QL 57/06/17 (August 4, 1792).

58. Tib. Lo sems dpa' 08 Blo bzang bshe gnyen grags pa rnam rgyal (d. 1793). See Luciano Petech, *Aristocracy and Government in Tibet: 1728–1959* (Serie Orientale Roma 35. Rome: Instituto Italiano Per Il Medio ed Estremo Oriente, 1973), 60.

59. *Drungkhor* (Tib. *drung 'khor*, Ma. *jungkor*): The corps of lay officials who staffed the Ganden Podrang government. All 175 of these men hailed from aristocratic families. See Petech, *Aristocracy and Government in Tibet*, 8.

60. Pandita (Ma. Bandida): This name is used in Manchu-language texts to refer to both the Gazhi (Tib. Dga' bzhi) household and Noyan Pandita, father of Doring Tendzin Peljor. Petech, *Aristocracy and Government in Tibet*, 50–64; Tsepon W.D. Shakabpa, *One Hundred Thousand Moons: An Advanced Political History of Tibet,* trans. Derek F. Maher (Boston: Brill, 2010), 536–538.

61. MWLF, 155:0207–0208.

62. Petech, *Aristocracy and Government in Tibet*, especially the description of the Lhalu (Tib. Lha klu) and Gazhi clans, 39–43, 50–64.

63. MWLF, 155:0208.

64. MWLF, 155:0209.

65. MWLF, 155:0208–0209: "*Dzang ni baita fuhali toktoho kooli akū.*"

66. See for instance, use of the similar rhetoric in a memorial from Fuk'anggan dated QL 57/12/11 (YYZDZZ, 795–83) and a later memorial from Agūi dated QL 57/12/28 (February 8, 1792) in YYZDZZ, 803–808.

67. MWLF, 154:0981–0982, Agūi memorial, September–October 1792 (QL 57/08).

68. YYZDZZ, 708–711, Fuk'anggan memorial, QL 57/01/22 (February 14, 1792).

69. YYZDZZ, 711.

70. See, for instance: William Woodville Rockhill, "The Dalai Lamas of Lhasa and Their Relations With the Manchu Emperors of China: 1644–1908," *T'oung Pao* XI (1910): 49–52; Hugh Richardson, *Ch'ing Dynasty Inscriptions at Lhasa* (Roma: Serie Orientalia, 1974), 29–48; Tsepon W.D. Shakabpa, *Tibet, A Political History* (New Haven: Yale University Press, 1967), 157–158. Fabienne Jagou, "Manzhou jiangjun Fu-kang-an: 1792 zhi 1793 nian Xizang zhengwu gaige de xianqu [The Manchu general Fuk'anggan: instigator of the reform of political affairs in Tibet from 1792–1793]," in *Bianchen yu jiangli,* ed. Li Guoqiang et al. (Beijing: Zhonghua shuju, 2007), 147–151.

71. It might also be useful to consider Qianlong's treatment of Geluk monks in 1792 against the events of the two Jinchuan campaigns, in which the Qing forces also had to contend with suspect lamas and their potential magical powers. Much as in 1792, during the Jinchuan campaigns the court perceived itself as aligned with Gelukpa hierarchs against non-Gelukpa monks who were allied with "rebellious" Tibetans in Jinchuan.

72. Philip Kuhn, *Soulstealers* (Cambridge, MA: Harvard University Press, 1990), 111.

73. Kuhn, *Soulstealers*, 42–3, 45, 109–111.

74. Kuhn, *Soulstealers*, 86–87.

75. Kuhn, *Soulstealers*, 64.

76. Jonathan Lipman, *Familiar Strangers* (Seattle: University of Washington Press, 1997), 107–115. Much like in 1792, the events of 1781 resulted in the extension of the legal codes of the Qing interior to populations previously exempted from them. See Ma Haiyun, "Fanhui or Huifan? Hanhui or Huimin? Salar Ethnic Identification and Qing Administrative Transformation in Eighteenth-Century Gansu," *Late Imperial China* 29, no. 2 (December 2008): 1–36.

77. Roger Jackson, "Triumphalism and Ecumenism in Thu'u bkwan's *Crystal Mirror*," *Journal of the International Association of Tibetan Studies* 2 (August 2006): 1–23.

78. Perdue, *China Marches West*, 440; and James Hevia, "Lamas, Emperors and Rituals: Political Implications in Qing Imperial Ceremonies," *Journal of the International Association of Buddhist Studies* 16 (1993): 249.

79. MSCB, 100.

80. MSCB, 393–394.

81. Nga dbang blo bzang rgya mtsho, *Rgyal dbang lnga pa'i rang rnam du kU la'i gos bzang* (Kawring, HP: Tobdan Tsering, 1979–1983, TIBRC W23956), Ka:28a. A painting recording major events in the life of the Fifth Dalai Lama contains a depiction of the *zentak* ceremony. See Rubin Museum C2003.9.2 (HAR 65275). Desi Sanggyé Gyatso's widely read biography of the Fifth Dalai Lama did not mention the use of the *zentak*. Only in the nineteenth century, after the Golden Urn became associated with *zentak* divination, did Tibetan sources begin noting the "precedent" of the Great Fifth. See the biography of the Third Jamyang Zhepa: JYZP03, 37.

82. Yu Hong and Zhang Shuangzhi, "Jinping cheqian yu shenpan wenhua," *Xizang yanjiu* 2 (2006): 48–49.

83. Gaozong [Qianlong emperor], *Yuzhi shiwen shiquanji* (Beijing: Zhongguo zangxue chubanshe, 1993), 642; and QSL QL, edict of QL 58/02/04 (1793–03–15).

84. YHGSL, 15:7, Fuk'anggan's memorial, QL 57/12/29 (February 9, 1793).

85. In this respect, Fuk'anggan's conception of fate (Ch. *ming* 命) seems broadly in line with the understanding circulating within elite Chinese culture during the mid-Qing: one's fate was determined at birth and had repercussions for the individual that could often be at odds with their innate moral qualities. From a neo-Confucian perspective, however, humans were not without the ability to shape their "allotment." Through self-cultivation it was possible to "devise a moral strategy for contending with predestined situations." See Richard J. Smith, *Mapping China and Managing the World* (London: Routledge, 2013), 136; also the discussion in Christopher Lupke, ed., *The Magnitude of Ming: Command, Allotment, and Fate in Chinese Culture* (Honolulu: University of Hawai'i Press, 2005), 1–20.

86. Brandon Dotson, "Divination and Law in the Tibetan Empire," in *Contributions to the Cultural History of Early Tibet*, ed. Matthew Kapstein and Brandon Dotson (Leiden: Brill, 2007), 30–32, 60.

87. Fernanda Pirie, "The Impermanence of Power," in *Ladakhi Histories*, ed. John Bray (Leiden: Brill, 2005), 379–394; and Charles Ramble, "Rule by Play in Southern Mustang," in *Anthropology of Tibet and the Himalaya*, ed. Charles Ramble and Martin Brauen (Zürich: Volker-kundemuseum der Universität, 1993), 287–301. See also

Robert B. Ekvall, "Some Aspects of Divination in Tibetan Society," *Ethnology* 2, no. 1 (January 1963): 31–39.

88. Tib: *rten 'brel*.

89. MWLF, 154:0982, Agūi, QL 57/8 (September–October, 1792).

90. See for example JYZP03, 37, passim.

91. E'erdete Heying 額爾德特和瑛 [Hening 和寧]. *Yijianzhai shichao* 易簡齋詩鈔, 1823 (Harvard-Yenching Library, 5508 3812). Hening, who toward the end of his life changed his name to Heying (和瑛) out of respect for a name taboo associated with the new Daoguang emperor, ended his career as grand councilor. He held a lifelong interest in Tibet that began prior to his assignment in Lhasa. Recent Chinese scholarship has identified him as the editor and author of much of the *Weizang tongzhi*. He also composed an epic prose poem dedicated to Tibet, the *Xizang fu* (Ode to Tibet). Chi Wanxing, "Hening ji qi 'Xizang fu,'" *Jinan daxue xuebao shehuikexueban* 18, no. 4 (2008): 30–33.

92. MWLF, 154:0982–0983.

93. A list of "sutra reading lamas" in residence at Yonghegong ("雍和宮念經喇嘛") dated QL 57/04R/05 is included among the documents of YHGSL 14:348. The list begins with the three leading *kūtuktu* currently in residence, listed according to rank: Galdan Siretu *kūtuktu* (噶爾丹錫呼圖呼圖克圖), Gomang *kūtuktu* (果蟒呼圖克圖), and Tongkhor *kūtuktu* (洞科爾呼圖克圖).

94. In the early communications concerning the urn the Manchu word *šusihe*, meaning a small square of wood, was used to refer to the lot. Later, as the vocabulary for the ritual became fixed, this term was replaced by *sibiya*, referring to a more elongated "tally" stick. The shifting vocabulary probably reflected the shifting design for the ritual. From the beginning, Qianlong and his officials referred to the urn in Manchu as a *bum*. This term is clearly borrowed from the Tibetan term for squat, bulbous vessels: *bum pa*. In the Board of Civil Appointments, the lottery was conducted using a tall cylindrical vase (Ch. *tong* 筒). The fact that Qianlong and his officials selected a golden *bum* as opposed to a *tong* provides another argument for the case that the ritual was the product of close consultations with Tibetans in the capital.

95. MWLF, 154:0978.

96. MWJXD, 03–138–3–050, QL 51/06/28 (July 23, 1786).

97. MWLF, 154:0979.

98. MWLF, 154:0985–0986.

99. MWLF, 154:0986.

100. This would be an allusion to the succession crisis that followed the death of the Seventh Dalai Lama (d. 1757). For a description, see Chen Qingying and Chen Lizhen, *Dalai lama zhuanshi ji lishi dingzhi* (Beijing: Wuzhou chuanbo chubanshe, 2003), 63–64.

101. MWLF, 154:0984.

102. MWLF, 154:0984–0985.

103. Much like *kūtuktu* and *hūbilgan*, the Manchu term for "protector deity," *sakigūlsu enduri*, was originally imported from Mongol: *sakigulsun*.

104. Ma. *gurdemba*, Tib. *sku rten pa. Gurdemba* is the Manchu transliteration of the Tibetan word for the human medium who channels the instructions of the protector deity. Qing authors found this term roughly parallel to their own concept of *saman* (i.e. shaman).

105. MWLF, 154:0491–0492, court letter, QL 57/07/25 (September 11, 1792).

106. YHGSL, 15:126, edict, QL 58/03/15 (April 25, 1793).

107. MWLF, 154:0492–0493.

108. MWLF, 155:0209, Heliyen memorial, QL 57/06/17 (1792–08–04).

109. MWLF, 154:0493.

110. *Qinding Kuo'erke jilüe*, 622–636, edict, QL 57/08/27 (October 12, 1792).

111. MWLF, 154:1352.

112. MWLF, 155:2856–2857, 2859.

113. *Qinding Kuo'erke jilüe*, 102, edict of QL 56/09/20.

114. MWLF, 155:2860–2861.

115. *Discourse*, line 11.

116. See for instance comments on this aspect by Patricia Berger, *Empire of Emptiness* (Honolulu: University of Hawai'i Press: 2003), 35–36; Johan Elverskog, *Our Great Qing: The Mongols, Buddhism, and the State in Late Imperial China* (Honolulu: University of Hawai'i Press, 2006) 3; and Rockhill, "The Dalai Lamas of Lhasa and Their Relations with the Manchu Emperors of China: 1644–1908," 54.

117. *Discourse*, line 34.

118. The Smallpox Stele, (Ch.) *zhengchi xizang fengsu pai* 整飭西藏風俗碑. Other examples of this would be the *Weizang tongzhi* and Hening's prose poem, *Xizang fu*. For a list of other stelae in Lhasa see Zhang Yuxin, *Qing zhengfu yu lama jiao: fu Qingdai lama jiao beikelu* (Lhasa: Xizang renmin chubanshe, 1988), and also Zhang Husheng, "Quanren xu chudou bei hanwen beiwen jiaozhu," *Zhongguo zangxue* 2 (2006): 180–187.

119. Reprinted in Zhang Yuxin, *Qing zhengfu yu lama jiao*, 497.

120. Gaozong, *Yuzhi shiwen shiquanji*, 644.

121. Gaozong, *Yuzhi shiwen shiquanji*, 644.

122. Gaozong, *Yuzhi shiwen shiquanji*, 645.

123. *Discourse*, lines 30–31.

124. "*Congsu bugong*" 從俗布公. Edict of 1794–6–22 (QL 59/05/25). Reproduced in Evelyn S. Rawski and Jessica Rawson, eds., *China: The Three Emperors, 1662–1795* (London: Royal Academy of the Arts, 2005), 144–145.

125. MWLF, 155:2862.

Act II: Shamanic Colonialism

1. MWLF, 156:1399.

2. "Ten thousand" silver taels (Ch. *liang*) was probably a hyperbolic statement. But travel to and from central Tibet would have incurred considerable expense and time. The base salary for a Manchu bannerman in the capital garrison during the late Qianlong period was around two taels per month.

3. MWLF, 156:1380–1381, 1401.

4. MWLF, 156:1402.

5. MWLF, 156:1385–1386.

6. During the Qing period, the Khalkha of Outer Mongolia were organized into eighty-six "banners." These banners were in turn grouped into four different "leagues" that

in principle represented the domains of the four leading Khalkha khans at the time they submitted to the Qing. By the late 1700s, however, the Khalkha khans were rulers in name only, since the power to appoint banner heads and delimit territories was reserved by the Qing court. By a similar logic, the league captains were often but not always the descendants of the Khalka khans (Christopher Atwood, *Encyclopedia of Mongolia and the Mongol Empire* [New York: Facts on File, 2004], 30–32).

7. MWLF, 156:1404.

8. The earliest report of receipt of the *Discourse on Lamas* edict was from the Qing official stationed in Uliasutai (YHGSL 15:14) on QL 58/02/02 (March 13, 1793). Although the exact date Nawangdasi's petition arrived in the Lifanyuan is unknown, it was certainly no later than March 16, 1793, the day the emperor ordered the investigation of the case (MWJXD 23:194–199).

9. MWLF, 156:1404. The lineage of the Erdeni Pandita *kūtuktu* was evidently one of many Mongol reincarnations that had not previously reported its rebirths to the Court of Colonial Affairs.

10. MWJXD, 23:194–195, QL 58/02/05.

11. Qianlong, *Discourse on Lamas* (*Lama Shuo* 喇嘛說), lines 19–21. In the 1750s the previous Tüsiyetü Khan, the father of Cedendorji, had publicly predicted that his pregnant wife would give birth to the reincarnation of the Jebtsundamba *kūtuktu*. Thus subsequent birth of a daughter not only embarrassed the khan but also served as evidence for why the Qing court should prohibit the search for the Jebtsundamba *kūtuktu* among noble Mongol families.

12. MWJXD, 23:195–196, QL 58/02/05 (March 16, 1793).

13. MWJXD, 23:200–206, QL 58/02/08 (March 3, 1793).

14. MWLF, 156:1403.

15. MWLF, 156:1400–1401. This document is a Manchu-language transcript of a deposition of Nawangdasi conducted by officials of the Lifanyuan. The archive catalog dates the document to QL 58/06, yet evidence indicates that it actually dates to QL 58/02 and is most likely the interrogation cited by Qianlong in his court letter dated QL 58/02/08.

16. MWJXD, 23:202–203, QL 58/02/08 (March 19, 1793).

17. As noted in act 1, Gelek Namk'a was also involved in the search for the reincarnation of Changkya Rolpé Dorjé in 1786 and seems to have been well known to the emperor.

18. Manchu-Mongol language edict of QL 57/08/20 (October 14, 1792).

19. Emphasis added. MWJXD, 23:204–205, QL 58/02/08 (March 19, 1793).

20. See for example the exchange of letters between Heliyen and Qianlong concerning the persuasion of the Dalai Lama: MWJXD, 23:236–238; YHGSL, 15:281–283. While discussing the Tüsiyetü Khan case Qianlong also used the phrase *gūnin bahabufi*, which expresses the idea of "planting an idea in someone's mind" (MWJXD, 23:197). Adding the passive voice infix *bu* to the Manchu verb *dahambi* ("to convince") results in *dahabumbi*, indicating the act of being convinced by someone else (i.e., "persuaded").

21. YHGSL, 15:85a (#28) (QL 58/03/15, 1793–04–25). Contemporaneous Manchu-language texts phrase this slightly differently: "The names of the four oracles will completely fade away of their own accord." Ma. *ini cisui duin cuijung ni gebu be šuwe manambuci ombikai*, MWJXD 23:262, QL 58/04/01 (May 10, 1793). For "*ini cisui nakambi*," see MWLF microfilm 156:0050, QL 58/04/19.

22. Robert E. Buswell, Jr., and Donald S. Lopez, Jr., *The Princeton Dictionary of Buddhism* (Princeton: Princeton University Press, 2014), entry on "śraddhā" (faith), 847–848.

23. MWLF 154:1351–1354, letter to Agūi, QL 57/06/30 (August 17, 1792).

24. MWLF, 154:0491–0492.

25. MWLF, 155:0314–315.

26. MWLF, 155:0315.

27. Fifth Dalai Lama, Lozang Gyatso, *Rgyal dbang lnga pa'i rang rnam du kU la'i gos bzang*, 53 (Ka:28a).

28. Hešen conveyed other contemporaneous documents containing the Galdan Siretu *kūtuktu*'s opinion on this matter to the emperor. For example, see MWLF, 155:0490, QL 57/07/25.

29. MWLF, 155:0316.

30. MWLF, 154:0491–0492. This line of reasoning reappears in a memorial from Fuk'anggan: YHGSL, 15:10–12, QL 58/01/08.

31. Approximately thirty such letters are listed in a catalog of Tibet-related materials at the First Historical Archives. See Zhongguo diyi lishi dang'anguan and Zhongguo Zangxue zhongxin, eds., *Zhongguo diyi lishi dang'anguang suocun Xizang he Zangshi dang'an mulu, Man, Zangwenbu* (Beijing: Zhongguo zangxue chubanshe, 1999), 480–481, 485–487. These letters, plus numerous other Manchu- and Tibetan-language letters that do not appear in the above catalog, can be located at the beginning of microfilm roll #155 of the reproductions of the Manchu-language Grand Council file copies of palace memorials held by the First Historical Archives. The existence of these letters suggests that the Qing court was maintaining surveillance of communications between Tibetan elites.

32. MWLF, 156:0043–0052, QL 58/04/19 (May 28, 1793). This edict was issued in Manchu and subsequently translated into Tibetan for distribution in Tibet. The emperor had, however, a month earlier demanded the end of the oracles in a Manchu-language court letter to Heliyen, MWJXD 23:236–239, QL 58/03/17 (May 27, 1793).

33. MWLF, 155:0315.

34. See edict dated QL 57/08/27 in *Qinding Kuo'erke jilüe* (Beijing: Zhongguo zangxue chubanshe, 2006), 622–626. In the earliest extant formulation of the ritual, the emperor states that "the *ambans* resident in Tibet together with the Dalai Lama et al. will observe as sutras are recited and one [name] is selected from the urn" (MWLF, 154:0981–0982). See also MWLF, 155:2862, QL 57/08/29. This document reads: "The Dalai Lama together with the *ambans* residing in Tibet shall supervise the identification of the *trülku* by drawing lots."

35. YHGSL, 14:382, QL 57/10/23 (December 6, 1792). This document was also reproduced in the *Weizang tongzhi* (Lhasa: Xizang yanjiu bianji bu, [reprint] 1982), 263–264.

36. YHGSL, 14:384a, QL 57/10/23.

37. YHGSL, 15:30b–31a.

38. YHGSL 14:383b, emperor's rescript QL 57/11/29 (January 11, 1793).

39. This court letter is quoted in Fuk'anggan's memorial dated QL 57/12/29 (February 9, 1793), YHGSL, 15:7b–8a. Having been unable to locate the original court letter, I am assuming from contextualizing evidence that the letter quoted is the "separate edict" noted in Qianlong's rescript to Fukanggan's memorial of QL 57/10/23.

40. YHGSL, 15:8a, QL 57/12/29 (February 9, 1793).
41. YHGSL, 15:8a.
42. The phrasing here reveals a certain degree of confusion. More accurately, a protector (chökyong) should descend to the human medium. The Qing officials are using the term chökyong to refer inaccurately to the human medium, whereas in Tibetan the term refers to the protector deity.
43. YHGSL, 15:8b.
44. YHGSL, 15:8a–b.
45. Fuk'anggan's report was written in Chinese and spoke of "sorcerers" (wushi 巫師). Subsequent Manchu-language memorials and bilingual imperial proclamations in Manchu and Tibetan employed the term saman (related to the English shaman) or kutenpa (Ma. gurdemba, Tib. sku rten pa) in Manchu and Tibetan, respectively, to refer to the human medium who served as the vessel or intermediary for the deity to speak through.
46. Homi Bhabha, "Of Mimicry and Man: The Ambivalence of Colonial Discourse" October 28 (Spring 1984): 125–133.
47. Bhabha, "Of Mimicry and Man," 126.
48. MWLF, 156:0049.
49. Bhabha, "Of Mimicry and Man," 132–133.
50. Nicola Di Cosmo, "Manchu Shamanic Ceremonies at the Qing Court," in State and Court Ritual in China, ed. Joseph McDermott (Cambridge: Cambridge University Press: 1999), 352–398. See also Evelyn Sakakida Rawski, The Last Emperors: A Social History of Qing Imperial Institutions (Berkeley: University of California Press, 1998), 240.
51. Rawski, The Last Emperors, 240.
52. Rawski, The Last Emperors, 240.
53. Donald Sutton, "From Credulity to Scorn: Confucians Confront the Spirit Mediums in Late Imperial China," Late Imperial China 21, no. 2 (December 2000): 1–39. In Tibet there also existed diverse traditions of spirit mediums and shamans, many of whom were also women (Hildegard Diemberger"Female Oracles in Modern Tibet," in Women in Tibet, ed. Janet Gyatso and Hanna Havnevik, 113–168 [London: Hurst & Company 2005], 113–168). But Qing officials seem to have ignored these people in their attack on the state oracles.
54. A similar process also occurred in Mongolia. The prosecution of shamans there, however, began before Qing incorporation and often with Gelukpa assistance. See Johan Elverskog, Our Great Qing (Honolulu: University of Hawai'i Press, 2006), 118–119.
55. YHGSL, 15:8a.
56. Donald S. Lopez Jr., Prisoners of Shangri-La: Tibetan Buddhism and the West (Chicago: University of Chicago Press, 1998), 37.
57. Zeff Bjerken, "Exorcising the Illusion of Bon 'Shamans': A Critical Genealogy of Shamanism in Tibetan Religions," Revue d'Etudes Tibétaines 6 (October 2004): 4–69.
58. Bjerken, "Exorcising the Illusion of Bon 'Shamans,'" 7.
59. Bjerken, "Exorcising the Illusion of Bon 'Shamans,'" 12–13.
60. "Higher tradition," shangcheng 上乘. While shangcheng and xiacheng could also be translated as Mahāyāna ("Great Vehicle") and Hīnayāna ("Lesser Vehicle") doctrines, respectively, in these documents Qing authorities are primarily making a

disparaging distinction between the beliefs and practices sanctioned by the state and state-supported Geluk scholars and unsanctioned popular beliefs. They are not weighing in on doctrinal debates among Buddhists.

61. YHGSL, 15:8b–9a. This memorial refers to Tibetans alternately as "Fanmin" and "Tanggute."

62. YHGSL, 15:0a–9b.

63. YHGSL, 15:11a–b, memorial, QL 58/01/08. This was not true, at least not in the case of the oracle of the Lamo *chökyong*. This job was held by inheritance within a single family.

64. YHGSL, 15:11a–b.

65. YHGSL, 15:11b.

66. YHGSL, 15:11b–12a. One wonders if there is not a second subtext here: that local Tibetans in Chamdo not only might not accept Qing interference in this matter but also were resistant to oversight by Tibetan authorities in Lhasa.

67. YHGSL, 15:12a.

68. YYZDZZ, 794.

69. YHGSL, 15:9b, 15:30b–31b.

70. YHGSL, 15:31a.

71. There is no reference in the Demo *kūtuktu*'s biography of the Eighth Dalai Lama (DLNT08) to this event.

72. See, for instance, the identification of the Pakpalha *kūtuktu* in 1796: MWLF 162:2467–2474, JQ 01/08/10 (September 10, 1796).

73. YHGSL, 15:31a–b.

74. YHGSL, 15:30a.

75. YHGSL, 15:33–36.

76. See the discussion of different editions of the *Twenty-Nine Articles* in Liao Zugui, Li Yongchang, and Li Pengnian, *Qinding zangnei shanhou zhangcheng ershijiutiao banben kaolüe* (Beijing: Zhongguo zangxue chubanshe, 2006).

77. Emphasis added. YYZDZZ, 821–822, QL 58/02/24 (April 4, 1793).

78. The Tibetan-language *wang shu'i deb*, reproduced in Liao Zugui, Li Yongchang, and Li Pengnian, *Qinding zangnei shanhou zhangcheng ershijiutiao banben kaolüe*, 15. Of the two versions of the *Twenty-Nine Articles* that exist, the version stored at the Jokhang Temple allows the oracles, but still accuses them of corruption. A later version that had been held in the archives of the Ganden Podrang government makes no mention of the possible corruption. See reproduction of this document in Liao Zugui, Li Yongchang, and Li Pengnian, *Qinding zangnei shanhou zhangcheng ershijiutiao banben kaolüe*, 16.

79. YZDZZ, 821.

80. DLNT08, 210–kha–05.

81. YHGSL, 15:9a.

82. YHGSL, 15:84a.

83. YHGSL, 15:70a. Qianlong's letter to Fukanggan, dated QL 58/02/04, is quoted in Fukanggan's memorial dated QL 58/03/13 (April 23, 1793).

84. YHGSL, 15:70b.

85. MWJXD, 23:194–199.

86. YHGSL, 15:86a, QL 58/03/15 (April 25, 1793). As noted above, the mediums of the Lamo protector were not incarnate lamas but members of a single household.

87. MWJXD, 23:194–199.

88. YHGSL, 15:83b.

89. YHGSL, 15:83b–84a.

90. YHGSL, 15:84a.

91. YHGSL, 15:84a–84b.

92. YHGSL, 15:84b.

93. YGHSL, 15:84b.

94. YHGSL, 15:84b.

95. YHGSL, 15:84b.

96. Cited in Elliot Sperling, "Awe and Submission: A Tibetan Aristocrat at the Court of Qianlong," *The International History Review* 20, no. 2 (June 1998): 329.

97. For a summary of the discourses surrounding the corruption crisis of the Qianlong court, see: David Nivison, "Ho-shen and His Accusers: Ideology and Political Behavior in the 18th Century," in *Confucianism in Action,* ed. David S. Nivison and Arthur F. Wright (Stanford: Stanford University Press, 1959), 209–243; and Wook Yoon, "Prosperity with the Help of 'Villains,' 1776–1799: A Review of the Heshen Clique and Its Era," *T'oung Pao* 98 (2012): 479–527.

98. MWJXD, 23:198, QL 58/02/05 (March 16, 1793).

99. MWJXD, 23:196–197. This court letter is a draft. Underlining indicates Qianlong's additions. The passage in parentheses indicates a phrase that was crossed out.

100. YHGSL, 15:89a. *"Aiman"* in this context most likely refers to Khalkha Mongol leagues.

101. YHGSL, 15:86a–90a, Heliyen memorial, QL 58/03/15). The "Transcript of the Dalai Lama's Answers" (*dalai lama huifu dan* 達賴喇嘛回覆單) can be found in both YHGSL, 15: 270a–271a, and MWLF, 156:1384–1386.

102. MWLF, 156:1385–1386. On the occasion of the confirmation of the selection by the Dalai Lama, the treasurer presented one thousand *liang* of silver, for which he accepted, on behalf of the estate of the Erdeni Pandita *kūtuktu*, eighteen *juan* of writings by Tsongkhapa, two bolts of fine cloth, a bowl made of precious wood, twenty lacquered vases, ten bolts of monk robe cloth, one hundred *liang* of saffron, eighty-four lots of Tibetan incense, three tubes of candles, ten sheets of woolen fabric (*pu pian* 氆片), fifteen cases of women's head ornaments (花細), ten further cases of a different type of headdress (*bulukeba huaxi* 布魯克巴花細), thirty-six bolts of woolen fabric (*pulu* 氆氌), a sack of sugar, and another package of Tibetan spices. The treasurer was separately given a number of items as well.

103. YHGSL, 15:272a. "Assistant" : Ma. *nirba*, Ch. *ye'erba* 業爾巴, Tib. *gnyer pa*. This "confession" (*gongdan* 供單) appears in both YHGSL, 15:272a–273b, and MWLF, 156:1380–1383.

104. YHGSL, 15:272a.

105. YHGSL, 15:272b–273a.

106. YHGSL, 15:87a. Although the medium never admitted guilt in writing, Heliyen submitted the transcript of his interrogation to the throne under the title "Confession of the Lamo Chökyong and his Assistant Döndrup Dorjé" (Ch. *gongdan*). In contrast, the deposition of the Dalai Lama was labeled "Answers" (Ch. *huifudan*).

107. MWJXD, 23:196–197. Qianlong proposed that the Dalai Lama had identified the Tüsiyetü Khan's son in order to elicit greater donations from the Khalkha.

108. If average postal time between Lhasa and Beijing is considered, receiving a response from Lhasa to a letter posted from Beijing in forty days would be extremely fast. The average turnaround time for a piece of correspondence to travel from Beijing to Lhasa and back seems to have been sixty-three to seventy-five days (or nine to ten weeks), even at a postal rate of 600 *li* per day.

109. MWJXD, 23:236–239, court letter to Heliyen, QL 58/03/17 (April 27, 1793).

110. MWJXD, 23:260–262.

111. MWJXD, 23:260–261; see also YHGSL, 15:124.

112. Manchu-language issued to Qing colonial officers dealing with Mongol affairs, YHGSL, 15:291–293 (QL 58/05/25). Information concerning the selection of the Erdeni Pandita *kūtuktu* first appeared in Chinese a day later, and only in the form of a private court letter from the emperor to Sun Shiyi, the governor-general of Sichuan. A similar edict was drafted on QL 58/05/08 (June 15, 1793) but not distributed. See YHGSL, 15: 278–280.

113. MWLF, 156:1404.

114. See Sungyun's memorial of QL 58/03/14 (YHGSL 15:71–74). These signs were also noted in the bilingual Manchu–Mongol edict of QL 58/03/15 (YHGSL 15:121) and the Manchu-language court letter to Heliyen, MWJXD 23:236–237, QL 58/03/17.

115. Jin Hai et al., *Qingdai menggu zhi* 清代蒙古志 (Huhehaote: Neimenggu renmin chubanshe, 2009), 221–225, 394.

116. Just two years later, in a similar case involving the search for the reincarnation of a *kūtuktu* who was historically the ruler of a nomadic banner in Qinghai, the Cagan Nomunhan *kūtuktu*, Qianlong conceded the right of the lama to reincarnate among local nobles, including his own relatives, provided that the final confirmation occurred using the Golden Urn in Lhasa. The title *nomunhan* carried with it recognition of the monk's temporal authority. See Max Oidtmann, "Overlapping Empires: Religion, Politics, and Ethnicity in 19th Century Qinghai," *Late Imperial China* 37, no. 2 (December 2016): 74.

117. YHGSL, 15:126, QL 58/03/15.

118. YHGSL, 15:126.

119. YHGSL 15:116–117. Since the results of Heliyen's investigation had yet to arrive in Beijing, the emperor cited Sungyun's memorials from Mongolia.

120. YHGSL, 15:118.

121. YHGSL, 15:120.

122. YHGSL, 15:124.

123. YHGSL, 15:112.

124. MWJXD, 23:238–239, QL 58/03/17 (April 27, 1793).

125. MWJXD, 23:238.

126. YHGSL, 15:158–157, QL 58/03/24 (May 4, 1793). The other significant public pronouncement issued in advance of the ritual was similarly vague on who would actually draw the lot: "Having reported the names to the Court of Colonial Affairs and written the names on lots and placed them in the urn, the seal-holding *jasak lama kūtuktus* will read sutras before the Buddha, after which the officials of the Court of Colonial Affairs will jointly oversee the confirmation by drawing a lot." YHGSL 15:124, QL 58/03/15. The "Eighth Prince" most likely refers to Yongxuan 永璇,

1746–1832 (Prince Yishen of the First Rank 億慎親王). Liobooju (Liu-bao-zhu 留保住), an eight-banner Mongol, was president of the Court of Colonial Affairs. Delek (De-le-ke 德勒克, d. 1794?) was an official in the Court of Colonial Affairs who had previously been in charge of the court's Tanggūt (i.e., Tibetan) language translation school for Manch and Mongol bannermen (thanks to Matthew Mosca for this reference).

127. MWJXD, 23:260–261, QL 58/04/01: "Having searched out and obtained the names of five boys, the Eighth Prince, Liobooju, and Delek were delegated to write their names on lots and place them in the vase that had been donated to Yonghegong. After reading prayers for three days, on the first day of the fourth month they watched together as a lot was drawn and the name of Ciwangjab, the son of the Khalkha layman, was selected."

128. YHGSL, 15:292, edict QL 58/05/25: "Having received [Kūišu's memorial reporting the names of the five candidates], I immediately commissioned the Eighth Prince to supervise together with Liobooju and Delek the reading of sutras by lamas, after which, from among the lots that had been placed in the Golden Urn, the lot of the fifth candidate, named Ciwangjab, was drawn without prejudice and confirmed [as the reincarnation]."

129. MWJXD, 23:260–261.

130. MWJXD, 23:261.

131. YHGSL, 15:277b–27a, 292–293.

132. YHGSL, 15:291–292, QL 58/05/25 (July 2, 1793).

133. Amitāyus: Ma. *ayusi fucihi*, Tib. *a yu She* or *tshe dpag med.*

134. Ferdinand Lessing, *Yung-ho-kung: An Iconography of the Lamaist Cathedral in Peking with Notes on Lamaist Mythology and Cult* (Stockholm: Elanders Boktryckeri Aktiebolag, 1942), 64–65.

135. The documentary record suggests that for the remainder of the dynasty, this was a role that the cathedral shared with the Chapel of Victory Over the Three Realms (Tib. *gzim chung sa gsum rnam rgyal*), a chamber in the older Red Palace section of the Potala. On the occasion of the enthronement of the Eighth Dalai Lama in 1762, Qianlong bestowed an image of himself that subsequently hung in this chamber. The room also housed a complete set of the Kangyur translated into Manchu. See Gyurme Dorje, *Footprint Tibet Handbook,* 4th ed. (Bath, UK: Footprint, 2009), 113–114.

136. Tib. *chu glung wang zhu tshur phul gyi deb gzhung.* This register contains fifty-eight documents and was reproduced in Chab spel tshe brtan phun tshogs et al., eds., *Bod kyi gal che'i lo rgyus yig cha bdams bsgrig* (Lhasa: Bod ljongs bod yig dpe rnying dpe skrun khang, 1991), 113–280.

137. This edict appears in *Bod kyi gal che'i lo rgyus yig cha bdams bsgrig*, 214–220, and Chab spel tshe brtan phun tshogs, *Bod kyi lo rgyus rags rim g.yu yi phreng ba* [BLRYP] (Lhasa: Bod ljongs bod yig dpe rnying dpe skrun khang, 1989), 335–340. Subsequent citations of this edict are from the latter source. Grand Council file copy of the original Manchu-language edict, MWLF, 156:0044–0052, QL 58/04/19 (May 28, 1793). For the Grand Council file copy of Heliyen's base memorial, see MWLF, 156:1395, QL 58/03/15 (April 25, 1793).

138. BLRYP, 334.

139. In chronological order, the main edicts announcing the Golden Urn are: 1) Manchu/ Mongol language edict, QL 57/08/29 (October 14, 1792), MWLF, 155:2855–2861 (also YHGSL, 14: 352); 2) the *Discourse on Lamas*, QL 57/10 (before November 10, 1792); and 3) the Manchu/Mongol edict of QL 58/03/15 (1793–04–25), YHGSL, 15:94–126.

140. For the Manchu–Mongol bilingual version of this edict: YHGSL, 15:212–230. The Xining *amban* Tekšin reported the translation and distribution of the *Discourse on Lamas* edict among the Mongol banners of Kökenuur and the Geluk monasteries of Amdo on April 25, 1793 (YHGSL 15:82–80, QL 58/03/15).

141. QSL QL 58/04/19 (May 28, 1793). Although the *Discourse on Lamas* stele dates the original proclamation to mid-November, 1792, the fact that the *Discourse* only appears in the *Veritable Records* in May 1793 suggests that it may not actually have been composed in November 1792.

142. *Weizang tongzhi*, 267–269.

143. BLRYP, 341–343.

144. Earliest report from Fuk'anggan of discussing the Golden Urn with the Dalai Lama: MWLF, 154:1350, QL 57/08/10 (September 25, 1792). Qianlong ordered Heliyen to update the Dalai Lama in several court letters: MWJXD 23:236–239, QL 58/03/17 (April 27, 1793) and MWJXD, 23:260–262, QL 58/04/01 (May 10, 1793).

145. The emperor had already issued injunctions to prevent Mongols from soliciting divinations from the Lamo *chökyong* and other state oracles in central Tibet. See bilingual Manchu–Mongol edict of QL 57/03/15 (YHGSL 15:94–126) and court letter to Lhasa *ambans* of QL 58/03/17 (MWJXD 23:236–239). However, these commands did not yet include a blanket prohibition of soliciting the help of oracles for searches for *trülku* within Tibet.

146. BLRYP, 335.

147. BLRYP, 335.

148. BLRYP, 335–336.

149. Although these confessions were submitted in Chinese, there are numerous Manchu words transliterated into Chinese, such as the term for "gift" (Ma. *belek*)—suggesting that there might have been Manchu-language originals, or the interrogations might have been conducted in Manchu and Tibetan.

150. BLRYP, 338.

151. Tib. *rgyal khab*, Ma. *daicing gurun*, Ch. *benchao* 本朝.

152. BLRYP, 336: The Manchu original contains a longer and stronger statement. MWLF 156:0046: "I have studied the Buddhist sutras in the Mongol and Tibetan script since the eighth year of my reign, which now amounts to over fifty years. In my spare time from handling affairs, I have acquired a general understanding of the Buddha's way through intense focus, explanation, and discussion. Our Great Qing state's continuous protection of the Yellow Doctrines stems from our observation that the Mongols in particular are by nature sincere believers in the Buddha, and thus we appropriately honor their teachings." The emperor may also have felt entitled to such claims because only three years earlier, in 1790, he had witnessed the printing of the complete Manchu translation of the Tibetan Buddhist canon, a major achievement of his reign that had taken some twenty years to bring to fruition. Qianlong had personally edited some of the translations.

153. BLRYP, 336–337.

154. Tib. *rgyal khag*, Ma. *gurun boo*, Ch. *guojia* 國家.

155. BLRYP, 337. The Manchu version of this edict speaks only of subjecting "Mongol *jasaks*" to the Court of Colonial Affairs. In Tibetan, the Court of Colonial Affairs is referred to here as the *mong gol sbyor khang* ("the court of Mongol affairs"). MWLF 156:0048.

156. BLRYP, 337. The Tibetan reads: "Similarly, the self-serving practice of [finding] rebirths among the descendants or brothers of royals is henceforth prohibited. With regard to this law, the Mongol *khans*, *beile*, *beise*, and *gong* already possess their own inheritable positions. Therefore it is not appropriate that they carry off the wealth of the reincarnated lamas as well."

157. As I will discuss in act 3, the lack of clarity about who was an aristocrat and whether this statute applied to central Tibet and Amdo turned out to be a source of confusion and contention.

158. BLRYP, 338–339.

159. MWLF, 156:0046. This phrase is used in several edicts to convey the sense that the Qing suppression of the oracles was achieved not through brute force, but through law.

160. MWLF, 156:0050. Qianlong used these verbs frequently to describe the overall effect he wished to have on Tibetan Buddhism.

161. BLRYP, 339.

162. Moreover, a question can be raised about whether the Qing officials were talking about Manchu shamans or Chinese sorcerers. In Manchu, Heliyen and Qianlong spoke of "shamans of the interior" (Ma. *dorgi ba i saman*, MWLF 156:0049). Their descriptions of their abilities would seem to place them firmly within the shamanic traditions with which bannermen like Heliyen would be most familiar: the traditions the Manchus inherited and adapted from Inner Asia. Still, the ambiguous meaning of "the interior" could indicate that they were speaking of the traditions of China proper as well. The final translation into Tibetan identifies the "people who are possessed by gods and ghosts" as clearly being of China (Tib. *rgya yul*; BLRYP, 338). From the perspective of the Tibetan translation, then, regardless of whether Tibetans appreciated a separate Manchu divination tradition in other contexts, here the Manchu tradition was indistinguishable from the "traditions of China," much in the same way that Tibetan texts seldom distinguished "China" from the Great Qing. The Chinese version of this text translated this expression as "*neidi shiwu* 內地師巫" (*Weizang tongzhi* 269).

163. MWLF, 156:1382–138.

164. MSCB, 432.

165. YHGSL, 15:84b.

166. MWLF, 156:1386.

167. In his report on the oracles of QL 57/12/29 (February 9, 1793), Fuk'anggan quoted Qianlong as referring to the oracles as the "lowest tradition of Buddhism."

168. BLRYP, 341.

169. BLRYP, 341.

170. DLNT08, 269a:2–269b:3.

171. BLRYP, 342. A similar statement from the Dalai Lama was reported in Heliyen's memorial of QL 58/03/15: "However, the customs of the Tanggūt are passed on from

generation to generation, and it is impossible to inform every household. Now having witnessed several trials, it is apparent that the [oracles] possess not even the slightest magical ability. The sanction of the Golden Urn by the emperor to be placed before the image of Tsongkhapa and used for drawing lots is both just and righteous. There are neither clergy nor laypeople who are not persuaded."

172. BLRYP, 342.

173. BLRYP, 343.

174. BLRYP, 342.

175. YHGSL, 15:138–139. Bilingual Manchu–Chinese Grand Secretariat copy of a memorial from Fuk'anggan and Heliyen dated QL 58/03/22 (May 2, 1793). The memorial was rescripted four days earlier, on QL 58/03/18.

176. YHGSL, 15:87b, QL 58/03/15.

177. YHGSL, 15:282a, QL 58/05/09 (June 16, 1793).

178. Heliyen quotes the Dalai Lama as referring to "my Tibet" (Ma. *meni Dzang*).

179. YHGSL, 15:282a–b.

180. YHGSL, 15:281a. With regard to the question of who would draw the lot, the statute drafted by Heliyen remained ambigious, stating that the lots would be drawn as the Dalai Lama et al. together with the *ambans* supervised.

181. YHGSL, 15:282b.

182. MWJXD, 23:291, QL 58/06/08 (July 15, 1793).

183. MWJXD, 23:292.

184. MWJXD, 23:316, Manchu-language court letter to Heliyen, QL 58/08/14.

185. *Weizang tongzhi*, 269.

186. For the emperor's court letter to Heliyen, see MWJXD, 24:48–51, QL 59/03/04 (April 3, 1793). For Fukanggan's original report on this matter, see YHGSL, 15:10.

187. MWLF, 158:3415–3416, Heliyen memorial, QL 59/08/18 (September 11, 1794).

188. YHGSL, 15:10.

189. MWLF, 159:1292–1295, Heliyen and Hening memorial, QL 59/11/10 (December 3, 1794).

190. *Weizang tongzhi*, 269–270.

191. MWJXD, 24:59–62, QL 59/03/10.

192. Samten Chhosphel, "The Seventh Pakpa Lha, Jigme Tenpai Gonpo," *Treasury of Lives*, accessed March 14, 2013, http://www.treasuryoflives.org/biographies/view/Jigme -Tenpai-Gonpo/3783.

193. The Qing court may, however, been confirming a title that the Dalai Lama had already granted to the Pakpalha. Previous generations of the Pakpalha had also held this title. Chhosphel, "The Seventh Pakpa Lha, Jigme Tenpai Gonpo."

194. For the argument that Sungyun was ejected from Beijing on account of his hostility to Hešen and so that the chief grand councilor could make space for the return of his younger brother from Tibet, see Zhang Yuxin, "Weizang Tongzhi de zhuozhe shi Hening," *Xizang yanjiu* 4 (1985): 102.

195. Sungyun was appointed Lhasa *amban* on QL 59/07/19 (August 14, 1794). Pakpalha had passed away on QL 59/07/11.

196. MWLF, 159:0525–0526, QL 59/10/04 (October, 27, 1794).

197. MWLF, 159:0528.

198. MWLF, 159:0527.

199. MWLF, 159:0529.

200. MWLF, 159:1209, QL 59/11/13 (December 5, 1794).

201. MWLF, 159:1209.

202. MWLF, 159:1210.

203. WLF, 159:1211. Sungyun wrote, "Your servant observes that things having been dealt with this way, not only is the Zhiwala *kūtuktu* persuaded, but, when the disciples, who had previously by themselves conducted the search for rebirths of the Pakpalha *kūtuktu*, were told that this time the determination would be made according to the emperor's edict and that this was entirely appropriate, thanked [the emperor] joyously with utter sincerity and true earnestness."

204. MWLF, 160:2028, QL 60/06/29 (August 13, 1795).

205. MWLF, 160:2027. In Manchu, this law was referred to as the "*aisin bumba tampin de sibiya tatami toktobure kooli.*"

206. See court letter to Heliyen, MWJXD, 23: 290–296, QL 58/06/08 (July 15, 1793).

207. MWLF, 160:2028–2029. In this memorial, *šaburung* is the Manchu transliteration of the Tibetan term *zhabs drung*, meaning "honored one." Sungyun appears to be using this term to refer to those *trülku* who had not been honored with the title *kūtuktu* by the Qing court. The "board" here refers to the Court of Colonial Affairs.

208. MWLF, 160:2029.

209. MWLF, 160:2030–2031.

210. MWLF, 162:2471–2472, memorial from Sungyun and Hening, JQ 01/08/10 (September 10, 1796).

211. MWLF, 162:2473–2474.

212. DLNT08, 250:kha–251:ka. These prayers were: 1) *dga ldan lha brgya ma*: "Hundred deities of Tushita," a guru yoga of Tsongkhapa; Ch. *doushuai shangshi yujiamu* 兜率上師瑜伽母, and 2) *dmigs brtse ma*: Miktsema prayer aiming at loving kindness, a prayer to Tsongkhapa; Ch. *yuanbeisong* 緣悲頌.

213. "Faith derived from conviction": Tib. *yid ches pa'i dad pa*. DLNT08, 251:ka–kha.

214. DLNT08, 250:kha.

215. Blo bzang chos kyi nyi ma [Tukwan *kūtuktu* 03], *Lcang skya rol pa'i rdo rje'i rnam thar* (Lanzhou: Kan su'u mi rigs dpe skrun khang, 1989 [1798]), 62.

216. Both possible translations of Tib. *yid ches pa'i dad pa*.

217. Elizabeth Kolsky, *Colonial Justice in British India: White Violence and the Rule of Law* (New York: Cambridge University Press, 2010), 13, 15.

218. MWLF, 160:2033, QL 60/06/29 (August 13, 1795).

Act III: Amdowas Speaking in Code

1. MWLF, 164:0390, Sungyun memorial of JQ 02/08/03 (September 22, 1797). The office of the Xunhua subprefect (Ch. Xunhua ting tongzhi 循化廳同知) had been established just forty years earlier, in 1762, to expand the civil administration of Gansu province to the Tibetan communities along the border. Its jurisdiction covered the area of modern Xunhua and Tongren counties in Qinghai Province and Xiahe County in Gansu Province.

2. MWLF, 164:0393.

3. The Tibetan translation of Sungyun's Manchu-language memorial puts Belmang Pandita's speech as follows: "The entourage of the Jamyang Zhepa with great respect knelt and said, 'We request to prostrate with folded hands before the treasured image of the Great Emperor. The Cakravartin Great Sovereign Emperor is truly the same as the Manjusri Bodhisattva [*gnam gyi lha Gong ma bdag po chen po nyid rje btsun 'jam pa'i dbyangs*]. It is difficult to imagine, but this judgment on the identification of the *trülku* by means of shuffling the wooden lots after having completed the rituals has occurred according to the decision by means of prophecy having gone directly to the lord Tsongkhapa'" (JYZP03, 54–55).

4. Paul Nietupski, *Labrang Monastery: A Tibetan Buddhist Community on the Inner Asian Borderlands, 1709–1958* (Lanham, MD: Lexington Books, 2011), 135. Several other studies echo this assessment. See Sonam Dorje, "Drakpa Gyeltsen," *Treasury of Lives*, accessed April 7, 2013, http://www.treasuryoflives.org/biographies/view/Drakpa -Geltsen/4720; and "The Third Jamyang Zhepa, Tubten Jigme Gyatso," *Treasury of Lives*, accessed July 21, 2017, http://www.treasuryoflives.org/biographies/view/Third -Jamyang-Zhepa-Tubten-Jigme-Gyatso/2506.

5. Nietupski, *Labrang Monastery*, 137.

6. This second note (MWLF, 164:0387) was most likely dispatched to Beijing as an attachment to the longer memorial from Sungyun (MWLF, 164:0390). Both documents are dated JQ 02/08/03 (September 22, 1797).

7. MWLF, 163:1352–1355, JQ 02/01/08 (February 4, 1797).

8. MWLF, 163:0645–0646, JQ 01/11/21 (December 19, 1796).

9. (Ma.) *tanggūda*. See note 35.

10. MWLF, 164:0388.

11. JYZP02: Gung thang bstan pa'i sgron me, *Kun mkhyen 'jam dbyangs bzhad pa sku 'phreng gnyis pa rje 'jigs med dbang po'i rnam thar* (Lanzhou: Kan su'u mi rigs dpe skrun khang, 1991 [1798]).

12. JYZP03: Mkhan po ngag dbang thub bstan rgya mtsho, *Kun mkhyen 'jam dbyangs bzhed pa sku 'phreng gsum pa'i rnam thar* (Beijing: Krung go'i bod kyi shes rig dpe skrun khang, [1859–1889]).

13. BMNT: Brag dgon pa dkon mchog bstan pa rab rgyas, *Yongs rdzogs bstan pa'i mnga' bdag rje btsun bla ma rdo rje 'chang 'kon mchog rgyal mtshan dpal bzang po'o zhal snga nas kyi rnam par thar 'dod 'jug ngogs zhes bya ba bzhugs so* (Beijing: Mi rigs dpe sgrun khang, 2001).

14. For a representative sample of such narratives, see: *Bla brang dgon pa'i lo rgyus mdor bsdus* (Lanzhou: Srid gros kan lho bod rigs rang skyong khul bsang chu rdzong u yon lhan khang rig gnas lo rgyus dpyad gzhi'i yig rigs u yon lhan khang gis bsgrigs, 1999), biographies of Labrang monks compiled by the Xiahe County branch of the People's Political Consultative Congress; Zha Zha, *Fojiao wenhua shengdi: Labuleng si* (Lanzhou: Gansu minzu chubanshe, 2010); Zha Zha, *Labuleng si huofo shixi* (Lanzhou: Gansu renmin chubanshe, 2000); Zhou Ta/'Brug Thar, *Lun Labulengsi de chuangjian ji qi liu da xueyuan de xingcheng* (Lanzhou: Gansu minzu chubanshe, 1998); Zhou Ta, *Mdo smad byang shar gyi bod kyi 'tsho ba shog pa'i lo rgyus dang rig gnas bcas par dpyad pa* (Beijing: Minzu chubanshe, 2002); and Zhou Ta and Qiaogao Cairang, *Gansu Zangzu tongshi* (Beijing: Minzu chubanshe, 2009).

15. See Max Oidtmann, "Between Patron and Priest: Amdo Tibet Under Qing Rule, 1792–1911" (PhD diss., Harvard University, 2014), and "A 'Dog-eat-dog' World: Qing Jurispractices and the Legal Inscription of Piety in Amdo," *Extrême-Orient Extrême-Occident* 40 (November 2016): 151–182; and Nietupski, *Labrang Monastery*, 126–127.

16. See the section on "lamas" in the Jiaqing edition (1817) of the *Daqing Huidian Lifanyuan zeli*, reprinted in Zhao Yuntian, annotator, *Qianglong chao neifu chaoben Lifanyuan zeli* (Beijing: Zhongguo Zangxue chubanshe, 2006), 368.

17. Wang Xiangyun, "The Qing Court's Tibet Connections: Lcang skya Rol pai'i rdo rje and the Qianlong Emperor," *Harvard Journal of Asiatic Studies* 60, no. 1 (2000): 125–163, 127.

18. Chen Xiaomin, "Qingdai zhujing lama zhidu de xingcheng yu yange," *Manzu yanjiu* 4 (2007): 111–121, 115–116.

19. Qianlong reign draft statutes of the Court of Colonial Affairs section on "Tibetan monk preceptors in the capital" (*jingshi fanseng* 京師番僧), in Zhao Yuntian, *Qianlong chao neifu chaoben Lifanyuan zeli*, 125; and Chen Xiaomin, "Qingdai zhujing lama zhidu de xingcheng yu yange," 117.

20. Jiaqing edition, *Lifanyuan zeli* section on "lamas resident in the capital" (*zhujing lama* 駐京喇嘛), in Zhao Yuntian, *Qianlong chao neifu chaoben Lifanyuan zeli*, 368.

21. Chen Xiaomin, "Qingdai zhujing lama zhidu de xingcheng yu yange," 111–121.

22. See Marina Illich, "Imperial Stooge or Emmissary to the Dge lugs Throne? Rethinking the Biographies of the Chankya Rolpé Dorjé," in *Power, Politics, and the Reinvention of Tradition; Proceedings of the Tenth Seminar of the International Association for Tibetan Studies, Königswinter,* ed. Bryan J. Cuevas and Kurtis R. Schaeffer (Leiden: Brill, 2006), 17–32. Studies by Berger and Wang present a more nuanced interpretation of the activities of Rolpé Dorjé but still largely catalog his activities according to the for/against dichotomy. See Wang Xiangyun, "The Qing Court's Tibet Connections: Lcang skya Rol pa'i rdo rje and the Qianlong Emperor," *Harvard Journal of Asiatic Studies* 60, no. 1 (2000): 125–163; and Patricia Berger, *Empire of Emptiness* (Honolulu: University of Hawai'i Press, 2003).

23. Paul Kocot Nietupski, "The 'Reverend Chinese' (*Gyanakpa tsang*) at Labrang Monastery," in *Buddhism Between Tibet and China*, ed. Matthew T. Kapstein (Boston: Wisdom, 2009), 181–213; and Nietupski, *Labrang Monastery*, 123–125, 128–129.

24. Nietupski, *Labrang Monastery*, 128; "The 'Reverend Chinese' (*Gyanakpa tsang*) at Labrang Monastery," 189.

25. Nietupski, *Labrang Monastery*, 128–129; see also MSCB, 278–281.

26. This "Galdan Siretu *kūtuktu*" is not to be confused with the regent to the Eighth Dalai Lama, Galdan Siretu Samadi Bakshi Ngawang Tsultrim, or the Galdan Siretu who advised the emperor in acts 1 and 2. See the Qianlong-period statutes on "Tibetan monk preceptors in the capital (*jingshi fanseng*)" in Zhao Yuntian, *Qianglong chao neifu chaoben Lifanyuan zeli*, 125.

27. Johan Elverskog, "Wutai Shan, Qing Cosmopolitanism, and the Mongols," *Journal of the International Association of Tibetan Studies* 6 (December 2011): 255. Matthew Kapstein has also noted the contributions of scholars from Amdo to an "Inner Asian cosmopolitanism" that arose during the eighteenth century. See Matthew T. Kapstein, "Just Where on Jambudvīpa Are We?" in *Forms of Knowledge in Early Modern Asia,* ed. Sheldon Pollock (Durham: Duke University Press, 2011), 336–364.

28. Elverskog, "Wutai Shan, Qing Cosmopolitanism, and the Mongols," 255.

29. Roger Jackson, "Triumphalism and Ecumenism in Thu'u bkwan's *Crystal Mirror*," *Journal of the International Association of Tibetan Studies* 2 (August 2006): 15–16.

30. Tsebak 策拔克: Mongol, Bordered Yellow Banner, d. 1812. Tsebak must have hailed from a family with strong Buddhist beliefs because he was named after the bodhisattva of long life, Amitāyus, or Tsepakmé (*Tshe dpag med*) in Tibetan.

31. MWLF, 163:0638, Tsebak, memorial, JQ 01/11/21 (December 19, 1796). There is also a rare and uncataloged map of the five Mongol banners situated to the south of the Yellow River attached to this memorial (*junwang Nahanduo'erji deng wu qi youmu dixingtu* 郡王納漠達爾濟等五旗遊牧地輿圖), MWLF, 163:0649–0653. Scattered Tibetan (Ch. *fan*, Ma. *aiman i fandze*) raiding began to come to the attention of the court in 1782, but intensified during the 1790s. Tsebak was cashiered in 1797 for mishandling the raiding. See Wenfu, *Qinghai shiyi jielüe* (Xining: Qinghai renmin chubanshe, 1993 [1810]), 10, 15–25; and Max Oidtmann, "Overlapping Empires: Religion, Politics, and Ethnicity in 19th Century Qinghai," *Late Imperial China* 37, no. 2 (December 2016): 41–91.

32. Although Tibetan sources confirm that the treasurer of the Jamyang Zhepa estate at this time was a Mongol, Lozang Dargyé, they provide little information about him. It is possible that he was the "Mongol doctor" who was invited to Labrang by the Second Jamyang Zhepa to help establish the monastery's medical college in 1784 and subsequently rose through the monastic bureaucracy to the position of treasurer. See Belmang Pandita's gazetteer of Labrang monastery: (Dbal mang dkon mchog rgyal mtshan), *Bla brang bkra shis 'khil gyi gdan rabs lha'i rnga chen* (Lanzhou: Gansu minzu chubanshe, 1987 [1800]), 258. Labrang's treasurers were often Mongol monks since they served at the discretion of not only the monastic community but also the neighboring Mongol prince (*qinwang*, later *junwang*) who had donated the original land and people around the monastery to the Jamyang Zhepa's estate.

33. MWLF, 163:0643.

34. For example, in 1836, the coordinators of the search for the reincarnation of the Fifth Cagan Nomunhan wrote to the Qinghai *amban* to request the use of the urn (MWLF, 206:2122–2125, DG 16/12/14). In 1890, representatives of the estate of the Tatsak *kūtuktu* (Ma. Jirung *kūtuktu*) also requested the use of the urn ritual (National Palace Museum, Taipei, *Qingdai gongzhongdang zouzhe ji junjichudang zhejian*, doc. #171082, GX 16/07/20 [September 3, 1890]).

35. Specifically a (Ma.) *tanggūda* (Ch. *baihu*), an imperially sanctioned local administrative rank in non-Han areas of the empire recognizing the chief of a hundred households. In practice, the actual number of households supervised by a "hundred-household-chief" varied widely. Such positions were usually hereditary (although succession generally required the approval of the court) and not formally part of the imperial government's civil bureaucracy.

36. The seven overarching ranks of the Qing imperially sanctioned Mongol aristocracy.

37. MWLF, 163:0646.

38. Bilingual edict in Mongol and Tibetan, issued from the office of the Xining *amban*, QL 60/04/15 (June 1, 1795), held at Qinghai Provincial Museum, photograph in collection of author.

39. Quoted in Sungyun's memorial, MWLF, 163:1352–1353, JQ 02/01/08 (February 2, 1797). Original instructions to Sungyun probably date to JQ 01/12/05, the day that Tsebak's original report was received at court.

40. MWLF, 163:1353–1355, Sungyun and Hening memorial, JQ 02/01/08 (February 4, 1797).

41. Gungtang kūtuktu 03 mentions a chamberlain to the Jamyang Zhepa estate named Sherab Gyatso who accompanied Belmang Pandita 02 to Lhasa in 1797. However, it is unclear if this is the same chamberlain discussed by Sungyun. JYZP02, 483.

42. MSCB, 411–428; also Sonam Dorje, "Konchok Sengge," Treasury of Lives, accessed March 22, 2013, http://www.treasuryoflives.org/biographies/view/Konchok-Sengge /3769.

43. MWLF, 163:1355.

44. Court letter quoted in Manchu-language memorial from Tsebak, MWLF, 163:1701, JQ 02/02/28 (March 26, 1797).

45. MWLF, 163:1701.

46. MWLF, 163:1701–1702.

47. MWLF, 164:0394.

48. MWLF, 164:1708–1710, Sungyun memorial, JQ 02/11/20 (January 6, 1798–I). Sungyun quotes Belmang as stating that he had recited prayers to Amitāyus Buddha to promote the emperor's long life and that he would return to the Xining area the following year (1798) "after the snow melted."

49. MWLF, 164:1710.

50. MWLF, 164:1710.

51. JYZP02, 490.

52. Dbal mang dkon mchog rgyal mtshan (Belmang Pandita 02), Bla brang bkra shis 'khil gyi gdan rabs lha'i rnga chen (Lanzhou: Gansu minzu chubanshe, 1987), 460–482; also Samten Chhosphel, "The Third Gungtang, Konchok Tenpai Dronme," Treasury of Lives, accessed March 27, 2013, http://www.treasuryoflives.org/biographies/view/ Konchok-Tenpai-Dronme/4730.

53. While this text has become enormously influential in post-1978 studies of the history of northwest China and Tibet, there have been few studies on the circulation of this text and similar historical works in Tibet prior to 1911.

54. MSCB, 782–783.

55. BMNT, 155. Drakönpa's description of the Golden Urn as a "sign" or "omen" (Tib. mtshan ltas) echoes that of Sungyun, who explained the importance of understanding the lottery as an "omen" (Ma. temgetu) in his memorial to Qianlong, MWLF, 160:2030, QL 60/06/29 (August 13, 1795).

56. Nietupski, Labrang Monastery, 162–163, n. 132, states that the author of this biography began his work in 1859. The colophon is unclear on the date of printing, but suggests that it occurred in or before 1889, the year the author passed away. See JYZP03, 382–383.

57. JYZP03, 17–32.

58. This monk is identified in both the biography of the Third Jamyang Zhepa and the biography of Belmang Pandita as a kachu, a monk who possessed the academic credentials of a geshé, perhaps from Trashi Lhünpo monastery. JYZP03, 37; BMNT, 155.

59. JYZP03, 37.

60. Samten Chhosphel, "Longdol Lama Ngawang Lobzang," *Treasury of Lives*, accessed March 22, 2013, http://www.treasuryoflives.org/biographies/view/Longdol-Lama -Ngawang-Lobzang/3877.

61. Samten Chhosphel, "Longdol Lama Ngawang Lobzang."

62. JYZP03, 37.

63. The Longdöl Lama also elaborated a list of specific texts and prayers that the disciples of the Jamyang Zhepa should recite both at Labrang and in Lhasa. In summary, he presented a detailed set of instructions for a full ritual cycle that was attentive to issues such as location, participants, texts, and temporal sequence. The correct outcome of the ritual hinged on the precise execution of all of these elements. See JYZP03, 37.

64. JYZP03, 37. The second sentence of this quote also appears in the biography of the Belmang Pandita. See Drakgönpa, BMNT, 155.

65. See BMNT, 155. The Gungtang *kūtuktu* recorded the Longdöl Lama as stating: "It is necessary to make the decision by conducting a dough ball investigation [here referred to as a *takdril*] before the Jowo Rinpoché. If the [recognition] is conducted in the same manner as that which [found] the previous Great Fifth [Dalai Lama], then there will be no possibility of deception." See Gung thang bstan pa'i sgron me, 482.

66. JYZP03, 38. The Tongkhor *kūtuktu* was not the same person as the monk from Tong-khor monastery with the *kachu* geshé degree.

67. JYZP03, 37.

68. JYZP02, 483.

69. The Golden Urn was referred to here as a "*zangyur*" divination. Drakgönpa, BMNT, 155.

70. BMNT, 156.

71. The four *trülku* lineages based at Labrang monastery that had achieved prominence when one of their lamas had been appointed (in one case nominally) to the "golden throne" (Tib. *serkhri*) of the chief abbot of Ganden monastery, outside of Lhasa. Niet-upski, *Labrang Monastery*, 139.

72. JYZP03, 40.

73. JYZP03, 40.

74. JYZP03, 40.

75. JYZP03, 41.

76. JYZP03, 41: "The *amban* reported three names from among the four candidates to the golden ear [i.e., the emperor] for testing. However, among these [he] extolled the supreme incarnation [i.e., the child who was ultimately identified as the rebirth, can-didate two] as being the most promising."

77. MWLF, 163:0642–0644.

78. JYZP03, 41–42.

79. MSCB, 431–432.

80. MSCB, 431.

81. In the case of the biography of the Third Jamyang Zhepa, Tukwan's dream does not appear in the text until the very end of the account of the search process. See BMNT, 165.

82. JYZP02, 482–483.

83. JYZP02, 483.

84. JYZP02, 482.

85. BMNT, 155.

86. JYZP02, 482.

87. JYZP02, 482. Even the concerned petitioners quoted by Gungtang also refer to emperor's method simply as "*takdril*" (483).

88. JYZP02, 483.

89. JYZP02, 482.

90. Drakgönpa and Khenpo Ngawang Tupten Gyatso both report that after the treasurer Lozang Dargyé backed out of leading the expedition, new leadership was selected by using a dough ball divination. See JYZP03, 42; BMNT, 157. With regard to the sudden withdrawal of the treasurer, Khenpo Ngawang Tupten Gyatso reports that the treasurer excused himself on account of old age and poor health. Nothing is mentioned about possible pressure to recuse himself from the search. Drakgönpa does not discuss this detail.

91. JYZP03, 42–43.

92. BMNT, 158–159.

93. The "sandalwood Jowo" (Tib. *tshan dan jo bo*) is a reference to the massive sandalwood (Ch. *zhantan* 旃檀) statue of Sakyamuni housed in Yonghegong temple in Beijing. It is striking that Tukwan has evidently interpreted the substatute relegating the selection of Mongol *kūtuktu* to Yonghegong and Tibetan *kūtuktu* to Lhasa not as an ethnic or geographical distinction but rather a status distinction between "low" and "high" *trülku*.

94. Tib. *khya dge dpon slob*: a monastic official named Khyagé.

95. Lhamo Sungjönma (Tib. *lha mo gsung 'byon ma*) is a painting before which important divinations are frequently conducted. Apparently this image is still possessed by the government of the Fourteenth Dalai Lama in exile and still used in divinations.

96. JYZP03, 43–44.

97. BMNT, 159.

98. See comments in Derek F. Maher, "The Eighth Dalai Lama Jampel Gyatso" and "The Ninth to the Twelfth Dalai Lamas" in *The Dalai Lamas: A Visual History*, ed. Martin Brauen (Chicago: Serindia, 2005), 117–127 and 129–135, especially 127, 130; Kapstein, "Just Where on Jambudvīpa Are We?" 159–160; and Nietupski, *Labrang Monastery*, 135–136. Blanket assessments such as "Tibetans disliked the interference intensely" (Maher 127) ignore the geographic diversity of views among Tibetans.

99. BMNT, 160. "Two Tibetan lay officials" (Tib. *Böpa drungkhor nyi*). This expression is typical for nineteenth-century Tibetan-language texts from Amdo that usually distinguish *Böpa*—"Tibetans" or officials from the Ganden Podrang government—from Amdo people.

100. JQ 02/08/01, BMNT, 160; JYZP03, 44.

101. JYZP03, 46; BMNT, 162.

102. BMNT, 162.

103. BMNT, 162; JYZP03, 45. Both of these sources record that similar feelings arose between Belmang and the junior *amban*, Hening, when they met a day later.

104. BMNT, 162; JYZP03, 45.

105. BMNT, 162; JYZP03, 45.

106. BMNT, 163.

107. JYZP03, 47. A similar concern is also expressed in MSCB, 432.
108. BMNT, 161.
109. The candidate originally favored by the treasurer and the Xining *amban*, the son of Dülagyel.
110. BMNT, 163.
111. I.e., Labrang monastery.
112. BMNT, 163. Khenpo Ngawang Tupten Gyatso also records parts of this conversation, JYZP03, 47–48.
113. JYZP02, 482; BMNT, 155; JYZP03, 43. MSCB merely records the emperor as stating that the ritual would have to occur in Ü-Tsang (431).
114. MWLF, 163:0643–0644, JQ 01/11/21 (December 19, 1796).
115. MWLF, 163:1354, JQ 02/01/08 (February 4, 1797).
116. Tenma (Tib. *bstan ma*). This female protector is identified as Drakgyelma (Tib. *drag rgyal ma*) in JYZP03, 45–46.
117. MSCB, 432. With regard to the oracles, the biography of the Belmang Pandita briefly states, "Then [Belmang] sought oracles from the Dga' gdong, Gnas chung, and Drag rgyal ma, and carried out all the ceremonies [*zhabs brtan*] as they instructed" (162). The biography of the third Jamyang Zhepa adds that, "When they sought out the prophecies of the chökyong, they were told that nowadays it was good to make the identification according to the [advice] of the Gadong [oracle]. Secretly make a recognition and the best one will appear" (45).
118. JYZP03, 47.
119. JYZP02, 483.
120. The monastic college located within the Potala Palace complex.
121. MSCB, 432. The *Bstan 'bar ma*, *chos rgyal*, and *Bdag bzhan ma* prayers. The last of the three is actually the last four lines of the *Bstan 'bar ma*. Brenton Sullivan assisted with the identification of these prayers.
122. JYZP02, 483.
123. BMNT, 164; JYZP03, 49.
124. JYZP03, 49.
125. JYZP03, 50: *ma non par bzo lta dang smra brjod*: unforced actions and speech.
126. BMNT, 164–165. The same statement can also be found in JYZP03, 50–51.
127. BMNT, 165.
128. JYZP03, 51.
129. JYZP02, 484.
130. See definitions of the "four faiths" (Tib. *dad pa gzhi*) and "faith of conviction" (Tib. *yid ches kyi dad pa*) in *Bod rgya tshig mdzod chen mo* (Beijing: Minzu chubanshe, 1993), 1242–1243, 2573. Also, "*yid ches kyi dad pa*," The THL Tibetan Dictionaries, accessed April 6, 2013, http://www.thlib.org/reference/dictionaries/tibetan-dictionary/translate .php.
131. For information on the intertwined cataloging and censorship activities in China, see Kent Guy, *The Emperor's Four Treasuries* (Cambridge, MA: Council on East Asian Studies, Harvard University Press, 1987). For censorship in Mongolia, see Walther Heissig, *Beiträge zur Übersetzungsgeschichte des Mongolischen Buddhistischen Kanons* (Göttingen: Vandenhoeck 6 Ruprecht, 1962), 43–53.

132. JYZP03, 19; BMNT, 156.

133. MWLF, doc. # 3–207–4442–047, XF 09/10/28 (November 22, 1859).

134. JYZP03, 51, 53.

Conclusion: Paradoxes of the Urn and the Limits of Empire

1. Wei Yuan, *Shengwuji* (Beijing: Zhonghua shuju, 1984), 218.

2. YHGSL, 14:352, Manchu-language edict of QL 57/08/29 (October 14, 1792).

3. YHGSL, 15:291–293, Manchu-language edict of QL 58/05/25 (May 28, 1793).

4. MWJXD, 23:290–296, QL 58/06/08 (July 15, 1793).

5. Despite complaining about the "unfamiliar laws of the interior," in both cases the treasurers opted to hold the ritual in Beijing (YHGSL, 17:305–307).

6. The most emblematic examples of this might be nineteenth-century rebirths within the Cagan Nomunhan and Jamyang Zhepa lineages. Gray Tuttle also observes that in the late eighteenth century elite families in Amdo appear to have taken a greater interest in identifying their sons as *trülku*. Tuttle, "The Role of Mongol Elite and Educational Degrees in the Advent of Reincarnation Lineages in Seventeenth Century Amdo," in *The Tenth Karmapa and Tibet's Turbulent Seventeenth Century*, ed. Karl Debreczeny and Gray Tuttle (Chicago: Serindia, 2016), 235–262. It would seem that at least in Amdo, the Qing government did not intend to use the Golden Urn to prevent reincarnation among elite families.

7. Among the archives of the Kundeling monastery, for instance, is a letter that reports on the consulation of the Lamo *chökyong* oracle concerning the location of the rebirth of the Eighth Tatsak *kūtuktu*, the former regent to the Eighth and Ninth Dalai Lamas. Bonn Collection, Kündeling archive, doc. # 594 (1812). Both the Lamo and Nechung oracles were consulted in the search for the Ninth Dalai Lama in 1807–1808. See biography of the Ninth Dalai Lama, Ngawang Lungtok Gyatso: De mo ho thog thu Blo bzang thub bstan 'jigs med rgya mtsho, *Sku phreng dgu pa lung rtods rgya mtsho'i rnam thar* (Beijing: Krung go'i bod rig pa dbe skrun khang, 2011), 12, 23, 32.

8. Qianlong, *Discourse on Lamas*, lines 22–23.

9. "Water-Ox Year Edict," in BLRYP, 338–339.

10. See *Lifanyuan zeli* from 1817. Reprinted in Zhao Yuntian, annotator, *Qianlongchao neifu chaoben "Lifanyuan zeli"* (Beijing: Zhonggguo Zangxue chubanshe, 2006), 369. Similar language is echoed in subsequent editions. See also *Qinding Daqing huidian shili lifanyuan* (Beijing: Zhongguo Zangxue chubanshe, 2006 [1899]), 173.

11. H. S. Brunnert and V. V. Hagelstrom, *The Present Day Political Organization of China* (Shanghai: Kelly and Walsh, Limited, 1912), 474. Ning Chia, "The Lifanyuan in the Early Ch'ing Dynasty" (PhD diss., The Johns Hopkins University, 1992), 213.

12. "Bod dang bar khams rgya sog bcas kyi bla sprul rnams kyi skye phreng deb gzhung dge," in Chap spel tshe brtan phun tshogs, *Bod kyi gal che'i lo rgyus yig cha bdams bsgrigs* (Lhasa: Bod ljongs bod yig dpe rnying dpe skrun khang, 1991), 282–369.

13. This is a conservative estimate. The editors of the *Princeton Dictionary of Buddhism* suggest that there were as many as three thousand incarnation lines in Tibet prior to the

1950s (Robert E. Buswell and Donald S. Lopez, Jr. *The Princeton Dictionary of Buddhism* [Princeton: Princeton University Press, 2014], 847). John Powers and David Templeman, the editors of the *Historical Dictionary of Tibet* (Lanham, MD: Scarecrow Press, 2012) place this number in the "hundreds" (658–659). Gray Tuttle, citing Pu Wenchang, estimates over 1,200 *trülku* lineages in Amdo alone by the early twentieth century ("The Role of Mongol Elite and Educational Degrees in the Advent of Reincarnation Lineages," 244). A recent authoritative PRC count estimated over 1,700 officially certified incarnate lamas in 2014 (Xiong Wenbin and Zhang Chunyan, eds., *Huofo zhuanshi: 2014 nian zang chuan fojiao huofo zhuanshi zhuanti zhan* [Beijing: Zhongguo zangxue chubanshe, 2014], 5).

14. A particularly important case was that of the Labrang-based monk Künga Gyeltsen (1835–1895), who was awarded the title of *kūtuktu* in 1867 and allowed to reincarnate as a reward for services rendered against Muslim rebels in Xinjiang. *Qinding Daqing huidian shili lifanyuan*, 155.

15. I arrived at this number after examining the published catalogs of Chinese- and Manchu-language palace memorials (*gongzhong zouzhe*) and Grand Council file copies (*lufu zouzhe*) and then checking them against the original documents in the FHA to be sure that the original document indeed nominally claimed to use the urn. This overall number also includes usages indicated in the sources cited in note 29. See Zhongguo diyi lishi dang'anguan and Zhongguo Zangxue zhongxin, eds., *Zhongguo diyi lishi dang'anguan suocun Xizang he Zangshi dang'an mulu, Man Zangwen bufen* (Beijing: Zhongguo Zangxue chubanshe, 1999), and *Zhongguo diyi lishi dang'anguan suocun Xizang he Zangshi dang'an mulu, Hanwen bufen* (Beijing: Zhongguo Zangxue chubanshe, 2000). The catalog of the Manchu-language materials (1999) lists two other usages of the urn that I could not confirm against the original document. This survey does not cover archival materials held at the National Palace Museum in Taibei. Quexi and Cao Ziqiang arrive at a similar number, but give no explanation of the sources or methods used: Quexi and Cao Ziqiang, "Jinping cheqian: yizun chuishi zhi tixian," in *Huofo ji zhuanshi zhidu yanjiu,* ed. Chen Qingying et al. (Beijing: Zhongguo zangxue yanjiu zhongxin zongjiaosuo, neibu ziliao, 2006), 350. Zeng Guoqing gives an estimate of seventy identifications of incarnations from thirty-nine different lineages using the urn: "Lun Qingting zhi Zang yu jinping cheqian," *Zangxue* 10 (2010): 8.

16. YHGSL, 23: 394–408, 417–432. The Harvard-Yenching Library possesses two registers of official business from the office of the Lhasa *ambans* that record usages of the urn: *Dzang de tefi dalafi baita icihiyara ambasa araha benebume badarangga doro-i sucungga aniya de deribume tetele manju hergen-i bithe be alime gaire cese* [1875–1900] and *Zhuzang banshidachen zouzhedang manhan heji yuanchaoben* [1879].

17. Beginning in 1817 the Qing court began using a similar lottery system to allocate administrative jobs among the Geluk lamas and monks resident in the capital. Zhao Yuntian, annotator, *Qinding Daqing huidian shili lifanyuan* (Guangxu edition), "lama fenghao," 153.

18. MWLF, doc. # 03–0197–3625–037.

19. Although I suspect that as a *kūtuktu* this lineage had a statutary obligation to use the urn, I have found no prior record of usage. MWLF, doc. # 03–0210–4583–025.

20. See for instance Canggeng and Šengtai's account of the selection of the Eleventh Tatsak *kūtuktu* in 1890. The *ambans* report the selection in detail, including an unsual

reference to having ostentatiously prayed before selecting the lot. National Palace Museum Grand Council Archive, doc. # 171082, GX 16/09/05.

21. See petitions from the Tenth Tatsak Lama to the Qing court concerning the search in 1877 for the Thirteenth Dalai Lama in Zhongguo Zangxue yanjiu zhongxin et. al. eds, *Yuan yilai Xizang difang yu zhongyang zhengfu guanxi dang'an shiliao huibian* (Beijing: Zhongguo Zangxue chubanshe, 1995), vol. 5, 1847–1853; and also a memorial from Sunggui in vol. 5, 1853; as well as a copy of the Manchu-language original of the latter document in *Dzang de tefi dalafi baita icihiyara ambasa araha benebume badarangga doro-i sucungga aniya de deribume tetele manju hergen-i bithe be alime gaire cese*, Harvard-Yenching Library, TMA 4664.88 7453, 10a–b. Also the biography of the Ninth Dalai Lama, Lungtok Gyatso: De mo ho thog thu Blo bzang thub bstan 'jigs med rgya mtsho, 31–32, 35, 36–37. Tsepon Wangchuk Deden Shakabpa, *One Hundred Thousand Moons: An Advanced Political History of Tibet,* trans. and annotated by Derek F. Maher (Boston: Brill, 2010), 562, 588, 628. In the case of the Thirteenth Dalai Lama, there was also discussion among Tibetan and Qing officials about whether malevolent deities might attempt to manipulate the ritual, thus undermining the reliability of the outcome.

22. The album reproduced here is from the collection of the Harvard Art Museums, Arthur M. Sackler Museum (1985.863.5). The album is unbound and the arrangement here reflects my best guess of the original order. The album is similar to one held by the library of the Institut des Hautes Études Chinoises, Paris, and analyzed by Isabelle Charleaux, Marie-Dominique Even, and Gaëlle Lacaze. This second document, which, unlike the Harvard album, is accompanied by a Mongol-language text and labels, was probably produced for the personal enjoyment of a Mongol prince, Manjubazar, who accompanied the official Qing delegation to Lhasa that witnessed the enthronement of the Ninth Dalai Lama. See Charleaux, Even, and Lacaze, "Un Document Mongol Sur L'intronisation du IXe Dalai Lama," *Journal Asiatique* 292, no. 1–2 (2004): 151–222.

23. Manchu-language edict to the Grand Council (First Historical Archives, Beijing, *junjichu shangyu dang*), Doc # 3-1-78-4. When the Xining *amban* first forwarded the names of the candidates to the court and Lhasa in 1822, he neglected to mention that one of the children was a Chinese commoner. The local community in Amdo must therefore have been quite surprised by this abrupt reversal. Subsequent editions of the regulations of the Court of Colonial Affairs noted this clarification. In 1825, the Lhasa *amban* Sungting reported that together with the Galdan Siretu Samadi Baksi (the Tsemonling *kūtuktu*), he had identified an alternate child using the Golden Urn (MWLF, doc. # 3-2-4016-047, DG 05/02/16). For entry in Guangxu *Huidian*, see Zhao Yuntian, annot. *Qinding Daqing huidian shili lifanyuan*, 153.

24. FHA *junjichu shangyudang* 91-2, DG 22/11/29 (1842–12–30); MWLF, 4245-052, DG 23/03/11 (1843–04–16).

25. Künga Gyeltsen, a Geluk monk from Amdo, served as a Qing military commander in Xinjiang. See his biography, Skal bzang legs bshad, *Rje bstun byams pa mthu stobs kun dga' rgyal mtshan gyi rnam thar* (Beijing: Zhongguo Zangxue, [c. 1895–1900] 1994).

26. In 1890, for instance, the Qing government resisted a request from the treasurer of the Tatsak lineage's estate not to employ the urn in the recognition of the Eleventh Tatsak *trülku*. Schwieger, *The Dalai Lama and the Emperor of China: A Political History*

of the Tibetan Institution of Reincarnation (New York: Columbia University Press, 2015), 195–198; also National Palace Museum (Taiwan) Archives MWLF doc. # 171082, GX 16/07/20.

27. During the Kangxi reign (1662–1722), for instance, Tibet was understood as comprising Ü, Tsang, Ali, and Kham. See text of the *Pingding Xizang bei* (Stele on the pacification of Tibet) and *Xizang ji* (Record of Tibet) cited in Li Fengzhen, *Qingdai Xizang junwangzhi chutan du qingshi zhaji* (Beijing: Zhongguo Zangxue chubanshe, 2012), 229. See also the description of Tibet in Fu-heng, et al., eds., *Huang Qing Zhigongtu: si juan* (Beijing: 1757–1790), Bibliothèque nationale de France, accessed February 16, 2018, http://catalogue.bnf.fr/ark:/12148/cb444768402, vol. 2, 4a–5b; and Fu-Heng et al., eds., *Qinding xiyu tongwenzhi*, Changchun: Jilin chuban jituan, 2005 [1763]), 323.

28. Fu-heng et al., eds. *Qinding xiyu tongwenzhi*, 265.

29. For a detailed discussion of the evolution of Tibetan geographical conceptions, see Gray Tuttle, "Challenging Central Tibet's Dominance of History: The *Oceanic Book*, a 19th Century Politico-Religious Geographic History," in *Mapping the Modern in Tibet; Proceedings of the Eleventh Seminar of the International Association for Tibetan Studies, Königswinter,* ed. Gray Tuttle (Andiast, Switzerland: International Institute for Tibetan and Buddhist Studies GmbH, 2011), 135–172.

30. See the Fifth Dalai Lama's preface to Güüshi Khan's legal code of 1647, in Ngag dbang Blo bzang Rgya mtsho, *gsung 'bum* (The collected works of the Great Fifth Dalai Lama), vol. *ma* (16) (Gangtok: Sikkim Research Institute of Tibetology, 1991–1995), 97–105 (TBRC W294).

31. In the 1720s, Nian Gengyao was perhaps among the first Qing officials to describe Qinghai as one of the four constituent parts of Tibet (specifically, as one of the four "tribes" of the "Tanggūt"). Nineteenth-century Qing sources widely accepted the idea that Qinghai/Kökenuur was one of the four constituent parts of Tibet. These were Ü, Tsang (these first two were sometimes combined), Kham, and Amdo. See, for example, Yu Zhengxie, *Dachen yuanshi,* in *Yu Zhengxie quanji* (Hefei: Huangshan shushe, 2005 [1807]),380, and Wei Yuan, *Shengwuji* (139). But even Qianlong continued to describe Tibet as composed of three parts (Kham, Ü, and Tsang), none of which was explicitly Qinghai/Kökenuur. See, for example, Qing Gaozong (Qianlong), *Yuzhi shiwen shiquan ji* (Beijing: Zhongguo Zangxue chubanshe, 1993), 644.

32. For the most systematic articulation of Amdo as a distinct region and component of "Greater Tibet," see Sumpa Khenpo, *General Description of Jambudvīpa* (1777), transcription by Turrel V. Wylie, *The Georgraphy of Tibet According to the 'dzam-gling-spyi-bshad* (Rome: Serie Orientale Roma XXV, 1962): 10, 38–43. The Second Gungtang *kūtuktu* described Amdo as one of the three provinces of Tibet in 1798 (JYZP02, 17). The Demo *kūtuktu* also wrote of "Tibet and Greater Tibet," the latter connoting the addition of the regions of Amdo and Kham. See his biography of the Ninth Dalai Lama, *Rgyal ba'i dbang po thams cad mkhyen pa blo bzang bstan pa'i 'byung gnas ngag dbang lung rtogs rgya mtsho dpal bzang po'i zhal snga nas kyi rnam par thar pa mdor mtshon pa dad pa'i yid 'phrog,* in *Rgyal dbang sku phreng rin byon gyi mdzad rnam* (Beijing: Krung go'i bod rig pa dbe skrun khang, 2011), 11, 14. For further discussion, see Max Oidtmann, "Overlapping Empires: Religion, Politics, and Ethnicity in 19th Century Qinghai," *Late Imperial China* 37, no. 2 (December 2016): 70–76.

33. DLNT08, 203ka.06; 205ka.06.

34. Emphasis added. DLNT08, 207kha.04–208kha.01.

35. DLNT08, 205ka.06.

36. DLNT08, 203kha.05–06.

37. Th'u bkwan 03 Blo bzang chos kyi nyi ma, *Ljang skya rol pa'i rdo rje'i rnam thar* (Lanzhou: Kan su'u mi rigs dpe skrun khang, 1989 [1798]), 613.

38. Funds derived, one suspects, from the successful campaign against the Gurkhas. Peter Schwieger, *The Dalai Lama and the Emperor of China: A Political History of the Tibetan Institution of Reincarnation* (New York: Columbia University Press, 2015), 171–172, passim; and Joachim Karsten, "On the Monastic Archives of Kun-bde gling, Lhasa, Including a Preliminary Analytical Historical Study of the Monastery Itself," accessed May 16, 2017, http://www.dtab.uni-bonn.de/articles/kunling.htm.

39. Luciano Petech, "The Dalai Lamas and Regents of Tibet: A Chronological Study," *Serie Orientale Roma* LX (1988): 125–147. Recent studies of the Tibetan army and Geluk medicinal colleges by Alice Travers and Stacey Van Vleet, respectively, represent a reversal of this tradition and a growing scholarly interest in the contacts between the Qing state and Tibetans. Travers, "The Tibetan Army of the Ganden Phodrang," in *Secular Law and Order in the Tibetan Highland*, ed. Dieter Schuh (Andiast: Monumenta Tibetica Historica, Abteilung III, Band 13, 2015), 249–266; Van Vleet, "Medicine, Monasteries, and Empire: Tibetan Buddhism and the Politics of Learning in Qing China," PhD diss., Columbia University, 2015.

40. For an early nineteenth-century usage of *bod pa* that clearly distinguishes the people of Kham and Amdo from those of central Tibet, see again the biography of the Ninth Dalai Lama, De mo ho thog thu Blo bzang thub bstan 'jigs med rgya mtsho, *Sku phreng dgu pa lung rtods rgya mtsho'i rnam thar*, 24. See also BMNT, 160; and Belmang Pandita's *History of India, Tibet, Eastern and Western Mongolia* (Dbal mang dkon mchog rgyal mtshan [Belmang Pandita 02 Könchok Gyeltsen], *Rgya bod hor sog gyi lo rgyus nyung brjod pa byis pa 'jug pa'i 'bab stegs.* In *The Collected Works of Dbal-maṅ dkon-mchog-rgyal-mtshan,* reproduced by Gyaltan Gelek Namgyal, vol. 4 [*nga*] [Delhi: New Laxmi Printers, 1974 (1809–1820)]), 607:1–2. A fascinating document from 1778 records a criminal from the Mongol banners of Qinghai referring to his accomplices from central Tibet as "*boba fanzi*" (撥巴番子, i.e., Tibetan Fan): MWLF microfilm 113–2106, QL 43/06R/17 (1778–07–29). Rockhill reports that Tibetan-speaking people across the Gansu borderlands referred to themselves as "Bod-pa." See William Woodville Rockhill, *Notes on the Ethnography of Tibet* (Washington, DC: Government Printing Office, 1895), 669. Perhaps the label had become popularized during the late nineteenth century.

41. For both Wei Yuan and Zhong-fan, the author of the *Fanseng yuanliao kao* (1843), *fan* and *tanggute* have lost the geographical distinctions of the Qianlong period and become broadly interchangeable ethnonyms. See Zhong-fan, *Fanseng yuanliao kao*, ed. Wu Fengpei (Lhasa: Xizang minzu chubanshe, 1982). Archival documents from Xunhua subprefecture dating from 1875 to 1911 refer to the Tibetan inhabitans of Amdo generally as *Fanmin* (Fan commoners) or *Fanzu* (Fan clans or Fan communities). The ubiquitous use of *fanzu* in the late 1800s may have paved the way for the adoption of *zangzu* 藏族 in the early 1900s, despite the changed connotations of *zu* (now, "race" or "people"). The first archival usage I have found for *zangzu* dates to 1905. By 1912,

the new ethnonym had been popularized to the degree that it had become the standard reference to Tibetans in the "Five Races Republic" (Ch. *wuzu gonghe* 五族共和) rhetoric of the new Republic of China.

42. A good example is the broad application of the imperially sanctioned *Fanlü* (Tibetan code) by Qing officials when dealing with "Tibetan cases" (*fan an*) in Qinghai and Gansu in the nineteenth century. See Max Oidtmann, "A 'Dog-eat-dog' World: Qing Jurispractices and the Legal Inscription of Piety in Amdo," *Extrême-Orient Extrême-Occident* 40 (November 2016): 151–182. For more detailed studies of Chinese-Tibetan contacts in Kham, see Wang Xiuyu, *China's Last Imperial Frontier* (Lanham, MD: Lexington Books, 2011); and Yudru Tsomu, *The Rise of Gönpo Namgyel in Kham* (Lanham, MD: Lexington Books, 2015).

43. Although we must be careful here to distinguish between Wei Yuan's understanding of "Chinese" sovereignty and that of twentieth-century nationalists. For Wei Yuan, China meant first and foremost the authority of the Confucian state, as embodied by the Qing monarchy. For the CCP in the 1990s, the urn was a symbol of the popular sovereignty of the "Chinese people" (*Zhonghua minzu*) in Tibet.

44. For the shifting goals and strategies of Qing officials, see Elliot Sperling, "The Chinese Venture in K'am, 1904–1911," in *The History of Tibet, vol. 3*, ed. Alex McKay (New York: RoutledgeCurzon, 2003), 69–91; Daphon David Ho, "The Men Who Would not be Amban and the One Who Would: Four Frontline Officials and Qing Tibet Policy, 1905–1911," *Modern China* 34, no. 2 (2008): 210–246; and also Wang Xiuyu, *China's Last Imperial Frontier: Late Qing Expansion in Sichuan's Tibetan Borderlands* (Lanham, MD: Lexington Books, 2011).

45. *Rgyal mchog bka' drin bla med sku phreng bcu gsum pa chen po mchog nas rtsal ba'i bod zhi bde rang dbang rgyal khab du gnas pa'i yongs kyab bka* (Thirteenth Dalai Lama's edict on Tibet as an independent country), February 13, 1913. Reproduced in Tsepon Wangchuk Deden Shakabpa, *Bod kyi srid don rgyal rabs* (Kalimpong: T. Tsepal Taikhang, 1976), vol. 2, 219–223. This document does not use the term "Tibetan" (*bod pa*) or "citizen." Instead, the people are referred to solely in religious and territorial terms: the "yellow and white people of all classes" (i.e., the *sangha* and laypeople) and as the residents of Tibet (Bod). Clause four, on the responsibility of the people to defend the frontiers, most succinctly captures the radical shift of responsibility (but not sovereignty) from the ruler to the people.

46. Scott Relyea provides a detailed account of these developments in Kham: "Yokes of Gold and Threads of Silk: Sino-Tibetan Competition for Authority in Early Twentieth Century Kham," *Modern Asian Studies* 49, no. 4 (2015): 963–1009.

47. Dbal mang dkon mchog rgyal mtshan (Belmang Pandita 02), *Rgya bod hor sog gyi lo rgyus nyung brjod pa byis pa 'jug pa'i 'bab stegs*, in *The Collected Works of Dbal-man dkon-mchog-rgyal-mtshan*, reproduced by Gyaltan Gelek Namgyal, vol. 4 (Delhi: New Laxmi Printers, 1974). The work lacks a clear statement of completion. Since Belmang lists the Jiaqing reign (1796–1820) but not the enthronement of the Daoguang emperor, and because the last event mentioned in the text is the ascension of the second Tsemonling reincarnation (Tshe smon gling 02 ngag dbang 'jam dpal tshul khrims rgya mtsho, 1792–1860?) to the position of regent in 1819 and subsequent search for the Tenth Dalai Lama, it appears that a date of 1819 through 1821 is appropriate. The translation of the title also poses problems. Modern PRC references to this text translate

the place name *rgya* as an abbreviation for "China" (i.e., Tib. *rgya nag*). Considering the ordering of content within the text as well as the titles of other contemporaneous books, I have chosen to view *rgya* as an abbreviation of *rgya dkar* or "India." In this text *hor* generally refers to Eastern Mongols and other Mongol groups ruled by descendants of Chinggis Khan. *Sog* refers primarily to Oirat or Western Mongols. For a full discussion see Max Oidtmann, "A Case for Gelukpa Governance: A Historian of Labrang Monastery, Amdo, and the Manchu Rulers of China," in *Greater Tibet: An Examination of Borders, Ethnic Boundaries, and Cultural Areas*, ed. Paul Christiaan Klieger (Lanham, MD: Lexington Books, 2016), 111–148, and "Overlapping Empires." The xylograph consulted for this text comes from Belmang's *Collected Works*, which were printed no later than 1864.

48. Nayancheng, *Pingfan zouyi* ([China]: Lanyuan a gong ci, 1853), 2:39b–40b; Oidtmann, "Overlapping Empires," 49–52.
49. See for instance, Sumpa Khenpo's *Annals of Kökenuur*: Sum pa ye shes dpal 'byor, *Mtsho sngon lo rgyus tshangs glu gsar snyan zhes bya ba bzhugs so* (Zi ling: Mtsho sngon mi rigs dpe sgrun khang, 1982 [1786]), 55.
50. Belmang Pandita 02, *History*, 578:4–5.
51. Belmang Pandita 02, *History*, 577:5–578:2, 581, 624:5.
52. Belmang Pandita 02, *History*, 607:2–608:2.
53. Belmang Pandita 02, *History*, 661:6–662:3.
54. Belmang Pandita 02, *History*, 662:3–5.
55. Belmang Pandita 02, *History*, 564:4–6.
56. Belmang Pandita 02, *History*, 579:1–3.
57. Belmang Pandita 02, *History*, 576, 625–627.
58. According to Belmang, Emperor Kangxi brought Kokonor under his control when the Khoshot princes of the region accepted his invitation to an audience in 1697: "From then on, Kokonor began to enter under the authority of China" (626:4–5). As for the Junghars: "The Junghars as well fell under the dominion of China in wood-monkey year [1764?]" (631:3–4).
59. Belmang Pandita 02, *History*, 519:4–520:1.
60. Matthew King, "Writing True Places in the Twilight of Empire and the Dawn of Revolution: The Buddhist Historiography of the Mongol Zawa Damdin Luwsandamdin (1867–1937)" (PhD diss., University of Toronto, 2014), 109, 166.
61. For a discussion of Mongol views of the Qing as "our" empire, see Johan Elverskog, *Our Great Qing: The Mongols, Buddhism, and the State in Late Imperial China* (Honolulu: University of Hawai'i Press, 2006).
62. Belmang Pandita 02, *History*, 482.
63. Belmang Pandita 02, *History*, 565.
64. For Belmang's supervision of Drakgönpa's work, see the colophon of the *Oceanic Book* (MSCB, 782–783).
65. Tuttle, "Challenging Central Tibet's Dominance of History," 137–138.
66. BMNT, 209.
67. Uradyn Bulag, "Going Imperial: Tibeto-Mongolian Buddhism and Nationalisms in China and Inner Asia," in *Empire to Nation: Historical Perspectives on the Making of the Modern World*, ed. Joseph Esherick, et al. (Lanham, MD: Rowman and Littlefield, 2006), 260–295.

68. Gray Tuttle, *Tibetan Buddhists in the Making of Modern China* (New York: Columbia University Press, 2005), 2, 4, 10–14, chapters 6–7.

69. The following section is based on interviews with Cheng Qingying and other scholars at the China Tibetology Research Center, as well as interviews with officials, monks, and scholars in Gansu and Qinghai Province.

70. Danzhu Angben, "Lun huofo," in *Huofo ji zhuanshi zhidu yanjiu*, ed. Chen Qingying and Ga Dawa Caireng (Beijing: Zhongguo zangxue zhongxin zongjiaosuo, 2006), 14–36.

71. Photograph and newspaper clipping displayed at the museum of the Zhongguo Zangxue zhongxin, June 2015.

72. Chen Qingying, interview, August 15, 2014.

73. This summary follows Robert Barnett's thorough account: "Authenticity, Secrecy and Public Space: Chen Kaiyuan and Representations of the Panchen Lama Reincarnation Dispute of 1995," in *Tibetan Modernities: Notes from the Field on Cultural and Social Change*, ed. Robert Barnett and Ronald Schwartz (Leiden: Brill, 2008), 353–424.

74. Arjia Rinpoché, *Surviving the Dragon* (New York: Rodale, 2010), 200–201.

75. See the discussion in Melvyn C. Goldstein, *The Snow Lion and the Dragon: China, Tibet, and the Dalai Lama* (Berkeley: University of California Press, 1999), 106.

76. Guojia zongjiao shiwuju (National Religious Affairs Bureau), "Zangchuan fojiao huofo zhuanshi guanli banfa," law no. 5 (July 18, 2007), article 8, accessed November 21, 2016, http://www.gov.cn/gongbao/content/2008/content_923053.htm.

77. The Fourteenth Dalai Lama, "Glang sa kyabs mgon sku phreng bcu bzhi pa chen po mchog nas gzhis byes bod mis mtshon bod brgyud nang bstan gyi rjes 'jug ser skya kun dang/bod dang bod mir 'brel chags kyi ske 'gro yongs la stsal ba'i gal che'i bka' yig," accessed October 25, 2011, http://www.gyalwarinpoche.com. For an insightful analysis of this document, see Robert Barnett, "Between the Lines: Interpreting the Dalai Lama's Statement on his Successor," *The China Beat*, accessed October 25, 2011, http://www.thechinabeat.org/?p=3873.

78. "Jizhehui, 'Zhengxie weiyuan tan cujin minsheng gaishan yu shehui hexie wending'" 记者会'政协委员谈促进民生改善与社会和谐稳定, accessed June 12, 2017, http://live .people.com.cn/note.php?id=1077150302125559_ctdzb_034.

79. See for instance, Chris Buckley, "China's Tensions with Dalai Lama Spill Into the Afterlife," *The New York Times*, accessed March 11, 2015, https://nyti.ms/2mLxVfa.

80. The assertions of this paragraph are largely based on my own conversations with Tibetans and Han since I first began traveling in the Tibetan regions of China in 2000. The fact that the Panchen Lama, Gyaincain Norbu, has a large body of Han followers only came to my attention in fall 2017 when I was asked by a Lhasa- and Shanghai-based art gallery to help them translate certificates of devotion and discipleship to the Panchen Lama from Chinese and Tibetan into English. The gallery had been commissioned to produce these certificates by the office that coordinates the affairs of the Panchen Lama. When asked just who they expected to market these documents to, the gallery owner replied that they would be distributed primarily to Han devotees.

81. Quantitative surveys of Tibetan religious beliefs and attitudes are very rare. One such study conducted in the early 2000s, however, found that belief in reincarnation was slipping among younger generations of Tibetans, especially those in urban areas, as a result of changes in state religious policy. Ga Dawa Cairen, *Dangdai Zangchuan fojiao*

huofo: xintu renting he shehui yingxiang (Beijing: Zhongguo Zangxue chubanshe, 2010), 8–9.

82. For a summary of these developments, see Mark C. Elliott, "The Case of the Missing Indigene: Debate Over a 'Second Generation Ethnic Policy," *The China Journal* 73 (2015): 186–213.

Translation of the Qianlong Emperor's *Discourse on Lamas*

1. O. Franke and B. Laufer, *Lamaistische Kloster-Inschriften aus Peking, Jehol und Si -ngan; mit unterstützung der Hamburgischen Wissenschaftlichen Stiftung* [Inscriptions from Lamaist temples in Beijing, Jehol, and Xi'an] (Berlin: Verlag von Dietrich Reimer, 1914), plate 4. Parentheses indicate interlinear commentary. Tibetan transcriptions follow the Wylie system.
2. Tib. *bod*.
3. Ch. 《輟耕錄》.
4. Ch. 陶宗儀
5. Ch. 《明武宗外記》.
6. Ch. 毛奇齡.
7. Tib. *gur*, Ma. *gurun*, Ch. *chao* 朝.
8. Tib. *bde skyid rgyal po*. Tibetan text does not use the term for emperor (*gong ma chen po*).
9. Tsongkhapa's actual dates: 1357–1419.
10. Tib. *yul dbus su dbang bsgyur nas*; Ch. *zhongguo* 中國.
11. Tib. *bod chos*.

Bibliography

Archives

First Historical Archives (Beijing). *Junjichu, Lufu zouzhe* 軍機處錄副奏摺.

First Historical Archives (Beijing). *Junjichu, Shangyudang* 軍機處上諭檔.

First Historical Archives (Beijing). *Manwen lufu zouzhe* 滿文錄副奏摺.

First Historical Archives (Beijing). *Yangxindian zaobanchu zuocheng zuohuo jiqingdang* 養心殿 造辦處作成做活計清檔.

National Palace Museum (Taipei). *Qingdai gongzhongdang zouzhe ji junjichudang zhejian* 清代 宮中檔奏摺及軍機處檔摺件.

Qinghai Provincial Archives (Xining). *Qingdai Xunhua ting dang* 清代循化廳檔.

Unpublished Manuscripts and Blockprints

Dzang de tefi dalafi baita icihiyara ambasa araha benebume badarangga doro-i sucungga aniya de deribume tetele manju hergen-i bithe be alime gaire cese 駐藏 辦事大臣抄送光緒元年至二十六年接 收文冊. Manuscript, Lhasa: 1875–1900. Harvard-Yenching Library, TMA 4664.88 7453.

E'erdete Heying 額爾德特和瑛 [Hening 和寧]. *Yijianzhai shichao* 易簡齋詩鈔, 1823. Harvard-Yenching Library, 5508 3812.

Fu-heng 傅恒, ed. *Huang Qing Zhigongtu: jiu juan* 皇清職貢圖, 九卷. Blockprint, Beijing: Qing Neiwufu, 1761–1805. Harvard-Yenching Library, T 2488 3202. Accessed February 16, 2018. http://nrs.harvard.edu/urn-3:FHCL:5022520.

"The Finding of a Dalai Lama." Loose-leaf album, 19th century after 1809. Harvard University Art Museums. Arthur M. Sackler Museum, 1985.863.5.

Lian-yu 聯豫. *Xizang zouzhe* 西藏奏摺. Guangxu reign, before 1908. Harvard-Yenching Library, T 4664.88 1455.

Na-yan-chang 那彥成. *Pingfan zouyi* 平番奏疏. [China]: Lanyuan a gong ci, 1853.

Yubi pingding Taiwan ershi gongchen xiangzan 御筆平定台灣二十功臣像贊. Illustrated handscroll, 1787–1788. Private collection.

Zhuzang bansidachen zouzhedang manhan heji yuanchaoben 駐藏辦事大臣奏摺檔滿 漢合集原抄本. Lhasa: 1879. Harvard-Yenching Library, Ma 4664.8 4121.

Published Sources

Ahmad, Zahiruddin. *Sangs rgyas rgya mtsho. Life of the Fifth Dalai Lama, Vol. IV, Part I.* New Delhi: International Academy of Indian Culture and Aditya Prakashan, 1999.

——. *Sino-Tibetan Relations in the Seventeenth Century.* Rome: Istituto Italiano per il Medio ed Estremo Oriente, 1970.

Arjia Rinpoché. *Surviving the Dragon: A Tibetan Lama's Account of Forty Years Under Chinese Rule.* New York: Rodale, 2010.

Atwood, Christopher. *Encyclopedia of Mongolia and the Mongol Empire.* New York: Facts on File, 2004.

——. "'Worshipping Grace': The Language of Loyalty in Qing Mongolia." *Late Imperial China* 21, no. 2 (2000): 86–139.

Barnett, Robert. "Authenticity, Secrecy, and Public Space: Chen Kaiyuan and Representations of the Panchen Lama Reincarnation Dispute of 1995." In *Tibetan Modernities: Notes from the Field on Cultural and Social Change,* ed. Robert Barnett and Ronald Schwartz, 253–424. Leiden: Brill, 2008.

Bartlett, Beatrice S. *Monarchs and Ministers: The Grand Council in Mid-Ch'ing China, 1723–1820.* Berkeley: University of California Press, 1991.

Bell, Christopher Paul. "Nechung: The Ritual History and Institutionalization of a Tibetan Buddhist Protector Deity." PhD diss., University of Virginia, 2013.

Benton, Lauren. *Law and Colonial Cultures: Legal Regimes in World History, 1400–1900.* Cambridge: Cambridge University Press, 2002.

Berger, Patricia. *Empire of Emptiness.* Honolulu: University of Hawaii Press, 2003.

Bhabha, Homi. "Of Mimicry and Man: The Ambivalence of Colonial Discourse." *October* 28 (Spring 1984): 125–133.

Bira, Sh. *Mongolian Historical Literature of the XVII–XIX Centuries Written in Tibetan.* Ed. Ts. Damdinsüren. Trans. Stanley N. Frye. Bloomington, IN: The Mongolia Society, 1970.

Bjerken, Zeff. "Exorcising the Illusion of Bon 'Shamans': A Critical Genealogy of Shamanism in Tibetan Religions." *Revue d'Etudes Tibétaines* 6 (October 2004) : 4–69.

Bla brang dgon pa'i lo rgyus mdor bsdus. Lanzhou: Srid gros kan lho bod rigs rang skyong khul bsang chu rdzong u yon lhan khang rig gnas lo rgyus dpyad gzhi'i yig rigs u yon lhan khang gis bsgrigs (夏河縣委員會文史資料委員會), 1999.

Bod kyi lo rgyus yig tshags dang gzhung yig phyogs bsdus dwangs shes me long. Beijing: Minzu chubanshe, 1989.

Brag dgon pa dkon mchog bstan pa rab rgyas [Drakgönpa Könchok Tenpa Rabgyé]. *Mdo smad chos 'byung (Deb ther rgya mtsho)*. Xining: Mtsho sngon mi rigs dpe skrun khang, 1987 [1865].

——. *Yongs rdzogs bstan pa'i mnga' bdag rje btsun bla ma rdo rje 'chang 'kon mchog rgyal mtshan dpal bzang po'o zhal snga nas kyi rnam par thar 'dod 'jug ngogs*. Beijing: Minzu chubanshe, 2001 [1864].

Brophy, David. "The Junghar Mongol Legacy and the Language of Loyalty in Qing Xinjiang." *Harvard Journal of Asiatic Studies* 73, no. 2 (December 2013): 231–258.

Brunnert, H. S., and V. V. Hagelstrom. *The Present Day Political Organization of China*. Shanghai: Kelly and Walsh, Limited, 1912.

Bstan po no mon han 'Jam dpal chos kyi bstan 'dzin 'phrin las. *'Dzam gling rgyas bshad*. Gangtok: Dzongsar chhentse labrang, 1981 [1820–30].

Bulag, Uradyn E. "Going Imperial: Tibeto-Mongolian Buddhism and Nationalisms in China and Inner Asia." In *Empire to Nation: Historical Perspectives on the Making of the Modern World,* ed. Joseph Esherick et al., 260–295. Lanham, MD: Rowman and Littlefield, 2006.

Burbank, Jane, and Frederick Cooper. *Empires in World History: Power and the Politics of Difference*. Princeton: Princeton University Press, 2010.

Buswell, Jr., Robert E., and Donald S. Lopez, Jr. *The Princeton Dictionary of Buddhism*. Princeton: Princeton University Press, 2014.

Cabezón, José Ignacio. "Introduction." In *Tibetan Ritual*, ed. José Cabezon, 1–36. New York: Oxford University Press, 2010.

Cankanjia 参看加. "Zangchuan fojiao huofo doushe zhuanshifa" 藏傳佛教活佛奪舍轉 世法. In *Anduo yanjiu zangxue lungwen,* vol. 2, ed. Gansu sheng zangxue yanjiu suo, 182–190. Beijing: Minzu chubanshe, 2006.

Chab spel tshe brtan phun tshogs. *Bod kyi lo rgyus rags rim g.yu yi phreng ba*. Lhasa: Bod ljongs bod yig dpe rnying dpe skrun khang, 1989.

——, ed. *Bod kyi gal che'i lo rgyus yig cha bdams bsgrigs*. Lhasa: Bod ljongs bod yig dpe rnying dpe skrun khang, 1991.

Chang, Michael G. *A Court on Horseback: Imperial Touring and the Construction of Qing Rule, 1680–1785*. Cambridge, MA: Harvard University Asia Center, 2007.

Charleux, Isabelle, and Gaëlle Lacaze. "L'intronisation du IXe Dalai lama vue par un prince mongol: un rouleau peint conservé à la bibliothèque de l'Institut des Hautes Etudes Chinoises." *Arts Asiatique* 59 (2004): 30–57.

Charleux, Isabelle, Marie-Dominique Even, and Gaëlle Lacaze. "Un Document Mongol Sur L'intronisation du IXe Dalai Lama." *Journal Asiatique* 292, no. 1–2 (2004): 151–222.

Chatterjee, Partha. *The Nation and Its Fragments: Colonial and Post-Colonial Histories*. Princeton: Princeton University Press, 1993.

Chayet, Anne. "A Propos de Notations Geographiques Dans L'Amdo Chos 'Byung." In *Tibet, Past and Present v. 1*, ed. Henk Blezer, 247–262. Leiden: Brill, 2002.

——. "À propos du règlement en 29 articles de l'année 1793." *Cahier d'Extrême-Asie* 15 (2005): 165–186.

Chen Qingying 陳慶英. *Dalai lama zhuanshi ji lishi dingzhi* 達賴喇嘛轉世及歷史定制. Beijing: Wuzhou chuanbo chubanshe, 2003.

——. "Hanwen 'Xizang' yi ci lai li jianshuo" 漢文 '西藏'一詞來歷簡說. *Yanjing xuebao* 5 (1999).

Chen Qingying 陳慶英 and Chen Lijian 陳立健. *Huofo zhuanshi: yuanqi, fazhan, lishi dingzhi* 活佛轉世: 緣起, 發展, 歷史定制. Beijing: Zhongguo zangxue chubanshe, 2014.

Chen Xiaomin 陳曉敏. "Qingdai zhujing lama zhidu de xingcheng yu yange" 清代駐京 喇嘛制度的形成與沿革. *Manzu yanjiu* 4 (2007): 111–121.

Chhosphel, Samten. "Longdol Lama Ngawang Lobzang." *Treasury of Lives*, accessed March 22, 2013. http://www.treasuryoflives.org/biographies/view/Longdol-Lama -Ngawang-Lobzang/3877.

——. "The Third Gungtang, Konchok Tenpai Dronme." *Treasury of Lives,* accessed March 27, 2013. http://www.treasuryoflives.org/biographies/view/Konchok-Tenpai -Dronme/4730.

——. "The Third Tukwan, Lobzang Chokyi Nyima." *Treasury of Lives*, accessed June 8, 2013. http://www.treasuryoflives.org/biographies/view/Lobzang-Chokyi-Nyima/3008.

Chi Wanxing 池萬興. "Hening ji qi *Xizang fu*" 和寧及其 '西藏賦.' *Jinan daxue xuebao (Shehui kexue ban)* 18, no. 4 (2008): 30–33.

Chia, Ning. "The Lifanyuan in the Early Ch'ing Dynasty." PhD diss., The Johns Hopkins University, 1992.

Cidan Lunzhu 次旦倫珠. "Huofo zhuanshi de chansheng ji lishi zuoyong" 活佛轉世的產生及歷史作用. In *Huofo ji zhuanshi zhidu yanjiu* 活佛及轉世制度研究, ed. Chen Qingying 陳慶英 and Ga Dawa Cairen 嘎達哇才仁, 1–13. Beijing: Zhongguo Zangxue zhongxin zongjiaosuo, 2006.

Cohn, Bernard S. *Colonialism and Its Forms of Knowledge.* Princeton: Princeton University Press, 1996.

Crossley, Pamela K. "Manzhou Yuanliu Kao and the Formalization of the Manchu Heritage." *The Journal of Asian Studies* 46, no. 4 (November 1987): 761–790.

——. "The Rulerships of China." *American Historical Review* 97, no. 5 (December 1997): 1468–1483.

——. *A Translucent Mirror: History and Identity in Qing Imperial Ideology.* Berkeley: University of California Press, 1999.

Dabringhaus, Sabine. "The Ambans of Tibet: Imperial Rule at the Inner Asian Periphery." In *The Dynastic Center and the Provinces: Agents and Interactions,* ed. Jeroen Duindam and Sabine Dabringhaus, 114–126. Leiden: Brill, 2014.

——. "Chinese Emperors and Tibetan Monks: Religion as an Instrument of Rule." In *China and Her Neighbors: Borders, Visions of the Other, Foreign Policy, 10th to 19th Century,* ed. Sabine Dabringhaus, Roderich Ptak, and Richard Teschke, Wiesbaden: Harrassowitz Verlag, 1997.

——. *Das Qing-Imperium als Vision und Wirklichkeit: Tibet in Laufbahn und Schriften des Song Yun (1752–1835).* Stuttgart: Franz Steiner Verlag, 1994.

Dalton, Jacob Paul. *The Taming of the Demons: Violence and Liberation in Tibetan Buddhism.* New Haven: Yale University Press, 2011.

Danzhu Angben 丹珠昂奔. "Lun huofo" 論活佛. In *Huofo ji zhuanshi zhidu yanjiu* 活佛 及轉世制度研究, ed. Chen Qingying 陳慶英 and Ga Dawa Cairen 嘎達哇 才仁, 14–36. Beijing: Zhongguo zangxue zhongxin zongjiaosuo, 2006.

Daowei Cairangjia 道幃才讓加. "Gandan pozhang shiqi Xizang de zhengzhi zhidu wen-hua yanjiu" 甘丹頗章時期西藏的政治制度文化研究. PhD diss., Zhongyang minzu daxue, 2007.

——. "Xizang gandan pozhang difang zhengfu jianli chuqi Gushihan banfa de zangwen tiejuan wenshu kaoshu" 西藏甘丹頗章地方政府建立初期顧實汗頒發的藏文鐵 卷文書考述. *Xizang dang'an* 21, no. 2 (2015): 24–31.

Das, Sarat Chandra. *Journey to Lhasa and Central Tibet*. London: John Murray, 1902.

Dbal mang dkon mchog rgyal mtshan [Belmang Pandita 02 Könchok Gyeltsen]. *Bla brang bkra shis 'khyil gyi gdan rabs lha'i rnga chen*. Lanzhou: Gansu minzu chubanshe, 1987 [1800].

——. *Rgya bod hor sog gyi lo rgyus nyung brjod pa byis pa 'jug pa'i 'bab stegs*. In *The Collected Works of Dbal-man dkon-mchog-rgyal-mtshan*, reproduced by Gyaltan Gelek Namgyal, vol. 4 (*nga*). Delhi: New Laxmi Printers, 1974 [1809–1820].

De mo 08 ngag dbang thub bstan 'jigs med rgya mtsho. *'Jam dpal rgya mtsho'i rnam thar*. Lhasa: Dga' ldan pho brang, Bras spungs, 1811. (TBRC W2CZ7847)

——. *Rgyal ba'i dbang po thams cad mkhyen pa blo bzang bstan pa'i 'byung gnas ngag dbang lung rtogs rgya mtsho dpal bzang po'i zhal snga nas kyi rnam par thar pa mdor mtshon pa dad p'i yid 'phrog*. In *Rgyal dbang sku phreng rin byon gyi mdzad rnam*. Beijing: Krung go'i bod rig pa dbe skrun khang, 2011.

Deng Chengwei 鄧承偉. *Xiningfu xuzhi* 西寧府續志. Xining: Qinghai renmin chubanshe, 1985 [1883].

Deng Ruiling 鄧銳齡. "1789–1790 nian Ehui deng Xizang shiyi zhangcheng" 1789–1790 年鄂輝等西藏事宜章程. *Zhongguo zangxue* 83, no. 3 (2008): 138–146.

——. *Qing qianqi zhi Zang zengce tanze* 清前期治藏政策探賾. Beijing: Zhongguo zangxue chubanshe, 2012.

Dennerline, Jerry. "The Shun-chih Reign." In *The Cambridge History of China, Volume 9, The Ch'ing Dynasty to 1800, Part One*, ed. Willard J. Peterson, 73–119. Cambridge: Cambridge University Press, 2002.

Di Cosmo, Nicola. "Manchu Shamanic Ceremonies at the Qing Court." In *State and Court Ritual in China*, ed. Joseph McDermott, 352–398. Cambridge: Cambridge University Press, 1999.

——. "Qing Colonial Administration in Inner Asia." *The International History Review* XX, no. 2 (June 1998): 287–309.

——. "The Qing and Inner Asia: 1636–1800." In *The Cambridge History of Inner Asia: The Chinggisid Age,* ed. Nicola Di Cosmo, Allen J. Frank, and Peter B. Golden, 333–362. Cambridge: Cambridge University Press, 2009.

Diemberger, Hildegard. "Female Oracles in Modern Tibet." In *Women in Tibet*, ed. Janet Gyatso and Hanna Havnevik, 113–168. London: Hurst & Company, 2005.

Dirks, Nicholas. "Imperial Sovereignty." In *Imperial Formations*, ed. Ann Laura Stoler, Carole McGranahan, and Peter C. Perdue, 311–340. Santa Fe: School for Advanced Research Press, 2007.

Dotson, Brandon. "Divination and Law in the Tibetan Empire: The Role of Dice in the Legislation of Loans, Interest, Martial Law, and Troop Conscription." In *Contributions to the Cultural History of Early Tibet,* ed. Matthew T. Kapstein and Brandon Dotson, 3–77. Leiden: Brill, 2007.

Duff, Tony. *The Illuminator Tibetan–English Encyclopaedic Dictionary*. Katmandu: Padma Karpo Translation Committee, 2000.

Ekvall, Robert B. "Some Aspects of Divination in Tibetan Society." *Ethnology* 2, no. 1 (January 1963): 31–39.

Elliott, Mark C. "The Case of the Missing Indigene: Debate Over a 'Second Generation Ethnic Policy.'" *The China Journal* 73 (2015): 186–213.

——. "The Manchu-Language Archives of the Qing Dynasty and the Origins of the Palace Memorial System." *Late Imperial China* 22, no. 1 (June 2001): 1–70.

——. *The Manchu Way: The Eight Banners and Ethnic Identity in Late Imperial China*. Stanford: Stanford University Press, 2001.

Elman, Benjamin A. "The Civil Examination System in Late Imperial China, 1400–1900." *Frontiers of History in China* 8, no. 1 (2014): 32–50.

——. "Political, Social and Cultural Reproduction via Civil Service Examinations in Late Imperial China." *Journal of Asian Studies* 50, no. 1 (February 1991): 7–28.

Elverskog, Johan. "China and the New Cosmopolitanism." *Sino-Platonic Papers* 233 (February 2013): 1–30.

——. *The Jewel Translucent Sūtra: Altan Khan and the Mongols in the Sixteenth Century*. Leiden: Brill, 2003.

——. *Our Great Qing: The Mongols, Buddhism, and the State in Late Imperial China*. Honolulu: University of Hawai'i Press, 2006.

——. "Wutai Shan, Qing Cosmopolitanism, and the Mongols." *Journal of the International Association of Tibetan Studies* 6 (December 2011): 243–274.

Farquhar, David M. "The Emperor as Bodhisattva in the Governance of the Ch'ing Empire." *Harvard Journal of Asiatic Studies* 38, no. 1 (June 1978): 5–34.

Feng Mingzhu 冯明珠. "Zouguo liuhen: Songyun zhu Zang de zhengji yu zhuoshu" 走過留痕:松筠駐藏的政績與著述. In *Bainian zhu Zang dachen yanjiu luncong* 百 年駐藏大臣研究論叢, ed. Zeng Guoqing 曾國慶, 448–479. Beijing: Zhongguo Zangxue chubanshe, 2014.

Fitzgerald, Devin. "Research Note: Between Paper and Wood, or the Manchu Invention of the *Dang'an*." *Saksaha* 13 (2015): 75–80.

Fletcher, Jr., Joseph. "Heyday of the Ch'ing Order in Inner Asia." In *The Cambridge History of China, Volume 10, Late Ch'ing 1800–1911,* ed. Denis Twitchett and John K. Fairbank, 351–408. Cambridge: Cambridge University Press, 1978.

Ford, Lisa. *Settler Sovereignty: Jurisdiction and Indigenous People in America and Australia, 1788–1836*. Cambridge, MA: Harvard University Press, 2010.

Franke, O., and B. Laufer. *Lamaistische Kloster-Inschriften aus Peking, Jehol und Si -ngan; mit unterstützung der Hamburgischen Wissenschaftlichen Stiftung* [Inscriptions from Lamaist temples in Beijing, Jehol, and Xi'an]. Berlin: Verlag von Dietrich Reimer, 1914.

Fu-heng 傅恒 et al., eds. *Huang Qing zhigongtu* 皇清職貢圖. Taibei: Taiwan shangwu yinshuguan, 1984.

——. *Qinding xiyu tongwenzhi* 欽定西域同文志. Changchun: Jilin chuban jituan, 2005 [1763].

Ga Dawacairen 嘎達哇才仁. *Dangdai Zang chuan fojiao huofo: xintu rentong he shehui yingxiang* 当代藏传佛教活佛:信徒认同和社会影响. Beijing: Zhongguo Zangxue chubanshe, 2010.

——. "Xizang difang zhengfu de si da hufashen" 西藏地方政府 的四大護法神. *Xizang dang'an* 20, no. 1 (2015): 92–101.

Giersch, C. Patterson. *Asian Borderlands: The Transformation of Qing China's Yunnan Frontier.* Cambridge, MA: Harvard University Press, 2006.

Goldstein, Melvyn C. *A History of Modern Tibet, 1913–1951: The Demise of the Lamaist State.* Berkeley, Los Angeles: University of California Press, 1989.

——. *The Snow Lion and the Dragon: China, Tibet, and the Dalai Lama.* Berkeley: University of California Press, 1999.

Gong Jinghan 龔景瀚. *Xunhua zhi* 循化志. Xining: Qinghai renmin chubanshe, 1981 [1792].

Goossaert, Vincent. "Counting the Monks: The 1736–1739 Census of the Chinese Clergy." *Late Imperial China* 21, no. 2 (December 2000): 40–85.

——. "Taoists, 1644–1850." In *The Cambridge History of China, Volume 9, Part Two, The Ch'ing Dynasty to 1800,* ed. Willard J. Peterson, 412–457. Cambridge: Cambridge University Press, 2016.

Grant, Bruce. *The Captive and the Gift: Cultural Histories of Sovereignty in Russia and the Caucasus.* Ithaca: Cornell University Press, 2009.

Grupper, Samuel M. "Manchu Patronage and Tibetan Buddhism During the First Half of the Ch'ing Dynasty." *The Journal of the Tibet Society* 4 (1984): 47–75.

Gser tog Blo bzang tshul khrims rgya mtsho. *Sku 'bum byams pa gling gdan rabs don ldan tshangs pa'i dbyangs snyan.* Xining: Mtsho sngon mi rigs dpe khang, 1983 [1903].

Gung thang bstan pa'i sgron me. *Kun mkhyen 'jam dbyangs bzhad pa sku 'phreng gynis pa rje 'jigs med dbang po'i rnam thar.* Lanzhou: Gansu People's Publishing House, 1990 [1798].

Guy, Kent R. *The Emperor's Four Treasuries: Scholars and the State in the Late Ch'ien-lung Era.* Cambridge, MA: Council on East Asian Studies, Harvard University Press, 1987.

Harrell, Stevan. "Civilizing Projects and the Reaction to Them." In *Cultural Encounters on China's Ethnic Frontiers,* ed. Stevan Harrell, 3–36. Seattle: University of Washington Press, 1995.

Harrison, Henrietta. "The Qianlong Emperor's Letter to George III and the Early-Twentieth-Century Origins of Ideas About Traditional China's Foreign Relations." *The American Historical Review* 122, no. 3 (June 2017): 680–701.

Hartley, Lauran. "Self as a Faithful Public Servant: The Autobiography of Mdo mkhar ba Tshe ring bang royal (1697–1763)." In *Mapping the Modern in Tibet; Proceedings of the Eleventh Seminar of the International Association for Tibetan Studies, Königswinter,* ed. Gray Tuttle, 45–72. Andiast, Switzerland: International Institute for Tibetan and Buddhist Studies GmbH, 2011.

Heissig, Walther. *Beiträge zur Übersetzungsgeschichte des Mongolischen Buddhistischen Kanons.* Göttingen: Vandenhoeck 6 Ruprecht, 1962.

Heller, Amy. "The Great Protector Deities of the Dalai Lamas." In *Lhasa in the Seventeenth Century,* ed. Françoise Pommaret, 81–98. Leiden: Brill, 2003.

Henss, Michael. "The Bodhisattva-Emperor: Tibeto-Chinese Portraits of Sacred and Secular Rule in the Qing Dynasty, Part 1." *Oriental Art* 47, no. 3 (2001): 2–16. Part 2, *Oriental Art* 47, no. 5 (2001): 71–83.

Heqiyeletu 賀其葉勒圖. "Zang chuan fojiao hutuketu zhixiang kaoshi" 藏傳佛教呼圖克圖職銜考釋. In *Huofo ji zhuanshi zhidu yanjiu* 活佛及轉世制度研究, ed. Chen Qingying

陳慶英 and Ga Dawa Cairen 嘎達哇才仁, 236–248. Beijing: Zhongguo Zangxue zhongxin zongjiaosuo, 2006.

Heuschert, Dorothea. "Legal Pluralism in the Qing Empire: Manchu Legislation for the Mongols." *International History Review* 20, no. 2 (1998): 310–324.

Hevia, James. "Lamas, Emperors and Rituals: Political Implications in Qing Imperial Ceremonies." *Journal of the International Association of Buddhist Studies* 16 (1993): 243–278.

Ho, Daphon David. "The Men Who Would Not Be Amban and the One Who Would: Four Frontline Officials and Qing Tibet Policy, 1905–1911." *Modern China* 34, no. 2 (2008): 210–246.

Hostetler, Laura. *Qing Colonial Enterprise: Ethnography and Cartography in Early Modern China.* Chicago: University of Chicago Press, 2001.

Huang Weizhong 黃维忠. "Zangchuan fojiao de huofo zhuanshi zhidu" 藏傳佛教的活佛轉世制度. In *Huofo ji zhuanshi zhidu yanjiu* 活佛及轉世制度研究, ed. Chen Qingying 陳慶英 and Ga Dawa Cairen 嘎達哇才仁, 98–115. Beijing: Zhongguo Zangxue zhongxin zongjiaosuo, 2006.

Illich, Marina. "Imperial Stooge or Emissary to the Dge lugs Throne? Rethinking the Biographies of the Chankya Rolpé Dorjé." In *Power, Politics, and the Reinvention of Tradition; Proceedings of the Tenth Seminar of the International Association for Tibetan Studies, Königswinter,* ed. Bryan J. Cuevas and Kurtis R. Schaeffer, 17–32. Leiden: Brill, 2006.

Ishihama, Yumiko. "The Conceptual Framework of the dGa'-ldan's War Based on the *beye dailame wargi amargi babe necihiyeme toktobuha bodogon i bithe,* 'Buddhist Government' in the Tibet-Mongol and Manchu Relationship." In *Tibet and Her Neighbours: A History.* ed. Alex McKay, 157–165. London: Edition Hansjorg Mayer, 2003.

——. "The Image of Ch'ien-lung's Kingship as Seen from the World of Tibetan Buddhism." *Acta Asiatica* 88 (2005): 49–64.

——. "New Light on the 'Chinese Conquest of Tibet' in 1720 (Based on the New Manchu Sources)." In *Tibetan Studies Vol. 1, Proceedings of the 7th Seminar of the International Association for Tibetan Studies, Graz 1995,* ed. Helmut Krasser, Michael Torsten Much, Ernst Steinkellner, and Helmut Tauscher, 419–426. Wein: Verlag der Österreichischen Akademie der Wissenschaften, 1997.

——. "A Study on the Seals and Titles Conferred by the Dalai Lama." In *Tibetan Studies: Proceedings of the 5th Seminar of the International Association for Tibetan Studies,* ed. Shōren Ihara and Zuiho Yamaguchi, 501–514. Narita: Naritasan Shinsoji, 1992.

Jackson, Roger. "Triumphalism and Ecumenism in Thu'u bkwan's *Crystal Mirror." Journal of the International Association of Tibetan Studies* 2 (August 2006): 1–23.

Jagou, Fabienne 谷嵐. "Étude des toponymes choisis par les Mandchous pour définir le territoire tibétain." In *Etudes tibétaines en l'honneur d'Anne Chayet,* ed. J. L. Achard, 127–146. Geneve: Droz, 2010.

——. "Manzhou jiangjun Fukang'an: 1792 zhi 1793 nian Xizang zhengwu gaige de xianqu" 滿洲將軍福康安:1792 至1793年西藏政務改革先驅. In *Bianchen yu jiangli* 邊臣與疆吏, ed. Li Guoqiang, Paola Calanca, and Fabienne Jagou, 147–167. Beijing: Faguo hanxue and Zhonghua shuju, 2007.

——. "The Thirteenth Dalai Lama's Visit to Beijing in 1908: In Search of a New Kind of Chaplain-Donor Relationship." In *Buddhism Between Tibet and China*, ed. Matthew T. Kapstein, 349–377. Boston: Wisdom, 2009.

——. "The Use of Ritual Drawing of Lots for the Selection of the 11th Panchen Lama." In *Revisiting Rituals in a Changing Tibetan World: Proceedings of the Seminar La transformation des rituels dans l'aire tibétaine à l'époque contemporaine held in Paris on November 8th and 9th, 2007*, ed. Katrine Buffetrille, 43–68. Leiden: Brill, 2011.

Jin Hai 金海, Qimude Dao'erji 齊木德道爾吉, Huricha 胡日查, and Hasibagen 哈斯巴根. *Qingdai menggu zhi* 清代蒙古志. Huhehaote: Neimenggu renmin chubanshe, 2009.

Jitsuzo, Tamura, Shunju Imanishi, and Hisashi Sato, eds. *Wuti Qingwen jian* 五體清 文鑑 (*Gotai Shimbun kan yakukai*). Kyoto: Institute for Inland Asian Studies, Kyoto University, 1966.

'Ju mi pham rgya mtsho. *Rgyal po lugs kyi bstan bcos sa gzhi skyong ba'i rgyan* [An Ornament for Worldly Kings: A Treatise on the Way of the King]. In *Gsum 'bum Ju mi pham rgya mtsho'i vol 1. (ka)*, 1–158. Paro, Bhutan: Lama Godrup and Sherab Drimey, 1984–1993.

Kanda Nobuo et al., eds. *Manbun Rōtō* 滿文老檔. Tokyo: Toyō Bunkyō, 1969.

Kapstein, Matthew T. "Just Where on Jambudvīpa Are We?" In *Forms of Knowledge in Early Modern Asia,* ed. Sheldon Pollock, 336–364. Durham: Duke University Press, 2011.

——. *The Tibetans*. Malden, MA: Blackwell, 2006.

Karmay, Samten G. "The Fifth Dalai Lama and His Reunification of Tibet." In *Lhasa in the Seventeenth Century*, ed. Francoise Pommaret, 65–80. Leiden: Brill, 2003.

——, trans. *The Illusive Play: The Autobiography of the Fifth Dalai Lama*. Chicago: Serindia, 2014.

Karsten, Joachim. "On the Monastic Archives of Kun-bde gling, Lhasa, Including a Preliminary Analytical Historical Study of the Monastery Itself." Accessed May 16, 2017. http://www.dtab.uni-bonn.de/articles/kunling.htm.

Katō Naoto. "Lobsang Danjin's Rebellion of 1723." In *The Tibetan History Reader*, ed. Gray Tuttle and Kurtis Schaeffer, 411–436. New York: Columbia University Press, 2013.

Kim Hanung. "Another Tibet at the Heart of Qing China: Location of Tibetan Buddhism in the Mentality of the Qing Chinese Mind at Jehol." In *Greater Tibet*, ed. P. Christiaan Klieger, 37–56. Lanham, MD: Lexington Books, 2016.

King, Matthew. "Writing True Places in the Twilight of Empire and the Dawn of Revolution: The Buddhist Historiography of the Mongol Zawa Damdin Luwsandamdin (1867–1937)." PhD diss., University of Toronto, 2014.

Köhle, Natalie. "Why Did the Kangxi Emperor go to Wutai Shan? Patronage, Pilgrimage, and the Place of Tibetan Buddhism at the Early Qing Court." *Late Imperial China* 29, no. 1 (June 2008): 73–119.

Kolla, Edward J. *Sovereignty, International Law, and the French Revolution*. Cambridge: Cambridge University Press, 2017.

Kolsky, Elizabeth. *Colonial Justice in British India: White Violence and the Rule of Law*. New York: Cambridge University Press, 2010.

Kuhn, Philip A. *Soulstealers: The Chinese Sorcery Scare of 1768*. Cambridge, MA: Harvard University Press, 1990.

Kung, Ling-wei. "The Secret History of Tibet: The Mindstream Transference from the Fifth to the Sixth Dalai Lamas and Its Manchu-Mongol Translations in the Qing Archives." Paper presented at Beyond Empire and Borders: The Third International Conference on the Qing and Inner Asia, Columbia University, September 6, 2017.

Leibold, James. *Reconfiguring Chinese Nationalism: How the Qing Frontier and Its Indigenes Became Chinese*. New York: Palgrave Macmillan, 2007.

Lessing, Ferdinand. *Yung-ho-kung: An Iconography of the Lamaist Cathedral in Peking with Notes on Lamaist Mythology and Cult*. Stockholm: Elanders Boktryckeri Aktiebolag, 1942.

Li Fengzhen 李鳳珍. *Qingdai Xizang junwangzhi chutan du qingshi zhaji* 清代西藏郡王 制初探讀清史札記. Beijing: Zhongguo Zangxue chubanshe, 2012.

Liao Zugui 廖祖桂 and Chen Qingying 陳慶英. "Qingchao jinping cheqian zhidu sheli ji qi lishi yiyi" 清朝金瓶掣簽制度的設立及其歷史意義. *Zhongguo Zangxue* 3 (1995): 38–46.

Liao Zugui, Li Yongchang 李永昌, and Li Pengnian 李鵬年. *Qinding zangnei shanhou zhangcheng ershijiutiao banben kaolüe* 欽定藏內善後章程二十九條版本考略. Beijing: Zhongguo Zangxue chubanshe, 2006.

Lin Jifu 林繼富. "Huofo zhuanshi yu Zangzu shen pan xisu" 活佛轉世與藏族神判習俗. *Xizang yishu yanjiu* 1 (1996): 56–62.

Lin, Hsiao-ting. *Tibet and Nationalist China's Frontier: Intrigues and Ethnopolitics, 1928–49*. Vancouver: University of British Columbia Press, 2006.

Lipman, Jonathan N. *Familiar Strangers: A History of Muslims in Northwest China*. Seattle: University of Washington Press, 1997.

Liu Limei 劉麗楣. "Guanyu zhu Zang dachen yu Dalai lama xianjian liyi wenti" 關於駐藏大臣與達賴喇嘛相見禮儀問題. In *Bainian zhu Zang dachen yanjiu luncong* 百年駐藏大臣研究論叢, ed. Zeng Guoqing 曾國慶, 348–356. Beijing: Zhongguo Zangxue chubanshe, 2014.

Liu Zhong 劉忠. "Shilun Qingdai zhu Zang dachen Songyun dui Xizang de gaige" 試論清代駐藏大臣松筠對西藏的改革. In *Bainian zhu Zang dachen yanjiu luncong* 百年駐藏大臣研究論叢, ed. Zeng Guoqing 曾國慶, 154–166. Beijing: Zhongguo Zangxue chubanshe, 2014.

Lopez, Jr., Donald S. *Prisoners of Shangri-La: Tibetan Buddhism and the West*. Chicago: University of Chicago Press, 1998.

Lupke, Christopher. "Diverse Modes of *Ming*: An Introduction." In *The Magnitude of Ming: Command, Allotment, and Fate in Chinese Culture*, ed. Christopher Lupke, 1–20. Honolulu: University of Hawai'i Press, 2005.

Ma Haiyun. "Fanhui or Huifan? Hanhui or Huimin? Salar Ethnic Identification and Qing Administrative Transformation in Eighteenth-Century Gansu." *Late Imperial China* 29, no. 2 (December 2008): 1–36.

Martin, Dan. "Bonpo Canons and Jesuit Cannons: On Sectarian Factors Involved in the Ch'ien-lung Emperor's Second Goldstream Expedition of 1771–1776 Based Primarily on Some Tibetan Sources." *Tibet Journal* 15 (1990): 3–28.

——. *Tibetan Histories: A Bibliography of Tibetan-Language Historical Works*. London: Serindia Publications, 1997.

Mayers, William Frederick. *The Chinese Government*. Shanghai: Kelly and Walsh, 1897.

McCleary, Rachel M., and Leonard W.J. van der Kuijp. "A Market Approach to the Rise of the Geluk School." *Journal of Asian Studies* 69, no. 1 (2010): 149–180.

Millward, James A. *Beyond the Pass: Economy, Ethnicity, and Empire in Qing Central Asia, 1759–1864.* Stanford: Stanford University Press, 1998.

Mkhan po Ngag dbang thub bstan rgya mtsho. *Kun mkhyen 'jam dbyangs bzed pa sku 'phreng gsum pa'i rnam thar.* Beijing: Zhongguo Zangxue chubanshe, 1991.

Morrison, Alexander. "Creating a Colonial Shari'a for Russian Turkestan." In *Imperial Cooperation and Transfer, 1870–1930,* ed. Volker Barth and Roland Cvetkovski, 127–149. London: Bloomsbury, 2015.

Mosca, Matthew. *From Frontier Policy to Foreign Policy: The Question of India and the Transformation of Geopolitics in Qing China.* Stanford: Stanford University Press, 2013.

——. "The Literati Rewriting of China in the Qianlong-Jiaqing Transition." *Late Imperial China* 32, no. 2 (December 2011): 89–132.

Namgyal, Tsering. "Sherab Gyatso." *Treasury of Lives.* Accessed June 9, 2013. http://www.treasuryoflives.org/biographies/view/Drungchen-Sherab -Gyatso/2495.

Nebesky-Wojkowitz, René de. *Oracles and Demons of Tibet: The Cult and Iconography of the Tibetan Protective Deities.* Graz, Austria: Akademische Druck, 1975.

Ngag dbang Blo bzang Rgya mtsho. *Gsung 'bum* vol. ma (16). Gangtok: Sikkim Research Institute of Tibetology, 1991–1995 (TBRC W294).

Nian Gengyao 年羹堯. *Nian Gengyao Zouzhe Zhuanji* 年羹堯奏摺專輯. Taibei: Guoli Gugong Bowuyuan, 1971.

Nietupski, Paul Kocot. "Bla brang Monastery and Wutai Shan." *Journal of the International Association of Tibetan Studies* 6 (December 2011): 327–348.

——. *Labrang Monastery: A Tibetan Buddhist Community on the Inner Asian Borderlands, 1709–1958.* Lanham, MD: Lexington Books, 2011.

——. "The 'Reverend Chinese' (*Gyanakpa tsang*) at Labrang Monastery." In *Buddhism Between Tibet and China,* ed. Matthew T. Kapstein, 181–213. Boston: Wisdom Publications, 2009.

——. "The World According to Belmang Pandita." Unpublished manuscript, 2012.

Nivison, David. "Ho-shen and His Accusers: Ideology and Political Behavior in the 18th Century." In *Confucianism in Action,* ed. David S. Nivison and Arthur F. Wright, 209–243. Stanford: Stanford University Press, 1959.

Norman, Jerry. *A Concise Manchu–English Lexicon.* Seattle: University of Washington Press, 1978.

Ocko, Jonathan, and David Gilmartin. "State, Sovereignty, and the People: A Comparison of the 'Rule of Law' in China and India." *Journal of Asian Studies* 68, no. 1 (February 2009): 55–133.

Oidtmann, Max. "Between Patron and Priest: Amdo Tibet Under Qing Rule, 1792–1911." PhD diss., Harvard University, 2014.

——. "A Case for Gelukpa Governance: A Historian of Labrang Monastery, Amdo, and the Manchu Rulers of China." In *Greater Tibet: An Examination of Borders, Ethnic Boundaries, and Cultural Areas,* ed. Paul Christiaan Klieger, 111–148. Lanham, MD: Lexington Books, 2016.

——. "A 'Dog-eat-dog' World: Qing Jurispractices and the Legal Inscription of Piety in Amdo." *Extrême-Orient Extrême-Occident* 40 (November 2016): 151–182.

——. "Overlapping Empires: Religion, Politics, and Ethnicity in 19th-Century Qinghai," *Late Imperial China* 37, no. 2 (December 2016): 41–91.

Osterhammel, Jürgen. *Colonialism*. Princeton, NJ: Markus Wiener Publishers, 2005.

Perdue, Peter. *China Marches West: The Qing Conquest of Central Eurasia*. Cambridge, MA: Harvard University Press, 2005.

——. "China and Other Colonial Empires." *The Journal of American-East Asian Relations* 16, no. 1–2 (Spring–Summer 2009): 85–103.

——. "Comparing Empires: Manchu Colonialism." *The International History Review* 20, no. 2 (1998): 255–262.

——. "Tea, Cloth, Gold, and Religion: Manchu Sources on Trade Missions from Mongolia to Tibet." *Late Imperial China* 36, no. 2 (December 2015): 1–22.

Petech, Luciano. *Aristocracy and Government in Tibet: 1728–1959*. Serie Orientale Roma 35. Rome: Instituto Italiano Per Il Medio ed Estremo Oriente, 1973.

——. *China and Tibet in the Early XVIIIth Century: History of the Establishment of the Chinese Protectorate in Tibet*. Leiden: Brill, 1972.

——. *The Dalai Lamas and Regents of Tibet: A Chronological Study*. Serie Orientale Roma 80. Rome: Instituto Italiano Per Il Medio ed Estremo Oriente, 1988.

Pirie, Fernanda. "The Impermanence of Power: Village Politics in Ladakh, Nepal, and Tibet." In *Ladakhi Histories: Local and Regional Perspectives*, ed. John Bray, 379–394. Leiden: Brill, 2005.

Powers, John. *The Buddha Party: How the People's Republic of China Works to Define and Control Tibetan Buddhism*. Oxford: Oxford University Press, 2017.

Powers, John, and David Templeman. *Historical Dictionary of Tibet*. Lanham, MD: Scarecrow Press, 2012.

Pu Wencheng 蒲文成. *Qinghai fojiao shi* 青海佛教史. Xining: Qinghai renmin chubanshe, 2001.

Qi Meiqin 祁美琴 and Zhao Yang 趙陽. "Guangyu Qingdai Zangshi ji zhu Zang dachen yanjiu de jidian kaolü 關於清代藏史及駐藏大臣研究的幾點思考." In *Bainian zhu Zang dachen yanjiu luncong* 百年駐藏大臣研究論叢, ed. Zeng Guoqing 曾國慶, 569–592. Beijing: Zhongguo Zangxue chubanshe, 2014.

Qi Yunshi 祁韵士. *Huangchao fanbu yaolüe* 皇朝藩部要略. Ha'erbin: Heilongjiang jiaoyu chubanshe, 1997 [1846].

Qinding Daqing huidian shili-lifanyuan 欽定大清會典事例, 理藩院. Annotated by Zhao Yuntian 赵云田. Beijing: Zhongguo Zangxue chubanshe, 2006 [1899].

Qinding Kuo'erke jilüe 欽定廓爾克紀略. Beijing: Zhongguo zangxue chubanshe, 2006.

Qinding Lifanbu Zeli 欽定理藩部則例. Tianjin: Tianjin guji chubanshe, 1998 [1908].

Qing Gaozong 清高宗 [Qianlong 乾隆]. *Yuzhi shiwen shiquanji* 御製詩文十全記. Beijing: Zhongguo Zangxue chubanshe, 1993.

Quexi 却西 and Cao Ziqiang 曹自強. "Jinping cheqian: yizun chuishi zhi tixian" 金瓶掣簽: 釋尊垂示之體現. In *Huofo ji zhuanshi zhidu yanjiu* 活佛及轉世制度研究, ed. Chen Qingying 陳慶英 and Ga Dawa Cairen 嘎達哇才仁, 350–358. Beijing: Zhongguo zangxue yanjiu zhongxin zongjiaosuo, 2006.

Ramble, Charles. "Rule by Play in Southern Mustang." In *Anthropology of Tibet and the Himalaya*, ed. Charles Ramble and M. Brauen, 287–301. Zürich: Völker- kundemuseum der Universität, 1993.

Rawski, Evelyn Sakakida. *The Last Emperors: A Social History of Qing Imperial Institutions.* Berkeley: University of California Press, 1998.

——. "Qing Publishing in Non-Han Languages." In *Printing and Book Culture in Late Imperial China*, ed. Cynthia J. Brokaw, Kai-Wing Chow, 304–331. Berkeley: University of California Press, 2005.

Rawski, Evelyn S., and Jessica Rawson, eds. *China: The Three Emperors, 1662–1795.* London: Royal Academy of the Arts, 2005.

Relyea, Scott. "Yokes of Gold and Threads of Silk: Sino-Tibetan Competition for Authority in Early Twentieth-Century Kham." *Modern Asian Studies* 49, no. 4 (2015): 963–1009.

Rgyal dbang lnga pa chen po Nga dbang blo bzang rgya mtsho. *Rgyal dbang lnga pa'i rang rnam du kU la'i gos bzang* [Autobiography of the Fifth Dalai Lama]. Kawring, HP: Tobdan Tsering, 1979–1983 (TIBRC W23956).

Richardson, Hugh. *Ch'ing Dynasty Inscriptions at Lhasa.* Serie Orientale Roma 37. Rome: Instituto Italiano Per Il Medio ed Estremo Oriente, 1974.

Rockhill, William Woodville. "The Dalai Lamas of Lhasa and Their Relations with the Manchu Emperors of China: 1644–1908." *T'oung Pao* XI (1910): 1–104.

——. *The Land of the Lamas: Notes of a Journey Through China, Mongolia, and Tibet.* New York: The Century Company, 1891.

——. *Notes on the Ethnography of Tibet.* Washington, DC: Government Printing Office, 1895.

Rose, Leo E. *Nepal: Strategy for Survival.* Berkeley: University of California Press, 1971.

Ruegg, D. Seyfort."mchod yon, yon chod and mchod gnas/yon gnas: On the Historiography and Semantics of a Tibetan Religio-Social and Religio-Political Concept." In *Tibetan History and Language: Studies Dedicated to Géza Uray on his Seventieth Birthday*, ed. Ernst Steinkellner, 441–454. Wien, Austria: Arbeitskreis fur Tibetische und Buddhistische Studien, Universitat Wien, 1991.

——. *Ordre Spirituel et Ordre Temporel Dan la Pensée Bouddhique de l'Inde et du Tibet: Quatre Conférences au College de France.* Paris: Collège de France, 1995.

——. "The Preceptor-Donor Relation in Thirteenth-Century Tibetan Society and Polity." In *The Tibetan History Reader*, ed. Gray Tuttle and Kurtis Schaeffer, 211–232. New York: Columbia University Press, 2013.

Sangs rgyas rin chen. "Laa mo bde chen dgon pa'i sku phyag gser khri rin po che'i sku phreng rim byon gyi lo rgyus mdo bsdus ngo sprod." *Mdo smad zhib 'jug* I (1999): 108–118.

Schaeffer, Kurtis R. "The Fifth Dalai Lama Ngawang Lopsang Gyatso, 1617–1682." In *The Dalai Lamas: A Visual History*, ed. Martin Brauen, 65–91. Chicago: Serindia, 2005.

——. "New Scholarship in Tibet, 1650–1700." In *Forms of Knowledge in Early Modern Asia*, ed. Sheldon Pollock, 291–310. Durham: Duke University Press, 2011.

——. "Ritual, Festival and Authority Under the Fifth Dalai Lama." In *Power, Politics, and the Reinvention of Tradition; Proceedings of the Tenth Seminar of the International Association for Tibetan Studies, Königswinter*, ed. Bryan J. Cuevas and Kurtis R. Schaeffer, 187–202. Leiden: Brill, 2006.

Schaeffer, Kurtis R., Matthew T. Kapstein, and Gray Tuttle, eds. *Sources of Tibetan Tradition*. New York: Columbia University Press, 2013.

Schwieger, Peter. *The Dalai Lama and the Emperor of China: A Political History of the Tibetan Institution of Reincarnation*. New York: Columbia University Press, 2015.

Shakabpa, Tsepon Wangchuk Deden. *Bod kyi srid don rgyal rabs* (2 volumes). Kalimpong: T. Tsepal Taikhang, 1976.

———. *One Hundred Thousand Moons: An Advanced Political History of Tibet*. Trans. and annotated by Derek F. Maher. Boston: Brill, 2010.

———. *Tibet: A Political History*. New Haven and London: Yale University Press, 1967.

Shneiderman, Sara. "Barbarians at the Border and Civilizing Projects: Analyzing Ethnic and National Identities in the Tibetan Context." In *Tibetan Borderlands*, ed. Christiaan Klieger, 9–34. Leiden: Brill, 2006.

Skal bzang legs bshad. *Rje bstun byams pa mthu stobs kun dga' rgyal mtshan gyi rnam thar*. Beijing: Zhongguo Zangxue, 1994 [c. 1895–1900].

Smith, Richard J. *Mapping China and Managing the World: Culture, Cartography, and Cosmology in Late Imperial Times*. London: Routledge, 2013.

Sonam Dorje. "Konchok Sengge." *Treasury of Lives*. Accessed March 22, 2013. http://www.treasuryoflives.org/biographies/view/Konchok-Sengge/3769.

———. "The Third Jamyang Zhepa, Tubten Jigme Gyatso," *Treasury of Lives*. Accessed July 21, 2017. http://www.treasuryoflives.org/biographies/view/Third-Jamyang-Zhepa-Tubten-Jigme-Gyatso/2506.

Song Tingsheng, ed. *Nayancheng Qinghai zouyi* [Nayancheng's memorials from Qinghai]. Xining: Qinghai renmin chubanshe, 1997.

Sørensen, Per K. "The Dalai Lama Institution: Its Origin and Genealogical Succession." *Orientations* (September 2005): 53–60.

———. "The Sacred Junipers of Reting: The Arboreal Origins Behind the Dalai Lama Lineage." *Orientations* (September 2008): 74–84.

Sperling, Elliot. "Awe and Submission: A Tibetan Aristocrat at the Court of Qianlong," *The International History Review* 20, no. 2 (June 1998): 325–335.

———. "The Chinese Venture in K'am, 1904–1911." In *The History of Tibet, Vol. 3*, ed. Alex McKay, 69–91. New York: RoutledgeCurzon, 2003.

———. "Pho-lha-nas, Khang-chen-nas, and the Last Era of Mongol Domination in Tibet." *Rocznik Orientalistyczny* 35 (2012): 195–211.

———. *The Tibet-China Conflict: History and Polemics; Policy Studies Number 7*. Washington: East-West Center, 2004.

Sullivan, Brenton. "Monastic Customaries and the Promotion of Dge Lugs Scholasticism in A Mdo and Beyond." *Asian Highlands Perspectives* 36 (2015): 84–105.

———. "The Mother of All Monasteries." PhD diss., University of Virginia, 2013.

Sum pa mkhan po ye shes dpal 'byor. *Chos 'byung dpag bsam ljon bzang*. Lanzhou: Kan su'u mi rigs dpe skrun khang, 1992 [1748].

———. *Mtsho sngon lo rgyus tshangs glu gsar snyan zhes bya ba bzhugs so*. Xining: Mtsho sngon mi rigs dpe sgrun khang, 1982 [1786].

———. *Sum pa ye shes dpal 'byor gyi rang rnam*. Lanzhou: Gansu minzu chubanshe, 1997.

Sun Zhenping 孫鎮平. *Qingdai Xizang fazhi yanjiu* 清代西藏法制研究. Beijing: Zhishi chanquan chubanshe, 2004.

Sutton, Donald S. "Ethnicity and the Miao Frontier in the Eighteenth Century." In *Empire
at the Margins: Culture, Ethnicity, and Frontier in Early Modern China*, ed. Pamela Kyle
Crossley, Helen F. Siu, and Donald Sutton, 190–228. Berkeley: University of California Press, 2006.

——. "From Credulity to Scorn: Confucians Confront the Spirit Mediums in Late Imperial China." *Late Imperial China* 21, no. 2 (December 2000): 1–39.

Teng, Emma Jinhua. *Taiwan's Imagined Geography: Chinese Colonial Travel Writing and
Pictures, 1683–1895*. Cambridge, MA: Harvard University Asia Center, 2004.

Th'u bkwan 03 Blo bzang chos kyi nyi ma. *Ljang skya rol pa'i rdo rje'i rnam thar*. Lanzhou:
Kan su'u mi rigs dpe skrun khang, 1989 [1798].

Travers, Alice. "The Tibetan Army of the Ganden Phodrang." In *Secular Law and Order in
the Tibetan Highland*, ed. Dieter Schuh, 249–266. Andiast: Monumenta Tibetica Historica, Abteilung III, Band 13, 2015.

Tsomu, Yudru. *The Rise of Gönpo Namgyel in Kham: The Blind Warrior of Nyarong*. Lanham,
MD: Lexington Books, 2015.

Tsyrempilov, Nikolay. "Dge Lugs Pa Divided: Some Aspects of the Political Role of Tibetan
Buddhism in the Expansion of the Qing Dynasty." In *Power, Politics, and the Reinvention
of Tradition: Tibet in the Seventeenth and Eighteenth Centuries: PIATS 2003: Tibetan Studies:
Proceedings of the Tenth Seminar of the International Association for Tibetan Studies*, Oxford,
2003, ed. Bryan J. Cuevas and Kurtis R. Schaeffer, 47–64. Leiden; Boston: Brill, 2006.

Tucci, Guiseppe. *Tibetan Painted Scrolls*. Bangkok: SDI Publications, 1999 [reprint of Rome:
La Libreria Dello Stato, 1949].

Tuttle, Gray. "Challenging Central Tibet's Dominance of History: The *Oceanic Book*, a
19th Century Politico-Religious Geographic History." In *Mapping the Modern in Tibet;
Proceedings of the Eleventh Seminar of the International Association for Tibetan Studies, Königswinter*, ed. Gray Tuttle, 135–172. Andiast, Switzerland: International Institute for
Tibetan and Buddhist Studies GmbH, 2011.

——. "The Role of Mongol Elite and Educational Degrees in the Advent of Reincarnation Lineages in Seventeenth-Century Amdo." In *The Tenth Karmapa and Tibet's Turbulent Seventeenth Century*, ed. Karl Debreczeny and Gray Tuttle, 235–262. Chicago:
Serindia, 2016.

——. "A Tibetan Buddhist Mission to the East: The Fifth Dalai Lama's Journey to Beijing,
1652–1653." In *Tibetan Society and Religion: The Seventeenth and Eighteenth Centuries*, ed.
Gray Tuttle, Bryan Cuevas, and Kurtis Schaeffer, 65–87. Leiden: Brill, 2006.

——. *Tibetan Buddhists in the Making of Modern China*. New York: Columbia University
Press, 2005.

Uspensky, Vladimir L. "Previous Incarnations of the Qianlong Emperor According to the
Panchen Lama Blo Bzang Dpal ldan Ye shes." In *Tibet, Past and Present, vol. 1*, ed. Henk
Blezer, Alex Mckay, and Charles Ramble, 215–228. Leiden: Brill, 2002.

——. *Prince Yunli: Manchu Statesman and Tibetan Buddhist*. Tokyo: Institute for the Study of
Languages and Cultures of Asia and Africa, 1997.

van der Kuijp, Leonard W. J. "The Dalai Lamas and the Origin of Reincarnate Lamas." In *The Dalai Lamas: A Visual History*, ed. Martin Brauen, 15–31. Chicago: Serindia, 2005.

Van Schaik, Sam. *Tibet: A History*. New Haven: Yale University Press, 2011.

Van Vleet, Stacey. "Medicine, Monasteries, and Empire: Tibetan Buddhism and the Politics of Learning in Qing China." PhD diss., Columbia University, 2015.

Vostrikov, A. I. *Tibetan Historical Literature*. Trans. Harish Chandra Gupta. Richmond, Surrey: Curzon Press, 1994.

Waddell, L. A. "Chinese Imperial Edict of 1808 A.D. on the Origin and Transmigration of the Grand Lamas of Tibet." *The Journal of the Royal Asiatic Society of Great Britain and Ireland* (January 1910): 69–86.

Wakeman, Jr., Frederic. *The Great Enterprise: The Manchu Reconsctruction of Imperial Order in Seventeenth-Century China*. 2 vols. Berkeley: University of California Press, 1985.

Waley-Cohen, Joanna. *The Culture of War in China: Empire and the Military Under the Qing Dynasty*. London: I. B. Tauris, 2006.

——. "Religion, War, and Empire-Building in Eighteenth-Century China." *The International History Review* 20, no. 2 (June 1998): 336–352.

Wang Jiapeng 王家鵬. "Qing gong cang youguan jinping cheqian de wuxi 清宮藏有關 '金瓶掣簽'文物析." In Chen Qingying 陳慶英 and Ga Dawa Cairen 嘎達哇才仁, *Huofo ji zhuanshi zhidu yanjiu* 活佛及轉世制度研究, 417–418. Beijing: Zhongguo zangxue yanjiu zhongxin zongjiaosuo, 2006.

Wang Xiangyun. "The Qing Court's Tibet Connections: Lcang skya Rol pai'I rdo rje and the Qianlong Emperor." *Harvard Journal of Asiatic Studies* 60, no. 1 (2000): 125–163.

Wang Xiuyu. *China's Last Imperial Frontier: Late Qing Expansion in Sichuan's Tibetan Borderlands*. Lanham, MD: Lexington Books, 2011.

Wang Yuping 王玉平. "Huofo zhuanshi de chansheng he jinping cheqian de zhiding" 活 佛轉世的產生和金瓶掣簽的制定. *Xizang yanjiu* 1 (1996): 29–33.

Wei Yuan 魏源. *Shengwu ji* 聖武記. Beijing: Zhonghua shuju, 1984 [1842].

Weizang tongzhi 衛藏通志. Lhasa: Xizang yanjiu bianjibu, 1982.

Wenfu 文孚. *Qinghai shiyi jielüe* 青海事宜節略. Xining: Qinghai shaoshu minzu guji congshu, 1993 [1810].

Will, Pierre Etienne. "Checking Abuses of Power Under the Ming Dynasty." In *China, Democracy, and Law*, ed. Mireille Delmas-Marty and Pierre-Étienne Will, trans. Naomi Norberg, 117–167. Leiden: Brill, 2011.

——. "Creation, Conflict, and Routinization: The Appointment of Officials by Drawing Lots, 1594–1700." Unpublished manuscript.

Williams, E. T. "Witchcraft in the Chinese Penal Code." *Journal of the North-China Branch of the Royal Asiatic Society* 38 (1907): 61–96.

Wu Fengpei 吳豐培, ed. *Lianyu zhu Zang zougao* 聯豫奏稿. Lhasa: Xizang renmin chubanshe, 1979.

——, ed. *Qingdai Zangshi zoudu* 清代藏事奏牘. Beijing: Zhongguo zangxue chubanshe, 1994.

——. "Qingdai zhuzang guanyuan de shezhi he zhiquan" 清代駐藏官員的設置和職權. In *Bainian zhu Zang dachen yanjiu luncong* 百年駐藏大臣研究論叢, ed. Zeng Guoqing 曾國慶, 105–107. Beijing: Zhongguo Zangxue chubanshe, 2014.

——, ed. *Qingji chou Zang zoudu* 清季籌藏奏牘. 3 vols. Changsha: Shangwu yinshuguan, 1938.

——. "Sheng-tai he You-tai" 升泰和有泰. In *Bainian zhu Zang dachen yanjiu luncong* 百年駐藏大臣研究論叢, ed. Zeng Guoqing, 280–301. Beijing: Zhongguo Zangxue chubanshe, 2014.

Wu Fengpei 吳豐培 and Zeng Guoqing 曾國慶. *Qingchao zhu zang dachen zhidu de jianli yu yange* 清朝駐藏大臣制度的建立與沿革. Beijing: Zhongguo zangxue chubanshe, 1989.

Wu Yuncen 吳雲岑. "Jinping cheqian de sheli ji qi yiyi" 金瓶掣簽的設立及其意義. *Xizang yanjiu* 1 (1996): 34–50.

Wylie, Turrell V. *The Geography of Tibet According to the 'dzam-gling-spyi-bshad.* Rome: Serie Orientale Roma XXV, 1962.

——. "Reincarnation: A Political Innovation in Tibetan Buddhism." In *Proceedings of the Csoma de Koros Memorial Symposium*, ed. Louis Ligeti, 581–586. Budapest: Akadémiai Kiadó, 1978.

Xiong Wenbin 熊文彬 and Zhang Chunyan 张春燕, eds. *Huofo zhuanshi: 2014 nian zang chuan fojiao huofo zhuanshi zhuanti zhan* 活佛轉世: 2014年藏傳佛教活佛 轉世專題展. Beijing: Zhongguo zangxue chubanshe, 2014.

Xizang zizhiqu dang'anguan 西藏自治區檔案館, ed. *Xizang lishi dang'an huicui* 西藏 歷史檔案 館薈萃. Beijing: Wenwu chubanshe, 1995.

Ya Hanzhang 牙含章. *Dalai lama zhuan* 達賴喇嘛傳. Beijing: Renmin chubanshe, 1984.

Yang Hongwei 楊紅偉. "Labulengsi yu qing zhengfu guangxi zonglun" 拉卜楞寺與清 政府 關係總論. *Jianghan Luntan* 4 (2012): 106–114.

Yu Hong 于洪 and Zhang Shuangzhi 張雙志. "Jinping cheqian yu shenpan wenhua" 金 瓶掣簽與神判文化. *Xizang yanjiu* 2 (2006): 43–49.

Yu Zhengxie 俞正燮. *Dachen yuanshi* 大臣原始. In *Yu Zhengxie quanji* 俞正燮全集, vol. 1, 379–414. Hefei: Huangshan shushe, 2005 [1807].

Zeng Guoqing 曾國慶. *Bainian zhu Zang dachen yanjiu luncong* 百年駐藏大臣研究論叢. Beijing: Zhongguo zangxue chubanshe, 2014.

——. "Lun Qingting zhi zang yu jinping cheqian" 論清廷治藏與金瓶掣 簽. *Zangxue yanjiu* 10 (March 2011): 1–8.

Zeng Guoqing 曾國慶 and Huang Weizhong 黃維忠. *Qingdai zangzu lishi* 清代藏族歷 史. Beijing: Zhongguo Zangxue chubanshe, 2012.

Zha Zha 扎扎. *Fojiao wenhua shengdi: Labuleng si* 佛教文化聖地: 拉卜楞寺. Lanzhou: Gansu minzu chubanshe, 2010.

——. *Labuleng si huofo shixi* 拉卜楞寺活佛世系. Lanzhou: Gansu renmin chubanshe, 2000.

Zhang Fan. "Grass-root Official on the Ideological Battlefield: Reevaluation of the Study of the Amban in Tibet." In *Political Strategies of Identity Building in Non-Han Empires in China*, ed. Francesca Fiaschetti and Julia Schneider, 225–253. Wiesbaden: Harrassowitz Verlag, 2014.

Zhang Husheng 張虎生. "Quanren xu chudou bei hanwen beiwen jiaozhu" 勸人恤出痘 碑漢文碑文校注. *Zhongguo zangxue* 2 (2006): 180–187.

Zhang Yisun 張怡蓀. *Bod rgya tshig mdzod chen mo.* Beijing: Minzu chubanshe, 1993.

Zhang Yun 張雲. "Helin zhu Zang: Qingchao zhu Zang dachen de yige dianxingxing fenxi 和琳駐藏一清朝駐藏大臣的一個典型性分析," 和琳駐藏: 清朝駐藏大臣 的一個典型性分析. In

Bainian zhu Zang dachen yanjiu luncong 百年駐藏大臣 研究論叢, ed. Zeng Guoqing曾國慶, 480–506. Beijing: Zhongguo Zangxue chubanshe, 2014.

Zhang Yuxin 張羽新. "*Weizang tongzhi de zhuozhe shi Hening*" 衛藏通志的作者是和 寧. *Xizang yanjiu* 4 (1985): 99–107.

——. *Qing zhengfu yu lama jiao: fu Qingdai lama jiao beikelu* 清政府與喇嘛教: 附清代喇嘛教碑 刻錄. Lhasa: Xizang renmin chubanshe, 1988.

——. *Qingchao zhi Zang dianzhang yanjiu* 清朝治藏典章研究. Beijing: Zhongguo Zangxue chubanshe, 2002.

Zhao Yuntian 趙雲田, annotator. *Qianlong chao neifu chaoben Lifanyuan zeli* 乾隆朝内 府抄本 理藩院則例. Beijing: Zhongguo Zangxue chubanshe, 2006.

Zhong-fang 钟方 and Wu Fengpei 吳豐培, eds. *Fanseng yuanliu kao* 番僧源流考. Lhasa: Xizang renmin chubanshe, 1982 [1843].

Zhongguo diyi lishi dang'anguan 中國第一歷史檔案館 and Yonghegong guanlichu 雍和宮 管理處, eds. *Qingdai Yonghegong dang'an shiliao* 清代雍和宮檔案史料. Beijing: Zhongguo minzu shying yishu chubanshe, 2011.

Zhongguo diyi lishi dang'anguan 中國第一歷史檔案館, Yonghegong guanlichu 雍和宮 管理 處, and Zhongguo Zangxue yanjiu zhongxin 中國藏學研究中心, eds. *Zhongguo diyi lishi dang'anguan suocun Xizang he Zangshi dang'an mulu, Hanwen bufen* 中國 第一歷史檔案館所 存西藏和藏事檔案目錄漢文部分. Beijing: Zhongguo Zangxue chubanshe, 2000.

Zhongguo diyi lishi dang'anguan 中國第一歷史檔案館 and Zhongguo Zangxue yanjiu zhongxin, eds. *Zhongguo diyi lishi dang'anguan suocun Xizang he Zangshi dang'an mulu, Man Zangwen bufen* 中國第一歷史檔 案館所存西藏和藏事檔案目錄滿藏文部分. Beijing: Zhong-guo Zangxue chubanshe, 1999.

Zhongguo Zangxue yanjiu zhongxin 中國藏學研究中心, Zhongguo diyilishi dang'anguan 中國第一歷史檔案館, Zhongguo di'er lishi dang'anguan 中國第二 歷史檔案館, Xizang zizhiqu dang'an guan 西藏自治區檔案館, and Sichuan sheng dang'anguan 四川省檔案館, eds. *Yuan yilai Xizang difang yu zhongyang zhengfu guanxi dang'an shiliao huibian* 元以來西 藏地方與中央政府關係檔案 史料匯編. Beijing: Zhongguo Zangxue chubanshe, 1995.

Zhongguo zhenxi falü dianji jicheng bingbian di'er ce 中国珍稀法律典籍集成, 丙编, 弟 二册. Beijing: Kexue chubanshe, 1994.

Zhou Ta 洲塔 ('Brug Thar), ed. *Labulengsi gaoseng zhuanlüe* 拉卜楞寺高僧傳略. Lanzhou: Gansu minzu chubanshe, 2010.

——. *Lun Labulengsi de chuangjian ji qi liu da xueyuan de xingcheng* 論拉卜楞寺的創建及其六大 學院的形成. Lanzhou: Gansu minzu chubanshe, 1998.

——. *Mdo smad byang shar gyi bod kyi 'tsho bas hog pa'i lo rgyus dang rig gnas bcas par dpyad pa*. Beijing: Minzu chubanshe, 2002.

Zhou Ta 洲塔 ('Brug Thar) and Qiaogao Cairang 喬高才讓. *Gansu zangzu tongshi* 甘肅藏族 通史. Beijing: Minzu chubanshe, 2009.

Index

Page numbers in *italics* refer to illustrations.

Agūi, 45, *85*; and *amban* system, 47; and Golden Urn origins, 60, 83–84, 228; and Gurkha war, 56; and Islam, 76; and Tibetan responses to Golden Urn, 54

Altan Khan (Tümed ruler), 31, 34, 35, 213, 254*n*75

ambans, 45–48; formal appointments of, 46–47, 257*n*122; and Ganden Podrang, 47, 258*n*127; Golden Urn role, 105, 269*n*34; and Gurkha war, 47, 56, 60; and information management, xii–xiii, 245*n*3; installation of, 13, 39, 45–46; and Pakpalha *kūtuktu* reincarnation search, 143, 144; and prostration, 53–54, 69–70; and Qing sovereignty imposition, 47, 55. *See also specific people*

anti-oracle campaign, 94; and Beijing *kūtuktus,* 103–105, 112, 269*n*28; chronological context, 228, 229; and criticisms of Dalai Lama VIII, 127; and Erdeni Pandita *kūtuktu* reincarnation search, 100, 101, 104, 117, 118, 121–126, 127, 228, 272*nn*100, 102, 106–107, 273*n*119; and faith, 101–102, 107, 268*nn*20–21; focus on Lamo Chökyong oracle, 50; formal edict (May 1793), 104, 229, 269*n*32; Fuk'anggan's investigation, 106–113, 117–118, 228, 270*nn*42, 45, 271*nn*61, 63, 276*n*167; and Golden Urn policy communications, 104, 135–136; Heliyen's investigation, 118–120, 121–125, 136, 228, 271*n*86; and legal order, 73; and Nechung oracle case, 155; overview, 101; and Pakpalha *kūtuktu* reincarnation search, 145–146; Qianlong emperor's instructions, 105–106, 269*n*39; and shamanism, 109, 113, 120, 135, 136, 270–271*nn*45, 53–54, 60, 276*n*162;

[313]

anti-oracle campaign (*continued*)
and Tibetan Buddhism
transformation goal, 136, 276n160;
and Tibetan elites, 104, 269n31
Atiśa, 26
A-Zha, *3*

Bahadur Shah, 10, 52
Bajung (*amban*), 10, 47, 55, 59, 262n44
Bartlett, Beatrice, xii
Beijing *kūtuktus*: and anti-oracle
campaign, 103–105, 112, 269n28; and
Golden Urn origins, 60, 83, 85–87,
266n94; and Golden Urn policy
communications, 18–19, 93; and
Jamyang Zhepa *kūtuktu* reincarnation
search, 161, 164, 194; and Kangxi
emperor, 48, 161, 258n128; origins
of, 48; Qianlong reign legal
framework, 161–162; scholarship on,
162–163, 280n22. *See also specific
people*
Belmang Pandita II Könchok Gyeltsen,
52; and *ambans*, 182, 284n103;
and Dalai Lama VIII, 187;
disillusionment with Qing state,
211–216, 291–292n47; and dough
ball divination, 190; and Golden Urn
policy communications, 175; and
Golden Urn request, 171–172; on
Qing colonial rule in Tibet, 213–214,
292n58; response to Jamyang Zhepa
kūtuktu identification, 157–158, 159,
170, 279n3, 282n48; and ritual
scheduling, 181–183; and search
party, 169; and secret preparations,
183, 185–186. *See also Life of the
Second Belmang Pandita*
Benton, Lauren, 42
Berger, Patricia, 246n6, 280n22
Bhahba, Homi, 109

Biography of the Eighth Dalai Lama.
See Demo *kūtuktu* VIII Ngawang
Tubten Jikmé Gyatso
Bjerken, Zeff, 110, 111
Bodhipathapradīpa (A Lamp for the Path
to Enlightenment) (Atiśa), 26
Bomandorji, 165
Book of Rites, 8
Bootai (*amban*), 56, 64–65, 227,
263–264n56
British India, 21, 40, 109, 154
Brunnert, H. S., 249n38
Bufu (*amban*), 63
Bulag, Uradyn, 216
Bumi Rinpoché, 1–2
Buswell, Robert E., Jr., 102

Cagan Nomunhan *kūtuktu,* 166, 196,
273n116, 281n34, 286n6
candidate criteria: and Cagan
Nomunhan *kūtuktu,* 166, 196,
273n116, 286n6; and Erdeni Pandita
kūtuktu reincarnation search, 96, 98,
126; exceptions, 196, 229, 286n6; and
Jamyang Zhepa *kūtuktu* reincarnation
search, 166, 169, 196, 281nn35–36;
Mongol nobility, 62–63, 96, 125,
133, 166, 268n11, 276n156, 281nn35,
36; nineteenth century, 196, 201,
204, 286n6, 288n23; and Pakpalha
kūtuktu reincarnation search, 196; and
Tibetan nationalism, 209–210;
"Water-Ox Year Edict" on, 133, 135,
276nn156–157
Cao Ziqiang, 287n15
Cedendorji. *See* Tüsiyetü Khan
Cengde (*amban*), 47, 66, 263n45
Changkya *kūtuktu* III Rolpé Dorjé: and
Beijing *kūtuktu* system, 162–163;
Belmang Pandita II on, 215; and
Dalai Lama VII reincarnation search,

84; and Jamyang Zhepa *kūtuktu* reincarnation search, 180; Qianlong emperor's trust in, 62; and Qianlong's Buddhist practices, 246*n*6; reincarnation search, 63–64, 83, 227, 268*n*17

Changkya *kūtuktu* IV Ngawang Lozang Chöden, 48, 227, 228, 258*n*128

Chapel of Victory Over the Three Realms, 274*n*135

Chatterjee, Partha, 40

Chen Qingying, 218

Chen Xiaomin, 162

Chiang Kai-shek, 216–217

Chinese language, 18, 23, 251*n*47

Chinese nationalism: and Confucianism, 210, 291*n*43; Golden Urn as symbol of, 210, 224; and PRC Tibetologists, 15, 16, 210, 248*n*27, 291*n*43

Chinese Nationalist Party, 216–217

Chinggünjab, 62

Chingisids, 50

Chödrup Gyatso (Tenth Zhamarpa), 52, 56, 62

Choktu Taiji (Khalkha ruler), 32

chöyön relation, 33–34, 35, 36–37, 254*n*79

Chuzang *kūtuktu* (Ngawang Tubten Wangchuk), 63, 64, 162

Collection of Poetry and Prose on the Ten Complete Victories (Qianlong emperor), 7–8

colonialism: applicability to Qing state, 40–42, 43, 249*n*38, 256*n*105, 256*nn*105, 108, 257*n*118; and Confucianism, 41–42; and legal order, 154; and mimicry, 109; and separation vs. assimilation, 5, 42–43, 257*n*117; and Tibetan Buddhism transformation goal, 21, 43–44. *See also* Qing colonial rule in Tibet

commoner candidates. *See* candidate criteria

Confucianism: and Chinese Buddhist clergy, 75; and Chinese nationalism, 210, 291*n*43; and colonialism, 41–42; on fate, 265*n*85; and Golden Urn policy communications, 8; and Qing administrative categories, 17; and shamanism, 110

Court of Colonial Affairs: and Beijing *kūtuktus*, 161–162; and colonialism term, 249*n*38; and Erdeni Pandita *kūtuktu* reincarnation search, 96–97, 129; and Golden Urn policy communications, 19, 135, 197, 276*n*155; and minor lineages, 197

Crossely, Pamela, 41

Cultural Revolution, 218

Dalai Lama III Sönam Gyatso, 31, 34

Dalai Lama IV Yönten Gyatso, 31, 254*n*75

Dalai Lama V Ngawang Lozang Gyatso: and doubts about *trülku* institution, 61–62, 63; and dough ball divination, 78, 103, 265*n*81; and Geluk church establishment, 32–33, 34, 61–62; and Jamyang Zhepa *kūtuktu* reincarnation search, 174–175; and Mongol-Geluk church relations, 32, 212, 254*n*76; and Mongols, 212; and Qing-Geluk church alliance, 30, 34, 36–37; and Tibetan civil wars, 31, 32, 254*n*76; and *trülku* institution, 25, 29, 253*n*69

Dalai Lama VI Tsangyang Gyatso, 37, 48

Dalai Lama VII Kelzang Gyatso, 255*n*97; and *amban* system, 46; and Beijing *kūtuktus*, 48; and Qing-Geluk church alliance, 12, 38–39; reincarnation search, 63, 266*n*100

Dalai Lama VIII Jampel Gyatso: and
anti-oracle campaign, 103, 119,
120; character of, 49; and doubts
about *trülku* institution, 140, 200,
276–277*n*171; elite belief in
divination of, 97–98, 100; and Erdeni
Pandita *kūtuktu* reincarnation search,
96, 100, 121, 124, 125, 126, 129, 142,
272*nn*102, 107; and Golden Urn
ritual details, 141; and Gurkha war,
49, 55–56, 58–59, 227; and Heliyen,
142, 228, 263*n*49; and Jamyang
Zhepa *kūtuktu* reincarnation search,
169, 170, 187, 188; and Lhalu clan, 72;
and minor lineage searches, 114,
271*n*71; and Nechung oracle case,
155; and Pakpalha *kūtuktu*
reincarnation search, 150; political
roles of, 9; and prostration, 53–54,
57, 69, 227, 261*n*15, 263*n*53; Qing
criticisms of, 55, 69, 74, 84–85, 88,
89–90, 127, 134, 263*n*54; Qing
evaluation of, 59, 60, 69, 71, 141–142,
263–264*n*56; and regents, 48–49;
responses to Golden Urn, 116–117,
133, 138–141, 142, 277*n*178. *See also*
Ganden Podrang

Dalai Lama IX Lungtok Gyatso, 50, 201,
202, 203, 286*n*7, 288*n*22

Dalai Lama XIII Tupten Gyatso, 201,
207–208, 210–211, 216, 217, 288*n*21,
291*n*45

Dalai Lama XIV Tenzin Gyatso, 1,
219–220, 223; future reincarnation
of, 2, 221–222

Dalai Lamas: and anti-oracle campaign,
114, 115; and early Qing views of
Tibet, 251*n*48; and Golden Urn
origins, 7, 11, 86; Golden Urn role,
105, 114, 269*n*34, 271*n*71; political
role of, 9; and Qing-Geluk church

alliance, 12, 30, 34, 35, 36–37,
38–39, 55; and *trülku* institution, 25,
27. *See also* Geluk church; *specific
lamas*

Daoguang emperor, 201, 204

Das, Sarat Chandra, 17, 110–111

Dayan Khan, 50

Dbal mang II Dkon mchog rgyal
mtshan, 254*n*76

Dejū *trülku* VI (Jamyang Sherab Paldan),
221

Delek, 274*n*126

de Magalhães, Gabriel, 6–7

Demo *kūtuktu* VII, 208

Demo *kūtuktu* VIII Ngawang Tubten
Jikmé Gyatso: background of, 50;
and doubts about *trülku* institution,
200; on geographical conceptions of
Tibet, 289*n*32; on Gurkha war, 56,
207; and oracle investigations, 119;
on Pakpalha *kūtuktu* reincarnation
search, 150, 151–152, 153; on
prostration, 57, 58, 59; on Qianlong
emperor's Buddhist practices, 140; on
Qing-Geluk church alliance,
205–207; and Twenty-Nine reforms,
116–117

Demo lineage, 27. *See also specific people*

Deng Ruiling, 263*n*54

Dharma. *See chöyön* relation

Discourse on Lamas: and anti-oracle
campaign, 104; and doubts about
trülku institution, 11, 62, 90, 97;
historians' reliance on, 18; and legal
order, 11, 68, 92, 93; on minor
lineages, 197; and Mongols, 90–91,
97; and oracle inclusion, 104; purpose
of, 18; and Qing-Geluk church
alliance, 77, 90, 91; and Qing
sovereignty imposition, 15, 54, 55,
92; and regional variations, 114–115;

stelae, 8, 93, 229; on Tibetan
Buddhism transformation goal, 8;
timing of, 89, 96, 132, 228, 268n8,
275n141; translation, 239–243; and
Trashi Lhünpo investigation, 64, 68
Dobis Tsering Gyal, 254n78
Döndrup Dorjé, 124
Doring Tendzin Peljor, 71–72, 121
doubts about *trülku* institution, 153;
and Dalai Lama V, 61–62, 63; and
Dalai Lama VIII, 140, 200,
276–277n171; and dough ball
divination, 181; and faith, 74, 76,
87; and Golden Urn origins, 6, 7,
60, 73–75, 79, 83, 87, 90;
and Golden Urn policy
communications, 11, 62, 89–90, 97,
276–277n171; and oracles, 60, 64,
71–73; and Qianlong emperor, 7,
62–64, 127; and Qing-Geluk
church alliance, 62, 261n24; and
Tibetan responses to Golden Urn,
153, 199–200, 276–277n171; and
Tüsiyetü Khan, 62, 97, 268n11
dough ball divination, 77–79; and Dalai
Lama V, 78, 103, 265n81; difference
from Golden Urn, 78–79, 81; and
divine intervention, 131–132; and
doubts about *trülku* institution, 181;
and lottery as omen, 178–179;
mistrust of, 181; PRC-era use of, 218;
and Trashi Lhünpo sack, 66, 78. *See
also* dough ball divination in the
Jamyang Zhepa *kūtuktu* reincarnation
search
dough ball divination in the Jamyang
Zhepa *kūtuktu* reincarnation search:
and complexity of oracles, 138; and
faith, 189–190; Longdöl Lama on,
174, 179, 283n65; oracles on, 186; and
semantic assimilation, 175, 178–179,

181, 190, 283n69, 284n87; Tatsak
kūtuktu's tests, 188–190; Tukwan
kūtuktu on, 17, 175–176, 180–181
Drakgönpa Könchok Tenpa Rapgyé,
29, 138, 175, 282n55. *See also Life of
the Second Belmang Pandita*; *Oceanic
Book*
"Drawing Lots from the Golden Urn to
Locate the *Trülku*" (Hening), 82
Drungpa *kūtuktu* Lozang Jinpa (Trashi
Lhünpo treasurer), 65, 66, 67, 68, 71,
72
Dülagyel (father of Wangchen Bum),
159, 165, 166, 176–177, 281n35

Eldemboo (*amban*), 263n45
Elliott, Mark, xii, 41
Elman, Benjamin, 248n22
Elverskog, Johan, 21, 163, 164, 254n79
Erdeni Pandita I Lozang Tenzin
Gyeltsen, 50, 126
Erdeni Pandita II, 50, 126. *See also*
Erdeni Pandita *kūtuktu* reincarnation
search
Erdeni Pandita *kūtuktu* III Ciwangjab,
126, 129, 130, 131, 274n127. *See also*
Erdeni Pandita *kūtuktu* reincarnation
search
Erdeni Pandita *kūtuktu* reincarnation
search, 95–100, 267n2; and anti-
oracle campaign, 100, 101, 104, 117,
118, 121–126, 127, 228, 272nn100,
102, 106–107, 273n119; and candidate
criteria, 96, 98, 126; and Golden Urn
policy communications, 96–97,
125–127, 130–131, 134, 228, 229,
268nn8–9, 273n112; identification,
125, 228, 229; lineage background,
50–51; and local elites, 52; ritual
details, 125, 128–129,
273–274nn126–28

faith, 21; and anti-oracle campaign, 101–102, 107, 268nn20–21; and doubts about *trülku* institution, 74, 76, 87; and Golden Urn origins, 61, 76, 77; and Golden Urn policy communications, 127, 140; and Jamyang Zhepa *kütuktu* reincarnation search, 189–190; and Pakpalha *kütuktu* reincarnation search, 153; and Tibetan responses to Golden Urn, 153–154

Fandze, 23, 251–252nn48–52

fate, 80–82, 265n85

First Historical Archive (FHA), xiii

Ford, Lisa, 42

Fuk'anggan, 45, *58*; death of, 229; evaluation of Ganden Podrang government, 59–60, 61, 69, 74, 141–142; on fate, 80–81, 265n85; and Golden Urn origins, 79–81, 85–86, 88, 228, 265n85; Golden Urn policy communications, 79–81, 93, 116–117, 228, 265n85; and Gurkha war, 10, 58–59, 74, 227; and Islam, 76; and minor lineage searches, 113, 114–115; on oracle inclusion, 104, 105–106, 112–114, 116, 271n63; oracle investigation, 106–113, 117–118, 228, 270nn42, 45, 271nn61, 63, 276n167; and Pakpalha *kütuktu* reincarnation search, 144; and prostration, 57–59, 261n15; and Qing-Geluk church alliance, 206–207; and Twenty-Nine reforms, 11, 47, 100, 101, 115–116, 228

Galdan Siretu *kütuktu,* 48, 266n93, 280n26; and anti-oracle campaign, 103–105, 186, 269n28; arrival in Tibet of, 227; and doubts about *trülku* institution, 200; and Golden Urn origins, 85–87; and Golden Urn

policy communications, 93; identification of, 258–259n129; on oracle inclusion, 54, 86, 102–104, 105, 112, 116; and Qing-Geluk church alliance, 208; scholarship on, 163; and Tibetan responses to Golden Urn, 54

Galdan Siretu *kütuktu* (Lozang Tenpé Nyima). *See* Ganden Tripa 45 Lozang Tenpé Nyima

Galdan Tsering (Junghar ruler), 213

Ganden Podrang: and *ambans,* 47, 258n127; Belmang Pandita II on, 214; *drungkor* (lay officials), 72, 264n59; founding of, 12, 32, 33; jurisdiction of, 115, 204–205, 271n66, 289n27; and Lhalu clan, 72; and Mongols, 14; and oracles, 50, 100; Qing evaluation of, 59–60, 61, 69, 71, 141–142, 263–264nn56, 59–60; regencies, 48–49, 208; and *trülku* institution, 27. *See also* Dalai Lama VIII Jampel Gyatso; Geluk church; Qing sovereignty imposition; Twenty-Nine reforms

Ganden Tripa XLV Lozang Tenpé Nyima, 163, 280n26

Gelek Namk'a, 99, 268n17

Geluk church: accusations of corruption in, 6, 60, 61, 122, 127; early Qing era status, 30, 253n72; establishment of, 14, 27, 32–34, 61–62, 254nn76, 78; fear of schism in, 14–15, 60, 76, 265n76; importance of, 9; and information management, xii; and Junghar wars, 37–38; origins of, 15; political roles of, 9, 247n17; PRC relations with, 15–16; and Tibetan civil wars (18th century), 31–32, 254n76; and Tibetan identity, 22,

250*n*44; and Tibetan nationalism, 15–16. *See also* Beijing *kūtuktus*; Ganden Podrang; Mongol-Geluk church relations; Qing-Geluk church alliance

geographical terms, 246–248*nn*8, 21

Gilmartin, David, 250*n*42

Golden Urn lottery: blank lot test, 105; Dalai Lama XIV on, 221–222; difference from dough ball divination, 78–79, 81; importance to Qianlong emperor of, 100–101; and minor lineage searches, ix, x, 50–52, 113–117, 197; as omen, 150, 178–179, 282*n*55; PRC policy (2007), 220–221; PRC resurrection (1995), 1–2, *3*, 218–220. *See also* Pakpalha *kūtuktu* reincarnation search

Golden Urn origins: Agūi on, 83–84; and Beijing *kūtuktus,* 60, 83, 85–87, 266*n*94; and bureaucratic appointment lottery, 5–8, 79, 80–81; chronological context, 228; and criticisms of Dalai Lama VIII, 84–85, 88, 89–90; and doubts about *trülku* institution, 6, 7, 60, 73–75, 79, 83, 87, 90; and dough ball divination, 81; and faith, 61, 76, 77; and fate, 80–82, 265*n*85; and Gurkha war, 9, 60–61, 74–75, 76; and legal order, 87–88, 92–93; and Manchu-language sources, 19, 81; and Qianlong's mistrust of clergy and divination, 75–76; and Qing-Geluk church alliance, 77; urn manufacture, 7, 79, 228

Golden Urn policy communications: and anti-oracle campaign, 104, 135–136; and Beijing *kūtuktus,* 18–19, 93; and bureaucratic

appointment lottery, 7–8; chronological context, 228; and Court of Colonial Affairs, 19; and doubts about *trülku* institution, 11, 62, 89–90, 97, 276–277*n*171; and dough ball divination, 103; and Erdeni Pandita *kūtuktu* reincarnation search, 96–97, 125–127, 130–131, 134, 228, 229, 268*nn*8–9, 273*n*112; and faith, 127, 140; and fate, 80–81, 265*n*85; formal edict (Oct. 1792), 11, 18, 89–90, 93, 249*n*37; gradual nature of, 18, 195–196; and legal order, 11, 22, 68, 92, 93, 148–150, 276*n*159; and Mongols, 90–91, 275*n*145, 276*nn*155–156; and oracle inclusion, 7, 94, 104, 116, 141, 271*n*78; overview, 275*n*139; Republic of China, 217; and ritual details, 131–132, 273–274*n*126, 277*n*180; shifting vocabulary for, 266*n*94; "Water-Ox Year Edict," 132–136, 139, 275*nn*149, 152, 276*nn*155–156, 157. *See also Discourse on Lamas*

Golden Urn ritual details: *ambans'* role, 105, 269*n*34; Dalai Lama VIII on, 141; Dalai Lama role, 105, 114, 269*n*34, 271*n*71; and divine intervention, 131–132; Erdeni Pandita *kūtuktu* reincarnation search, 125, 128–129, 273–274*nn*126–28; Jamyang Zhepa *kūtuktu* reincarnation search, 187–188, 285*nn*120–121; and minor lineage searches, 113–114; ongoing changes in, 89, 196, 286*n*5; Pakpalha *kūtuktu* reincarnation search, 150–153, 278*n*212; and policy communications, 128–129, 131–132, 273–274*n*126, 277*n*180

Imperially Sanctioned Twenty-Nine Articles of Reconstruction. See Twenty-Nine reforms

incarnate lamas. See Geluk church; trülku institution

incarnation lineages. See trülku institution

information management: and ambans, xii–xiii, 245n3; and Jamyang Zhepa kūtuktu reincarnation search, 191–192; and Qing colonial rule in Tibet, xii–xiii, 44–45, 47–48, 69, 263n46; Qing state internal, xii, 44–45, 245n3

Ishihama Yumiko, 36, 250n44

Islam, 76, 265n76

Jamyang Zhepa kūtuktu I, 78, 175; reincarnation search, 160, 200

Jamyang Zhepa kūtuktu II, 175

Jamyang Zhepa kūtuktu III Lozang Tupten Jikmé Gyatso, 157, 158, 192, 229, 278n1. See also Jamyang Zhepa kūtuktu reincarnation search

Jamyang Zhepa kūtuktu IV Lozang Jigmé Tubten Chökyi Nyima, 218, 224

Jamyang Zhepa kūtuktu reincarnation search, 155–156; and Beijing kūtuktus, 161, 164, 194; and candidate criteria, 166, 169, 196, 281nn35–36; chronological context, 229; and faith, 189–190; final identification, 157, 169–170, 229, 278n1; Golden Urn request, 165, 171–172; identification of Wangchen Bum (son of Dülagyel), 166–167, 176–177, 183, 190, 192–193, 285n109; and information management, 191–192; Labrang community alternate plans, 173–175, 176–177,

282n58, 283nn63–66; lineage background, 50, 51, 51, 52, 192, 259–260nn143–144; and Longdöl Lama, 174, 175, 176, 178, 179, 182, 187, 283n63; and Lozang Dargyé, 165, 166–167, 169, 281n32, 284n90; Manchu-language sources on, 158, 165–170, 190–191; nineteenth-century Tibetan-language sources on, 158, 159–160, 170–173, 175–181, 186–189, 190–191, 283n81, 285n117; and oracles, 138, 186–187, 193, 285nn116–117; and Qing-Geluk church alliance, 163–164, 171–172; ritual details, 187–188, 285nn120–121; ritual location, 185–186, 285n113; ritual manipulation, 158–159, 167–170, 194, 229, 279n6, 282nn39, 41; ritual scheduling, 181–183, 284nn99, 103; secret preparations, 183, 185–186, 285n113; Sixteen Spheres sadhana, 174, 179, 187; sources for, 159–161; and Tibetan courtesy theory, 158; and Tibetan opposition theory, 164, 181, 284n98; Tibetan responses, 157–158, 159, 160–161, 170, 175–176, 193, 279n3, 282n48; and Tukwan kūtuktu's dream, 175–178, 283n81, 284nn93, 95. See also dough ball divination in the Jamyang Zhepa kūtuktu reincarnation search

Jamyang Zhepa lineage nineteenth-century reincarnation searches, 286n6

Jebtsundamba lineage, 9, 25, 62, 72, 97, 204, 268n11

Jiaqing emperor, 44, 45, 160, 213, 291n47

Jinchuan campaigns, 11, 261nn8, 24, 264n71

Jokhang Temple: Golden Urn installation in, 113–114, 132; and Jamyang Zhepa *kūtuktu* reincarnation search, 185; oracle investigation in, 111, 119; as site of Golden Urn resurrection (1995), 1; stelae, 91–92, 93, 229

Junghar wars, 14, 15, 37–39, 161, 213, 214

justice, 250*n*42

Kadampa order, 26, 62

Kangxi emperor: and Beijing *kūtuktus*, 48, 161, 258*n*128; and Ganden Podrang jurisdiction, 289*n*27; and Qing colonial rule in Tibet, 39; and Qing-Geluk church alliance, 36–37, 38; and Qing views of Tibet, 251*n*47

Kapstein, Matthew, 248*n*31, 280*n*27

Karma Kagyü order, 25, 26–27, 31, 32, 35, 252*n*56

Karmapa II Karma Pakshi, 252*n*56

Karmapa III Rangjung Dorje, 25

Karmapa IV, 25

Karma Püntsok Namgyel (Tsang ruler), 31

Karma Tenkyong (Tsang ruler), 31–32

Kelzang Bum, 157, 158–159, 165, 278*n*1. *See also* Jamyang Zhepa *kūtuktu* III Lozang Tupten Jikmé Gyatso

Khalkha Mongols, 30, 32, 37, 267–268*n*6; Jebtsundamba lineage, 9, 25, 62, 97, 204, 268*n*11. *See also* Erdeni Pandita *kūtuktu* reincarnation search

Khenpo Ngawang Tupten Gyatso. *See Life of the Third Jamyang Zhepa*

Kim Hanung, 69

Kökenuur Mongols: Belmang Pandita II on, 215–216, 292*n*58; Cagan Nomunhan *kūtuktu* reincarnation search, 166, 196, 273*n*116, 281*n*34, 286*n*6; and Ganden Podrang jurisdiction, 205; and Qing colonial

rule in Tibet, 39; and Sumpa *kūtuktu* reincarnation search, 115

Kolsky, Elizabeth, 42, 154

Könchok Senggé, 168–169, 170, 174, 187

Kuhn, Philip, xii, 75

Kūišu, 99, 128, 130, 131

Kündeling monastery, 49, 208, 290*n*38

Künga Gyeltsen, 287*n*14, 288*n*25

kūtuktu status, 24, 72, 197. *See also trülku* institution; *specific people*

Labrang Monastery Gazetteer, 159, 170, 171, 282*n*53

Labrang Trashi Khyil monastery, 51, *51, 192*; and Beijing *kūtuktus,* 163; Golden Throne holders, 175, 283*n*71; size of, 259–260*nn*143–44. *See also* Jamyang Zhepa *kūtuktu* reincarnation search

labrang (trülku estates), 27–28, 29

The Ladder for Guiding the Youth, 211–216, 291–292*n*47

Lamo Chökyong oracle: anti-oracle campaign focus on, 50; and Changkya *kūtuktu* reincarnation search, 64; and doubts about *trülku* institution, 72, 73–74; and Erdeni Pandita *kūtuktu* reincarnation search, 95–96, 100, 121, 125, 134, 228; and Fourth Changkya *kūtuktu,* 227; nineteenth-century use, 286*n*7; Qianlong emperor's earlier respect for, 64; Qing campaign against, 94, 118, 228, 271*n*86; responses to Golden Urn, 137–139. *See also* anti-oracle campaign

law. *See* legal order

"Law on the Method of the Reincarnation of Lamas" (Republic of China), 217 legal order: and anti-oracle campaign, 73; Belmang Pandita II on, 214–215; and Golden Urn origins, 87–88, 92–93; and Golden Urn policy communications, 11, 22, 68, 92, 93, 148–150, 276*n*159; and Han interior, 250*n*42; and Manchu-language sources, 250*n*44; and Mongol-Geluk church relations, 212–213; and nineteenth-century Golden Urn, 201, 204; and oracles, 139; and PRC policies, 222; and Qing sovereignty imposition, 22, 88, 92, 136, 154–155, 201, 276*n*159; and Tibetan Buddhist doctrines, 250*n*44; and Tibetan responses to Golden Urn, 148–150, 154, 278*nn*205, 207; and Trashi Lhünpo investigation, 67–68

Lhalu clan, 72

Lhazang Khan, 37

Li Fengzhen, 250*n*46

Life of the Second Belmang Pandita, 159, 170, 171–172, 178, 179–180, 182, 187, 188, 284*n*90, 285*n*117

Life of the Second Jamyang Zhepa, 48, 159, 160, 161, 170–171, 177–178, 179, 188, 189, 283*n*65, 289*n*32

Life of the Third Jamyang Zhepa, 158, 159, 170, 172–174, 175–176, 186, 187, 188, 193, 282*nn*56, 58, 283*n*81, 284*n*90

Ligdan Khan (Chahar ruler), 31, 32

Liobooju, 274*n*126

Longdöl Lama, 174, 175, 176, 178, 179, 182, 187, 283*n*63

Lopez, Donald S., Jr., 102, 247*n*17

Lo Sempa *trülku* VIII, 71–72

Lozang Dargyé, 165, 166–167, 169, 281*n*32, 284*n*90

Lozang Tenpé (Trashi Lhünpo *jedrung lama*), 64, 66, 67, 75, 78, 262*nn*31, 39

Lubsang-Danzin, 38, 39

Luo Gan, 2

Mahāyāna Buddhism, 25–26

Manchu-language sources, ix; and anti-oracle campaign, 101; on faith, 101–102, 268*nn*20–21; formal edict on Golden Urn, 18, 89–90, 93, 249*n*37; and Golden Urn-dough ball divination differences, 81; and Golden Urn origins, 19, 81; Golden Urn policy communications, 89; on Jamyang Zhepa *kūtuktu* reincarnation search, 158, 165–170, 190–191; lack of attention to, xiv, 18; and legal order, 250*n*44; and Mongols, 22–23; and oracle investigations, 118, 270*n*45; and shamanism, 111; on Tibetan Buddhist doctrines, 22, 250*n*44; and "Water-Ox Year Edict," 275*n*149

Mao Zedong, 216–217

"Method for Managing the Reincarnation of Living Buddhas of Tibetan Buddhism" (State Bureau of Religious Affairs), 220–221

Ming state, 6, 30, 35

Mongol-Geluk church relations: and *chöyön* relation, 33–34, 254*n*79; and Dalai Lama V, 32, 212, 254*n*76; and Geluk church establishment, 14, 32–33, 254*nn*76, 78; history of, 13; nineteenth century, 212–213, 248*n*24; and Tibetan civil wars, 31, 32

Mongols: and anti-oracle campaign, 228; and geographical terms, 247*n*8; and Golden Urn policy communications, 90–91, 275*n*145, 276*nn*155–156; Jebtsundamba lineage, 9, 25, 62, 97, 204, 268*n*11; and *kūtuktu* status, 24; lack of threat from, 77; and minor lineage searches,

Orientalist scholarship, 110–111
ornamentalism, 257n117
Osterhammel, Jürgen, 40, 43, 257n118

Pakpa Lama, 33–34
Pakpalha *Kūtuktu* VII Jigme Tenpai
  Gonpo, 145, 277n193. *See also*
  Pakpalha *kūtuktu* reincarnation
  search
Pakpalha *kūtuktu* reincarnation search,
  143–148; and anti-oracle campaign,
  145–146; and candidate criteria, 196;
  chronological context, 229; lineage
  background, 27, 50, 51, 52; ritual
  details, 150–153, 278n212; and
  Sungyun, 146–148, 153, 229,
  278n203; and Zhiwala *kūtuktu* IV,
  52, 148, 278n203
Panchen Lama VI, 52, 63, 72, 84,
  263n52
Panchen Lama VII, 59, 64–65, 72, 103,
  183
Panchen Lama IX, 217
Panchen Lama X, 217, 218–219
Panchen Lama XI Gyaincain Norbu,
  1–2, 218–220, 223, 293n80
Panchen Lamas: and anti-oracle
  campaign, 114; and Golden Urn
  origins, 7, 86; Golden Urn role, 105;
  and Gurkha war, 52, 64–65; political
  roles of, 9; and *trülku* institution, 25,
  27. *See also specific lamas*
People's Republic of China (PRC),
  217–225; archive policies, xiii–xiv,
  245n5; and Fifth Jamyang Zhepa
  kūtuktu reincarnation search, 218;
  and Geluk church, 15–16; Golden
  Urn law (2007), 220–221; Golden
  Urn resurrection (1995), 1–2, *3*,
  218–220; Han population, 223,
  293–294nn80–81; and legal order,

222; Maoist revolution, 15; and
  minority peoples, 4, 16, 216–217,
  224–225, 248n27; *trülku* institution
  policies, 217–218, 220–221, 223. *See
  also* PRC Tibetologists
Perdue, Peter, 41, 62
Petech, Luciano, 4, 38–39, 208, 257n122
Polhané, 38
PRC Tibetologists, 2, 4; and Chinese
  language, 18; and Chinese
  nationalism, 15, 16, 210, 248n27,
  291n43; and Jamyang Zhepa *kūtuktu*
  reincarnation search, 160; on number
  of lineages, 287n13; and PRC archive
  policies, xiii; and Tibetan
  nationalism, 15–16
Prithvi Narayan Shah (Gurkha king), 52
prostration, 53–54, 57–58, 69–70,
  260n1, 261n15, 263nn52–53
Pu Wenchang, 259n130, 287n13

Qianlong emperor: abdication of, 44,
  229; and *amban* system, 46–47,
  257n122; and anti-oracle campaign,
  101, 105–106, 113, 117–118, 119,
  268n20, 269n39; and Beijing
  kūtuktus, 161–162; and Buddhist
  practices, 76, 134, 140, 246n6,
  275n152; and bureaucratic
  appointment lottery, 5–6, 7–8, 79;
  and Cagan Nomunhan *kūtuktu,*
  273n116; and Confucianism, 41;
  criticisms of Dalai Lama VIII, 89–90,
  127, 134, 263n54; death of, 164; and
  doubts about *trülku* institution, 7,
  62–64, 127; and early Qing views of
  Tibet, 251n49; and Erdeni Pandita
  kūtuktu reincarnation search, 97–100,
  122, 125, 228, 229, 272n107, 273n108;
  fear of Geluk schism, 14, 76; and
  Gurkha war, 55–56, 58–59, 74–75,

Qianlong emperor (*continued*)
91, 261*n*9; and Heliyen, 68–69,
263*n*45; importance of Golden Urn
to, 100–101; and information
management, xii, 44–45; and
Jamyang Zhepa *kūtuktu* reincarnation
search, 159, 160, 166–167, 169,
192–193; and Junghar wars, 38; and
legal order, 67–68, 87–88, 92–93,
148–149; mistrust of clergy and
divination, 75–76; and Mongols,
90–91; and Pakpalha *kūtuktu*
reincarnation search, 144–145, 148;
and prostration, 53–54, 57, 63,
69–70, 227; and Qing evaluation of
Ganden Podrang government, 60,
71; and Qing-Geluk church alliance,
14; on Qing sovereignty imposition,
91, 92; and regents, 12, 49; and ritual
details, 128–129, 131–132, 150,
273–274*n*126; Tibetan
disillusionment with, 213; and
Tibetan responses to Golden Urn,
143; and Trashi Lhünpo
investigation, 65–68; voice of,
44–45. *See also Discourse on Lamas*;
Golden Urn origins; Golden Urn
policy communications
Qing colonial rule in Tibet:
applicability of colonialism term to,
40–42, 43, 249*n*38, 256*nn*105, 108,
257*n*118; Belmang Pandita II on,
213–214, 292*n*58; and Court of
Colonial Affairs, 19, 249*n*38; Dalai
Lama XIII on, 207–208; early Qing
views, 22–24, 250*nn*44, 46, 251*n*47;
establishment of, 38–40, 45–46,
256*nn*103–104; evaluation of
Ganden Podrang government,
59–60, 61, 69, 71, 141–142,
263–264*nn*56, 59–60; and

information management, xii–xiii,
44–45, 47–48, 69, 263*n*46; and
Junghar wars, 37–38; and
ornamentalism, 257*n*117; and
prostration, 53–54, 57–58, 69–70,
260*n*1, 261*n*15, 263*n*53; stelae, 8,
91–92, 93, 267*n*118; tensions in, 5,
42–43, 257*n*117. *See also ambans*;
Qing sovereignty imposition;
Tibetan Buddhism transformation
goal; Twenty-Nine reforms
Qing-Geluk church alliance: and *chöyön*
relation, 35, 36–37; and Dalai Lama
V, 30, 34, 36–37; and Dalai Lama
VIII, 55; and doubts about *trülku*
institution, 62, 261*n*24; evidence of,
ix; and faith, 21; and fear of schism,
14–15, 60; and Golden Urn origins,
77; and Gurkha war, 56, 207,
261*nn*8–9; history of, 11–12, 13–14;
and Jamyang Zhepa *kūtuktu*
reincarnation search, 163–164,
171–172; and Jinchuan campaigns, 11,
261*nn*8, 24, 264*n*71; and Junghar
wars, 12, 38–39; and Mongols,
90–91; and Qing legitimization, 35;
and regents, 208, 290*n*38; sources
on, 255*n*94; and Tibetan nationalism,
208–209; and Tibetan responses to
Golden Urn, 149–150, 156, 205–207;
and Trashi Lhünpo investigation, 68;
and *trülku* institution, 24, 35; as
unifying project, 35. *See also* Beijing
kūtuktus
Qing History Project, xiii
Qing sovereignty imposition, 20–21,
54–55; and *ambans*, 47, 55; and fear
of Geluk schism, 15, 60, 76, 265*n*76;
and Golden Urn policy
communications, 15, 54, 55, 92,
134–135; and Gurkha war

(1791–1792), 54, 55; and Gurkha war, 54, 55; and legal order, 22, 88, 92, 136, 154–155, 201, 276n159; and minor lineage searches, 114; as new strategy, 91–92; nineteenth century, 201, 204, 288nn23, 26; PRC Tibetologists on, 16; and prostration, 53–54, 69–70; Wei Yuan on, 194

Qing state: administrative categories under, 16–17; appointment lottery, 6–8, 79, 80–81; censorship by, 192; civil examination system, 12, 248n22; collapse of, 210; cosmopolitanism, 163, 164, 193, 280n27; establishment of, 30, 36; and geographical terms, 246–248nn8, 21; information management, xii, 44–45, 245n3; and Islam, 76, 265n76; Jinchuan campaigns, 11, 261nn8, 24, 264n71; and Khalkha Mongols, 267–268n6; nineteenth-century priorities of, 204, 288n25; nineteenth-century Tibetan disillusionment with, 211–216, 291–292n47; and shamanism, 109–110. See also PRC Tibetologists

Qing views of Tibet, 22–24; ambiguity in, 23, 251–252nn48, 50–51; and Chinese language, 23, 251n47; and culture, 23, 250n46; geographical terms, 247–248n8, 21; and legal order, 250n44, 252n52; limited understanding, 121–122; and Mongol perspectives, 22–23; and nonbelligerence, 24, 252n53; and Tibetan Buddhism, 22, 24, 250n44, 251n48; and Tibetan nationalism, 209, 290–291n40–42. See also Tibetan identity

Qubilai Khan, 34, 258n128

Quexi, 287n15

Rawski, Evelyn S., 109

regencies, 29, 37, 39, 49, 55

reincarnation searches. See trülku institution; specific searches

Republic of China, 217

Rinchin Gyatso, 165

Rolpé Dorjé. See Changkya kütuktu III Rolpé Dorjé

Ruegg, David Seyfort, 33

Sachen Künga Nyingpo, 26

šajin, 250n44. See also suwayan šajin

Sakya order, 26, 33–34, 36, 258n128

Sanggyé Gyatso, 25, 37, 62, 265n81

Schwieger, Peter, 25, 36, 208, 254n76, 262n31

Shakabpa, Tsepon W. D., 17, 201

shamanism, 109–111; and anti-oracle campaign, 109, 113, 120, 135, 136, 270–271nn45, 53–54, 60, 276n162; Han interior, 109–110, 135, 136, 276n162; Mongols, 270n54

Sherab Kanjur, 168, 169, 282n41

Shérap Gyatso, 179

Shunzhi emperor, 30, 35, 36–37, 161

Siretu Kurun Jasak Lama, 259n129

Siretu kütuktu, 259n129

Sixteen Spheres sadhana, 174, 179, 187

Sönam Rapten, 34

sovereignty, 93

Sperling, Elliot, 121

spirit mediums, 110. See also shamanism

Sufi Muslims, 76

Sumpa kütuktu, 114–115

Sungyun (amban): arrival in Tibet of, 277nn194–195; and Erdeni Pandita kütuktu reincarnation search, 99, 273n119; and faith, 153; and Jamyang Zhepa kütuktu reincarnation search, 157–159, 160, 167–170, 182–183, 185–186, 229, 279nn3, 6, 282n48;

Sungyun (amban) (*continued*)
    and legal order, 148–150, 278*n*207;
    and lottery as omen, 150, 282*n*55;
    and Nechung oracle case, 155; and
    Pakpalha *kütuktu* reincarnation
    search, 146–148, 153, 229, 278*n*203;
    and prostration, 53; and ritual details,
    150–151, 152–153; and Twenty-Nine
    reforms, 48
Sutton, Donald, 110
suwayan šajin (Yellow Doctrines), 22,
    250*n*44

Tanggūt, 22–23, 250*n*46, 251*nn*48–52
Tatsak *kütuktu* VII, 49
Tatsak *kütuktu* VIII Lozang Tenpé
    Gönpo, *184;* appointment of, 55, 227;
    background of, 49; and doubts about
    trülku institution, 200; and Erdeni
    Pandita *kütuktu* reincarnation search,
    121; and Jamyang Zhepa *kütuktu*
    reincarnation search, 170, 183,
    188–189; and legal order, 149; and
    oracle investigations, 119; and
    Pakpalha *kütuktu* reincarnation search,
    150; and Qing-Geluk church alliance,
    208; recall proposals, 141; and Trashi
    Lhünpo investigation, 66, 67
Tatsak *kütuktu* IX, 286*n*7
Tatsak *kütuktu* XI, 287–288*n*20, 288*n*26
Tatsak lineage, 27. *See also specific people*
Tibetan Buddhism transformation goal:
    and anti-oracle campaign, 136,
    276*n*160; and colonialism, 21, 43–44;
    and Golden Urn policy
    communications, 8
Tibetan civil war (1727), 38, 45
Tibetan civil wars (18th century), 31–32,
    254*n*76
Tibetan identity: and culture, 23,
    250*n*46; and Ganden Podrang

jurisdiction, 204–205, 289*n*27; and
    Geluk church, 22, 250*n*44;
    geographical terms, 247–248*nn*8, 21;
    inconsistency of, 17–18. *See also* Qing
    views of Tibet; Tibetan nationalism
Tibetan nationalism: Dalai Lama XIII
    on, 207–208, 210–211, 216, 291*n*45;
    and Dalai Lama XIV, 219, 221;
    and Geluk church, 15–16; and
    nineteenth-century Golden Urn use,
    209–210; and Qing-Geluk church
    alliance, 208–209; and Qing views of
    Tibet, 209, 290–291*n*40–42
Tibetan responses to Golden Urn, 5,
    86–87; advisor concerns about, 54,
    83–84, 113, 121, 271*n*66; courtesy
    theory, 158; Dalai Lama VIII,
    116–117, 133, 138–141, 142, 277*n*178;
    and doubts about *trülku* institution,
    153, 199–200, 276–277*n*171; and
    faith, 153–154; and geographical
    conceptions of Tibet, 204–205,
    289*nn*27, 31–32; Heliyen report,
    142–143, 277*n*178; and Jamyang
    Zhepa *kütuktu* reincarnation search,
    157–158, 159, 160–161, 170, 175–176,
    193, 279*n*3, 282*n*48; Lamo
    Chökyong oracle, 137–139; and legal
    order, 148–150, 154, 278*nn*205, 207;
    and lottery as omen, 150, 178,
    282*n*55; nineteenth century, 199,
    200–201, 287–288*nn*17, 19–20;
    opposition theory, 4, 17, 164, 181,
    246*n*6, 248*n*31, 284*n*98; Qianlong
    emperor concerns, 143; and Qing-
    Geluk church alliance, 149–150, 156,
    205–207; requests for lottery, 165,
    171–172, 193, 281*n*34; and ritual
    details, 150–151
Toin Tutop Nyima (Kharachin Lama),
    259*n*130

Tongkhor III Gyelwa Gyatso,
reincarnation of, 28–29, 253*n*69
Tongkhor *kūtuktu* VI Jamyang Tendzin
Gyatso, 48, 174, 176, 200, 201, 204,
266*n*93, 283*n*66, 288*n*23
Trashi Lhünpo monastery sack (1791),
10, 56; chronological context, 227;
and dough ball divination, 66, 78;
investigation of, 60, 65–68, 228,
262*nn*31, 39; overview, 64–65
Travers, Alice, 290*n*39
trülku institution, 24–29; and candidate
criteria, 126, 166, 273*n*116, 281*nn*35–
36; and Cultural Revolution, 218;
and estates, 27–28, 29; and Geluk as
church, 9, 247*n*17; history of, 24–25;
importance of, 9; and Mongols,
62–63; nineteenth century, 197–198,
286–287*nn*13–14; number of lineages,
197–198, 286–287*n*13; PRC policies,
217–218, 220–221, 223; prohibition
of Mongol reincarnations, 62–63, 96,
268*n*11; and Qing-Geluk church
alliance, 24, 35; regencies, 29, 37;
reincarnation search process, 28–29,
50–52, 253*n*68. *See also* doubts about
trülku institution
Tsebak (*amban*), 165–166, 169, 229,
281*nn*30–31
Tsemönling *kūtuktu* I Samadi Baksi
Ngawang Tsültrim, 49, 59, 153, 208,
227, 258*n*129, 280*n*26, 288*n*23
Tsewang Rabtan (Junghar ruler), 213
Tukwan *kūtuktu* III Lozang Chökyi
Nyima, 48; and Beijing *kūtuktu*
system, 162; and doubts about *trülku*
institution, 63, 200; and Jamyang
Zhepa *kūtuktu* reincarnation search,
164, 175–178, 190, 283*n*81, 284*nn*93,
95; and *Life of the Second Jamyang
Zhepa,* 170–171; and Pakpalha *kūtuktu*

reincarnation search, 153; Qianlong
emperor's patronage of, 76; on
shamanism, 110–111
Tüsiyetü Khan, 62, 97, 268*n*11. *See also*
Erdeni Pandita *kūtuktu* reincarnation
search
Tuttle, Gray, 216, 286*n*6, 287*n*13
Twenty-Nine reforms (1793), 132, 205,
228; and *ambans,* 47; focus on Golden
Urn, 100–101; and Gurkha war, 10,
11; and oracle inclusion, 116, 271*n*78;
Tibetan responses to, 115–117

van der Kuijp, Leonard W. J., 252*n*56
Van Vleet, Stacey, 290*n*39

Waley-Cohen, Joanna, 261*nn*8, 24
Wangchen Bum (son of Dülagyel), 159,
165, 166–167, 176–177, 183, 190,
192–193, 281*n*35, 285*n*109
Wang Feng, 218
Wang Xiangyun, 280*n*22
"Water-Ox Year Edict," 132–136, 139,
275*nn*149, 152, 276*nn*155–156, 157
Wei Yuan, 194, 195, 210, 251*n*48,
290*n*41, 291*n*43
Weizang tongzhi, 266*n*91, 267*n*118

Xi Jinping, 222
Xizang, 23, 250*n*46, 251*n*47

Yamantai (*amban*), 56, 65
yangsi. See trülku institution
Yongxuan, 273–274*n*126
Yongzheng emperor, xii, 38, 39–40,
45–46
Yotai (*amban*), 199
Yuan dynasty, 11, 34, 67, 68
Yutok Trashi Döndrup, 71
Yu Xiaodong, *3*
Yu Zhengxie, 251*n*48

The Social Life of Inkstones: Artisans and Scholars in Early Qing China, by Dorothy Ko. University of Washington Press, 2017.

Darwin, Dharma, and the Divine: Evolutionary Theory and Religion in Modern Japan, by G. Clinton Godart. University of Hawaii Press, 2017.

Dictators and Their Secret Police: Coercive Institutions and State Violence, by Sheena Chestnut Greitens. Cambridge University Press, 2016.

The Cultural Revolution on Trial: Mao and the Gang of Four, by Alexander C. Cook. Cambridge University Press, 2016.

Inheritance of Loss: China, Japan, and the Political Economy of Redemption After Empire, by Yukiko Koga. University of Chicago Press, 2016.

Homecomings: The Belated Return of Japan's Lost Soldiers, by Yoshikuni Igarashi. Columbia University Press, 2016.

Samurai to Soldier: Remaking Military Service in Nineteenth-Century Japan, by D. Colin Jaundrill. Cornell University Press, 2016.

The Red Guard Generation and Political Activism in China, by Guobin Yang. Columbia University Press, 2016.

Accidental Activists: Victim Movements and Government Accountability in Japan and South Korea, by Celeste L. Arrington. Cornell University Press, 2016.

Ming China and Vietnam: Negotiating Borders in Early Modern Asia, by Kathlene Baldanza. Cambridge University Press, 2016.

Ethnic Conflict and Protest in Tibet and Xinjiang: Unrest in China's West, coedited by Ben Hillman and Gray Tuttle. Columbia University Press, 2016.

One Hundred Million Philosophers: Science of Thought and the Culture of Democracy in Postwar apan, by Adam Bronson. University of Hawaii Press, 2016.

Conflict and Commerce in Maritime East Asia: The Zheng Family and the Shaping of the Modern World, c. 1620–1720, by Xing Hang. Cambridge University Press, 2016.

Chinese Law in Imperial Eyes: Sovereignty, Justice, and Transcultural Politics, by Li Chen. Columbia University Press, 2016.

Imperial Genus: The Formation and Limits of the Human in Modern Korea and Japan, by Travis Workman. University of California Press, 2015.

Yasukuni Shrine: History, Memory, and Japan's Unending Postwar, by Akiko Takenaka. University of Hawaii Press, 2015.

The Age of Irreverence: A New History of Laughter in China, by Christopher Rea. University of California Press, 2015.

The Knowledge of Nature and the Nature of Knowledge in Early Modern Japan, by Federico Marcon. University of Chicago Press, 2015.

The Fascist Effect: Japan and Italy, 1915–1952, by Reto Hofmann. Cornell University Press, 2015.

Empires of Coal: Fueling China's Entry into the Modern World Order, 1860–1920, by Shellen Xiao Wu. Stanford University Press, 2015.